THE JEWISH PEOPLE
4000 YEARS OF SURVIVAL

THE JEWISH PEOPLE

4000 YEARS OF SURVIVAL

by MAX WURMBRAND
in collaboration with CECIL ROTH

with 600 illustrations

SHENGOLD PUBLISHERS, INC.
NEW YORK CITY

Designed by Martin Brandt, TEL-AVIV

© MASSADA PRESS LTD., TEL-AVIV, ISRAEL, 1966

PUBLISHED 1967 BY SHENGOLD PUBLISHERS, INC. NEW YORK

BY ARRANGEMENT WITH MASSADA PRESS LTD., ISRAEL

PRINTED IN ISRAEL BY PELI-P.E.C. PRINTING WORKS LTD.

LIBRARY OF CONGRESS CATALOG CARD NO. 67 — 16635

THE PATRIARCHS

It is with the patriarch Abraham that, according to ancient tradition, the course of Hebrew Jewish history begins. At some period early in the second millennium before the current era, he left his home in Ur of the Chaldees on the Euphrates, ultimately to settle in what was then called the Land of Canaan, and later Palestine.

The Bible, our only source for early Hebrew history, indicates no political or economic reasons for this migration. It seems that foreign incursions had rendered the position of the inhabitants of southern Mesopotamia, in the region of Ur, insecure and had driven the Semitic tribes northward. After a lengthy stay at Haran on the banks of the Belikh, a tributary of the Middle Euphrates, Abraham and his family proceeded in a south-westerly direction and reached the Land of Canaan. This latter stage of his migration was due, the Bible informs us, to a Divine call.

Abraham had abandoned the polytheistic and idolatrous beliefs of his tribe for a belief in One God, the Creator of heaven and earth, of whom there could be no representation, either in wood or in stone. This God demanded of his followers that they "keep the way of the Lord to do righteousness and justice" (*Genesis 18:19*). Feeling, no doubt, that it was advisable to leave a country in which he was regarded as a renegade, Abraham looked for a new home, where he could live in accordance with his beliefs and freely disseminate them. On the stage of history, he appears as the first prophet of the true way of life amidst a pagan world. As the father of monotheism, he towers in Hebrew history and legend,

The route of Abraham's wanderings from Ur of the Chaldees via Haran to Canaan, where he took up his residence in Beersheba.

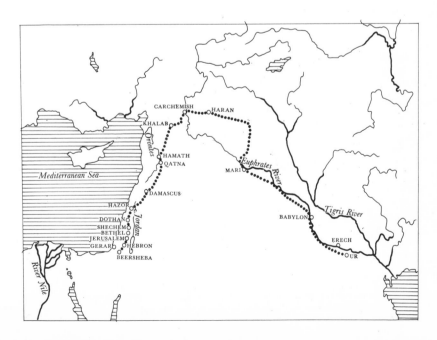

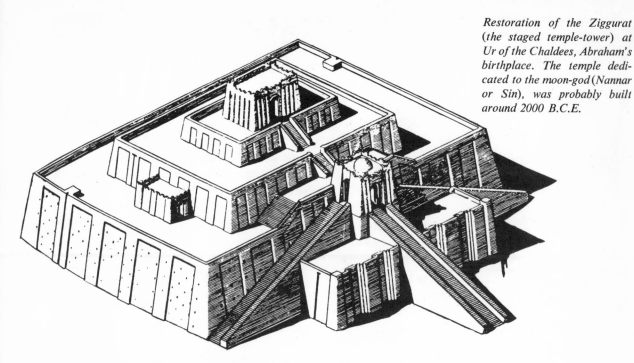

above his own and succeeding ages for his epoch-making repudiation of idolatry and for the realization of the monotheistic principle, which became the distinguishing mark of his descendants after him.

Abraham is depicted in the Book of Genesis as the wealthy owner of many sheep, oxen, asses and camels, tended by numerous shepherds and herdsmen. He lived a nomadic life, journeying through Canaan from north to south in search of suitable pasture-land. Wherever he pitched his tent, he built an altar to the Lord and called upon His name. When a famine ravaged the Land of Canaan, he went to Egypt, where he sojourned for a while, until the food was again to be had. He then returned to Canaan to resume his wanderings, this time from south to north.

The "Standard" of Ur, a mosaic in lapis lazuli and shell on a wooden background, consisting of two panels, found in one of the royal tombs. On the "Peace" panel, reproduced below, the royal family is seen in the top row at a feast. The two lower rows show attendants bringing in spoils captured from the enemy. (British Museum).

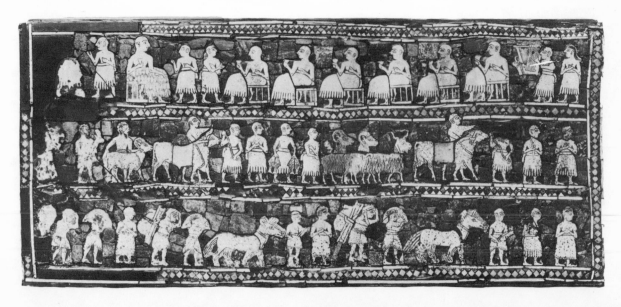

Lyre (restored) found in the tomb of Queen Shub-ad (ab. 2900 B.C.E.) at Ur of the Chaldees. The sound-box is adorned by a beautiful bull's head in gold. (University Museum, Philadelphia).

It would, nevertheless, be a mistake to consider Abraham merely a nomadic shepherd. Ur of the Chaldees, the land which he had left, was high on the scale of contemporary culture. Palestine, too, is now known to have been one of the cradles of human civilization, southern Palestine having provided some of the earliest artistic manifestations of man known to us, while Jericho, for example, represented the oldest type of town-civilization. In Canaan, as in Mesopotamia, Abraham was always associated with an important urban center, and in his new homeland his name was linked especially with the ancient city of Beersheba. He must, therefore, be looked upon as having been aware of the best in the culture of his times.

Abraham's contemporaries in Canaan did not regard him as an unwelcome intruder. Enjoying friendly relations with all the petty kings in

The stairs leading to the entrance of the Machpelah Cave at Hebron, the traditional tomb of the Patriarchs (from a painting by M. Lander).

the center and in the south of the country, he even helped them repel a massive invasion led by Amraphel king of Shinar, and recovered the booty taken by the enemy. He was highly respected by the citizens of Kiriath-Arba, later known as Hebron, who addressed him as "a mighty prince among us" (*Genesis 23:6*). From one of them he bought a field and its twin cave of Machpelah as a burial place for his wife Sarah. There he himself was later buried, and there, too, were buried his son Isaac and Isaac's wife Rebekah, his grandson Jacob and one of Jacob's wives, Leah. The Cave of Machpelah at Hebron subsequently became a venerated Jewish shrine.

According to the Biblical account, the crowning point in Abraham's career was his unshakeable readiness to fulfill a Divine command bidding him sacrifice his only son Isaac. This command, however, had only the purpose to prove the extent of Abraham's faith. When Isaac was already bound upon the altar, a voice from heaven, saying: "Lay not thine hand upon the lad", marked the repudiation among the Hebrews of the barbarous custom of human sacrifice.

In contrast to both his father Abraham and his son Jacob, Isaac, the second of the Patriarchs, played but a minor role in the Biblical narrative. His lifetime marked the transition from nomadic wanderings to a settled agricultural life, so that digging wells and searching for sources of water became a major occupation of his. He sowed, and in fruitful years reaped a hundredfold, and grew exceedingly rich. True, we hear of friction with powerful neighbors, but, on the whole, his seems to have been a peaceful life. It was on terms of equality that he dealt with city-kings and was referred to as "the blessed of the Lord." He lived in the country as of right, for there he was born and knew no other land.

The traditional Tomb of Rachel on the road from Jerusalem to Bethlehem. The building is probably medieval but was restored by Sir Moses Montefiore in the 19th century.

Consequently, the idea of even temporarily leaving Canaan never occurred to him, not even in time of famine.

The greater part of the Book of Genesis is devoted to the description of Jacob's stormy life and to the vicissitudes of his twelve sons, the ancestors of the Twelve Tribes of Israel.

Driven out of his father's home by the animosity of his brother Esau, Jacob was obliged to spend twenty years with his mother's Aramean relatives at Haran. There he married two sisters, Leah (who bore him six sons and a daughter) and Rachel. The latter, his favorite, was, however, barren and only gave birth to a son, Joseph, after many years. Jacob also took his wives' two handmaids as concubines. In all, he had eleven sons and one daughter when he left Mesopotamia to return to his homeland, where he became reconciled with Esau. Before entering Canaan, the name Israel ("he who strives with God") was bestowed upon him in a mysterious incident, in which "there wrestled a man with him until the breaking of the day." In Canaan, on the way to Hebron, Rachel died in giving birth to her second son Benjamin, and was buried "in the way to Ephrath — the same is Bethlehem". Throughout the centuries, the traditional tomb of Rachel, on the road from Jerusalem to Bethlehem, has been a much frequented and highly venerated shrine.

In Canaan, Jacob was first associated with the city of Shechem, in the hill country of Ephraim, where he acquired a portion of land which he bequeathed to Joseph. Following a feud between two of his sons and the inhabitants of Shechem, Jacob moved southward and settled in Hebron.

Especially significant is the career of Joseph, which is recounted in the Book of Genesis in great detail. His brothers, resenting their father's preference for him, sold him into slavery and persuaded Jacob into believing that an evil beast had devoured him. Joseph was brought by the slave-dealers to Egypt and there sold to the captain of Pharaoh's guard, who put the intelligence of his Hebrew slave to good use. But Joseph's good looks brought him into trouble, for his master's wife fell in love with him, and when Joseph, unwilling to betray his master's trust, rejected her overtures, the scorned and angry woman took her revenge by accusing him of having tried to violate her. Thrown into prison as a result of this false accusation, Joseph met there two court dignitaries who had fallen from favor. He interpreted their dreams, foretelling that the one would suffer capital punishment, while the other would be reinstated in his former position. Both predictions were fulfilled and when Pharaoh subsequently had a strange dream which defied interpretation, the rehabilitated court official remembered Joseph. The Hebrew youth was brought out of the dungeon and having explained the dream, offered Pharaoh statesmanlike advice, in consequence of which he was elevated to a position of eminence in Egypt.

The story of Joseph depicted in miniatures in a Franco-Spanish Haggadah of the 13th century, now at the British Museum (Add. 27210). Upper row. Right panel: Joseph is cast into a pit by his brethren, who kill a goat and dip his coat in its blood, in order to make their father Jacob believe that an evil beast has devoured him.
Left Panel: Joseph's brethren sell him to a travelling company of Ishmaelites who are on their way to Egypt.
Lower row. Right panel: Joseph's bloodstained coat is presented by his brethren to Jacob.
Left panel, above: Joseph rejects the overtures of his Egyptian master's wife and flees, leaving his garment in her hand.
Below: Joseph in prison, interpreting the dreams of Pharaoh's dignitaries.

A severe famine led Jacob to send his sons to Egypt, where, thanks to Joseph's wise administration, corn was available. There they met their brother, whom they failed to recognize, but who immediately knew who they were. Having ultimately revealed himself to his brothers and having assured them that he bore them no grudge, since God had intended it all for a higher purpose, Joseph bade them bring their father and their families to live in Egypt, where he would provide for them.

The story of Joseph is probably to be assigned to the period of the rule of the Hyksos or Shepherd Kings. Being themselves aliens, they encouraged the settlement of kindred elements. Coming to Egypt, Jacob and his sons made their homes in the province of Goshen, which, situated in the north-eastern corner of the country, became the center of Hebrew settlement. It was in Egypt that Jacob died, but in accordance with his last wish, his body was brought to Canaan, to be buried with his fathers in the cave of Machpelah.

After his death, Jacob's descendents multiplied in Egypt and lived there for several generations.

The family of an Asiatic chieftain called Absha (probably an Amorite and approximately a contemporary of Abraham) is permitted to enter Egypt; about 1900 B. C. E. Mural painting from the tomb of an Egyptian dignitary at Beni-Hasan.

THE EXODUS

It was probably immediately after the fall of the Hyksos rule in Egypt (about 1580 B.C.E.) that a change took place in the policy of the Egyptian rulers towards the Hebrews, who had prospered and multiplied in the province of Goshen. In the eyes of the Egyptians, but recently liberated from the yoke of the Asiatic invaders, this alien people occupying a border region, represented a grave risk to the security of the country. In order, therefore, to crush their morale and prevent them from making common cause with foreign foes, the Egyptian rulers reduced them to a position of servitude and, at the same time, instituted drastic measures to curb their increase in numbers. In their ambitious building projects, the Pharaohs utilized the cheap slave labor provided by the merciless subjugation of whole tribes and peoples, including the Hebrews, who were associated especially with the construction of the two "store-cities" of Pithom and Raamses.

Pharaoh Merenptah II (1225–1215 B.C.E.), believed to be the Pharaoh of the Exodus.

It was probably under the Pharaoh Rameses II (1292–1225 B.C.E.) that the Hebrews experienced the greatest sufferings. They were liberated during the reign of his successor Merenptah II (1225–1215 B.C.E.), through the great and inspiring leadership of Moses, a descendent of Levi the son of Jacob.

According to the narrative in the Book of Exodus, Moses was brought up in the royal court by Pharaoh's daughter. On reaching manhood and witnessing the privations and misery of his people, he threw in his lot with them. In sublime and heroic proportions, the Biblical account, picturesquely elaborated in later Jewish legend, describes Moses' career and his subsequent epoch-making achievements.

Only after the Egyptians had been smitten with ten terrible plagues, did the Pharaoh relent and grant Moses permission to lead the children of Israel out of Egypt. However, the Hebrews had barely started upon their march from slavery to freedom, when Pharaoh regretted his decision. He pursued the Hebrews at the head of his army, but was unable to prevent their reaching the Desert of Sinai, since they miraculously passed through the Red Sea, while he perished in its waves together with all his host. The exodus from Egypt, still commemorated annually in the Feast of Passover, marked the beginning of the Hebrews as a free and independent people.

The aim of Moses was to bring the children of Israel back to the Land of Canaan, the land of their forefathers. From a military point of view, however, the most convenient route, running along the Mediterranean coast — "the Way of the Sea" — was hazardous. Moses therefore, led the people into the Sinai Desert, in order to enter the Land of Canaan by a circuitous route from the east.

"They made their lives bitter with hard service in mortar and in brick" (Exodus 1 : 14). Brickmaking in Egypt. Wall painting from the tomb of Rekh-mi-Re, vizier of Upper Egypt, at Thebes, about 1450 B. C. E. (Metropolitan Museum of Art, New York).

צְפַרְדֵּעַ   דָם

עָרוֹב   כִּנִּים

שְׁחִין   דֶּבֶר

אַרְבֶּה   בָּרָד

מַכַּת בְּכוֹרוֹת: חוֹשֶׁךְ

The Ten Plagues, from the Venice Haggadah of 1609.
First row: The transformation of water into blood and the appearance of the plague of frogs.
Second row: Plague of lice and attacks by wild animals.
Third row: Cattle plague and boils.
Fourth row: Hail and locusts.
Fifth row: The days of darkness and the death of all Egyptian first-born.

15

It was at Mount Sinai, amidst awe-inspiring manifestations, that Moses proclaimed to the people their Divine mission. There they received the Ten Commandments, a brief code of principles regulating man's relationship with God and with his fellow-men; there they entered into a covenant to give concrete expression to these principles in every aspect of life. All the numerous prescriptions that constitute the Law (the Torah) are based on these fundamental principles and the whole Law is, therefore, traditionally considered as having been implicitly revealed at Mount Sinai.

Moses on Mount Sinai, receiving the Tables of the Law. From the 14th century Sarajevo Haggadah.

The Tabernacle or Tent of Meeting, according to a miniature in the Alba Bible (a manuscript Spanish Bible translation of the early 15th century). The miniature shows the Ark of the Covenant, the table with the loaves of shewbread, the altar and the seven-armed candlestick. Aaron the High Priest is offering incense before the Ark, while one of his sons is preparing an animal sacrifice.

Under the leadership of Moses, the children of Israel wandered in the wilderness for forty long years. Their wanderings, in the Biblical account, were especially associated with the oasis of Kadesh-Barnea in the southern Negev, on the border between Sinai and the Land of Canaan. As the center of their imageless worship, Moses constructed a portable sanctuary, the Tabernacle or Tent of Meeting, which housed, in its innermost recess, the Ark of the Covenant. This chest, constructed of acacia wood that was overlaid with pure gold, both within and without, had a highly ornamented cover and was carried on two staves during the journeyings of the Israelites. In the Ark were placed the two tables of stone engraved with the Ten Commandments. A sacrificial ritual was instituted and the priesthood was conferred on Aaron, Moses' brother, and his descendants, while auxiliary services were assigned to the other members of the tribe of Levi, the Levites.

The Pillar of Merenptah II (Cairo Museum), erected in his fifth year to celebrate his wars and victories. The Pharaoh boasts of having defeated and destroyed Israel. This is the first historical document in which the name of Israel is mentioned.

The years of wandering were punctuated by periods of discontent on the part of the people, who had soon forgotten the sufferings in Egypt. Disquiet was fomented by internal rivalries and the frequent attacks of hostile desert tribes. Ultimately, however, all these hardships served to weld the Hebrew tribes into a single, united people.

After defeating Sihon, the king of the Amorites, and Og, the king of Bashan, Moses occupied the country between the Arnon and Jabbok rivers, east of the Jordan and of the Dead Sea. But it was not given to Moses to attain his goal and lead the children of Israel into the Promised Land. He was permitted but a distant view of it from the summit of Mount Nebo. There he died, at the conclusion of the years of wandering, "and he was buried in the valley in the land of Moab over against Beth Peor; and no man knoweth of his sepulchre unto this day" (*Deuteronomy 34:6*).

ISRAEL IN CANAAN

Under Joshua, who had succeeded to the leadership upon the death of Moses, the Hebrew tribes crossed the River Jordan, a short distance above the point where it flows into the Dead Sea. Then, achieving their first great triumph on the western side of the river, they captured Jericho, an ancient seat of Canaanite culture.

From the Jordan Valley, Joshua began his conquest of the central portion of the country, later known as the hill-country of Ephraim, after the name of the Israelite tribe that settled there. Following an initial setback, Joshua succeeded in taking the fortress of Ai, thereby opening the hill-country to the Hebrews and permitting them to advance to Mount Ebal, near the town of Shechem. There, in fulfilment of the injunction of Moses (*Deuteronomy 27:4 ff*), Joshua built an altar, on which sacrifices were offered and where he solemnly read the Law before the assembled Israelites.

The kings of the southern part of the country, fearful of the invading tide of Hebrews, were the first to form a league, led by Adoni-Zedek, king of Jerusalem, for the purpose of destroying the growing threat to their domains. They were, however, decisively defeated in battle at Gibeon, in the Valley of Aijalon, where the sun is reported to have stayed its course, in order to allow Joshua to complete his victory.

Seeing that Joshua was in possession of central and southern Canaan, the kings of the northern cities banded themselves together into a confederation, headed by Jabin, king of Hazor, and mobilized a vast army, equipped with many horses and chariots. Battle was joined at the waters of Merom, but the league sustained a crushing defeat at the hands of the Israelites who, having stormed and burnt Hazor, occupied northern Canaan.

The Conquest of the Promised Land, from the Venice Haggadah of 1609. On the left the defeat of Sihon, king of the Amorites, and Og, king of Bashan (Numbers 21 : 21-35); on the right the capture of Jericho (Joshua 6 : 12-20); in the middle the capture of Ai (Joshua 8 : 1-29).

Despite these military victories, the establishment of the Hebrews in the country was, even now, a slow and painful process, and Canaanite enclaves still held out in many places. Not until several generations later were the last Canaanite strongholds reduced.

Before his death, Joshua allotted the land among the twelve tribes, nine of whom, together with half the tribe of Manasseh, received their inheritance in western Canaan, while the remaining two tribes and half of Manasseh were allowed to return and settle on the other side of the Jordan, in keeping with a promise made to them by Moses.

Joshua's period of leadership was followed by that of the Judges, a succession of leaders who exercised authority over the whole or part of

Joshua bidding the sun and the moon to stand still in the Valley of Aijalon, to allow him to complete his victory over the Canaanites (Joshua 10 : 11-15). Wall painting in the synagogue of Dura-Europos (3rd century C.E.).

Palestine in the period of the Judges.

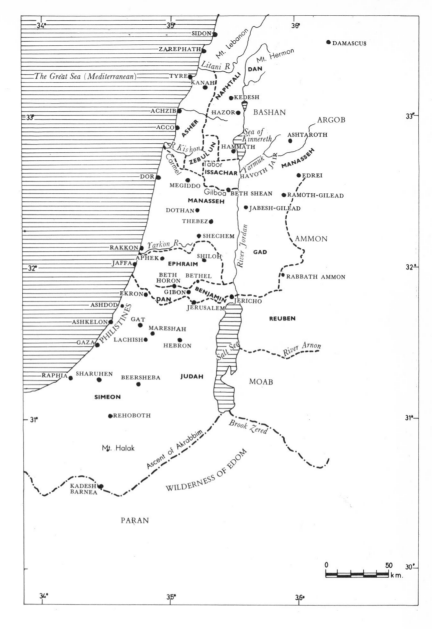

Basalt Stele with relief, from the Canaanite Shrine at Hazor (14th-13th century B.C.E).

the country. Generally speaking, these Judges arose during times of national crisis and were instrumental in repulsing an alien invasion or in delivering the people from foreign domination. One of them, a woman — the prophetess Deborah — had to face a powerful adversary, the king of Hazor, whose name was again Jabin. This city that had been conquered and razed by Joshua, had been rebuilt and was once again in the possession of the Canaanites. Jabin, who had oppressed Israel for twenty years, appointed Sisera to command his 900 iron chariots. With the assistance, however, of Barak, Deborah defeated the enemy in a pitched battle near Mount Tabor and delivered Israel from the Canaanite menace in a victory celebrated in the famed song of Deborah, which has been preserved in the Book of Judges.

21

SAMSON·PORTAS·VRBIS·PORTAT·IN·MONTEM

During the period of the Judges, no single power, however, menaced the independence of the Hebrews as much as did the Philistines, a highly civilized sea people from the Greek islands, who possessed new and formidable weapons. Having been repulsed by Egypt, they had seized the coastal plain, where they had established themselves and from which they advanced inland. With Samson's single-handed struggle serving only as a local check on their progress, the Philistines subsequently subjugated large sections of the country and threatened the very existence of the entire Hebrew people.

One of Samson's feats in his struggle against the Philistines. "He laid hold of the doors of the gate of the city (of Gaza) . . . and carried them up to the top of the mountain that is before Hebron" (Judges 16 : 3). Mosaic floor in the Church of St. Gereon, Cologne (12th century).

THE FOUNDATION OF THE MONARCHY: SAUL, DAVID AND SOLOMON

As the period of the Judges drew to its close, the impressive personality of the prophet Samuel emerged into the forefront of Israelite history. Samuel had witnessed the defeat of Israel at the battle of Aphek, where the Ark of the Covenant had fallen into the hands of the victorious Philistines. He had doubtless beheld the downfall of the national sanctuary at Shiloh, destroyed, as archaeological investigations have revealed, by the Philistines. He had seen the subjugation of his people by the Philistine invader. After these disasters, Samuel devoted a lifetime of patient work to the difficult task of restoring the shattered morale of his people, and succeeded not only in rekindling the religious and national enthusiasm of the tribes of Israel, but also in encouraging them to victorious action against the Philistines in a battle near Mizpah. But Samuel was growing old, and in such critical times the people were averse to relying on the occasional leadership of Judges. The Israelites, therefore, insisted on the appointment of a king, in the belief that only a unified rule could cope with the dangers besetting them. Seeing, at first, in this desire of the people a manifestation of lack of confidence in Divine guidance, an attempt at detracting from God's sovereignty over the Israelites, and a dangerous act of assimilation into the ways of other nations, Samuel was reluctant to agree to such a step. However, events pressed hard, one upon the other, and compelled him to accede to the will of the people.

The Ark of the Covenant, captured by the Philistines in the battle of Aphek, has wrought havoc in their country and is restored by them to the Israelites (I. Samuel 6 : 1-16). Wall painting in the synagogue of Dura-Europos (3rd century C.E.).

The first king of Israel was Saul the son of Kish of the tribe of Benjamin. Anointed by Samuel, Saul established his headquarters at his native town of Gibeah, about $3\frac{1}{2}$ miles north of Jerusalem. He proved his military prowess by conducting a victorious campaign against the Ammonites, who had menaced the people of Jabesh Gilead on the eastern side of the Jordan. Later, despite their preponderance in arms and men, he inflicted a decisive defeat upon the Philistines at Michmash. This victory was, in large measure, due to a daring act of bravery on the part of Jonathan, Saul's son and heir apparent. As a result of this battle, the hill-country of central Palestine was liberated from Philistine domination.

The war against the Philistines led, however, to the first rupture in the relationship between Saul and Samuel. Saul had usurped certain powers which Samuel regarded as symptomatic of an autocratic monarchy, that was the antithesis of a kingdom bound by allegiance to Divine authority and command. The breach became final when Saul, in his campaign against Amalek in the Negev, failed to comply with the Biblical injunction, totally to destroy all the Amalekites, together with all their cattle and sheep. "Hath the Lord," said Samuel, "as great delight in burnt-offerings and sacrifices, as in hearkening to the voice of the Lord? Behold, to obey is better than sacrifice, and to hearken than the fat of rams. For rebellion is as the sin of witchcraft, and stubbornness is as iniquity and idolatry" (*I Samuel 15:22-23*). Because Saul had arrogated to himself the role of an absolute, despotic ruler, he had forfeited his right to kingship over the Israelites. In consequence, Samuel secretly anointed David the son of Jesse, of the tribe of Judah, as king in his stead.

David gained distinction and renown in the war against the Philistines, particularly by his victory in single combat over the giant Philistine warrior Goliath. Rising to high military rank, David, by his physical comeliness, moral virtues and bravery, won the hearts of the people, the enduring friendship of Jonathan, and the hand of Saul's daughter Michal. At times, David even enjoyed the personal favor of Saul, playing to him to soothe his dark and disturbed moods. Saul, however, overcome with jealousy of David's growing popularity and his increasing prestige resulting from his successes against the Philistines, tried to rid himself of the young hero. Pursued by Saul through the Wilderness of Judah, David became an outlaw, and was finally compelled to seek asylum in Philistine territory.

These events profoundly affected the excitable and unstable mind of Saul, so that he became susceptible to fits of temper bordering on insanity, and reverted to superstitious practices which, earlier, he had severely condemned. After a comparatively short reign, Saul, together with his son Jonathan, met a tragic end on Mount Gilboa in an ill-fated battle against the Philistines, who had attacked the hill-country through

David slays the giant Philistine warrior Goliath (I. Samuel 17: 23-51). Mosaic floor in the Church of St. Gereon, Cologne (12th century).

the Valley of Jezreel from the north. Mourning the heroic death of Saul and Jonathan, David composed a dirge (*II Samuel 1:19–27*), which bears witness to his nobility of sentiment and his poetical genius.

There now ensued a struggle between the house of David and that of Saul, whose son Ish-Bosheth was placed on the throne by the dead king's general and reigned for a few years over all Israel, with the exception of David's own tribe, Judah, which followed him. The conflict finally ended in a victory for David. Upon the death of his rival, he was anointed king at Hebron over all the land. Not only was the Philistine menace finally crushed during David's reign, but his military conquests extended the borders of the kingdom on all sides, from Ezion-Geber on the Red Sea, in the land of Edom in the south, to Aram-Zobah in the north. His crowning achievement was the capture of Jerusalem, the Jebusite fortress which had for so long held out against the Hebrews. To this city he transferred his capital from Hebron, also making it the religious center of the kingdom by bringing there the Ark of the Covenant, which had been housed at different places after it had been recovered from the Philistines. Ever since then, even during centuries of exile, Jerusalem has been the emotional and spiritual center of the Jewish people, the focal point of all its hopes and yearnings.

The Queen of Sheba visits King Solomon. Detail from a painting by Piero della Francesca (15th century) in the church of San Francesco at Arezzo.

King Solomon on his throne, sitting in judgement (I. Kings 3 : 16-28). Miniature from a 13th century illuminated manuscript in the British Museum. (MS Add. 11639).

Megiddo, one of King Solomon's "chariot-cities". Stables at the Solomonian level of the excavations at Megiddo. (Courtesy of the Oriental Institute, University of Chicago).

Reconstruction of King Solomon's stables at Megiddo.

Though victorious in his foreign campaigns and, by dint of his administrative talents and personal charm, successful in welding the tribes of Israel into a strong, united nation, David's personal life was less happy. His liaison with Bath-Sheba aroused resentment against him in many circles. His weakness and vacillation in the face of his ambitious and impatient sons' rivalries almost cost him his crown, as well as his life, when one of them, Absalom, raised the standard of revolt. Before his death, David succeeded, however, in securing the throne for Solomon, his son by Bath-Sheba.

In the history, legend, and folk-lore of his people, David is the ideal of a perfect king, acceptable both to God and to men. The Psalms, traditionally composed by him, have immortalized his name as one of mankind's greatest religious poets.

David's choice of Solomon as heir to the throne was challenged by Adonijah, another of David's sons, but Solomon crushed the opposition, thereby assuring himself of a long and peaceful reign. By dividing the country into administrative districts, he helped further to weaken the ancient tribal divisions. Notwithstanding his peaceful intentions, he did not neglect the military strength of the state; he organized a large force of cavalry and fortified a number of strategically important positions. In his foreign policy, he employed diplomacy rather than arms. Thus

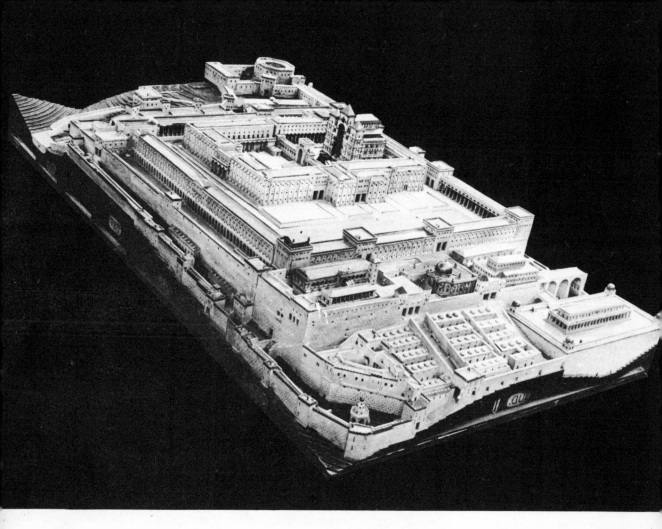

he secured Egyptian friendship by marrying the Pharaoh's daughter, and cultivated amicable personal relationships with Hiram king of Tyre and other neighboring countries. The development of international trade, which brought the country immense wealth and raised the standard of life and culture, received his especial attention. His fame as a wise and mighty ruler spread to distant lands, as witnessed by the visit paid to him by the Queen of Sheba. He adorned Jerusalem with public buildings and with magnificent palaces for himself and his many wives. But his immortal fame rests, first and foremost, on his building the Temple, an edifice on which he lavished the most precious building materials and embellishments.

Solomon's luxurious court and ambitious building projects could be maintained only at the cost of heavy taxation, which aroused wide-spread discontent. This led to several revolts during the last years of his reign and brought about, after his death, the division of the monarchy into two separate kingdoms, never again to be united.

History has been severe in its judgment of Solomon's prodigality that produced such fateful consequences. In Jewish legend, however, as well as in the folk-lore of other peoples, he is represented as the embodiment of wisdom and science, of justice and the fear of God. To him have been attributed the Biblical books of Proverbs, Ecclesiastes, and the Song of Songs, as well as several apocryphal works.

Reconstruction of the Temple ("The House of the Lord" I Kings 6 : 1) built by King Solomon in Jerusalem (model prepared by Dr. Schick).

THE DIVISION OF THE KINGDOM AND KINGDOM OF ISRAEL

Upon the death of Solomon, in the year 928 B.C.E., his son Rehoboam succeeded to the throne. There was, however, unrest among the northern tribes, which demanded relief from the severity of Solomon's policy of taxation and forced labor. When the new king refused to promise any reforms, the northern tribes, constituting the greater part of the state, broke away and established a separate kingdom. As their first king, they elected Jeroboam, the son of Nebat of the tribe of Ephraim, formerly one of Solomon's officers, who had rebelled against him and had afterwards spent several years in exile in Egypt. The southern tribes, Judah and Benjamin, however, remained faithful to Rehoboam and the Davidic dynasty.

Rehoboam's attempt to restore unity by force of arms proved unsuccessful. Henceforth, for two centuries, there were two separate Hebrew kingdoms: the kingdom of Israel in the north, later to have its capital at Samaria, after which it is often named, and the kingdom of Judah in the south, centering on Jerusalem and its Temple. In order to ensure the religious independence of his kingdom, Jeroboam king of Israel prohibited pilgrimages to Jerusalem and established two royal sanctuaries at Dan and Bethel, where the worship of golden calves was instituted.

Samaria (now Sebastieh). Site of the Capital of the Kingdom of Israel from the days of King Omri (882-871 B.C.E.) to the downfall of the kingdom in 722 B.C.E.

The northern kingdom was not only by far the larger of the two, but also economically more prosperous and politically more important. It suffered, however, from a fundamental drawback. No royal house that came to power had the mystical appeal of the Davidic dynasty. Permanent internal stability could, therefore, not be achieved and changes of rule were frequent. During the two centuries of the existence of the kingdom of Israel, nine dynasties, some of them extremely short-lived, followed one another in rapid succession, the two longest and most enduring being those of Omri (882–842 B.C.E.) and Jehu (842–747 B.C.E.).

It was Omri who transferred the capital from Tirzah to Samaria, a city founded by him and imposingly built to be worthy of a royal place of residence. Remains uncovered in the course of recent excavations bear out the Biblical picture of Samaria's luxurious court life. Particularly interesting are the fragments of ivory carvings that confirm the Biblical account of the 'ivory house' built by Ahab the son of Omri (*I Kings 22:39*).

The kings of the dynasty of Omri were martial rulers who waged both defensive and offensive wars, chiefly against the Arameans and the Moabites. The attempt of Mesha, king of Moab, to regain his independence after the death of Ahab, is vividly depicted in the famous Moabite Stone, discovered in the ruins of Dibon in Transjordan and now in the Louvre at Paris. This is the earliest external evidence of importance bearing directly on Biblical history.

During the reign of the dynasty of Omri, relations between the kingdoms of Israel and Judah became so cordial, that the house of Omri even allied itself with the Davidic dynasty through marriage.

The Book of Kings furnishes ample information about the reign of Omri's son Ahab (871–851) and the evil influence exerted on him by his wife Jezebel, daughter of Ethbaal, king of Tyre, as well as about his relations with the prophet Elijah, the uncompromising champion of the monotheistic faith and of the traditional moral standards of the nation. Vigorously Elijah opposed the king's indulgent attitude towards the cult of Baal, which was promoted by the idolatrous Jezebel, and he

Carved Ivory Tablets from the excavations at Samaria. They belonged probably to the palace built by King Ahab (871-851 B.C.E.), the so-called "Ivory House" (I Kings 22 : 39). On the left: a robed figure, perhaps the Egyptian god Osiris. On the right: a lion.

The Black Obelisk of Shalmaneser III, king of Assyria
(859-825 B.C.E.), found at
Kalah on the Tigris, now in
the British Museum. On the
second panel from above,
Jehu, king of Israel, is seen
paying homage to Shalmaneser. Jehu, who had overturned
and destroyed the dynasty of
Omri, is erroneously designated in the inscription as
"Jehu son of Omri".

The Stele of Mesha, king of Moab, discovered at Diban
(the Biblical Dibon) in Transjordan, now in the Louvre at
Paris. In this inscription the Moabite king boasts of his
rebellion against Israel (II. Kings 3 : 4-5) and his other
achievements. The inscription is in Moabite, a language
closely akin to Biblical Hebrew.

fearlessly denounced the judicial crimes committed by royal decree. Numerous legends grew up around the dominating figure of this towering personality, whose deeds and memory bestride the centuries, and who, we are told, was taken up to heaven in a chariot of fire. He, who never experienced the pangs of death, has remained forever alive in the folk-lore of the Jewish people. At every ceremony of circumcision, he, the zealous defender of Jewish tradition, is believed to be present. Synagogues in which he appeared to the faithful, were subsequently called after his name. At the Passover Seder, commemorating the liberation of the people from Egyptian oppression, he is an honored guest, and he is destined to be the forerunner and associate of the Messiah.

While the kingdom of Israel was expending much of its wealth and energy in constant fighting with its neighbors, in particular with the Aramean kingdom of Damascus, its existence was menaced by the advancing power of Assyria. In 841 B.C.E. Jehu king of Israel, who had ruthlessly annihilated the entire dynasty of Omri, was compelled to pay homage to Shalmaneser III, king of Assyria. The episode is portrayed on the well-known Black Obelisk, now in the British Museum, which depicts the earliest identifiable figure of a Hebrew. After almost half a century, the prestige of Omri was still so great in the eyes of neighboring peoples, that the usurper Jehu is referred to in the Black Obelisk as 'the son of Omri.'

Under Jeroboam II (789–748) the great-grandson of Jehu and the fourth king of the dynasty founded by him, the Assyrian advance was temporarily halted. There was a revival of trade and industry and an influx of wealth, bringing with it a corresponding growth of luxury. But thereafter, the kingdom deteriorated rapidly, ruler succeeding ruler with bewildering rapidity. The kings of Israel tried again and again to challenge Assyrian supremacy in the Middle East. A first warning of the impending doom came in 734, when Tiglath Pileser III, king of Assyria, captured a number of Israelite cities and carried away their inhabitants into captivity in Assyria. Hoshea, the last king of Israel, did not, however, profit by the lesson and became involved in anti-Assyrian intrigues. In 722, Sargon of Assyria took Samaria, razing it to the ground. A vast number of the population was now, in accordance with the usual Assyrian practice, deported and sent to distant parts of the empire. The subsequent fate of these exiles is not known. Some probably assimilated, becoming absorbed among the people of their countries of exile. Others may have joined, 135 years later, the exiles who came from the kingdom of Judah, thus contributing to the formation of the large Jewish diaspora in the Babylonian and, afterwards, in the Persian Empire. In Jewish legend, the greater number of the exiles from the kingdom of Israel continue to live as the "Lost Ten Tribes of Israel," whom the Messiah is to restore to their homeland.

The prophet Elijah (*first half of the 9th century B.C.E.*) is alive forever, according to Jewish popular tradition. He is believed to witness every circumcision ceremony and a chair is reserved for him near the godfather's chair. Artistically embroidered "Chairs of Elijah" are still preserved in some old synagogues. This one is in the synagogue of Carpentras (*Southern France*).

The seal of "Shema the servant of Jeroboam" found at Megiddo. It belonged probably to a minister of King Jeroboam II of Israel (789-748 B.C.E.) and is a fine example of artistic skill and taste in the heyday of the kingdom of Israel.

33

Sargon II, king of Assyria (722-705 B.C.E.), who destroyed Samaria, put an end to the Kingdom of Israel and carried part of its population into exile to distant provinces of the Assyrian empire. From a relief discovered at Khorsabad (Iraq).

In the devastated territory of the former kingdom of Israel, Assyrian military colonists were settled to maintain order. The remnant of the Israelite population intermarried with the colonists, whom they converted to monotheism. From this mixed population there originated the Samaritans, a Jewish sect which, surviving to the present day, bases its beliefs on the Pentateuch alone and rejects the other sacred writings of Judaism. Once the powerful rivals of the Jews, they are now reduced to 300–400 in number. About half of them still live concentrated around their traditional religious center. Mount Gerizim, situated near Nablus in the Arab kingdom of Jordan and in the immediate neighborhood of the once luxurious city of Samaria, from which they derive their name. The other members of this sect live in the State of Israel. Annually, they make a pilgrimage to their sacred mountain to celebrate Passover together with their brethren.

THE KINGDOM OF JUDAH

Being less wealthy and less important than the kingdom of Israel, the southern kingdom of Judah had, perhaps for this very reason, a far more tranquil history. It enjoyed the inestimable advantage of that internal stability which was denied the kingdom of Israel. From beginning to end, the throne was occupied, on the whole peacefully, by the same dynasty, and so strong was the people's attachment to it, that even after the fall of the kingdom the hope of the national restoration always centered around the figure of the Messiah (i.e., the anointed king) of the house of David.

As far as the external policy of the kingdom of Judah was concerned, its record was less glorious. Only five years after the secession of the northern tribes, the Egyptian Pharaoh Shishak (Sheshonk) invaded Judah. An account of this campaign has been preserved on the walls of the gateway that Shishak erected at the Temple of Karnak (*Upper Egypt*). Jerusalem itself was apparently not captured, but king Rehoboam was obliged to pay the Pharaoh a large tribute, which denuded the Temple and the palace of all the treasures accumulated by Solomon.

The center of the national worship was the Temple at Jerusalem. Remnants of old Canaanite folk-worship, however, survived and re-emerged to combine with foreign influences in maintaining or introducing rival cults. Sometimes, when the kings were under the sway of gentile mothers or wives, these cults were encouraged by the reigning dynasty itself. "High places" were set up here and there throughout the country for the practice of the revolting rites of Baal-worship. Children were sacrificed to Moloch, particularly at his shrine, called Topheth, in the valley of the Son of Hinnom in the immediate vicinity of Jerusalem. This situation provoked the intense indignation of the prophets, religious leaders who opposed the penetration of foreign ways and influences that were sapping the very foundation of the people's religious and moral life. The prophets advocated the return to strict monotheism and to the moral principles inseparably connected with it.

The relations between the northern and the southern kingdoms, which had been hostile during the reign of the first three kings of Judah, Rehoboam (928–911), Abijah (911–908) and Asa (908–867), became friendly after the accession of Omri to the throne of Israel (882). Jehoshaphat king of Judah (867–846) even concluded a treaty of alliance with Ahab king of Israel, while his son Jehoram, the heir to the throne of Judah, married Athaliah, the daughter of Ahab and Jezebel. On the whole, the alliance produced no advantage for Judah and all but brought disaster upon the Davidic dynasty. The dominant role was played by the more powerful kingdom of Israel, and Judah's participation in Israel's wars against the Arameans and the Moabites weakened her own strength, so that she was unable to prevent the vassal state of Edom from regaining its independence. Religious chaos increased in Judah as a result of

ESAIAS

the authority exercised by Athaliah who, like her mother, was a fanatical adherent of Baal-worship. When, in 842, her son Ahaziah, king of Judah, perished together with the descendants of Omri in the massacre which followed the revolt of Jehu, Athaliah usurped the throne of Judah and killed all the members of the Davidic dynasty. The only survivor was one of Ahaziah's sons, still a babe, who was hidden from the murderers thanks to the devotion of relatives and the cooperation of the high priest of the Temple at Jerusalem. The legitimate dynasty was restored in 836, when the seven years old Jehoash was proclaimed king and Athaliah was seized and put to death.

The Prophet Isaiah, the adviser and warner of the kings and the people of Judah in the second half of the 8th century B.C.E. Painting by Michelangelo in the Sistine Chapel, Rome.

The moral decay which the alliance with the kingdom of Israel had intensified in Judah, continued to pursue its tragic course. Although the people remained loyal to the house of David and no further dynastic revolt was attempted, both king Jehoash and his son Amaziah died at the hands of regicides. These assassinations probably expressed the violent indignation of patriots at the adversities that Judah suffered during the reign of these two kings. Jehoash was compelled to pay a humiliating tribute to Hazael king of Damascus, who had invaded his country and had threatened the capital. As for Amaziah, he recklessly provoked Joash, king of Israel, but was defeated and taken prisoner, while Jerusalem was captured and plundered.

After a long peaceful interlude (785–743), that extended through the reigns of Azariah and of Jotham and was contemporaneous with the prosperous rule of Jeroboam II in Israel, Judah became involved in the political turmoil caused by the Assyrian policy of expansion towards the west. Unlike the kings of Israel, who brought ruin on their country

Inscription discovered in 1931 in the Russian Monastery on the Mount of Olives. It marked the place to which the remains of King Uzziah (or Azariah) of Judah were transferred, some time in the period of the Second Temple.

The Siloam Tunnel, which brings the water of the Gihon spring, outside the walls of Jerusalem, to the inner pool of Siloam. The construction of the tunnel, by order of King Hezekiah, is mentioned in II Kings 20 : 20. The length of the tunnel is about 1700 feet and its height about 6 feet.

Inscription found in 1880 in the Siloam Tunnel, now in the Archeological Museum of Istanbul. It describes how the stone-cutters, who bored the tunnel from both sides simultaneously, met "drill upon drill, and the water flowed from the source to the pool" The inscription is in Biblical Hebrew and in the ancient Hebrew script.

Sennacherib, king of Assyria (705-681 B.C.E.), sitting on his throne, while the spoil of the city of Lachish passes before him. From the great relief in the palace of Nineveh, now at the British Museum.

by their futile opposition to Assyria, Ahaz king of Judah (743–727) chose peace by voluntarily submitting and paying tribute to Tiglath Pileser III. In an endeavor to appease Assyria, he even erected in the Temple at Jerusalem a copy of the altar he had seen at Damascus, when doing homage to his overlord. It is also possible that it was Ahaz who introduced figures of sacred horses into the Temple in honor of the Assyrian sun-god Shamash.

Under his son, the virtuous and God-fearing king Hezekiah (727–698), whose faithful, but not always heeded, adviser was the prophet Isaiah, the country seemed about to share the fate of Samaria, in consequence of the king's vacillating foreign policy. To prepare his capital for an emergency, he had a conduit cut through the rock, to bring an additional supply of water into the city, into the pool of Siloam (*II Kings 20:20*). The conduit and the inscription, written in ancient Hebrew and recording this remarkable feat of engineering, were re-discovered in 1880. The stone bearing the inscription was transferred to the Archaeological Museum at Istanbul.

The crisis came in 701. Sennacherib, king of Assyria, invaded Judah and, after a prolonged siege, captured the strongly fortified town of Lachish, southwest of Jerusalem, where recent excavations uncovered the remains of some 2,000 human bodies that had, at that time, been flung through a hole in the roof of a tomb-chamber. The siege of Jerusalem that now

39

One of the famous Lachish Letters written on potsherds. This letter (No. 4), written on both sides, is addressed to Yeush, the military commander of Lachish, by an outpost commander named Hoshayahu. He reports that he and his men are watching for light-signals from Lachish, but that the communications with Azekah by light-signals have been interrupted. The Lachish Letters date from the days of the decisive campaign of Nebuchadnezzar against Judah (588-586 B.C.E.).

A Building Inscription of Nebuchadnezzar II, king of Babylonia (604-562 B.C.E.), inscribed on a clay-cylinder. Such cylinders used to be buried in the foundations of restored temples. This king, who destroyed Jerusalem, was a great builder in his own country.

followed was, however, suddenly abandoned, and the people saw in this unexpected relief the result of direct Divine intervention.

Hezekiah's successors, Manasseh (698–642) and Amon (641–640), reverted to the policy of loyal submission to Assyrian suzerainty. On the one hand, this brought fifty years of undisturbed peace to Judah. On the other, however, it also increased Assyrian cultural influence, which was felt by conservative elements to endanger religious values and the traditional way of life. The reaction came in 640, when Amon was murdered and his eight years old son Josiah was enthroned. Priestly and prophetic circles assumed control of the young king's education and he proved an enthusiastic pupil. When, in 622, the Book of Deuteronomy was re-discovered in the Temple, he enforced the Law of Moses as the law of the State. "High places" were destroyed and all vestiges of paganism forcibly uprooted. Jewish sacrificial worship was centralized in the Temple at Jerusalem, and ever since remained indissolubly associated with the Holy City, outside of which it was inadmissible even after the destruction of the Temple.

The former Assyrian threat had meanwhile been succeeded by another, now emanating from the resuscitated Babylonian empire. For a time, Judah was the battlefield on which forces from the south and the north marched and countermarched. In an attempt to intercept an Egyptian army, king Josiah fell in battle at Megiddo (609). Pharaoh Necho II did not recognize the legitimate successor Jehoahaz and in his stead placed Jehoiakim (608–598), another son of Josiah on the throne.

In 598, Nebuchadnezzar king of Babylonia invaded Judah for the first time. Jehoiakim having died just before, his son Jehoiachin surrendered and was taken, together with a section of the population, into exile by Nebuchadnezzar. The Babylonian monarch then placed Zedekiah (597–586) on the throne. But when the latter showed signs of independence and began intriguing against him, Nebuchadnezzar once more marched upon Judah. The course of that campaign of 588–586 is reflected in the Lachish letters, which, written on potsherds, consist of a series of communications addressed by an outpost commander to his superior officer at Lachish and are among the oldest written documents of Jewish history extant.

The resistance was easily overcome. The Babylonians laid siege to Jerusalem in the winter of 587–586, and in the following summer the city was captured and the best and ablest inhabitants deported to Babylonia. The mounting tragedy of these events, extending from the reign of Josiah down to the destruction of Jerusalem, forms the bitter, agonizing subject of the prophet Jeremiah's unhappy predictions.

As far as any creative activity or any vital religious life was concerned, the land now lay desolate for one long generation. The indelible memory of that great national disaster is still to this day mournfully recalled in the Fast of Tishah be-Av — the Ninth of Av.

HIEREMIAS

Failure attended upon a last attempt by Nebuchadnezzar to organize the remnant of the population, by appointing a Judaean nobleman, Gedaliah the son of Ahikam, as governor of the country which was now a Babylonian province. Gedaliah did not succeed in appeasing the extremist elements, who saw in him a collaborator with the national enemy. He was murdered and many of those who had been left in the country, now afraid of Babylonian reprisals, fled to Egypt.

The Prophet Jeremiah, who predicted and witnessed the downfall of Jerusalem. Painting by Michelangelo in the Sistine Chapel, Rome.

42

THE BABYLONIAN EXILE

The exiles in Babylonia found themselves in a land very different from their native southern Palestine. Instead of the rolling hills and valleys of Judaea and the rocky river-beds and parched expanses of the south, they were now living in an immense, irrigated and incredibly fertile plain, in a rich country of large towns and a thriving trade and industry. The highly developed economic life of the Babylonian empire offered countless opportunities to the exiles' spirit of enterprise. Apart from the actual deportation and dispersion, it does not appear that any particular hardship was imposed upon the exiles, who seem to have been free to engage in trade and in the professions, and even to organize themselves in communities.

The Ishtar Gate (as reconstructed in the Staatliche Museen of Berlin), one of the gates of Babylon, dating probably from the time of Nebuchadnezzar.

The destruction of Jerusalem by Nebuchadnezzar and the deportation of the people of Judah, which marked a turning-point in Jewish history, were not deemed important enough by the victor to be commemorated by a monument. But a stele of Ashurbanipal, king of Assyria (669–631 B.C.E.), now in the Louvre at Paris, conveys an idea of the Assyro-Babylonian practice of displacing whole populations to far-off countries .

Nebuchadnezzar's successor, Evil-Merodach, released Jehoiachin king of Judah from imprisonment, in which he had been kept since 597, and bestowed special favors on him. Together with other members of the old Judean royal dynasty, Jehoiachin received official allocations from the household of the king of Babylon, as we learn from Biblical sources (II Kings 25:29–30) as well as from cuneiform administrative documents. Among the exiles there were, naturally, implacable nationalists, who could not forget the humiliation of defeat and dreamt only of revenge, as, for example, the author of Psalm 137, which opens with the tender, yearning lament: "By the rivers of Babylon, there we sat down, yea, we wept, when we remembered Zion," and closes with a fierce, embittered cry for retaliation: "O daughter of Babylon, that art to be destroyed, happy shall he be, that repayeth thee as thou hast served us. Happy shall he be, that taketh and dasheth thy little ones against the rock." The majority of the exiles, however, adapted themselves to the new environment, and many became prosperous. That they were not absorbed, under the circumstances, by the highly developed material and spiritual civilization of the Babylonians, among whom they lived, was mainly due to the activity of the prophets who continued among them.

The outstanding prophet of the period of the Babylonian exile was Ezekiel the son of Buzi. Of priestly descent, he had been led into exile in 597, in the first deportation. By the brilliant description of his mystical visions of the Godhead, by his stern condemnation of religious aberrations, and by his fiery assurance of national rebirth, he nurtured and preserved in the exiles loyalty to their ancestral monotheistic faith and adherence to their traditional values and to their hopes of a renewed national life of liberty in their ancient homeland.

Little is known about the predictions of the prophet Daniel, who was apparently a contemporary of Ezekiel and lived to see the downfall of Babylon. His obscure, shadowy figure subsequently assumed deep significance, on account of the later interpretations placed on his mysterious visions.

One of the greatest exilic prophets is not known to us by name, but a part of his work has been preserved in the Biblical book of Isaiah (*mainly chapters 40–55*). His prophetic activity coincided with the rise of the Persian empire under Cyrus, which portended the decline of Babylonian power. This anonymous prophet followed Cyrus' victories with enthusiasm and greeted him as the future liberator of the exiles.

It is the merit of these prophets that the great majority of the Jewish exiles retained their cohesion and their faith in the one God, who had brought disaster on them because of their sins, but would restore them in due course to their ancient land.

In 538, the Babylonian empire fell before the new power, the highly cultured, resplendent civilization of the Persians.

THE RETURN FROM EXILE

Cyrus, king of Persia and now master of the vast Babylonian empire, adopted a policy of reconciliation and pacification towards the numerous nationalities under his sway — a policy that contrasted sharply with the rude Assyrian and Babylonian practice. Favoring a decentralized administration and the restoration of regional cults in the various provinces of the empire, he directed the conquered peoples to take back to their former shrines the images of the gods that had been carried to Babylon, and allowed exiled national groups to return to their homelands. In conformity with this policy, one of the first acts of the victorious king, after the conquest of Babylon, was to issue a decree permitting the Judean exiles to go back to their country and rebuild the Temple at Jerusalem that had been destroyed.

Although the decree aroused great enthusiasm among the Jews, its immediate result was by no means a general exodus, since many of the exiles had become firmly established in their new land and now found it difficult to uproot themselves. According to the account contained in the second chapter of the Book of Ezra, the first wave of immigration from Mesopotamia to Judea consisted of about 50,000 people under the leadership, first of Sheshbazzar, the prince of Judah, and, shortly afterwards, under that of his successor Zerubbabel, likewise a scion of the

The Ruins of Persepolis, the capital of the Persian Empire. The town was founded by Darius I (521-486 B.C.E.) and destroyed by Alexander the Great in 330 B.C.E.

A Samaritan Torah Scroll. The Samaritans, who accept only the Pentateuch as Holy Scripture, still use the old Hebrew alphabet, while the rest of the Jewish people adopted, after the Babylonian exile, the so-called "square" characters.

Davidic royal house. These men were both invested with the official Persian dignity of governor of Judaea. The exiles who remained behind in Babylon proved their attachment to the ideal of national restoration by liberal contributions of gold, silver, and beasts of burden, and there was a continual flow of money, visitors, and individual immigrants during the subsequent centuries.

The process of resettlement and organization was a slow, gradual, and difficult one. The first task undertaken by the immigrants was to lay the foundation for the rebuilding of the Temple and to re-institute the sacrificial service on an altar set amid the ruins. This, however, aroused the suspicions of the local Persian administration, while intrigues on the part of the leaders of the Samaritan community increased the uneasiness of the situation.

The Samaritans descended, as already mentioned, from the remnant population of the kingdom of Israel, that had not been taken into exile

Detail from the Behistun Inscription of Darius I, cut in the living rock, near Hamadan, the ancient Ecbatana, 225 feet above the road. Above the inscription, which is an autobiography of the Great King in three languages (Persian, Elamite and Babylonian), King Darius is represented crushing his enemies, while the God Ahuza-Mazda hovers over their heads.

and had intermarried with the gentile colonists brought into the country by the Assyrians. At first they volunteered to collaborate in the rebuilding of the Temple. Since, however, the returning exiles did not consider them to be genuine Jews, they rejected the help offered, thereby precipitating the final breach between the Samaritans and the main body of Israel.

In view of these and other difficulties, the construction of the Temple was greatly delayed. The prophets Haggai and Zechariah accused the people of lack of zeal in the service of God and urged the completion of the enterprise. Appealing to Darius I, who had ascended the throne of Persia in 521, the Jews obtained from him confirmation of Cyrus' decree. In 516, more than 20 years after the return, they were finally able to celebrate the dedication of the Second Temple. This was a simple building in comparison with the former one, but was to attain great magnificence. when it was later entirely rebuilt by Herod at the end of the first century B.C.E.

Ezra, "a ready scribe in the Law of Moses... had set his heart to seek the law of the Lord and to do it." In the days of Artaxerxes I, King of Persia, he came from Babylon to Jerusalem on an official mission, "to teach in Israel statutes and judgements." (Ezra 7:1–10) From a miniature in the Codex Amiatinus, Laurentian Library, Florence.

Jewish coin of the Persian period, bearing on the reverse, to the right of the owl, the inscription "Yehud" in ancient Hebrew characters. The coin proves the status of an autonomous province enjoyed by Judaea under Persian rule.

The dedication of the Temple did not bring an end to the difficulties of the settlers. Intermarriage with gentile neighbors soon created religious and social problems. These were further aggravated by an acute economic crisis, as a result of which a large section of the settlers became financially dependent on the class of rich landed proprietors, who proved to be harsh usurers. Thanks to the consistently favorable attitude of the Persian court, help came from the Babylonian community .About the middle of the 5th century, Ezra, the priest and scribe, arrived in Jerusalem. He had been invested by King Artaxerxes I with full powers to organize the Judaean settlement in accordance with the Law of God. A few years later, the king appointed his Jewish cup-bearer, Nehemiah the son of Hacaliah, governor of Judea. Through the combined efforts of Ezra and Nehemiah, the various problems were solved. The walls of Jerusalem were restored, bringing some measure of physical security, and the Law of Moses was solemnly proclaimed as binding upon the new Commonwealth.

Judaea, the province Yehud, as it was designated on contemporary coins, was now governed by the high priest as the supreme head of the Jewish people. During the following century, apart from some incidents, the country pursued a tranquil existence under Persian rule, until Alexander the Great, having defeated the Persian empire in 333, brought the challenge of Greek culture to Palestine.

Xerxes I, King of Persia
(485–465 B.C.E.) from a
relief at Persepolis. According
to the opinion of many scholars, he is the king referred
to as Ahasuerus in the Book of
Esther.

"Then took Haman the (king's)
apparel and the horse and
caused Mordecai to ride
through the streets of the city
and proclaimed before him:
Thus shall it be done unto the
man whom the king delighteth
to honor" (Esther 6:11). Purim
dish of the 18th century,
Musée de Cluny, Paris.

The island of Elephantine in the Nile, opposite Assuan. This was the site of a Jewish military colony in the 6th-5th century B.C.E. The discovery, here, of documents written on papyrus threw a new light on the Jewish history in the period of Ezra and Nehemia.

The spirit of tolerance that characterized the Persian administration seems to have assured, on the whole, an undisturbed, dignified life to the Jewish communities in all parts of the empire. But there is a fundamental element of insecurity in the life of an ethnic and religious minority, and dramatic clashes are bound to occur from time to time. The Book of Esther tells of the attempt of an anti-Semitic minister, Haman, to exterminate the Jews with the sanction of a capricious king, Ahasuerus. But the plot was foiled by the prudence of the Jew Mordecai and the courage and charm of the Jewish queen Esther. The historical authenticity of the book is still problematic, and it is difficult to say exactly which Persian king is meant by Ahasuerus. The book has, however, been regarded by the Jews as an unceasing reminder of the danger inherent in life in the Diaspora, and the feast of Purim, commemorating the miraculous deliverance of the Persian Jews, has been observed since then by the Jewish communities throughout the world.

In addition to the exiles who remained in Babylonia, there was also a considerable settlement of Jews in Egypt. The discovery of the Elephantine papyri has brought to light the history of one group of Egyptian Jews, who formed a military colony that existed for a lengthy period on the island of Elephantine (called in Egyptian Yeb) opposite Syene (now Assuan), near the first cataract of the Nile. The colony, which spoke Aramaic and had its own temple, was probably founded by the Pharaoh Psammetichus II at the beginning of the 6th century, and may have been augmented by Judaean refugees who left their country in 586 after the assassination of Gedaliah. When Cyrus' son and successor, Cambyses, conquered Egypt in 525, he is said to have destroyed all the Egyptian temples, but to have spared that of the Jews at Elephantine.

The Elephantine papyri reveal a thriving economic life, as well as a certain degree of literary interest. Towards the end of the 5th century, in the days of Darius II, a group of fanatical Egyptians, taking advantage of the absence of the Persian governor, destroyed the temple, whereupon the community appealed to the high priest in Jerusalem and to the governor of Judea for help in rebuilding it. Although the governor's reply was a favorable one, we do not know whether the temple was ever restored or what later became of this isolated outpost of Judaism.

The Book of Esther is usually written on scrolls of parchment. Such scrolls were often artistically illuminated. This is part of a Scroll of Esther written in Southern France about 1600. (Roth Collection)

THE HASMONEAN REVOLT

The rise of Alexander the Great and the overthrow of the Persian empire at the battle of Issus (333 B.C.E.) completely altered the face of the Middle East. After his victory at Issus, Alexander, turning southward to conquer Egypt, occupied Palestine on his way there. The Jews peacefully accepted the change of rule and, led by the High Priest Simon the Just, went out to meet the conqueror. A Talmudic legend tells that Alexander alighted from his chariot to bow to the High Priest. When his generals questioned him on his strange behavior, Alexander replied, that the figure of that venerable old man had appeared to him in a vision before a battle and had led him on to victory. The historian Josephus adds that Alexander went up to Jerusalem, where he offered

The battle of Issus, in which Alexander the Great defeated Darius III Codomanus, king of Persia, in 333 B.C. Wall-painting from Pompei, in the Museo Nazionale, Naples. The battle sealed the triumph of Alexander over the Persian Empire and brought Palestine, among other territories, under his rule.

One of the Hellenistic cities which sprung up in Palestine under Ptolemaic rule was Philadelphia, so called after its founder, Ptolemy II Philadelphus, built on the site of the Biblical Rabbath-Ammon. In Amman, the present capital of the Kingdom of Jordan. impressive remains from the Hellenistic and Roman periods still testify to Philadelphia's past grandeur.

sacrifices to God. He permitted the Jews to live in accordance with their ancestral laws and exempted them from paying tribute every seventh year (the sabbatical year, when tilling the soil was forbidden).

The conditions under which the Jews had henceforth to live, were entirely different from those that had previously existed. Palestine now became the scene of a pervasive Greek culture, which made deep inroads on the Jewish way of life.

Alexander's career was a short one. He died in 323, barely ten years after Issus, and his empire did not survive him. After bloody conflicts between Alexander's ambitious generals, one of them, Ptolemy, secured the sovereignty over Egypt, and another, Seleucus, the rule over both Syria and part of the remaining Asiatic territories that had been conquered by Alexander. For more than a century, Palestine was subject to the Ptolemies of Egypt who, on the whole, favored and protected their Jewish subjects. Under their rule, close contact between Jews and Greeks inevitably exerted a considerable influence on Judaism. The Hellenistic outlook affected first and foremost the highest levels of society — the priestly aristocracy and the well-to-do tax-farmers and merchants. Knowledge of the Greek language spread among the Jews, who learned to participate in Greek gymnastic games, to frequent the Greek theater, and to appreciate Greek literature and philosophy. Respect for religious observance grew lax and scepticism tended to destroy tradition.

On the other hand, there were those who vehemently opposed this tendency towards Hellenism. Among these were the Hassidim (the pious ones), as well as the high priestly family of the Oniads. But the control of secular matters gradually passed out of the hands of the high priest into those of the Hellenizing Tobiads, descendants of Tobiah the Ammonite, who is mentioned in the Biblical book of Nehemiah. This family had accumulated great wealth by successful tax-farming and had gained political power through close ties, first with the Egyptian and subsequently with the Syrian court. At Arak-el-Amir in Transjordan, there still stand the impressive ruins of the palace of the Tobiad family, while exquisite coins of some of the Greek cities in the area bear additional testimony to the powerful Hellenistic influence. Interesting details about this period and about the Tobiads have been revealed by the Zenon Papyri, an Egyptian archive discovered in 1915 in the Fayyum province.

The Ptolemies, who were amicably disposed towards the Jews of Palestine, also favored the settlement of Jews in Egypt and employed them in their armies, where the highest ranks were open to them. The community of Alexandria became one of first importance, the splendor of its great synagogue being recalled in the Talmud.

The Ptolemies even took an interest in Jewish culture, as is evident from the famous Greek translation of the Bible, which was commenced under the auspices of Ptolemy II Philadelphus (285–246 B.C.E.). This translation

Northern entrance to the palace of the Tobiads at Arak-el-Amir in Transjordan (Reconstruction). From the 3rd-2nd centuries B.C.E.

Page from the Codex Sinaiticus (British Museum), a 4th century manuscript of the Greek version of the Bible, known as the Septuagint. This manuscript is called "Sinaiticus", because it was discovered, about the middle of the 19th century, in the Monastery of St. Catherine on Mount Sinai.

is known as the Septuagint, "the version of the Seventy." However, the correct name should, perhaps, be "the version of the Seventy-two," since, according to the apocryphal book "Letter of Aristeas" and to Talmudic tradition, 72 Jewish elders were sent by the high priest to Alexandria, at the king's request, to translate the Pentateuch.

From the outset, the Seleucid dynasty of Syria had contested the right of Egypt over Palestine. It was, however, only in 218 B.C.E. that Seleucid claims to Palestine were translated into action by Antiochus III. After a lengthy war, in the course of which his army was once defeated by the Egyptians in the battle of Raphia (on the border between Egypt and the Gaza Strip), Antiochus won a brilliant victory at Paneas, near the sources of the Jordan, and entered Jerusalem in 198. The change from Egyptian to Syrian rule pursued a peaceful course, since Antiochus III adopted a friendly attitude towards the Jews. The Syrian court, however, encouraged the process of Hellenization more actively than had been done by the tolerant Ptolemies, with the result that the Hellenistic Jewish circles now took the lead, and the breach between them and the conservative Hassidim widened considerably.

With the death of Antiochus III in 187, the idyllic relations between the Seleucid dynasty and its Jewish subjects came to an end. His successor, Seleucus IV, attempted to seize the treasures of the Temple at Jerusalem, but was, according to legend, thwarted in his attempt through a miraculous intervention. A few years later, when Antiochus IV Epiphanes ascended the Syrian throne, matters reached a crisis. The new ruler, a fanatical Hellenist, sought to Hellenize his dominions in every conceivable way, not excepting religion. He first interfered with Jewish religious life by deposing and appointing high priests at will and by plundering the Temple treasury. The legitimate high priest Onias was murdered. His son, likewise called Onias, fled to Egypt where, at Leontopolis, he founded a rival Temple, in which, contrary to the Deuteronomic principle, sacrificial services were held for about two and a half centuries.

The extreme Hellenists now had the upper hand in Jerusalem and spared no effort to "modernize" the Jewish religion and to transform it in conformity with the king's wishes. Encouraged by their compliance, Antiochus Epiphanes took the final step. In 168 B.C.E., he erected an altar to the Olympian god Zeus in the Temple at Jerusalem and forbade the practice of the fundamental Jewish religious observances.

This profanation sparked off a revolt led, in the first instance, by Mattathias the Hasmonean, an old priest of Modiin (a village in the hill country east of Lydda). With his five sons and with the zealots who had joined him, he retired into the mountains, whence he launched raids on the country, attacking Jewish apostates, destroying heathen altars, and forcibly circumcizing Jewish children found to be uncircumcized. The Syrian forces declared war against the rebels. At first Mattathias went so far in the observance of the Law, that he forbade any fighting, even in self-defence, on the Sabbath. The Syrians, taking advantage of these scruples, attacked principally on Sabbaths, when they could, without risk to themselves, inflict heavy losses on their adversaries. As a consequence, the Jews soon abandoned their previous policy in favor of permitting defensive fighting at all times.

Mattathias died, less than a year after the outbreak of the revolt. Before his death, he exhorted his followers to appoint, as his successor, his third son Judah, surnamed "the Maccabee." The meaning of the appellation is uncertain, the popular interpretation being "The Hammerer."

In accordance with Mattathias' wishes, Judah the Maccabee assumed military command and proved himself to be so inspired a leader, that he achieved everlasting fame among the Jewish people. With but modest forces, Judah defeated vastly superior Syrian armies in the battles of Beth Horon (north-west of Jerusalem) and Emmaus (near Latrun). After these victories, he entered Jerusalem and cleansed the desecrated Temple. In December (25th Kislev) 165 B.C.E., the Temple was re-dedicated, in memory of which the Feast of Hanukkah is, to this

Coin of Antiochus III, King of Syria (223–187 B.C.E.). The reverse shows an elephant, the formidable weapon of the Syrian army. The Syrians used elephants in their warfare against the Hasmoneans, although they were forbidden by the Romans to employ them, after the battle of Magnesia (190 B.C.E.).

The purification and re-dedication of the Temple of Jerusalem by Judah the Maccabee in 165 B.C.E. is commemorated every year by the feast of Hanukkah observed in the month of Kislev. During eight days lights are kindled, beginning with one light at the eve of the first day and adding one on each successive evening. The Hanukkah Lamp became a favourite theme of Jewish ritual art.

Above: a bronze Hanukkah lamp from Southern France, 14th or 15th century (Roth Collection).

Below: a bronze Hanukkah lamp dated 1574, made bei Meir Heilperin, Germany. Israel Museum, Jerusalem.

day, observed by the Jews throughout the world. It is celebrated as a feast of lights, when "Menorot" or "Hanukkiyyot" — Hanukkah lamps with eight lights — are lit in commemoration of the miracle which, according to tradition, occurred on that occasion. For the lighting of the golden candlestick in the Temple, just one small cruse of holy oil was found, normally sufficient for one day only, which, however, by a miracle, burnt throughout the eight days of the ceremony of dedication.

But final victory was yet to be achieved. Judah the Maccabee had to wage war against neighboring peoples, who sided with the Syrians; he had once more to face an army, sent against him by Antiochus V Eupator, who had meanwhile succeeded Antiochus IV Epiphanes. In a battle fought at Beth Zechariah (south-west of Jerusalem, on the way to Beth Zur), the Syrians made use of elephants. Eleazar, one of Judah's brothers, was killed in this battle, crushed beneath the weight of an elephant he had slain by running his spear through its belly.

In 161, the new ruler of Syria, Demetrius I Soter, dispatched against Judah a powerful army, led by one of Syria's ablest generals, Nicanor. By his superior military genius, however, Judah once again won the day at Beth Horon. This was his most brilliant, but also his last victory. A few months later, he fell in battle at that very place, when he heroically pitted 800 men against the Syrian force that had been sent to avenge the defeat of Nicanor.

The command was taken over by Jonathan, his brother. Demetrius I, finally realizing the hopelessness of quelling the revolt, came to terms with Jonathan and allowed him to enter Jerusalem, while Demetrius' successor went still further and recognized him as high priest. Partly by diplomacy, partly by arms, Jonathan enlarged the territory under his control, gained access to the sea by conquering Jaffa, and established friendly ties with Rome. But his successes found no favor with the Syrians, who treacherously seized him and murdered him and his sons.

The leadership now passed to Simon, the eldest of the Hasmonean brothers (142–135). He was recognized as high priest, prince, and military commander of the Jewish people. Simon succeeded in occupying the Akra, the fortress in Jerusalem, from which the Syrians had for so long dominated and menaced the city.

Coin of Antiochus VII Sidetes (139–129 B.C.E.), King of Syria in the days of the Hasmoneans Simon and John Hyrcanus. who reasserted his claim on Judaea.

The Story of Judith. Miniatures in the "Siddur Mainz" (Cod. Hebr. 37, Hamburg Library).
Above: Judith cutting the head of Holofernes, who lies intoxicated on the couch.
Below: Judith returns with Holofernes' head to the city of Bethulia. The story reflects the patriotic and warlike mood which prevailed in the early Hasmonean period.

These dramatic events left a profound impression on Hebrew folk-lore. The legendary story of Judith, the devoted woman who saved her people by killing the pagan general Holofernes in his tent, presumably refers to this period.

Simon's conquests were not limited to purely Jewish areas, nor were they always welcomed by the inhabitants of those regions. A graffito — a writing scratched on a wall — found at Gezer, which he captured and annexed, calls down fire from heaven on his house.

In a battle near Jabneh, Simon's sons inflicted a severe reverse upon the Syrian army sent by Antiochus VII to compel him to renounce all his conquests beyond the borders of Judaea. But Simon was treacherously murdered by his own son-in-law and was succeeded as high priest and prince by his son John Hyrcanus.

THE HASMONEAN KINGDOM

Like his predecessors, John Hyrcanus (known as Hyrcanus I) had to defend himself against Syrian attacks. Taking personal command of the army, Antiochus VII Sidetes invaded Palestine and besieged Jerusalem. Although the Syrians failed to capture the city, hunger, nevertheless, compelled Hyrcanus to sue for peace and to accept onerous conditions. But with the outbreak of grave disorders in Syria, following on the death of Antiochus VII, Hyrcanus began to disregard the terms of the treaty imposed upon him and embarked upon a series of triumphant campaigns against his neighbors. To finance this war, he is said to have opened the tomb of king David and to have used the treasures found there. By his military operations, Hyrcanus enlarged the borders of the Jewish State in every direction. Occupying once again the ancient boundaries of Biblical times, the re-established commonwealth gave expression to its newly acquired sense of independence by striking coins bearing conventional Jewish symbols. Everywhere in the conquered territories, the heathen population was forced to adopt Judaism.

His reign marked the first open breach between the two parties of the Sadducees and the Pharisees. The Sadducees, consisting mainly of members of the priestly aristocracy, were reactionary in the religious sphere and opportunists in the political, which two, they held, were to be kept separate and apart. On the other hand, the Pharisees, a popular faction led by the sages of the Law, maintained that there could be no separation between religion and politics, and that all life in its many and varied aspects, whether political or economic, had to be governed by revealed Law and tradition. Both groups were represented in the Sanhedrin, the Supreme Council of 71 members, which assisted the Hasmonean prince in political, legislative, and religious matters. But as the Pharisees opposed his policy, John Hyrcanus relied upon the Sadducees, who thus gained the upper hand, both in the Sanhedrin and at court.

Inscription from Gezer, of the Hasmonean period. The Hebrew text reads: "Boundary of Gezer". It has been suggested that the inscription was one of the signs marking the boundaries of the territory within which the citizens of Gezer could move about freely on Sabbath-days.

Bronze coin struck by John Hyrcanus. The inscription on the obverse reads: "Yohanan the High Priest and the Community of the Jews". The reverse bears a double cornucopia with a poppy-head in the middle.

The so-called "Tomb of Absalom", one of the funerary monuments in the Kidron Valley, outside Jerusalem, at the foot of the Mount of Olives. The square substructure is hewn out of the rock. The monument dates probably from the beginning of the 1st century C.E. (Drawing by J. Böhm, 1924).

One of the remarkable rock-hewn funerary monuments at Petra, the capital of the Nabataeans. The Nabataetan king, Aretas III, supported Hyrcanus II in his struggle with his brother Aristobulus.

John Hyrcanus was succeeded by his son Judah Aristobulus (104–103), the first Hasmonean to assume the title of king. The fact that he adopted a Greek name and that Greek authors called him a Philhellene (a friend of the Greeks) is symptomatic of a strange, but not infrequent phenomenon. The Hasmoneans, who had arisen as champions in the struggle against Hellenism and had carved out an immortal name for themselves by their undaunted bravery and by their unswerving devotion to Judaism and to their people's values, had themselves become Hellenized!

After a brief reign, Aristobulus was succeeded on the throne by his brother Alexander Yannai (*Jannaeus:* 103–76), who married the deceased king's widow (in accordance with Jewish law, since Aristobulus had died leaving no offspring). Alexander Yannai, who shared his father's bent for military adventures, but not always his good fortune in battle, was successful in extending the territory of his kingdom. But his costly campaigns and his despotic regime estranged his subjects who, under the leadership of the Pharisaic party, rose in revolt against him. It was only by using the utmost cruelty against the rebels, that Alexander Yannai was able to preserve his throne. He died while campaigning in Transjordan.

After his death, his widow Salome Alexandra (76–67) ruled for nine years with prudence and energy. Adopting a new approach in internal affairs, she reversed the course pursued by the Hasmonean rulers since the days of John Hyrcanus and, instead, favored the popular Pharisaic party, while in her external policy she succeeded in maintaining the safety and security of her kingdom by peaceful means. Her short reign was remembered as a period of peace and prosperity.

When she died, her two sons, Hyrcanus and Aristobulus, disputed the succession. Civil war broke out. At first Aristobulus was victorious and Hyrcanus was obliged to waive his claims to the throne in favor of his brother. But Hyrcanus soon regretted this renunciation of his rights and, taking refuge at Petra, at the court of Aretas III, king of the Nabateans, he induced the latter to support his claims and to attack Aristobulus in Jerusalem. A long and unsuccessful siege ensued, whereupon the rival brothers appealed to the Roman general Pompey who, having conquered Syria, was then in Damascus. Pompey solved the problem, as was to be expected, by making Judaea a Roman province. Entering Jerusalem, he took Aristobulus prisoner and sent him to Rome, while Hyrcanus, who had to forego the title of king, was confirmed as high priest and ethnarch (head of the people).

Such was the melancholy finish to a century of Maccabean struggle for independence — a century that had begun so bravely and proudly, but ended so ingloriously and pathetically.

Pompey, called "the Great" (Museo Capitolino, Rome), who put an end to Hasmonean independence by annexing Judaea to Rome in 63 B.C.E.

THE ROMAN TYRANNY

Henceforth, for seven centuries in effect, Palestine was, with some brief interludes, under the rule of Rome (during the second half of this period, under that of the Eastern Roman Empire, i.e., Byzantium). Always tight and oppressive, the control that was exercised assumed various forms.

While Hyrcanus bore the title of ethnarch, conceded to him by Pompey, Judaea was, in actual fact, under the jurisdiction of the proconsul of Syria and its real ruler was Hyrcanus' all-powerful adviser and minister Antipater, descended from a family of Idumaean proselytes, who enjoyed the confidence of Rome. In his hands Hyrcanus was a mere puppet.

Hyrcanus was called upon to defend his position, with Roman help, first against his brother Aristobulus' son, Alexander, who had contrived to elude his Roman captors and now claimed the high priesthood; next, against Aristobulus himself, who had likewise escaped from captivity; and finally against Aristobulus' second son, Antigonus, who, with the

Masada, the site of Herod's magnificent constructions. The place was to become a symbol of Jewish heroism, when it held out against the Romans three years after the destruction of Jerusalem.

Corinthian capital in Herod's palace at Masada.

assistance of the Parthians, succeeded in conquering Judaea. Having sent his uncle Hyrcanus captive to Parthia, he occupied the throne of Judaea (40–37 B.C.E.) and struck his own coinage bearing Jewish national symbols. He was, however, deposed with the aid of the Romans by Herod, the son of Antipater.

After the assassination of his father (in 43 B.C.E.), Herod inherited the confidence and support of Rome and allied himself with the Hasmonean family by marrying Hyrcanus' grand-daughter, the beautiful Mariamne. Proclaimed king of Judaea by the Roman Senate (40 B.C.E.), Herod conquered his kingdom, with the help of Roman troops placed at his disposal, and finally entered Jerusalem in 37 B.C.E. For a third of a century (37—4 B.C.E.), he reigned over Judaea, an energetic, capable and, in certain respects, far-sighted ruler, who was skilful in weathering the vicissitudes and storms of Roman civil wars and in siding, at the opportune moment, with the victor. As far as his foreign policy was concerned, his reign was a peaceful one. With Roman approval, he annexed Idumaea in the south, Samaria and Galilee in the north, and large territories east of the Jordan. His ambitious projects filled the land with splendid new buildings and cities in the Roman manner. At Masada, on an almost inaccessible crag overlooking the Dead Sea, he erected a luxurious

Greek inscription from the Herodian temple at Jerusalem, marking the confines of the holy precincts, the entry of which was forbidden to strangers under penalty of death. (Archeological Museum Istanbul).

palace-fortress that dominated the area. He built Caesarea on the sea-coast, north of Jaffa, transforming it into a great city rivaling Alexandria as a port and Jerusalem as the center of the country's life. The former Israelite Samaria now became Sebaste, a resplendent Greco-Roman city.

Herod's major achievement was, however, the rebuilding of the Temple at Jerusalem, executed with a lavish magnificence that became proverbial. The impressive remains of the Temple, which may still to-day be seen, are substantially part of the edifice he constructed.

In one sphere, however, Herod failed — and failed tragically. He was unable to gain the love of the Jewish people, who saw in him only an alien, a usurper and a servant of Rome. His gloomy character and his suspiciousness, which led him to suspect plots and conspiracies everywhere, account for an appalling series of domestic tragedies that cost the lives of his wife Mariamne, her brother Alexander, her grandfather Hyrcanus and three of Herod's own sons, so that his name has gone down in history as an unscrupulous and bloodthirsty tyrant.

After his death in 4 B.C.E., the Romans brought the monarchy to an end and divided the country among his three sons, Archelaus, Antipas, and Philip. Archelaus, who was given the title of ethnarch instead of that of king, was assigned Judaea, Samaria, and Idumaea, while Antipas was granted the rule of Galilee, and Philip, that of the territories east of the Jordan. Antipas and Philip had to content themselves with the rank of tetrarch (governor of a tetrarchy or district), a title often bestowed by the Romans on petty foreign princes.

The circumstances prevailing in Palestine under Herod's successors are, to some extent, reflected in the New Testament narratives.

From the outset, tension and conflict marked the relationships between Archelaus and his subjects. After enduring his tyrannical rule for ten years, the people appealed against him to Rome, whereupon the emperor Augustus deposed him and banished him to Gaul. (6 C.E.).

The "Wailing Wall", in Hebrew "The Western Wall", the only remnant of the Temple of Jerusalem. It has been considered, throughout the ages, as a Holy Place to which Jews from all over the world used to go on pilgrimage.

Inscription of Pontius Pilate discovered at Caesarea in 1964. This is the only extant inscription mentioning the name of this most famous Roman procurator.

Antipas succeeded in maintaining himself in Galilee during the reign of the emperors Augustus and Tiberius. Like his father, he was a zealous builder and founded the city of Tiberias. On the accession of Gaius Caligula to the imperial throne, Antipas tried to obtain the royal title for himself. This aroused the emperor's suspicions and in 37 C.E, Antipas, like Archelaus before him, had to go into exile to Gaul.

Philip was the only one who enjoyed a peaceful reign to his death (34 C.E.). Having likewise inherited Herod's love of building, he had founded, near the sources of the Jordan, the city of Caesarea Philippi (close to the present Syrian town of Banias, the ancient Paneas).

After Archelaus' banishment, the Romans resumed direct control of the country and ruled Judaea through procurators. The most famous of these was Pontius Pilate (26–36), under whom, according to the Gospels, the crucifixion of Jesus of Nazareth took place. His predecessor, Valerius Gratus, had already created profound discontent among the Jews by abusing his powers through interfering in the nomination of the high priest. Pilate behaved with even greater tactlessness and lack of statesmanship. He missed no opportunity of offending Jewish religious suscepti-bilities, and whenever he succeeded in provoking a riot, repressed it with the utmost severity and cruelty. Even Rome, at last, found that he had exceeded the bounds of his authority, and Pilate was recalled.

There was again a critical moment, when the emperor Caligula tried to enforce the cult of his person and the erection of his effigy in the Temple of Jerusalem. The famous Jewish philosopher Philo of Alexandria went to Rome to plead the Jewish cause and the emperor's assassination, in 41, finally averted the threat.

Portrait-coin of Herod Agrippa, I King of Judea (37–44 C.E.)

Between the years 37 and 44, there was an interlude in the direct Roman rule. Herod's grandson, Herod Agrippa I, was awarded the royal title and the territories east of Jordan, after the death of his uncle Philip. He was granted Galilee after Antipas' deposition and, finally, also Judaea and Samaria, so that his rule extended at last almost as far as that of Herod. Because of his punctilious observance of Jewish law, Herod Agrippa I was extremely popular with his Jewish subjects.

The country once more reverted to direct rule by procurators on the death of Herod Agrippa, whose son, Agrippa II, was consoled with the title of king of Chalcis. A few years later, he was assigned the Trans-jordanian territories, where his father had commenced his rule, as well as the supervision of the Temple at Jerusalem and the right to appoint the high priest.

THE GREAT REVOLT

The rule of the procurators, which became increasingly harsh and oppressive from the middle of the first century, was destined to have profound repercussions on Jewish life. That the transition, from the apparent autonomy under king Agrippa I to the reinstatement of direct Roman administration, met with resistance on the part of large circles of the Jewish people, is easy to understand. Even honest, capable, and well-intentioned procurators would have found their task a difficult one. What made matters worse, was the fact that the choice of procurators was most unfortunate. They were crude and venal, bent on enriching themselves by any means, and devoid of the slightest consideration for Jewish national and religious susceptibilities. Under these circumstances, relations between the Jews and the Romans were bound rapidly to deteriorate, and the situation moved irresistibly towards the final catastrophe.

In his works, "Antiquities of the Jews" and "Wars of the Jews," the Jewish historian Josephus, who lived through this period and took an active part in political life, has left an eyewitness account of contemporary events. Although often biased and unobjective, this record is,

Presumed bust of Flavius Josephus. (Ny Carlsberg Glyptothek, Copenhagen). Unreliable as a military leader in the Jewish revolt against Rome, Josephus achieved high merit as a historian of his people.

nevertheless, of the greatest historical and human interest. According to Josephus, the Jewish people was divided into three "philosophical sects," a term used by him in order to make the difference of outlook of the various Jewish groups more explicable to the gentile Greco-Roman world, for whom Josephus intended his writings. These "philosophical sects" were, in reality, religious groupings in which opposing interpretations of Judaism, conflicting social practices, and differing political activity were inextricably interwoven.

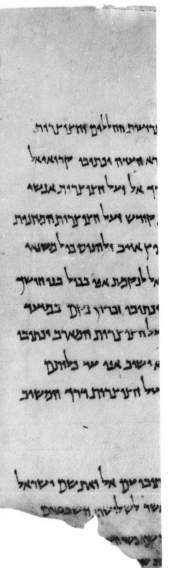

A column from the Scroll of the "War of the Sons of Light against the Sons of Darkness," one of the manuscripts discovered in 1947 in a cave near the Dead Sea. This is a plan of campaign for the war which Israel will have to sustain against the powers of darkness, before the final triumph of God is achieved.

We have already encountered the Pharisees and Sadducees as antagonistic parties in the reign of the Hasmonean rulers. Comprising mainly the priests and the aristocracy and representing wealth and power, the Sadducees held that God is not concerned with man's deeds in this world and that each one is permitted to act as he pleases (*Wars II, 8, 14*). They did not share the Messianic hopes of the Pharisees and of the people, concentrating rather on their own worldly success, largely through political activity. Furthermore, they rejected all laws that were not contained in the written Law, holding that the observances and enactments which the Pharisees derived from tradition, were without authority (*Antiquities XIII, 10, 6*). Because they were concerned with maintaining their own position, they were prepared to come to terms with the Roman conqueror, even at the expense of national interests.

On the other hand, the Pharisees, who had "the multitude on their side" (*ib., loc. cit.*), represented progress and religious democracy. In the belief that the teachings of God are to pervade and sanctify all life, they sought to spread the knowledge of the Torah among the masses and adopted the principle of the dynamic development of the written Law. Living simple, spiritual lives that were bound up with the welfare of the people as a whole, the Pharisees, while embracing the great Messianic hopes of the nation, were, in the main, opposed to an armed conflict with the Romans. They felt that the times were not yet ripe for the coming of the Messiah and that such a conflict with Rome would only lead to national disaster. When that disaster occurred and the Second Temple was destroyed, the Sadducees disappeared as a party, leaving the Pharisees to shape the character and future survival of the Jewish people. In the achievement of this task the Pharisaic movement proved its abiding significance.

The third group, the Essenes, is first mentioned by Josephus during the reign of Jonathan, and then again during that of Herod. The Essenes, desirous of dedicating themselves to the highest standards of holiness in preparation for the imminent coming of the Messiah, formed themselves in a society that had "no one certain city, but many of them dwell in every city" (*Wars II, 8, 4*). They shared their possessions in common, practised extreme piety as well as loving-kindness towards brethren and strangers, studied the ancient writings, purified themselves by frequent immersions and earned their bread by manual labor. Marriage was not usual among them, and membership, with its initiation into the higher mysteries of the group, was permitted only after a lengthy probationary period. It was possibly an offshoot of the Essenes which produced the apocalyptic literature recently discovered in caves near the Dead Sea, and built the buildings excavated at Wadi Qumran.

Josephus also mentions a "fourth sect of Jewish philosophy," founded, according to him, by Judah the Galilean in the first years of the common era and called the Zealots or Sicarii. "These men," says Josephus of them, "agree in all other things with the Pharisaic notions but they have an inviolable attachment to liberty" (*Antiquities XVIII, 1, 6*), being prepared bravely and unflinchingly to face death for their principle "that God is to be their only Ruler and Lord" in the kingdom of God, about to be established on earth, and not idolatrous Rome. Some scholars have identified these Zealots with the Qumran sect.

There was no relief from the increasingly heavy yoke of Roman oppression. These sufferings were interpreted by some as the *Ḥevle ha-Mashiaḥ*, the birthpangs of the Messiah, whose coming they sought to hasten by the overthrow of the wicked kingdom of Rome. The Romans, naturally seeing in all this a rebellion against their rule, put down these Messianic-inspired risings with a heavy hand. Armed revolt did not, however, flare up until 66, when the exactions and financial maladministration of the procurators, the last of whom, Gessius Florus, was the most venal and unscrupulous, occasioned yet greater distress and led to a general uprising in Jerusalem and to the expulsion of the Roman garrison. In order to suppress the revolt, the legate of Syria, G. Cestius Gallus, marched into Palestine at the head of a large force. However, inexplicably withdrawing from under the walls of Jerusalem, he was overwhelmed during his retreat on the classical battleground at the pass of Beth Horon. This remarkable success seemed almost to presage the dawn of Messianic days. A revolutionary government was set up in Jerusalem and assumed control of the administration of the entire country. Bearing symbols of redemption, finely minted coins were issued, including, for the first time, a silver currency. The country was divided into districts and organized for defence. One of the most important of these regions, Galilee, was entrusted to the command of Joseph ben Mattathias the Priest (the already mentioned historian Josephus Flavius).

Following the defeat of the legate of Syria, the emperor Nero appointed Vespasian, one of the ablest Roman generals, to conduct the military operations in Palestine. Soon after he had invaded Galilee in the spring of 67, resistance in that decisively important northern sector crumbled, due, in large measure, to the treachery of its commander Josephus. The latter went over to the Romans and subsequently became, when living in Rome as a protégé of the imperial family, the historian of the war in which he had played so inglorious a part.

The tragic and unexpected defeat in Galilee discredited the revolutionary government formed by the more moderate aristocratic elements. It was replaced by those who held more extreme views on the means of hastening the coming of Messianic times by the overthrow of the evil, pagan rule of Rome. However, comprising various groups, the extremists soon became locked within Jerusalem in a grim struggle for supremacy, with John of Gischala, Eleazar ben Simon, and Simon bar Giora and

Jewish coins struck during the Great Revolt (66–70 C.E.).

Silver half-shekel of the first year. On the obverse a chalice and the inscription "Half-Shekel — 1". On the reverse a bunch of three pomegranates and the inscription "Jerusalem the Holy".

Bronze coin of the second year. On the obverse an amphora and inscription "Year two". On the reverse a vine branch with leaf and the inscription "Deliverance of Zion".

Bronze coin of the third year. On the obverse an amphora with lid and the inscription "Year three". On the reverse vine branch with leaf and the inscription "Deliverance of Zion".

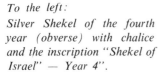

To the left:
Silver Shekel of the fourth year (obverse) with chalice and the inscription "Shekel of Israel" — Year 4".
To the right:
Bronze half-shekel of the fourth year (obverse) with palm-tree and two fruit-baskets. The inscription reads "Deliverance of Zion".

73

Masadah, the crag near the Dead Sea on which Herod built his fortified palace and which was to become the last stand of the Jewish patriots after the fall of Jerusalem (Aerial photograph by Dr. B. Rutenberg.)

Relief from the Arch of Titus at Rome, erected as a memorial of the victory over the Jews. Spoils from the Temple of Jerusalem, among them the seven-branched candelabrum, are carried in the triumphal procession.

their followers forming three armed camps that fought one another for leadership. John of Gischala and Simon bar Giora, in particular, clashed in bitter civil warfare. It was not a conflict of personalities, but of ideologies. Each faction had its own social-religious programme, and considered that only when this had been carried into effect, would God give victory to his people.

In the meantime, Vespasian, having conquered almost all the remainder of the country and having isolated Jerusalem, delayed his final assault upon the city, in order to allow the defenders to weaken themselves yet more by their internal conflicts and internecine fighting. He was, moreover, prevented from taking further action by the political disorders and struggles in Rome that followed the death of Nero. When Vespasian finally departed for Rome to become emperor, he left his son Titus in charge of the conduct of operations in Judea. Only when the latter besieged Jerusalem in the spring of 70, did the Jews, at long last, close their ranks.

Described in great detail by Josephus, the siege was one of the classical battles of ancient history. There were attacks and counter-attacks, there were engines of war, attempts at breaching the walls with battering rams, catapults that discharged huge missiles, and bombardment with ballistae capable of hurling large stones over great distances.

Besides the enemy without, dread famine stalked within the city and took its fearful toll of the population of Jerusalem, swollen by the arrival of large numbers of pilgrims for the Passover. The Jews, weakened by hunger and starvation, were unable, despite their stubborn bravery, to hold out for very long, and when the Romans ultimately succeeded in breaching the wall, the end was not far off. In August, almost on the exact anniversary of the destruction of Jerusalem by Nebuchadnezzar 656 years earlier, on the fast-day of the Ninth of Av, the Temple was destroyed by fire; whether on the instructions of Titus or against them, is uncertain. The upper city, defended by John of Gischala and Simon bar Giora, resisted for some weeks longer, but before the autumn armed opposition had ceased everywhere, except at Herod's fortress-palace of Masada, near the Dead Sea. There, a handful of Zealots under Eleazar ben Jair, who was a descendent of Judah the Galilean, the founder of the Zealot party, held out for another three years, until the spring of 73, when the defenders died by their own hands, rather than surrender to the hated enemy of their people.

Two years previously, Vespasian and Titus had celebrated their triumph in Rome. Spoils taken from the Temple were borne in the triumphal procession, in which Simon bar Giora, put to death immediately afterwards, and John of Gischala walked in chains. Soon the Arch of Titus, depicting some of these scenes, was to rise near the Forum, a visible symbol of the apparently final downfall of the Jewish people.

Roman coin struck in commemoration of the victory over the Jews. The inscription reads "Judaea capta" (Judaea subdued).

Judaea became an imperial province under a legate, who had his seat at Caesarea. Amid the ruins of Jerusalem and in its environs, a Roman legion (the Legio X Fretensis) was garrisoned. The traditional voluntary tax paid by the Jews, since early times, to the Temple in Jerusalem, was converted into the "Fiscus Judaicus," a compulsory contribution to the temple of Jupiter Capitolinus in Rome. Coins were struck, showing a captive Jewess (Judaea) seated under a palm-tree. They bore the inscription "Judaea devicta" or "Judaea capta" (subjugated Judaea).

Roman coin with the portrait of Titus, the conqueror of Jerusalem, remembered in the Jewish tradition as "Titus the Wicked".

AFTER THE DESTRUCTION

The Romans tightened their hold on the country even more drastically after the destruction of Jerusalem and the Temple, but the people continued to be in a state of unrest. The ferment spread to the Diaspora, where Jews had learnt, with stunned grief, of the downfall of their homeland and of their religious center. In Egypt, where the Temple of Leontopolis, founded by Onias about two and a half centuries earlier, was now closed, and in Syria and Cyrenaica, refugees from Judea succeeded in stirring up Messianic expectations and in inciting anti-Roman riots that were ruthlessly suppressed. Throughout the empire, especially during the tyrannical reign of Domitian (81–96), the "Fiscus Judaicus", that particularly galling and ignominious tax, was rigorously exacted from Jews and even from proselytes to Judaism.

Although conditions improved somewhat under Nerva (96–98), as well as during the first 16 years of the reign of Trajan (98–117), the turmoil subsided only superficially. In 115, while Trajan was engaged in a war against the Parthians on the far eastern border of the empire, revolts simultaneously broke out among the Jewish population of Egypt,

Hadrian, Roman emperor (117–138), who suppressed Bar Kokhba's revolt against Roman tyranny.

79

Cyrenaica and Cyprus and seemed for a time to threaten Roman rule. The objective was probably to march on Palestine from all sides and liberate it from the evil oppressor's hands. In Cyrenaica, where the Jews even had a king-Messiah Andreas (also called Lukuas), several inscriptions are extant, commemorating the subsequent restoration of various public buildings that had been destroyed by the Jews in the course of their revolt against the pagans. In Cyprus, they laid the flourishing city of Salamis waste. The reports, however, by Roman historians, of the great number of Greeks and Romans killed and of Jewish acts of violence and cruelty, are to be treated as gross exaggerations.

For Rome, the situation had taken an extremely serious turn, all the more so since Trajan was, at that time, experiencing considerable difficulties at the hands of the Mesopotamian Jews who, siding with the Parthians, menaced the Roman army from the rear. Trajan was, therefore, obliged to take immediate action against this wide-spread menace to Roman rule, and delegated two of his ablest generals to stamp out the spreading conflagration of resistance. Lusius Quietus quelled the uprising in Mesopotamia, where the ensuing Roman massacres heavily decimated the Jewish population, and in 117 C.E., Marcius Turbo suppressed, with utter ruthlessness, the attempt of the Jews in Egypt, Cyrenaica and Cyprus, to throw off the yoke of the hated idolatrous oppressor, the destroyer of their holy Temple and the ravager of their sacred, national homeland.

While the Jews of the Diaspora fought, Palestine remained ominously quiet. Fifteen years later, however, in 132, under the reign of Trajan's successor Hadrian (117–138), a general revolt flared up in the country and, for a time, achieved remarkable success. The immediate cause of the uprising was the issue of two decrees that outraged Jewish religious sentiments. The first was a decree prohibiting circumcision under penalty of death, while the second ordered the rebuilding of Jerusalem as a Roman city and the erection, on the ruins of the Temple of a pagan shrine dedicated to Jupiter Capitolinus.

The revolt, which was filled with Messianic expectations, was led by Simon bar Koseba (the son of, or more probably, the man of, Koseba: cf. *I Chronicles 4:22*), who became known as Bar Kokhba, the son of the star, in reference to the Messianic prediction in Numbers 24:17. "There shall step forth a star (*kokhav*) out of Jacob." Having overwhelmed the Roman forces in the south, he succeeded in liberating Jerusalem. To signalize the victory, silver and bronze coins were struck that are among the finest examples of ancient Jewish craftsmanship. On one side they bear the legend: "First (or second) year of the freedom of Israel" or "The freedom of Jerusalem." and, on the other, the name either of the leader "Simon Nasi (Prince) of Israel" or of "Eleazar the Priest," identified by some with Eleazar of Modiin, who was an uncle of

Jewish coins struck during the revolt of Bar Kokhba:

Tetradrachm. Front of Temple and the name "Simon" on the obverse, and lulab and ethrog on the reverse, with the inscription "For the freedom of Jerusalem".

Bronze Coin. On the obverse the inscription within the wreath reads: "Simon, Prince of Israel", and on the reverse, around the amphora: "First year of the redemption of Israel".

Bronze Coin. On the obverse a bunch of grapes and the inscription: "First year of the redemption of Israel". On the reverse a palm-tree and the inscription: "Eleazar the Priest".

Denarius. On the obverse, in a wreath, the name "Simon". On the reverse, a three-stringed lyre with the inscription "For the freedom of Jerusalem".

Bundle of documents on papyrus found in the caves of Bar Kokhba.

Bar Koseba and is well known from the Talmud. The legends are in ancient Hebrew characters, a further indication of the intensity of the feeling of national liberation which was thought to announce the advent of the Messiah.

There have recently been discovered, in caves near the Dead Sea, some of Bar Koseba's administrative archives, containing personal letters that vividly illustrate his forceful personality and leadership.

Ultimately, however, the Romans assembled a large force under Julius Severus, the most brilliant general of his day, whom the emperor Hadrian had been compelled to summon from Britain to take command of the military operations. Following long and bitter fighting, during which the Romans reduced one stronghold after another, only the mountain-fortress of Betar, six miles south-west of Jerusalem, remained in Jewish hands. There, Bar Koseba made his last stand. After a heroic resistance, the town fell, through treachery, to the Romans in 135 — on the Ninth of Av, according to tradition. Bar Koseba was killed in battle. The defenders were put to the sword, permission to bury the slain being withheld by the Romans for a considerable time.

Great was the havoc and terrible the devastation wrought by the war and its aftermath. Nearly 600,000 Jews are said to have fallen in battle, besides those who died of famine and disease. Of the survivors, so many

Letter on papyrus from Simon bar Koseba (Bar Kokhba) to the local commander in Ein Gedi.

were sold into slavery that a Jew fetched no more than the price of a horse. Palestine was left desolate, its Jewish settlements almost entirely wiped out. The fortifications of Betar, the ruins of which can still be traced, were torn down, to destroy the last brave symbol of the Jewish fight for freedom.

After the capture of Betar, resistance still continued in the caves and mountains near the Dead Sea, south of Ein Gedi. In this region, ghastly evidence has recently been discovered of the manner in which the last survivors were starved to death by the legionaries, unable to storm the defenders' mountain refuge.

The losses sustained by the Romans in putting down the Bar Koseba revolt were so heavy, that Hadrian, in his report of the victory presented to the Senate, thought it advisable to omit the traditional formula: "I and the army are well."

Exploration of the caves of Bar Kokhba in the mountains near the Dead Sea (Photo D. Harris-W.Braun, Jerusalem). In these caves Jewish patriots continued to resist, after the fall of Betar and the death of the leader.

Betar, the site of Bar Kokhba's last stronghold.

The Romans now rebuilt Jerusalem as a pagan city and named it Aelia Capitolina, in honor of the emperor Hadrian, whose family name was Aelius, and of Jupiter Capitolinus, the patron-god of Rome. A shrine dedicated to Jupiter was erected on the ruins of the Temple of God. Although forbidden, under pain of death, to enter the city, the Jews used to bribe the guards on the Ninth of Av, the fast day commemorating the destruction of the First and Second Temples, as well as the fall of Betar, and thus, as we learn from the Church Father Jerome, "they bought the privilege of shedding their tears on the ruins of their town," pouring out their hearts before the Western ("Wailing") Wall, the sole surviving remnant of the Temple.

The Ark of the Covenant. Relief from the Synagogue of Capernaum (Kfar Nahum). 2nd century C.E.

THE AGE OF THE MISHNAH AND THE PALESTINIAN TALMUD

The Synagogue of Capernaum (Kfar Nahum), on the northwest shore of the Lake of Tiberias, built in the 2nd century.

Under the reign of Herod, Hillel the Elder, a teacher of the Law, was elected to the dignity of president of the Sanhedrin. According to tradition, he descended from the Davidic royal family and was famous not only for his vast and profound learning but also for his modesty and gentleness. The high office that carried with it the title of Nasi (prince), remained, except for brief intervals, a hereditary one in Hillel's family also after the fall of Jerusalem.

The most prominent among Hillel's disciples was R. Johanan ben Zakkai, who rose to be one of the most influential and distinguished members of the Sanhedrin. At the outbreak of the Great Revolt, he belonged to the party that opposed an armed conflict with Rome. When war became inevitable, he was under no illusions as to its outcome, and the one aim of the aged Rabbi was to secure the survival of Judaism despite the impending national disaster. Having succeeded in leaving

Detail of mosaic floor from the Synagogue of Maon, near Nirim (western Negev). This synagogue is from the Byzantine period, probably 6th century, but it obviously continues an established tradition. There is literary evidence of mosaic floors with representation of living creatures in synagogues in the first half of the 4th century.

the besieged city, he obtained permission from Vespasian, to establish an academy for himself and his disciples at Jabneh (a coastal city between Jaffa and Ashdod). There, R. Johanan ben Zakkai and, after him, Rabban Gamliel II of Jabneh, a descendent of Hillel, succeeded in the stupendous task of laying the indispensable spiritual foundations for the continued survival of the Jewish people, in face of the overwhelming loss of the Temple and of Jerusalem and in spite of the violent disruption of Jewish life caused by the war and its tragic aftermath. There, they patiently re-created the authority of the Sanhedrin, gathering around themselves the most celebrated of contemporary scholars.

It was during this period that the canon of the Bible, traditionally divided into 24 books, was fixed. The books which were not admitted to the canon, the so-called Apocrypha, were since regarded as neither representative of nor normative for traditional Judaism.

After the overthrow of Jerusalem, the president of the Sanhedrin, the Nasi, bearing the title of Patriarch, was recognized by the Romans as the official representative of the Jewish people.

Although the Sanhedrin now consisted of Pharisaic scholars who were opposed to violence and favored peaceful relations with the Roman authorities, there were also exceptions. R. Akiba lent the support of his prestige to the revolt of Bar Koseba, whom he confidently regarded as the harbinger of the dawn of Messianic fulfilment. He suffered a martyr's death at the hands of the Romans and belongs to the group of heroes enshrined in their people's memory as the Ten Martyrs. R. Simon bar Jochai remained to the end of his days the inveterate and implacable enemy of Rome.

After Bar Koseba, attempts at hastening the advent of the Messiah by violent means were discredited. Patiently reconciling themselves to the reality of the situation, the people gradually recovered, to some extent, from the crushing blow.

As a result of Bar Koseba's revolt, the center of the Jewish population in Palestine, and with it the Sanhedrin, moved from Judaea in the south to Galilee in the north. Impressive evidence of the contemporary flourishing Jewish life in that area is to be found in the stately remains of ancient synagogues, to be seen in Galilee, at Capernaum, Meron, Chorazin, and elsewhere. At Beth Alpha and other places, mosaic floors have been uncovered, showing that figurative art was not alien to the Jews, nor banished from their places of worship.

Detail of mosaic floor from the Synagogue of Beth Alpha, in the Valley of Jezreel, not far from Beth Shean. The mosaic floor was laid, according to an inscription, in the days of the Byzantine emperor Justin I (518–527), but the synagogue is probably of an earlier date.

עמוד ימין

שה שכר הליכה בידה עושה ואינו
לך שכר מעשה בידו הלך הלך ועשה
זה לא הלך ולא עשה רשע רשע
כו׃ ארבע מידות ביושבים
... חכ׳ ספוג משפך ומשמרת
פה ספוג שהוא סופג את הכל
שפך שהוא מכניס בזו ומוציא בזו
זו משמרת שהיא מוציאה את
יין וקולטת את השמרים נפה
שהיא מוציאה את הקמח וקולטת
את הסלת׃ יו כל אהבה שהיא
תלויה בדבר בטל דבר ובטילה אה..
אהבה ושאינה תלויה בדבר אינה
בטילה לעולם׃ יז אי זה היא
אהבה שהיא תלויה בדבר אהבת
אמנון ותמר ושאינה תלויה בדבר
אהבת דוד ויהונתן׃ יח כל מחלוקת
שהיא לשם שמים סופה להתקיים
ושאינה לשם שמים אין סופה
להתקיים׃ יט אי זו היא מחלוקת
שהיא לשם שמים מחלוקת שמי והלל
ושאינה לשם שמים וו מחלוק קרח
ועל עדתו׃ כ כל המזכה את הרבים
אין חטא בא על ידו וכל המחטיא
את הרבים אין מספיקין בידו
לעשות תשובה׃ כא משה
זכה וזיכה את הרבים זכות הרבים
תלויה בו שנ׳ צדקת יי עשה ומשפטיו
עם יש׳ ירבעם חטא והחטיא את
הרבים חטא הרבים תלויה בו שעל

עמוד שמאל

חטאות מרבעם אשר חטא ואשר
החטיא את ישראל׃ כב כל מי שיש בו
שלושה דברים תלמידו של אברהם
אבינו ושלשה דברים תלמידו של
בלעם עין טובה ונפש שפלה ורוח
נמוכה תלמידיו של אברהם עין רעה
ונפש רחבה ורוח גבוהה תלמידיו
של בלעם מה בין תלמידיו של אברהם
אבינו לתלמידיו של בלעם תלמידיו
של בלעם יורדין לגיהנם שנאמר
אלהים תורידם לבאר שחת אנשי
דמים ומרמה לא יחצו ימיהם ואני
אבטח בך אבל תלמידיו של אברהם
אבינו יורשים גן עדן שנ׳ להנחיל
אהבי יש ואוצרותיהם אמלא יהודה
בן תימא אומ׳ הוי עז כנמר וקל
כנשר ורץ כצבי וגבור כארי לעשות
רצון אביך שבשמים כד הוא
היה אומ׳ עז פנים לגיהנם ובושת
פנים לגן עדן יהי רצון מלפניך
יי אלהינו ואלהי אבותי שתבנה עיר
במהרה ויתן חלקינו בתורתך כה
בן בג בג או׳ הפך בה והפך בה דכלא
בה וכלא בך ומנה לא תזוע שאין
לך מידה טובה ממנה בן הא הא
לפם צערא אגרא

חסל צבות
פירקא ה׳

Burial chamber in the Beth Shearim catacombs. Beth Shearim, which was the seat of the Sanhedrin in the days of R. Judah ha-Nassi and where R. Judah himself and many other scholars were buried, became a hallowed burial ground, to which the remains of pious Jews were brought, sometimes from far off countries.

Page from the Mishna manuscript called Codex Kaufmann, in the Library of the Hungarian Academy at Budapest.

Through the accumulated labors and legal discussions and decisions of generations of scholars, there had, side by side with the written law of the Pentateuch, come into being an oral law that embodied age-old traditions and that interpreted and amplified the enactments and provisions of the Pentateuch, adapting them to the changing conditions of life. About the year 200, the greatest of the patriarchs, R. Judah ha-Nasi (the Prince), codified, and most probably set down in writing, the oral law which had, until then, been transmitted mostly by word of mouth. This compilation, the work of the Tannaim (the teachers), known as the Mishnah (the teachings), later became the basis of the Gemara, which incorporated discussions on it and which, together with the Mishnah, constitutes the Talmud.

There has recently been brought to light at Beth Shearim (near Kiriath Amal, not far from Haifa) a great complex of catacombs in which R. Judah ha-Nasi, many prominent scholars of the period, and members of his family were buried and above which there once stood an imposing monument. To these catacombs were also brought the remains of Jews from many other lands, who desired to be laid to rest near these venerated scholars.

The Massorah, critical notes on the text of the Bible compiled by the Massorites of Tiberias, became a feature regularly accompanying Bible manuscripts. A 10th century Oriental manuscript of the Pentateuch, now in the British Museum (Or. Ms. 4445), shows the so-called "Little Massorah" on the margins and between the columns, and the "Great Massorah" at the top and bottom of the page.

During the centuries following the redaction of the Mishnah, Jewish spiritual life continued to be creative in Palestine, centering in the main on Tiberias. Palestine, through Yose ben Yose, Yannai, and perhaps also Kallir, was the birth-place of the synagogal poetry, the Piyyut, as well as of compilations of the Midrash, the homiletic interpretation of Biblical verses that reveals a deeper meaning and a wider application of the words and spirit of the Scriptures. In Tiberias, the Massorah, the scientific study of the actual Biblical text, was virtually brought to a close, thanks to the labors of Aaron ben Moses ben Asher, who lived there in the first half of the tenth century and whose manuscript of the Bible, complete with vowels and accents, came to be adopted, with minor exceptions, as the standard codex. There in Tiberias, the Tiberian system of Hebrew vocalization, which superseded rival systems and has survived in use to our day, was developed. The so-called Palestinian Talmud, too, was elaborated mainly in the academy of Tiberias, and received its definite form at the beginning of the fifth century. Consisting of the discussions, comments and amplifications of the sages known

Meron, near Safed. The shrine of Rabbi Simon bar Jochai, the traditional author of the Zohar, the classical cabbalistic textbook. The anniversary of his death is celebrated every year on the day of Lag ba-Omer.

as the Amoraim on the text of the Mishnah, it reflects the development of Jewish oral law during the two centuries that had elapsed since the compilation of that code.

Traditionally, Galilee was also the place of origin of the great mystical classic, the Zohar. The authorship of this book, in fact of medieval composition, was traditionally ascribed to the second century scholar R. Simon bar Jochai and his school. Simon's tomb can still be seen at Meron, near Safed, and the anniversary of his death is celebrated every year on Lag ba'Omer (the 33rd day of the Counting of the Omer, corresponding to the 18th of Iyyar) by the kindling of bonfires and ecstatic dances.

When, at the beginning of the fourth century, Christianity became the state religion of the Roman empire, anti-Jewish legislation soon made its appearance and state-supported Christian religious institutions were established throughout the land. As a result of these circumstances, coupled with the growing impoverishment of the country, conditions for the Jews in Palestine rapidly deteriorated. The Christian state could not tolerate even the vestige of Jewish autonomy still obtaining, more especially in Palestine, which the Church regarded as its Holy Land. Finally, in 425, the Byzantine emperor Theodosius II abolished the patriarchate.

This spelt the end of Palestine as the chief center and authority in Jewish life. At the same time, the Jewish population began to dwindle still more. The Jews, however, never entirely abandoned the country. In Upper Galilee, in the village of Pekiin, for instance, there has survived through the centuries the remnant of a peasant community, grouped around an ancient synagogue and boasting that their ancestors were never uprooted from the sacred soil.

The Tomb of R. Simon bar Yohai at Meron, near Safed, is a venerated shrine, to which pious Jews go on pilgrimage to light candles and to pray. A general pilgrimage is celebrated on the day of Lag ba-Omer (18th Iyyar), when bonfires are kindled and ecstatic dances performed.

THE AGE OF THE
BABYLONIAN TALMUD

During all this time, there had remained in Mesopotamia a large proportion of the Jewish people, descendants of those carried into exile by Nebuchadnezzar after the destruction of Jerusalem in 586 B.C.E. While retaining their loyalty to their people's traditions and unique way of life, they had struck roots in their new land, and had preferred not to avail themselves of the opportunity of returning to Palestine that had been offered them by Cyrus in 536 B.C.E., after the conquest of Babylon by the Persians. Although by now subjects of the Persian empire, the "Babylonian" Jews, as they continued to be called, maintained close links with the reborn Jewish community in Palestine. In the person of Ezra, who went to Jerusalem in about 458 B.C.E. to organize the life of the young body politic in accordance with the prescriptions of the Torah, they provided the spiritual leadership that guided Judaism on the path of its future development, while the consolidation of the political situation was the work of Nehemiah, who was a contemporary of Ezra and likewise came from the Babylonian diaspora. Emigration from Babylonia, although not on a large scale, was a continuous process during succeeding centuries. Hillel, the ancestor of the Palestinian patriarchs, as well as some of the most distinguished scholars, who shed luster upon Palestine Jewry during the age of the Mishnah and the Palestinian Talmud, were Babylonians by birth.

Jewish settlements in "Babylonia" in the Talmudic period.

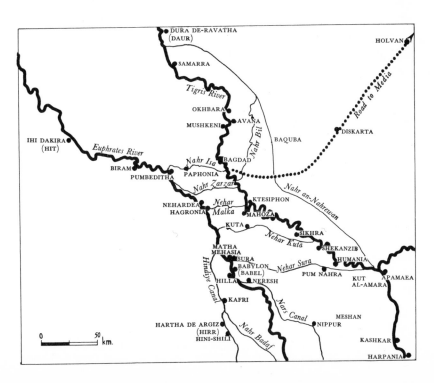

From the wall-paintings of the Synagogue of Dura-Europos: Moses addressing the people of Israel, when descending from Mount Sinai with the Book of the Law in his hands.

At times, there was also a movement in the reverse direction. After the destruction of the Temple and of Jerusalem by Titus in the year 70, and following the tragic end of the Bar Koseba revolt in 135, the Babylonian Diaspora absorbed fugitives and emigrants from Palestine. But when the situation became quiet again, emigration from Babylonia to Palestine was once more resumed.

After the overthrow of the Persian empire by Alexander the Great, the Babylonian Jews experienced a relatively short period of Greek rule. From the middle of the third century B.C.E., however, the territory became part of the empire of Parthia that had arisen on the ruins of the Persian empire and shared the same type of culture. Under the tolerant rule of the Arsacid dynasty, the Jews were permitted to develop a remarkable degree of local and national autonomy. There were towns, like Nehardea on the Euphrates, with an almost exclusively Jewish population, and others, like Sura and Pumbeditha, with very large Jewish communities, which became, in the course of time, the seats of renowned academies of Jewish learning. With the exception of the townsmen engaged in a variety of professions and trades, the Babylonian Jews were still in the main an agricultural population.

That the Babylonian Jews were by no means indifferent to aesthetic values is evident from the remarkable synagogue frescoes which have been discovered in excavations at Dura Europos on the Euphrates, on the fringe of their area of settlement, and have revolutionized our ideas of early Jewish art.

From the wall-paintings of the Synagogue of Dura-Europos: The Story of Mordecai and Esther. To the left: Haman leading Mordecai's horse. To the right: Ahasuerus and Esther sitting on their thrones.

The central authority of Babylonian Jewry was the exilarch, whose Aramaic title was *Resh Galuta*. Traditionally descended from the last king of Judah, the exilarchs enjoyed great authority among the Jews and were held in high esteem at the Parthian court.

These favorable conditions continued even after the reassumption of Persian control over Mesopotamia, when, after a brief period of Persian

הַמְקַנֵּא
לְאִשְׁתּוֹ ר' אֱלִיעֶזֶר אוֹ
מְקַנֶּה לָהּ עַל פִּי שְׁנַיִם
וּמַשְׁקֶה לָהּ עַל פִּי עֵד
אֶחָד אוֹ עַל פִּי עַצְמוֹ
ר' יְהוֹשֻׁעַ אוֹ מְקַנֶּה עַל
פִּי שְׁנַיִם וּמַשְׁקֶה עַל פִּי
שְׁנַיִם כֵּיצַ מְקַנֶּה לָהּ אַל
לָהּ בִּפְנֵי שְׁנֵי אַל תְּרַב
עִם אִישׁ פְּלוֹ' וְרִכְּרָה
עִמּוֹ עֵרֵי כּוֹתֵר לְבֵית
וּמוֹתֵר לֵיאָכוֹ בַּתְרוּם
נִכְנַס עִמּוֹ לְבֵ' הַסֵּתֶר
וְשָׁהָה עִמּוֹ כְּרֵי טוּם
אָסוּר לְבֵיתָהּ. וְאָסוּר
לֶאֱכֹל בַּתְרוּם/ וְאִם מֵת
חוֹלֵץ וְלֹא מְתַיֵּבַּם/
אֵלּוּ אֲסוּרוֹ לֵאָכוֹ
בַּתְרוּם/ הָאוֹמֵר טְמֵא
אֲנִי וְשֶׁבָּאוּ לָהּ עֵדִים
שֶׁטְּמֵא וְהָאוֹמֵר
אֵינִי שׁוֹתָה אוֹ שֶׁאֵי
בַּעַל רוֹץ לְהַשְׁתּוֹתָהּ

religious fanaticism, the Sassanid kings restored order and resumed the traditional policy of tolerance towards their Jewish subjects.

With the decline of Jewish Palestine, Babylonia represented the greatest concentration of Jewish population, and from the third century onwards, Rabbinic scholarship began to flourish there, more even than it had done in its former home. This was chiefly due to two great scholars, Abba Arikha (usually called Rab) and Samuel Yarhinaah (generally known as Mar Samuel), both disciples of R. Judah ha-Nasi, the compiler of the Mishnah. After their return from Palestine, they founded the Academies (Yeshibot) of Sura and Nehardea, where the discussions centered on the text of the Mishnah, on which thereby an extensive commentary, known as the Gemara, accumulated. The elaboration of this commentary was continued for nearly 300 years in these two academies and in others that were later established (Pumbeditha, Mahoza, etc.). When, towards the end of the fifth or early in the sixth century, the Babylonian Talmud finally received its definitive form, it constituted the cumulative result of the life-work of seven generations of Babylonian Amoraim (the interpreters of the Mishnah), whose activities extended until about the end of the fifth century, as well as of a long series of Saboraim ("reasoners"), who completed the task of editing the Talmud, previously redacted by the Amoraim Rav Ashi and Rabina II. Among the numerous Babylonian Amoraim whose opinions are recorded in the Talmud, at least Abbaye and Raba should be especially mentioned. They lived in the first half of the fourth century and their subtle and spirited debates enliven many a page of the Gemara.

In addition to the Halakhah, the legal enactments, the aim of which is to make all life the concrete expression and embodiment of the Divine teachings of the Torah, the Babylonian, like the Palestinian Talmud, contains much Aggadah, homiletic interpretations of Biblical passages, historical and legendary traditions, secular knowledge, and folk-lore, that served to imbue the people with the deeper, underlying spirit of the Torah and of the Divine purpose of Jewish life and historic experience. What may be regarded by a modern reader as lacking in pertinence, was incorporated into the Talmud by its redactors on the principle that everything concerning Judaism is relevant and may, moreover, serve to elucidate problems arising in later generations.

The Babylonian Talmud is more elaborate and much more voluminous than the Palestinian one. It, therefore, assumed a higher authority and a greater significance in the development of Judaism. Henceforth, the Babylonian Talmud regulated Jewish life in all lands, thereby conferring an essential unity upon the Jews, wherever they lived. The study of the Talmud became a religious duty and long characterized Jewish life, despite attempts made by Christian authorities throughout the ages, to destroy the Talmud by censorship or burning.

Page from the Munich manuscript (Cod. Hebr. 95) of the Babylonian Talmud, written in 1343, the only virtually complete Talmud manuscript.

קורין את שמע בערבין מסעה שהכהני'
בכבפי' לאכול בתרומה כהני' שנטמאו ו
וטבלו והעריב שמסן והגיע עתם לאכול
בתרומה : עד סוף האשמורה הראשונה שלים הנמונה כדמפרש בגמ' ומפס

[inner right margin — Rashi's commentary, in Rashi script]

קרין את שמע בערבים משעה שהכהני נכנסים
לאכול בתרומתן עד סוף האשמור הראשונה
דברי ר' אליעזר וחכמים אומר עד חצות רבן
גמליאל אומר עד שיעלה עמוד השחר מעשה
ובאו בניו מבית המשתה אמרו לו לא קרינו
את שמע אמר להם אם לא עלה עמוד השחר
חייבין אתם לקרות ולא זו בלבד אמרו אלא
כל מה שאמרו חכמים עד חצות מצותן עד
שיעלה עמוד השחר הקטר חלבי ואברי מצותן
עד שיעלה עמוד השחר וכל הנאכלים ליו' אחד
מצותן עד שיעלה עמוד השחר אם כן למה
אמרו חכמים עד חצות כדי להרחיק אדם מן
העבירה   גמ'   תנא היכא קאי דקתני
מאימתי ותו מאי שנא דתני בערבית ברישא
לתני דשחרית ברישא תנא אקרא קאי דכתיב
בשכבך ובקומך והכי קרתני זמן קש דשכיב
אימת משע שהכהני נכנסין לאכול בתרומתן
ואי בעי אימא יליף מברייתו של עולם דכתיב
ויהי ערב ויהי בקר יו' אחד אי הכי סיפ' דקתני
בשחר מברך שתי' לפני' ואחת לאחרי' בערב
מברך שתים לפניה ושתים לאחרי' לתני דערבי'
ברישא תנא פתח בערבי' והדר תני בשחרית
עד דקאי בשחרי' פריש מילי דשחרי' והדר פרי

מילי דערבית אמר מר משעת שהכהני נכנסי' לאכול בתרומה מכדי כהנים אימת
קא אכלי תרומה משע' צאת הכבבים לתני משע' צאת הכבבי מלתא אגב אורחי'
קמל כהני' אימת קא אכלי בתרומה משעת צאת הכבבים והא קמל   דכפר

[lower margin and outer left margin — Tossafot, in Rashi script]

Page from the Babylonian Talmud printed by Daniel Bomberg in Venice in 1520–1523. Bomberg's pagination of the Talmudic text (middle column in square letters), accompanied by Rashi's commentary on the inner (here right) margin and the Tossafot on the outer (here left) margin, has become the prototype of all subsequent editions of the Talmud, down to our days.

THE FORMATION
OF THE DIASPORA

Jews are known to have settled in the central and western provinces of the Roman empire before the beginning of the current era.

We have important literary evidence that Jews were to be found in *Italy* in the republican period. In addition to voluntary immigrants, the wars of Pompey in the first century B.C.E. and of Titus and Hadrian in the first and second centuries C.E. brought numerous Jewish prisoners to Italy as slaves. In the course of time, they were either freed by their masters or ransomed by fellow-Jews. Besides the city of Rome, in which naturally, the largest number of Jews lived, there were Jewish communities in the main towns of northern Italy, in southern Italy, and on the islands of Sicily and Sardinia. The remains of a synagogue, apparently founded in the early imperial period, have recently been discovered at Ostia, the port of ancient Rome.

The most impressive evidence of the life of Jews in Rome in the classical period is to be found in the various series of catacombs (or underground

Burial-niche in the Jewish catacomb of Villa Torlonia at Rome. The mural painting represents the Ark of the Law between two seven-branched candelabra. To the right an ethrog and a circumcision knife (?), to the left a palm-branch and a pomegranate.

Relief from a Jewish marble sarcophagus found in the Villa Randanini at Rome. The seven-branched candelabrum upheld by two genii represents an interesting mixture of Jewish and Roman decorative motives.

burial places), some decorated with murals, which have been discovered there. Each of these catacombs served numerous different synagogues. Inscriptions which have come to light there, are mostly in Greek and Latin, with an occasional Hebrew formula. Some of the sarcophagi are finely carved in a combination of classical and Jewish motifs.

Outside Rome, too, catacombs have been unearthed in many other places, including Sicily, Sardinia, and southern Italy. Of particular interest is the one in Venosa, birthplace of the Roman poet Horace. Tombstone inscriptions in Latin have also been preserved in southern Italy.

Inscription on a Jewish tombstone from Narbonne (southern France), dated in the 2nd year of the Visigothic king Egica (689). The Latin inscription begins with a branched candelabrum and includes the formula "Peace on Israel" in Hebrew.

Tombstones of Roman legionaries of the Ituraean Cohort, found at Mainz (Mayence), Germany. Ituraea, in the northernmost corner of Palestine, having been conquered and Judaized by the Hasmonean king Aristobulus (about 104 B.C.E.), it has been assumed that these legionaries were Jews.

In the first century C.E., there were Jews in *Spain*, where they may have been living since before the beginning of the current era. Funerary inscriptions in Latin, dating from the Visigothic period (fifth century), have been discovered there.

From the period of the Roman republic, Jews were to be found in *Gaul* (now France), particularly in the Mediterranean coastal towns. When, in the course of time, their numbers increased, they spread inland and founded flourishing communities. Tombstone inscriptions in Latin are extant from the end of the Merovingian period (seventh century).

Unsubstantiated reports declare that Jews settled in *Germany* before the beginning of the current era. It is more probable, however, that they followed in the wake of the Roman legions which, in the first century, conquered the western part of the country. It is even believed that there were Jews among the legionaries who formed the Roman army of occupation. If this be true, their effigies on tombstones, like those found at Mainz, are among the oldest identifiable likenesses of Jews known to us. A famous rescript of the emperor Constantine, issued in the year 321 to the city of Cologne, emphasizes the duties and privileges of the Jewish group, and shows that organized communities, recognized by the state, existed already in the Rhineland, and certainly in other places as well.

The Jews also spread, possibly from Egypt, over the whole coastal strip of *North Africa*. Jewish catacombs, dating from Roman times, have been found at Cyrene (Libya) and near Carthage (Tunisia). Relics of a fine synagogue floor in mosaic, reminiscent of those in Palestine, have come to light at Naro (present-day Hammam-Lif) in Tunisia.

There were Jewish communities in *Greece*, as well as in the Greek towns of the *Balkan Peninsula* and of *Asia Minor*, since the first century B.C.E. Remains of ancient synagogues, that bear witness to the presence of Jews throughout the eastern half of the Roman empire, have been discovered at Miletus and Priene in Asia Minor, at Stobi in Yugoslavia, on the islands of Aegina and Delos in the Aegean, and such of a probably much older one most recently at Sardis.

Living usually in close proximity to one another in a Jewish quarter, the Jews, wherever they settled, would form closely-knit groups, united by a common way of life that was fashioned by the teachings of the Torah and its developing rabbinic interpretation. There was the rich, varied pattern of customs and ceremonies, the rhythm of the weekly Sabbath and of annual feast- and fast-days, the uniform standards of the laws and high moral values of Judaism, the certain faith in the coming of Messianic times, and, after the destruction of the Temple and the loss of Palestine, the assurance too of the restoration of the homeland and the former glory. All this permeated the life of the Jews, in all the lands of their dispersion, with an inward meaning, a greatness

Mosaic floor from the synagogue of the ancient town of Naro, now Hamam Lif near Tunis, dating from the 4th century C.E.

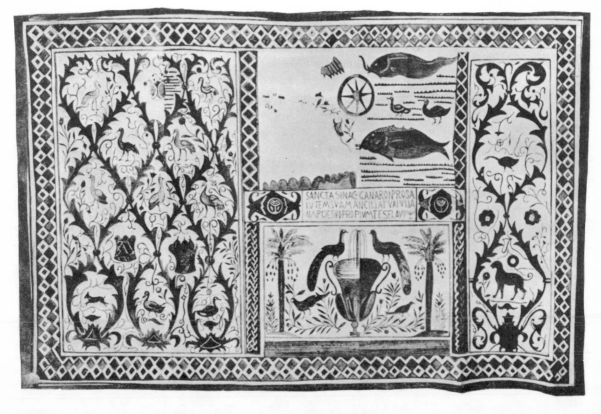

Above on the left:
Ancient Jewish tombstone from Southern Italy with Hebrew inscription and a primitive design of the seven-branched candelabrum, now in the Archeological Museum of Bari.

On the right:
Marble relief of the seven-branched candelabrum from the synagogue of Priene (now Samsoon) on the Aegean coast of Asia Minor. To the right, a shofar and a lulav. To the left, an ethrog. The two rolls on the basis of the candelabrum may symbolize Scrolls of the Law.

of purpose, a stubborn persistence that brought cohesion among the scattered members of the Jewish people, and a will to survive through all the vicissitudes of good and evil fortune, through tranquil days, as well as periods of suffering and persecution.

Wherever they settled, they founded synagogues and schools in which the Torah was taught, established all the ancillary organizations of a community, and devoted themselves to assisting their poorer brethren in their misfortune and need.

Until the destruction of the Temple in 70 C.E., they sent the traditional annual capitation tax of half a shekel to Jerusalem, and after the destruction of the Temple, they supported the Palestinian patriarchate with voluntary contributions.

In most places, a considerable amount of anti-Jewish feeling existed among the pagan neighbors of the Jews, and renowned Roman authors did not hesitate to express their hatred or contempt. The Roman government, however, generally proved tolerant and even granted the Jews, out of consideration for their religious scruples, certain privileges, such as, for instance, exemption from compulsory military service and from the cult of the emperor.

The position of the Jews, however, deteriorated in the fourth century, in the diaspora like in Palestine, when Christianity became the state religion of the Roman empire, and the emperors gradually adopted the view of the Church that Jews were to be deprived of civil rights and ostracized from Christian society.

THE AGE OF THE GEONIM

The Arab conquest of Mesopotamia, in the first half of the seventh century, did not greatly affect the position of the Jews. In return for the payment of the special tax imposed on unbelievers, they continued to enjoy religious liberty and communal autonomy. There was henceforth an increasing tendency for the Jews to become concentrated in the cities, with the result that Bagdad, the new capital founded in 762 by Al-Mansur, the second caliph of the Abbassid dynasty, soon came to have probably the greatest Jewish community, not only in Mesopotamia (to-day known as Iraq), but also in the world, a position it maintained for generations. Bagdad became the seat of the exilarchate, which was recognized by the Arab conquerors as the supreme authority of Mesopotamian Jewry. Bostanai, the youthful scion of the Davidic line of exilarchs, was confirmed in this dignity by the caliph Omar in 634, his descendents continuing to exercise the office down to the middle of the eleventh century.

Under Arab rule, the exilarchate attained its greatest resplendence. Nathan ha-Babli, a Babylonian scholar of the tenth century who emigrated to North Africa, has left an impressive description of the exilarch's manner of life, the brilliant ceremony of his installation, his relations with the caliph and the honor in which he was held at court.

In the intellectual sphere, primacy was enjoyed by the heads of the academies of Sura and Pumbeditha, styled Geonim ("excellencies"), whose moral authority extended throughout the Jewish world, far beyond the boundaries of Mesopotamia. From all over the Diaspora, communities as well as individual scholars turned to them for guidance as the fount-heads of Jewish tradition. Their Responsa (replies to questions addressed to them) decided the mode of application of this tradition to legal and ritual matters, and diffused everywhere the spirit and decisions of the Babylonian Talmud, which they thereby made paramount and authoritative in Jewish life.

The Geonim and their disciples were the first to compile legal codes. They commented on the Bible and the Talmud, wrote the first Talmudic dictionary and fixed the order of the Jewish liturgy, accepting into it the first products of synagogal poetry (piyyutim). In addition to translating the Bible into Arabic, Saadyah, Gaon of Sura in the first half of the tenth century, was the first systematic philosopher of the Jewish Middle Ages, while Sherira, Gaon of Pumbedita in the second half of the same century, compiled a history of the oral tradition. The Geonim thus guided the Jews to an inner cohesion and vitality, at a time when they were beset by new and bewildering problems and by the danger of internal disruption.

Formerly to a great extent obscure, this period has been illuminated by a vast mass of Responsa and other literary works discovered at the end of the last century in the Genizah (the depository of books and manus-

A famous manuscript from the Cairo Genizah. One of the few fragments of the Greek version of the Bible by Aquila the Proselyte, 2nd century C.E. The Greek text has been rubbed out (fortunately not carefully enough), and the parchment has been used again to copy Hebrew synagogal poems by the 6th century Palestinian poet Yannai. (University Library, Cambridge).

cripts worn out by use) of the earliest synagogue of Old Cairo. The manuscripts and fragments, now stored in England, mainly at Cambridge and Oxford, in Russia at Leningrad, and in the United States at the Jewish Theological Seminary and Dropsie College, have been studied and partly published during the past sixty years, and have considerably enriched our knowledge of this significant period in Jewish history.

The age of the Geonim may be said to have ended in the middle of the eleventh century. Dissension between the two academies of Sura and

A page of the Hebrew text of the apocryphal book Ecclesiasticus or the Wisdom of Jeshua son of Sirach, from the Cairo Genizah. Until the discovery of the Genizah, the book was known only in ancient translations (Greek, Syriac, Latin). The Genizah fragments supplied about two thirds of the lost Hebrew original.

Pumbeditha, mostly on questions of precedence, and friction between the Geonim and the exilarchs contributed to the decline of the Gaonate's prestige. Moreover, the study of the Talmud had meanwhile spread throughout the Diaspora and there were now in existence, not only in Palestine, but also in Europe and North Africa, Talmudical schools which had become independent of Babylonian tutelage and felt no need for accepting the Geonim as the supreme authority. The title Gaon was assumed by the head of the Bagdad academy, and Geonim there succeeded one another to the end of the thirteenth century, although they enjoyed by now no more than local importance.

The exilarchate, too, continued, with varying vicissitudes of fortune, until 1258, when Mesopotamia was overrun by the Mongols and Bagdad sacked.

THE KARAITES

It was in the eighth century, in the age of the Geonim, that the sectarian movement of the Karaites (the adherents of the Bible, from *kara*, to read or study the Scriptures) was founded. The sect's name, coined in the following century, indicates the character of its tenets. Repudiating the rabbinic tradition embodied in the Talmud, the Karaites endeavored to base their beliefs and practices wholly on the Bible. They were, however, unable to apply this principle consistently and systematically.

The founder of the sect was Anan ben David, whose open defection from traditional Judaism is attributed to his animosity against the Geonim who, despite his higher claims to the exilarchate on the grounds of both his seniority and his greater learning, nominated his younger brother to that dignity in about 765, probably because Anan was known to hold heterodox views.

As the leader of a new movement, for which he provided a basis and a code through his "Sefer ha-Mitzvot" (The Book of Commandments), Anan united around himself the followers of several existing sects that shared a general opposition to rabbinic tradition and a common adherence to the written word of the Bible. This outlook has previously been encountered as characteristic of Sadduceeism. Vestiges of it doubtless continued to exist throughout the centuries following the destruction of the Temple, giving birth, under the impact of the ferment prevailing in the Muslim world, to sectarianism among the Jews of Babylonia also. Thus, the Shiite rejection of the Sunna (the tradition), as of equal sanction with the Koran, undoubtedly influenced the emergence of the contemporary Jewish anti-Talmudic sects.

Rejecting the rabbinic interpretation of the Bible, the followers of Anan adopted their own system, which assigned exclusive authority to the Pentateuch, the Prophets, and the Hagiographa and led to a rigorous application of the laws derived from them. It was, for example, forbidden, on the basis of Exodus 35:3, to have any light burning on the Sabbath, even if it had been kindled before the advent of the Day of Rest; or through a literal interpretation of Exodus 16:29, it was forbidden to leave one's home on the Sabbath. The effect of all this was to introduce a rigorous, ascetic spirit into the teachings and practices of the sect. Karaism also observed its own calendar. It is not, however, to be assumed that Karaism was really based exclusively on the literal meaning of the Bible. The movement adopted many rabbinic rules of interpretation and developed its own body of oral traditions.

Profoundly attached to the Jewish Messianic idea centering on Zion, many Karaites left Babylonia to settle in Palestine. According to Karaite tradition, Anan himself went to Palestine and founded a Karaite Synagogue at Jerusalem. This spirit of practical devotion to the Holy Land was to have a profound influence on the Rabbanite Jews also.

After the death of Anan, the sect was rent by divisions and sub-divisions. Various leaders arose, the most important being Benjamin al-Nahawendi (first half of the ninth century) and Daniel al-Kumisi (second half of that century). The former, who with Anan was regarded as the co-founder of the sect, consolidated Karaism in a somewhat less rigorous form.

The tenth and eleventh centuries saw the most brilliant period in Karaite literature. In the fields of theology, Biblical exegesis, lexicography, codification, grammar and polemics, Karaite scholarship flourished and produced works of great significance.

Owing partly to the inclination to sectarianism prevalent in the East, and partly also to the passive attitude of the Rabbanites, who failed to counter its attacks on traditional Judaism, Karaism, despite internal dissensions, soon made considerable progress, spreading to Palestine, Syria, and Egypt.

The Gaon of Sura in the first half of the tenth century, Saadyah ben Joseph, not only towered above his contemporaries, but was also one of the most brilliant minds in all Jewish history. To meet the Karaites on their own ground, he devoted his vast talents to Hebrew grammar, lexicography, Talmudic methodology, halakhah, the calendar, Jewish philosophy, Biblical interpretation. He translated the Bible into Arabic, and wrote anti-Karaite polemical tracts. In all these varied fields, he sought to combat the prevailing ignorance that provided a fertile ground for the propagation of Karaism. Saadyah Gaon may, therefore, be said to have been the chief defender of Rabbinic Judaism, and consequently the arch-foe of the Karaite movement, the adherents of which did not hesitate to stigmatize him as such.

Due to the vicissitudes of history, the center of the Karaite sect moved, in the course of time, from one country to another, at first, from Babylonia to Palestine, then to Egypt, and, in the twelfth century, to Cons-

Karaite cemetery in the Crimea, where Karaites were established from ancient times. Towards the middle of the 18th century, the Crimea became the spiritual center of the sect.

tantinople, where a number of prominent authors flourished between
the twelfth and sixteenth centuries, creating a rich and varied literature.
From the sixteenth century on, the Karaite communities in Lithuania
and Poland rose to importance, engaging in a certain amount of
literary activity, mainly in the town of Troki. Finally, in the eighteenth
century, the Crimea became the spiritual and intellectual center of the
sect. There, some 10,000 of them were settled, out of a dwindling total
of about 14,000 adherents of Karaism.

In Czarist Russia, the Karaites were granted the privilege of not being
considered Jews and exemption from the vexatious anti-Jewish restrictions. When, however, the German army invaded the Crimea during
World War II, no such privilege was accorded them by the Nazis, and
many of the Karaites, consequently, shared the tragic fate of Russian
Jewry. Some 6,000, however, still live in the U. S. S. R. under much
the same conditions as the Jews.

In the Orient the principal Karaite community surviving after the war
was that of Cairo (about 4,000 souls). There was also an ancient Karaite
synagogue in the Old City of Jerusalem, in which, however, a quorum
for prayer could seldom be mustered. When the Old City surrendered
to the Arab Legion in 1948, there were only three Karaites left who,
after having been prisoners in Jordan for a time, finally settled in Israel.
Since then, large numbers of the Egyptian Karaite community, as well as
the remnant of Iraqi Karaites, have migrated to Israel, where they have
two cooperative villages. Loyal to the Jewish State, the community
maintains its religious particularism and continues faithful to its traditions, although the younger people tend to adopt traditional Jewish
practices adhered to by the country as a whole.

THE ISLAMIC AGE

The Arab conquest in the 7th century brought not only Mesopotamian and Palestinian Jewry, but also all the communities throughout the whole Middle East under the sway of Islam. It also wrought a profound change in Jewish life over a great part of the Mediterranean world. In the course of one generation, between 640 and 670, the Arab hosts overran, first Egypt and Lybia, then the Maghreb, i.e. the western half of North Africa as far as the Atlantic Ocean. In this part of the world there were old Jewish communities, which forthwith became wholly Arabicized in speech and culture.

Morocco, which had a considerable Jewish population and where many Berber tribes had been converted to Judaism, became a great center of Jewish life under Arab rule.

In Ifriqiya (now Tunisia), Kairouan was for several centuries one of the intellectual centers of Judaism. The North African communities supported the Babylonian academies of Sura and Pumbeditha and stood in active correspondence with them on religious and legal matters. It was in answer to inquiries directed from these new centers of learning in the west, that many of the Gaonic responsa were penned. When, towards the end of the ninth century, a strange traveller, Eldad the Danite, appeared in North Africa and spread fantastic reports on the Lost Ten Tribes of Israel, the community of Kairouan turned to Zemah, Gaon of Sura, for advice. The Epistle of the Gaon Sherira (about 990),

Imaginative reconstruction of a Khazar meeting. The Khazars were a Tartaric tribe in southern Russia, which was won over to Judaism in the 8th century. Their dwellings and meeting places were the Tartaric tents called "kibitka".

which is, in effect, the oldest Jewish literary history, was a reply to the question submitted by Jacob ben Nissim of Kairouan on the formation of the oral law.

But at that time, North Africa was already on the way to independent Talmudic scholarship. A Babylonian scholar, Hushiel ben Elhanan, who, according to a legend, had been captured by pirates and ransomed by the community of Kairouan, founded in this town a Talmudic school, which soon acquired renown. His son, Hananel ben Hushiel, was among the first commentators on the Talmud.

Jewish intellectual activity flourished in the Maghreb until the middle of the 12th century, when the rigidly unitarian and fanatically intolerant Mohammedan sect of the Almohades declared pitiless war on all un-believers and forced the Jews, either to embrace Islam or to leave the country. Many Jews turned Moslem to save their lives, but continued to practice Judaism in secret.

At the beginning of the eighth century, when the conquest of the Maghreb was completed, the Arab hosts burst into Spain and, before long, they subjected (it was said, with the help of the Jewish population) nearly the whole of the Iberian Peninsula. Jews followed on their heels in some numbers, many of them even serving in the Arab army and taking an active part in the conquest. In the tenth century, when in the days of Abd-ar-Rahman III (912-961) Islamic Spain reached its brilliant apogee, a large and active Jewish community flourished under his rule, centered around the resplendent capital of Cordova.

The tenth century marks, in fact, the beginning of what is usually called the Golden Age of Spanish Jewry. The outstanding Jewish personality in this century was Hasdai ibn Shaprut, physician and minister to the Caliph Abd-ar-Rahman III. He was sent on delicate diplomatic missions and became one of the most influential persons in the state. As the recognized head of the Jewish communities, he did much to foster Jewish scholarship and literature. Spanish Jewry's assiduous application to Hebrew grammar, belles-lettres, and other endeavors, for which they were to be so famous in the future, began in his day. Among his protégés were the poets and grammarians Menahem ben Saruk and Dunash ben Labrat. He also patronized the Talmudic school established by Moses ben Enoch, a Babylonian scholar who, according to the legend already mentioned in connection with the school at Kairouan, travelled on the same boat with Hushiel ben Elhanan, was captured by pirates together with him and ransomed by his co-religionists at Cordova. Hasdai himself was a distinguished scholar and translated into Arabic the writings of the first-century Greek physician Dioscorides.

A touching episode in Hasdai's life is his exchange of letters with Joseph, King of the Khazars. The Khazars were a Tartaric tribe established in southern Russia, who had been won over to Judaism towards the middle

Illuminated Oriental Bible Manuscript (Egypt, 11th century) in the Leningrad Library.

of the eighth century. When Hasdai learnt of the existence of an autonomous Jewish state in the east, he addressed a letter to the Khazar king, describing the condition of the Jews in Spain and expressing his yearning for a life of political independence for himself and his people. King Joseph replied, eagerly inviting Hasdai to come and be his minister. But a few years later, the kingdom of the Khazars was overthrown by the Russian Prince of Kiev.

In Spain, as in North Africa, much of Jewish culture found its vehicle in Arabic, which had become almost a second sacred tongue among the Jews. Their mastery of this language, in addition to their ancestral Hebrew and often the Romance languages of the environment, made it possible for Jews to carry out a remarkable activity as intellectual mediators and translators, which was to become so significant afterwards.

It was not only in speech that the Spanish Jews became Arabicized, but also in every aspect of their culture. Their names and dress were Arabic and their synagogues continued to express their complete adaptation to Arab tastes in architecture and decoration, even after Arab dominance had passed. In their illuminated manuscripts, with exquisite decoration in the Arab style, they rigorously eschewed any human representation, in accordance with the conventions of the Mohammedan environment. After the capture and sack of Cordova by the Berbers in 1013, its Jewish community became dispersed, most of its members finding refuge in Granada, Toledo, Malaga, and Saragossa. Moslem Spain was now divided in numerous petty states, whose courts competed among themselves in brilliance, almost like the courts of the Italian states of the Renaissance. In some of these courts, Jews played a prominent role. The outstanding name in the eleventh century is Samuel ibn Nagdela, known as Samuel ha-Nagid (Samuel the Prince), who was over many years vizier of the kingdom of Granada, administering the realm and leading its armies in war. Besides his activity as a statesman and soldier, Samuel found time to act as head of the Jewish community of the kingdom in matters both secular and religious. Himself a versatile author and poet, who wrote inter alia an "Introduction to the Talmud" as well as accounts of his escapes and victories in well polished verse, Samuel was also a generous Maecenas of science and art. He was interested in architecture too. According to a recent theory, he personally took part in the construction of the Court of Lions in the Alhambra of Granada. Solomon ibn Gabirol, who achieved in a short lifetime immortal fame, both as a poet and as a philosopher, was for a while his protégé and bewailed his death in an elegy. In his days, Jonah ibn Janah of Saragossa marked considerable progress in Hebrew philology, and Bahya ibn Pakuda, likewise of Saragossa, initiated Jewish moral theology.

Samuel ibn Nagdela was succeeded, on his death, by his son Joseph as vizier of Granada. But Joseph's inclination to promote mostly Jews to high dignities, aroused against him the violent hate of the Moslems, which vented itself in 1066 in anti-Jewish riots in Granada. Joseph lost his life and the Jews were expelled.

Jewish life continued, however, to flourish in Moorish Spain. The first half of the twelfth century still produced an ardent religious poet like Judah ha-Levi, who expressed his nostalgia for Zion in enthusiastic hymns. He also wrote the "Book of the Kuzari," a philosophic treatise which is an eloquent defence of Judaism. At the age of 60, he decided to realize his dream and set out for the Holy Land, but nobody knows whether he ever reached his goal. His last known station was Egypt. The further progress of the voyage and Judah ha-Levi's end remain a mystery. There is a legend saying that he was trampled to death by an Arab knight in sight of Jerusalem, while reciting one of his Zionides.

The Court of Lions in the Alhambra of Granada (Spain). Samuel ha-Nagid (990–1055), vizier of the kingdom of Granada since 1027, is believed to have taken part in the planning of the earliest part of the Alhambra. The fountain is remembered in one of the poems of Solomon ibn Gabirol.

Moses ben Maimon, known also as Maimonides (1135–1204), the great Jewish philosopher and authoritative codifier of Jewish religious law, Bronze medallion said to be from the Renaissance period.

His contemporaries were Moses ibn Ezra, conspicuous as a prolific religious and secular poet, and Abraham ibn Ezra, a poet too, but famous above all as a commentator of the Bible.

Towards the middle of the twelfth century, Jewry in Moorish Spain received a heavy blow, The Almohades, whom we have already seen at work in North Africa, had reached Spain and here, too, presented the Jews with the cruel choice of apostasy or exile. Henceforth, Spanish Jewish life was concentrated in the north of the Peninsula, in the Christian principalities, which now began to expand southward, bent on driving the Arabs out of Spain.

The man who was to become a celebrated philosopher and codifier of Judaism, the genius whom a grateful posterity used to remember as "the Great Eagle," Moses ben Maimon, was barely 13 years old when the Almohades sacked his native city of Cordova in 1148. The Maimon family set out to find a new home. Ultimately, they reached Fez in

Page from Maimonides' religious code "Mishneh Torah". Spanish manuscript dating from the 15th century. British Museum. (MS Harl. 5698).

בסימנא טבא

פעמי

הכן באמרתך ואל תשלט בי

כל און

ספר חמישי והוא ספר קדוש

Morocco, in 1160. Although the Jews suffered greatly from Moham-medan intolerance in Morocco, young Moses ben Maimon stayed there for a while and even embarked on literary work. In his "Epistle on Apostasy" (Iggeret ha-Shemad) he took up the defense of those Jews who had accepted the Mohammedan creed under duress, but continued to practise Judaism in secret, against Jewish fanatics who held that they must be considered as final and irremediable apostates. At that time, he also began his famous Arabic commentary on the Mishnah. But Moses ben Maimon soon felt that he could not stand any longer the oppressive atmosphere of Morocco. He went to Palestine in 1165, and from there to Egypt, establishing himself as a physician in the Cairo suburb of Fostat, where a considerable Jewish community had been flourishing since the eighth century. There he engaged in fruitful activities, besides his official tasks as court-physician to the Sultan of Egypt, and raised the prestige of Egyptian Jewry.

Highly esteemed by Jews and Moslems, Moses ben Maimon now completed his Arabic Commentary on the Mishnah and his great code of religious law, the Mishneh Torah. He also published his philosophic magnum opus the "Guide of the Perplexed." His fame had spread over the whole Jewish world, reaching even the distant communities of Yemen in South Arabia, whose Jews he warned against pseudo-Messianic agitation and exhorted to patience and calm reliance on divine deliverance. Moses ben Maimon died in 1204 and his body was transferred to Palestine, to be buried at Tiberias, where his tomb is still a place of pious visitation.

One of the squares of the old Jewish Quarter (the "Juderia") of Cordova now bears the name of Maimonides, "the town's most famous son".

THE DARK AGES

Merchant caravan on the way to China. From the Catalan Atlas (in the Bibliothèque Nationale of Paris), executed by Abraham and Judah Cresques of Majorca, in 1376/7.

The fate of the Jews of western Europe in the twilight of the classical period is obscure. When the Roman Empire became Christian in the fourth century, and there were outbreaks of violence against Jews, many of them were doubtless converted and absorbed in the general population. But part of them survived to carry on the traditions of their people.

In those areas which were conquered by the Arabs in the eighth century, the Jews adopted the Arabic language and helped to build up the great Arab-Jewish cultural world, of which some account has been given above. The Arab conquest had, however, a profound influence on the entire structure of Jewish life, even outside the Moslem orbit. The eastern and southern Mediterranean coasts were now cut off from the sphere of western Latin civilization, and this situation offered the Jews, who were already very active in commerce, new opportunities of putting to use their international potentialities.

To some extent, the Jews were at home in all lands, they possessed an international language and culture and theirs was a feeling of reciprocal solidarity which transcended all frontiers. Hence there emerged at this time a class of Jewish international merchants. Basically, they were engaged in exchanging the precious commodities of the Orient with the raw materials and hoarded treasures of the West. Jews from Asia and Africa reached western and central Europe and contributed considerably to the reinforcement of the Jewish communities everywhere. Arab authors of the ninth century mention Jewish merchants, whom they call "Radanites," a name of mysterious origin. These

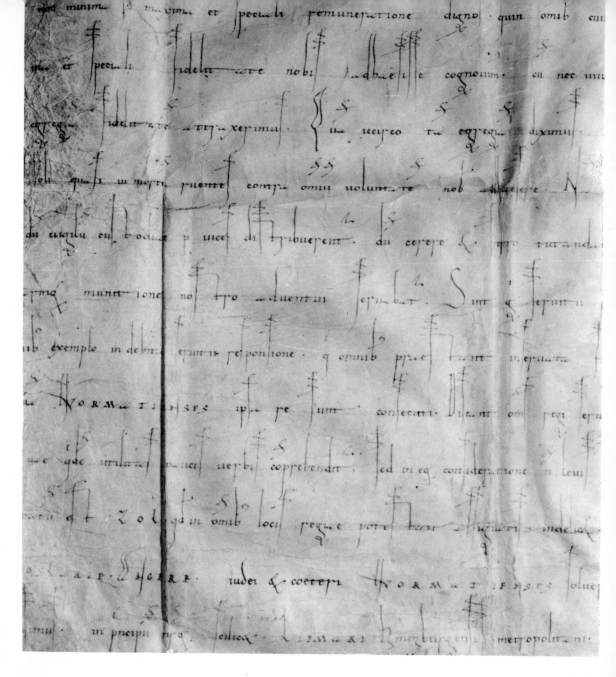

merchants played a most significant part in international trade. They spoke many languages and travelled by land and by sea between central Europe and India, calling at numerous ports and market-places on their way for the purpose of trade.

The Carolingian house, Charlemagne and his successors, seem especially to have patronized Jewish commercial activity, which was beneficial to the economy of their State. Many charters are extant testifying to their benevolence. There are also Jewish legends telling how they favored specific Jewish scholars and leaders. One tale relates that, in return for loyal service, Charlemagne permitted the leader of the Jewish community of Narbonne to possess freeholds of land and to exercise a semi-autonomous rule over his co-religionists as "King of the Jews" in this locality. This office survived until the thirteenth century.

Privilege granted by the German Emperor Henry IV (1056-1106) in the year 1074 to the city of Worms. As a reward for their loyalty to the Crown, "the Jews and other citizens of Worms" are exempted from certain taxes.

The City of Worms. Imaginative wall-painting of the 18th century wooden synagogue of Kapust, near Mohilev (White Russia). Worms was famous throughout the Diaspora as an ancient seat of Jewish learning and an example of Jewish martyrdom.

The same favorable attitude towards Jewish merchants and scholars seems to have obtained in the tenth century, under the emperors of the Saxon dynasty. According to a tradition, it was the emperor Otto II who rewarded the faithful services of a Jew named Kalonymus by transferring him and his family from their original home in Lucca, North Italy, to Mainz (Mayence) in the Rhineland. The family subsequently produced famous Talmudists, mystics, and poets and was, for many centuries, associated with Mainz and other towns in the valley of the Rhine, like Worms and Speyer.

A late echo of the famous Jewish international traders and travellers is to be found in the productions of the Jewish map-makers of Majorca, such as the renowned Catalan Atlas, which reflect vivid memories of the

The window of the so-called Kalonymus House at Mainz (Mayence) in the Rhineland. The Kalonymus family, which produced famous Talmudists and poets, originated in Italy and settled at Mainz in the Dark Ages.

121

trade-routes throughout the Mediterranean world and deep into the Sahara, which afterwards disappeared for many generations from men's recollections.

Not all the western Jews in the Dark Ages, however, were merchants. There were also artisans, concentrating on advanced techniques, such as those used in silk-weaving, dyeing, glass-blowing and so on. There were still also solidly established agricultural colonies all over Europe. Their existence is commemorated in place-names such as Judendorf or Villejuif. Jews were particularly active in vine-growing and wine-manufacture. They also traded in horses, cattle and poultry.

There was a considerable concentration of Jews in north-eastern France, where the great international trade-fairs of the period were held. This fact accounts for the emergence, in the eleventh century, of the great rabbinical schools there. The towering personality of the epoch is Rabbi Gershom ben Judah, "the Light of the Exile" (960–1028). He was born in France, but spent most of his years in Mainz, as the head of the local Talmudic school. Jews everywhere considered him the highest European authority. Rabbi Gershom is responsible for the ordinance proscribing, under sanction of excommunication (herem), polygamy among the western Jews (monogamy was, in fact, already generally practised). In his day, the conversion of a priest to Judaism provoked an outburst of violence against the Jews at Mainz. His son is said to have been

Interior of the Rashi Chapel of the Synagogue of Worms, destroyed by the Nazis in 1938. Against the wall the traditional chair of Rashi.

Exterior view of the Rashi Chapel at Worms.

forcibly baptized and to have died, before those Jews christened against their will were allowed to return to their faith.

Another outstanding figure was Rabbi Solomon ben Isaac (1040–1105) of Troyes in northern France, who studied at Worms and Mainz and prided himself on having been taught by the pupils of Rabbi Gershom. Rabbi Solomon ben Isaac, known, after the initials of his name, as Rashi, has become famed for his commentaries on the Bible and Talmud. Rashi's commentary on almost all the books of the Bible is distinguished by the conciseness of its style, the lucidity of its explanations and by the exquisite taste in its choice of haggadic quotations. It soon became, and remained to this very day, the pabulum of every Jewish student of the Bible. No wonder this was the first Hebrew book to be printed (Reggio 1475). As to Rashi's commentary on the Talmud, this is generally regarded as a master-piece in the art of explaining a difficult and complicated text in a minimum of words. In both commentaries he sometimes added the translation of obscure terms in the medieval French of his native province. His contemporaries exalted Rashi's deserts, by attributing to his commentary the merit of having preserved the Talmud from oblivion.

The city of Worms, where he studied and taught, cherished his memory with particular love. There is a Rashi chapel in the local synagogue (reconstructed after its destruction by the Nazis) and the chair on which

הנלגול שמרו לורתך לבך הוצרך כאן לומר וכשנתחות לבורש מלך פרם
מכל עמ': יהי א' אלהי עמו ויעל ולכך מוספהגוו: ד
ועתנח לפ' שוספר רבוטל מספיק בנתים שהרי ספר עורא חתור נפרור
אחר ספר רבוטל וכן ז'ן חוסב מזה לזה: העיך יש יות רא' פורש עלונגומ'
יועמד קול כרוך הכביך לכל בו מלכותו מי בכם מכל עמו יהוא עמו עמי
וגם בכתבה שלח לכל עשו ולכל מלכותן על רבר זה לחוזר וכן יומרו להם
נהכרות מבדו שהכריד להם ובהעגרת מכתבן משר שלח לפם כה אמר
מלך פרם וגו' כל המלכות הוזרן נתן יה ל' שווב מלך על כל התרמלכותחמ
פקד עלי והוא עמה עלי על ישעיה לבנות לו בית המקרש בירושלם שני כך
יומיר יא לאשיאן לכורש וגו' ובכר עוד לו נבומה זן וכל ישעיה אשר פומזה
פורושלם שהיא מרעת יהרה מ' בגם מכל עשו יעזו עדיך לאמר הרם פו יל
להיר עמך ועשר בוות בן הוד ותעירוהו וכן מיעון בעבדך טאמ' לאיר
כונש אני: עריך תורימ' בבה כך הבריך לכל הומלותמלי בגם בכביל
עמון של הפבה יה א' אלה עמן ויעל ומל לבנות כי ת יה אשר בירושלם:

חזק ונתחזק ישחק לא יוזק ובתורה לבו יחזק
ועינינו יזהירו כמראה הכזק
יעו יצחק לב מיזר זלאה כתבתי מיע עיזושי כתוביב ושיזמתיתן בכריל
ליזח יוזר שנתר' לאלא שישי כרוך עזוך ליעק לב ולוין מועמ ד
עשיה ירבה:

Rashi's Bible commentary. Manuscript dated 1250, in the Bibliothèque Nationale at Paris.

he used to sit while delivering his lectures is still there. Members of Rashi's family, the most important of whom were Rabbi Samuel ben Meir (Rashbam) and Rabbi Jacob ben Meir Tam (Rabbenu Tam), as well as a number of his and their disciples, supplemented the work of their great master. Their glosses on the Talmud, known as Tosaphoth (Addenda), were collected and published later. The period of the "Tosaphists" (twelfth and early thirteenth centuries) coincided with the cruel persecutions of Jews in Europe which were touched off by the First Crusade, and some of them died as martyrs.

The tombstone of the twelve Councillors (Parnassim) of the Community of Worms, who died as martyrs at the hands of the Crusaders in 1096.

THE CRUSADES

Battle between Crusaders and Saracens. Stained glass window (now destroyed) *in the Abbey of St. Denis, Paris:* (*From Lassine & Parmentier, Album Historique.*)

The Crusades were a landmark in Jewish history. There had previously been persecutions of Jews in western Europe, but they had been sporadic. Henceforth, they were to become a perpetual feature of Jewish life there. Towards the end of the eleventh century, Christian pilgrims returning from Palestine brought back tales of desecration of the holy places and ill-treatment of their visitors by the Moslems. These reports, exaggerated by fanatics, roused indignation in Europe and gave birth to the idea that the Holy Land must be liberated from the yoke of the unbelievers. In 1095, pope Urban II, addressing the Council of Clermont, formally invited the Christian princes and knights to undertake the deliverance of Jerusalem. His call had a mighty echo and in the spring of 1096, an army of Crusaders was already on the march eastwards, to fight the redoubtable infidels who were in possession of the Holy Sepulchre. Besides knights driven by genuine religious enthusiasm, the army included a large contingent of common adventurers.

While on their way through the Rhineland, it occurred to the Crusaders that there were infidels at home too, less formidable than the Moslems.

יבכר רבינו גרשון

יזכור רבינו שמעון הגדול ב"ר יצחק

יזכור רבינו שלמה ב"ר יצחק

יזכור רבינו יעקב תם

יזכור רבינו פרץ ורבינו שמואל בונאיר

יזכור רבינו חננאל ורבינו יצחק

יזכור רבינו מאיר בנו ד"ו ברוך

יזכור מוהר"ר מאיר ב"ה הקדוש ר' ברוך הלוי

יזכור רבינו יעקב בנו מוהר"ר משה הלוי

יזכור שאלתני בת מוהר"ר

יזכור שלמה

יזכור שנילן

יזכור יואל

יזכיר חנוך

יזכור שלמה

יזכור נתן

יזכור וזלן

יזכור יעקב

יזכור איזק

These were the harmless, defenseless, and reputedly wealthy Jews. Consequently, they began their Holy War by attacking Jews, wherever they encountered them on their route. In place after place, the Jews were compelled to choose between baptism and death. Most of them preferred death. They either took their own lives or were brutally slain by the Crusaders. Whole communities, such as Trier, Worms, Mainz, Speyer, and Cologne, were practically wiped out. Many Jews were forcibly baptized at Metz and Regensburg. There were Jewish settlements, our first knowledge of which dates from the record of one of those sanguinary episodes. After the Rhineland came the turn of Bohemia. At Prague and other places, the Jews were either forcibly baptized or massacred. However, in one place in Bohemia—unfortunately, its name is not given by the chronicler who relates the episode—the Jews took up arms and put the Crusaders to flight. The number of Jewish victims in Europe is estimated to have been about twelve thousand. The booty was divided between Crusaders and local secular and ecclesiastical authorities.

A new category of Hebrew literature now began to make its appearance, the "Memorbuch," in which honor is done to the memory of the victims of these depredations. Scores of place-names and thousands of individual martyrs are sometimes commemorated as having perished in the course of a few months.

When the Crusaders finally reached Palestine, in 1099, they annihilated the Jewish community in Jerusalem, re-established since the Moslem conquest. The synagogue in which the Jews had taken refuge was set on fire and the whole community perished in the flames.

Attacks on Jewish communities in central Europe now became a regular feature of the Crusades. Fifty years after the first Crusade, the Kingdom of Jerusalem, established by the Crusaders, was in such a sorry plight, that a second Crusade was preached by pope Eugenius III and the saintly abbot Bernard of Clairvaux. Zealous monks in France and Germany did their best to incite the Crusaders against the infidels at home too. King Louis VII of France and Emperor Conrad III of Germany contented themselves, however, with impoverishing the Jews by exempting the Crusaders from their obligations towards Jewish money-lenders, but granted the Jews at least a measure of protection from physical harm. Bernard of Clairvaux, too, made use of his authority to stem the frenzy of the Crusaders to some extent. Even so, both in France and Germany, many Jews were murdered. In Ramerupt (France) the famous Tosaphist Rabbenu Tam had a narrow escape from a martyr's death, thanks to the intervention of a friendly knight.

The Second Crusade did not save the Kingdom of Jerusalem, which was conquered in 1187 by Sultan Saladin of Egypt. The Third Crusade was organised in 1189 for the purpose of delivering Jerusalem anew. This time the fever reached England, whose king, Richard the Lion-Hearted,

Page from the Frankfort Memorbuch. Such books were used in the synagogues for the memorial prayers. They included lists of martyrs, benefactors of the community and prominent Jewish personalities, for whose souls prayers were recited. The page reproduced mentions Rabbi Gershom "the Light of the Exile", R. Solomon ben Isaac (Rashi), R. Jacob Tam, R. Meir of Rothenburg and others. (University Library, Jerusalem).

Clifford's Tower, York, where the Jews of York took refuge in 1190, dying at one another's hands, when resistance became hopeless.

also took the cross. In 1190, on Shabbat Hagadol (The Sabbath preceding Passover), which coincided with the Christian Holy Saturday, the Jewish community of York met its fate. They had taken refuge in the tower of the royal castle, where they resisted for several days. When there was no more hope of escape, they determined to anticipate massacre by dying by one another's hands.

There were outbreaks of violence elsewhere as well—at Norwich, Stanford Lynn, etc., but none of them reached the dimensions of the tragedy at York.

The Crusaders were less successful in their fight against the Saracens. They did not succeed in delivering Jerusalem from Saladin's hands.

No particular outburst of fanaticism marked the still-born Crusades of 1202–4 and 1228–9, known as the Fourth and Fifth. But the previous Crusades had fundamentally changed the relations between Jews and Christians in Europe. They had engendered the blind hate of Jews which characterized the Christians throughout the Middle Ages. On the other hand, they had also produced a deep estrangement of the Jews from their Christian surroundings. Mysticism found fertile soil in their cruelly wounded hearts and the echo of their suffering still resounds in the religious poetry of the period.

Ruins of the Crusaders' castle at Athlit, their last stronghold on Palestinian soil. Its evacuation in August 1291 marked the triumph of Moslem rule in Palestine for more than six centuries.

FALSE ACCUSATIONS

Once the appetite for blood was whetted, it was not easily assuaged. Before long, the pretext of a crusade was no longer necessary in order to assault the Jews. Horrible charges began to be levelled against them. For example, they were accused of "sacrificing" Christian children at Passover or Easter-tide, holidays which frequently coincided, in mockery of the Passion of Jesus. Later on, the refinement was added, that they made use of the blood in the manufacture of their unleavened bread (mazzoth) or in other paschal ceremonies.

This fantastic accusation, always bringing grim devastation in its trail, was formulated for the first time in England, in the case of "Saint" William of Norwich in 1144. In that year, the Jews of Norwich, envied and hated by their Christian neighbors on account of their prosperity, were accused by some monks of having martyrized a Christian boy on the eve of Passover. Although the authorities did not believe the charge and even protected the Jews, the "martyred" boy was proclaimed a saint and his body was said to have wrought miracles. Like accusations

Ritual murder at Trent (1475), according to a 15th century engraving. The Jews were said to need the blood of Christian children for the manufacture of the unleavened bread for the Passover ceremonial.

with similar effects were made against the Jews of Gloucester (1168) and Bury St. Edmunds (1181).

The seed spread by English monks fell on fertile soil in Continental Europe. The most notorious case of the blood-libel in the twelfth century occurred in 1171 at Blois, in France. Here the whole Jewish community of 21 men and 17 women were jailed on the charge of having murdered a Christian boy. Their guilt was "proved" by submitting the only witness for the prosecution to the ordeal of water, and all the Jews were burned alive together at a huge stake, after having refused to save themselves by accepting baptism. The date of the execution (20th Sivan) was long observed as a fast day by Jewish communities in France and the Rhineland.

It would lead too far astray, even to enumerate all the cases of blood-libel, but two of the most notorious should be mentioned.

The medieval Jew's House and Synagogue in Steep Hill, Lincoln.

In Lincoln, a boy named Hugh disappeared in 1255 and his body was found in a well in the courtyard of a Jewish house. The possibility of an

Lincoln Cathedral. The shrine of "Little St. Hugh", allegedly crucified by Jews in 1255.

accident was never considered, and the Jews were accused of having crucified the youngster. The boy's body was solemnly buried in the Cathedral and ninety-two members of Lincoln's Jewish community were sent to London for trial. Eighteen of them were hanged and the others allowed to ransom their lives at a high price. The event was the subject of contemporary ballads, and Chaucer recalled it as the case of "Little St. Hugh."

The other case occurred more than 200 years later at Trent (in northern Italy). On the first day of Passover 1475, a three years old Christian boy named Simon disappeared. It seems that a Christian who had lost a lawsuit against a Jew and had sworn to take revenge, murdered the boy with the intention of puting the blame on the Jews. Of course, Jews were accused and arrested as responsible for the ritual murder. They were submitted to atrocious torture, for the purpose of wringing confessions

Jews burnt at the stake, a frequent spectacle in the Middle Ages. From Schedel's "Liber Chronicorum", Nuremberg, 1493.

from them. After months of suffering, six of the accused were burnt alive and two, who had accepted baptism, had their sentence alleviated from burning to decapitation. The ninth accused died in prison and his body was subsequently burnt. In this case, Pope Sixtus IV opposed the ritual murder charge and vainly tried to save the innocent victims. Afterwards, he declined the insistent demand of the Trent clergy for the canonization of little Simon, who was made a saint of the Catholic Church only about 100 years later by Pope Gregory XIII. There is still a chapel named after him in St. Peter's Church, Trent, in which services

Tombstone of a young Jewish woman who died as a martyr. Speyer, second half of 14th century.

133

were discontinued in our days only, following the new spirit in the Catholic Church manifested in the Second Vatican Council (1962–65). The era of ritual murder accusations, ushered in by the case of Norwich, was destined to continue down to our own century, always with tragic sequels, especially in Germany, where the charge was endemic. It was of no avail that kings, emperors, and even popes recognized the absurdity of the accusation and issued formal edicts condemning it.

The doctrine of transubstantiation, recognised by the Church in 1215, provided a further fertile source of libel and a pretext for massacres. The Jews were accused of deliberately profaning the consecrated elements of the eucharist, thus renewing on the flesh of Jesus, into which the bread is believed to be converted in the mass, the pains and tortures he had undergone during the Passion. The first recorded instance of this accusation, bringing additional suffering and massacre in its train, occurred at Beelitz, near Berlin in 1247.

There were other famous incidents. In 1290, a Jewish couple in Paris was sentenced to death by burning for having pricked a host. According to a contemporary record, blood poured out of the perforated wafer. The church in the Rue des Billettes, where the desecrated host was exposed, became a celebrated place of pilgrimage.

In Deggendorf, Bavaria, the charge of host-profanation raised against the local Jews, led to the wholesale massacre of the entire community. The bodies of the Jews were burnt and their property was divided among the murderers. The Deggendorf accusation was followed by a wave of massacres throughout Germany.

In 1410, Jews were tortured and murdered at Segovia, Spain, for the desecration of a host, and in 1420, all the Jews of Austria were imprisoned on the same charge. A number committed suicide in jail, more than a hundred were burnt at the stake, and the remainder were expelled from Austria.

It is now believed that the presence of a minute scarlet fungus may have been responsible for the formation of red spots on hosts, which gave rise to the idea that the consecrated bread was bleeding, owing to ill-treatment by Jews.

The most ludicrous of these false accusations was that made in 1321, when the Jews of France were charged with having instigated the lepers, who were very numerous at the time, to poison wells and rivers. They allegedly had done so at the behest of the Moorish kings of Granada and Tunis. This charge gave rise to wide-spread murderous attacks, in which whole communities, for instance that of Chinon, were cruelly annihilated. Moreover, a heavy fine was imposed on all the Jewish communities of France.

Well-poisoning became a standing accusation against the Jews during the years 1347–1350, when the Black Death decimated the population

German 15th century broadsheet describing the host-desecration of Passau in 1478. As a consequence of this accusation, the convicted desecrators were burnt and the other Jews expelled from Passau, except those who accepted baptism. The synagogue was destroyed and on its place the church of St. Salvator was erected.

Ein grawſamlich geſchicht Geſchehen zu paſſaw Von den Juden als hernach volgt:

he ſtylt Criſtoff acht partickel des ſa-
cramét auß der kirché. legt das in ſein
taſché. hatby darinné drei tag behalté

Hye ſchuef er die ſacrament den ſuden
auff den niſch die vnuermayligt gewel-
ſen ſein. darumb ſy im ein guldé gaben

Hye tragen die iudé vñ ſchulklopffer.
die ſacrament yn ir ſynagog. vnd vber-
antwurten dye den Juden.

Hye ſtyche pfeyl Jud des ſacrament
auff irem altar.iſt plut darauß gangen
das er vñ ander ſuden geſehen haben.

Hye teylten ſy auß dye ſacramét ſchick-
ten zwen partickel gen Prag.zwé gen
ſaltzpurg.zwen yn die Newenſtat

Hye verprenten ſy die ſacramét verſu-
chen ob vnſer glaub gerecht wer flogé
auß dem offen zwen engel.vñ.ij.tauhé

Hye vecht man all Juden zu paſſaw
die dy ſacramét gekaufft verſchicki ge-
ſtolen vnd verprant haben.

Hye furt má ſy fur gericht. verurtaylt
die vier getaufft.fackel mano.kolmá
vnd walich.ſein gekopft worden.

Hye zereyſt man den pfeyl vnd vertel
die das ſacramét bebylté. dz darnach
geſtochen vnd verprant haben.

Hye verprent man ſy mit ſamproé ju-
den.die yn irem glauben blyben. vnd
vmb das ſacrament gewyſt haben.

Hye wirt der Criſtoff des ſacraments
verkauffer.auff einem wagé zeryſſen
mit gluenden zangen.

Hye hebt man an zw pawen. vnſerm
herren zu lob eyn gotzhauß. Auß der
juden ſynagog ꝛc.

of Europe. Although the Jews too suffered, the blame for the dissemina-
tion of the epidemic was attributed to them. The result was a wave of
massacres of unprecedented virulence throughout Germany and the
adjacent lands. Hundreds of communities were devastated (three hundred
communities were exterminated in Germany alone) and the victims of
the massacres reached proportions of tens of thousands.

ECONOMIC DEGRADATION

Hand in hand with the persecutions provoked by false accusations went the economic degradation of the Jews. It was not long before they lost the position as international merchants and skilled artisans, which they had occupied in Europe in the Dark Ages. Christian artisans in most countries, particularly in France and Germany, formed craft-guilds which wholly controlled industry. They were organized, to a great degree, on a semi-religious basis, with their patron saints and their church celebrations, which afforded no place for persons of other faiths. In Germany, Jewish artisans were allowed to practise their trade in the Jewish quarters only and to sell their products solely to their co-religionists.

Christian merchants, too, everywhere organized merchant-guilds, which increasingly controlled, or even monopolized, trade. They easily displaced their Jewish competitors, because the growing insecurity of life for Jews rendered travel for commercial purposes more and more dangerous. This happened just when the Crusades were giving an enormous stimulus to communications and, in the long run, to international trade between East and West. The great Italian trading-republics (especially Venice

Ich bitt euch jud leicht mir zů hand/   Was eüch gebürt gebt mir verstand·
Bar gelt auff bürgen oder pfand/

Jewish money-lender and German peasant. Woodcut from Cicero, De Officiis Augsburg 1531.

Jewish money-changer. Woodcut from Breydenbach, Die Heiligen Reisen gen Jerusalem, Strassburg 1487.

One of the earliest caracatures of a Jew. Aaron ,,Fil-Diaboli'' (son of the devil) of Colchester, whose son was involved in an offence against the Forestry Laws in 1277. He wears the Jewish badge in the form of the two tables of the Law, as usual in England (Public Record Office, London).

and Genoa), which developed and flourished in this period, made, from the beginning of their expansion, a determined attempt to squeeze their Jewish competitors out of existence. Religious zeal was, of course, the official disguise of their greed for profits.

The feudal system, as well as the growing insecurity, simultaneously put an end to the existence of most of the surviving Jewish peasants and farmers, who hitherto had remained attached to the soil in many regions. Excluded from the land and eliminated from commerce and industry over a great part of Europe, the Jews could find a return for their capital only in the classical and inevitable fashion of the retired merchant, that is, in investment. In the context of those days, this meant lending out their money for interest. The Third Lateran Council (1179), in a fit of somewhat impractical and impracticable idealism, had attempted to put an end to the "unnatural" practice of usury among the Christians. The Church, however, left a loop-hole open for the Jews to engage in money-lending at interest, and thus save society from the all but disastrous implications of the ecclesiastical economic doctrine.

While the ban of the Church did not prevent Italian bankers (the Lombards) from continuing to practise usury on a large scale, it opened before the Jews, superseded in other domains, a wide field of activity into which they were practically pushed. In northern Europe, most comprehensively in England, to a somewhat lesser degree in France and Germany, but only to a slight extent in Spain or, in the period with which we are now dealing, in Italy, the Jews became, for a while, the typical money-lenders of the age, officially recognized, and indeed encouraged

to follow this calling only. The term "Jew" was colloquially used as an equivalent for money-lender, with the result that the Jews acquired a reputation for vast wealth, for however short a time they could actually enjoy their riches. Their clients, so light-hearted and adulatory when they needed a loan, became filled with hatred when they received demands for payment, and imagined that their creditors had battened on their misery. Thus, the unpopularity of the Jews became greater and greater. To the hatred based on religious reasons, a social antagonism was now added, offering a further perpetual pretext for persecution and massacre.

Kings and rulers welcomed, for a time, the development of the Jewish money-trade. They relied on the Jewish capitalists to pay heavily for the protection granted to them and to make solid monetary advances to their treasuries in time of need. In due course, they became the sleeping partners in the transactions of their Jews. However much they stigmatized them in public, they did not shrink from relieving them of a great— sometimes an overwhelmingly great—part of their profits by means of confiscatory taxation. It has been well said, that in the Middle Ages the Jews constituted a sort of "financial sponge", which soaked up the floating capital of the country and was relentlessly squeezed, from time to time, into the royal exchequer. It might be added that, when the period of the sponge's usefulness had passed, it was mercilessly tossed away.

In England, an elaborate apparatus for Jewish financial operations, under Government organization and supervision, came into existence. The Jews carried on their business virtually for the benefit of the exchequer. It might almost be said that money-lending was converted into a government-monopoly. After the events at York in 1190, mentioned in the chapter on the Crusades, the mob had destroyed all the Jewish records and burnt the promissory notes of Christian debtors deposited in the local churches. This resulted in a heavy loss to the royal treasury. To prevent such losses in future, Richard the Lion-Hearted established an overall organization known later as the Exchequer of the Jews, under the control of Justices or Justiciars of the Jews with their seat at Westminster. All

Medieval caricatures showing English Jews (Isaac of Norwich and his family). Exchequer Issue Roll 1233 (Public Record Office, London).

138

Jewish transactions had to be registered and recorded by this office, and copies of the deeds, known by the Talmudic term *shetar*, latinized as *starrum* or Anglicized as *starr*, were locked in special chests for safe-keeping. When the debt was discharged, the deed would be endorsed to this effect in Hebrew. Hundreds of such documents are extant.

A similar institution was organized in France, in 1198, by King Philip Augustus. It was known as the "Produit des Juifs" (Jewish Revenue).

The most lucrative Jewish operations were those on the security of land. Their ultimate result was, in some countries, the concentration of feudal holdings in the hands of the wealthier nobility, who bought out the Jewish creditors.

Financial agreement written in Latin and endorsed by the Jewish money-lender in Hebrew. A typical medieval Anglo-Jewish "starr" (Public Record Office, London).

THE LATERAN COUNCILS

The position of the Jews was meanwhile deteriorating in other respects as well. In the twelfth century, the Catholic Church underwent a serious crisis, on account of the rise of the Albigensian heresy and related sects. Some of the sectarians preached a return to the Old Testament and practised certain Jewish rites. In the process of the reaction of the Church against the threat presented by these heresies, the Jews were bound to suffer. The Church held the sincere, though mistaken idea, that the Jews, the arch-unbelievers, were responsible for fomenting the heretical movements. So far as there was any truth at all in this, it consisted merely in the fact that the heretics studied the Old Testament and sometimes sought guidance from the Jews in this endeavor. It must also have seemed suspicious in the eyes of the Church, that Albigensian nobles did not mind having Jews in their employment as agents and bailiffs.

Church discipline was now generally stiffened and anti-Jewish Church legislation more systematically enforced. The Dominican order, especially brought into existence to fight heresy, before long extended its activity to a calculated offensive against Jews and Judaism.

Pope Innocent III, who convoked the Fourth Lateran Council of 1215 and promoted its drastic anti-Jewish regulations.

Jews wearing the distinctive badge and pointed hats. From an engraving in Pierre Comestor's Bible Historiale, 1499.

Although Pope Alexander III (1159–1181) was personally no enemy of the Jews, and even condemned violence against them and their forcible conversion, the Third Lateran Council, convoked by him in 1179, refurbished some of the old ecclesiastical measures against the Jews. For example, it insisted that Jews and Christians should not live together, lest the former exercise too strong an influence on their neighbors. Jews were forbidden to employ Christian servants and to build new synagogues or renovate old ones.

The policy of the Church became much grimmer after the accession of Pope Innocent III (1198–1216), a great papal figure, but a ferocious hater of Jews. The Fourth Lateran Council, which met in Rome in 1215 under his aegis, enacted a series of drastic regulations intended to minimize the influence of Jews over Christians and to emphasize their inferiority. Jewish money-lenders were warned that they would be forbidden any commercial relations with Christians, if they asked a high rate of interest. Jews who acquired Christian estates were obliged to pay to the Church the tithes and other dues formerly paid by the previous Christian owners. It was ordered that Jews should henceforth be set apart from their neighbors by a distinctive badge. The external identifying mark was meant to isolate the Jews from their Christian neighbors, for the purpose of obviat-

ing the unspeakable offense of unwitting sexual intercourse between adherents of the two faiths. The Council also prohibited Jews from occupying public office. Against Jewish converts coercion was declared permissible, to prevent or punish their adherence or their relapse to the rites and customs of their former creed.

The most cruel and humiliating of the Fourth Lateran Council's decisions was, of course, the introduction of the distinctive badge. This was the origin of the Badge of Shame, which was to have a pathetic history in Europe, with intervals, for over seven hundred years. It was not consistently enforced down to a relatively late period. In some cases the Jews were able to buy themselves a respite or secure personal dispensations from the obligation. But in due course, it became the rule in every part of Europe which owed obedience to the Catholic Church.

The Council had laid down the principle that unbelievers must be recognizable by their dress, without, however, fixing the form of the distinctive mark. This was left to subsequent regulation. Generally, it was a yellow ring known as the "rouelle" or "rotella" (wheel). Sometimes it was a solid circle, in certain countries partially colored. In England it had the traditional form of the Two Tables of Stone bearing the Ten Commandments, usually of a saffron hue. It may be added that the sign formed by inverted triangles, named the "Shield of David" and enforced by the Nazis in the twentieth century, was not used as a Jewish badge in the Middle Ages. Sometimes, in addition to the badge, Jews were obliged to wear hats or caps of a peculiar shape.

The result of the introduction of the badge was to mark the Jews apart from other men as a different and inferior race, liable at all times to insult or attack.

The increasing tendency to restrict the Jews to separate quarters in the towns where they lived, in which, moreover, the houses were sometimes similarly stigmatized, contributed to the isolation and degradation of the Jews in the eyes of their Christian fellow-citizens.

Above to the left: English Jew wearing the distinctive badge in the form of the two Tables of the Law. Miniature in a 14th century manuscript in the Cotton Collection, British Museum, London.
Above to the right and below: The Jewish badge in France and Spain, according to miniatures in 14th century manuscripts.

THE JEWS OF THE
MIDDLE AGES

Thus the typical medieval Jewish community came into existence in the countries of northern and western Europe. For the convenience of their economic operations, the Jews lived not only in the major towns, but scattered in many hundreds of places, which to-day would not be considered much more than villages. The communities were consequently, on the whole, rather small, for the most part probably not numbering one hundred souls and in very few cases exceeding one thousand.

The Jews tended to live huddled together in their own areas. This was not due primarily to obedience to the restrictive regulations of the Church. There were other motives, too, for this voluntary segregation. On the one hand, the Jews desired to avoid the manifestations of gentile hostility; on the other, Jewish feelings of solidarity and the exigencies of their communal organization made it necessary for them to live together in compact groups. To this day, the Jewish quarters in many old towns in various countries are still known by such names as Jewry, rue des Juifs, Judengasse, Via dei Giudei or Giudecca, and Juderia.

It is important, however, to note that, on the whole, the Jewish quarter was not restricted to Jews only, nor were Jews completely confined to it. In a few places in Spain, the Juderia, like the Moreria of the Moham-

The Synagogue of Fuerth (Bavaria). The building to the right, the Alte Schul, dated from the beginning of the 14th century. Engraving of the year 1705.

A Jewish physician and his patient. From Schobser's Plenarium, Augsburg 1487.

medans, was a self-contained, walled area, provided with gates which converted it into a stronghold in cases of necessity.

The focal point of the Jewish quarter was, of course, the Synagogue, which was also the center of religious and communal life. It was generally small and unimpressive, sometimes no more than a room in the house of one of the communal magnates. Occasionally, however, it attained a certain stateliness and significance. In such cases, the synagogue was, inevitably, built in the dominant architectural style of the area. By the side of the synagogue, in large communities at least, there was a hospice for strangers or the sick, with a hall in which weddings and other communal festivities were held.

In northern Europe, the principal economic mainstay of the Jewish quarter was money-lending. But money-lenders would inevitably be interested in the sale of precious objects they had taken in pawn. Thus, they became jewel merchants. They also traded in other merchandise which they imported from abroad. In addition, there were everywhere among the Jews goldsmiths and metal craftsmen who worked for the wider public. There were also Jewish ballad-singers. In Spain there were even Jewish lion-tamers. Jewish musicians were to be found everywhere. Jewish poets wrote in the local vernacular. Among the famous German Minnesingers, at least one, Süsskind of Trimberg (13th century), was a Jew.

On the other hand, it has already been pointed out, that in southern Europe money-lending made relatively little headway. Here the Jews were still largely concentrated in the traditional handicrafts, such as weaving, silk-manufacture, dyeing, and tanning.

In Spain, Jewish apothecaries brought up in the Moorish tradition seem to have been common. The Jewish physician was everywhere famous for his skill and devotion. The Church made great efforts to persuade Christians not to consult Jewish doctors, but in vain. Kings, bishops, and even Popes, overlooked the Church canons, when their health or life were at stake, and consulted them. Many Jews who attained high positions, especially in Spain and Portugal, began their careers as court-physicians.

Süsskind of Trimberg, the Jewish Minnesinger (second half of the 13th century). Six of his poems in medieval German have been preserved in the 14th century "Manessian" manuscript, in the Library of the Heidelberg University. The miniature in the same manuscript portrays Süsskind as a bearded Jew wearing the distinctive pointed hat.

Jews performing the Tashlikh ceremony. Woodcut from "Der gantz Juedisch Glaub" (The whole Jewish faith), Augsburg 1531, by the Jewish renegade and anti-Jewish polemist Anthonius Margaritha. The ceremony, performed on the first New Year's day, consists of shaking the garments while standing at the bank of a river, symbolically casting the sins into the depths of the water. The woodcut represents the garb of Jewish men and women in Germany towards the end of the Middle Ages.

Outwardly, the Jews were not unlike their neighbors. But for this, the institution of the Jewish badge would have been unnecessary. Long beards and earlocks, distinctive of a later period, do not seem to have been in fashion. In some regions and in various periods, beards were not grown at all. There was also no specific Jewish costume, except for synagogal worship. Characteristic, however, was the pointed Jewish hat, which we find all over northern Europe as the typical feature of the Jewish garb. In the mind of contemporary miniature painters, this head-gear was so closely connected with the Jews' image, that they anachronistically also dressed the Hebrews of the Biblical period in pointed hats.

Throughout the Middle Ages, it was usual to humiliate the Jews in all possible ways. Conventional church sculpture, for instance, included

...iniatures from the Mahzor ...osia, 14th century (Univer-...y Library Leipzig, Cod. V. ...02), illustrating Jewish garb ...medieval Germany. Below: ...ws at prayer in the syna-gue. The distinctive feature ...the pointed hat.

figures of the despised Synagogue confronted by the upright and radiant Church. The most wide-spread image derisively representing the Synagogue was, particularly in Germany, the "Jews' sow", the relief of which adorns many a church, sometimes accompanied by appropriate inscriptions.

Among the incidental humiliations to which the Jews were subjected, was that of being compelled to serve as executioners. Jews were executed by being strung up by the heels and left to die thus, in order to draw out the agony for days.

In the law-courts, Jews had to take the oath "more judaico", to the accompaniment of an elaborate and degrading formula.

Symbolic statues of the Church and the Synagogue, from the Liebfrauenkirche at Trier (Treves), Germany. In contrast with the proud, upright figure of the Church, the Synagogue is represented blindfold in a humble posture, with the crown tumbling down from her head, the sceptre broken and the Tables of the Law upside down.

The oath "more judaico" (according to Jewish custom). Woodcut from Tengler's Laienspiegel ("Mirror of the Layman"), Augsburg 1509. Jews appearing in court were obliged to take the oath in a most humiliating form. The particulars varied in the course of time and from country to country, but they all aimed at degrading the Jew. In some countries the oath "more judaico" was enforced down to the 19th century.

The Church meanwhile continued its unrelenting pressure on the Jews, in the hope of eventually making them acknowledge the error of their ways. The newly established mendicant orders of friars, particularly the Dominicans, were employed for this purpose. The thirteenth century marked the inauguration of the series of great formal disputations staged under high auspices, at which Jewish representatives were compelled to defend themselves and their faith against opprobrious onslaught. In these disputations Jewish apostates often cut a sad figure as the chief accusers of their former faith and co-religionists.

In the Disputation of Paris of 1240, the renegade Nicholas Donin undertook to prove that the Talmud contains attacks and calumnies against the person of Jesus and the Christian faith, and blasphemous

Disputation between Jewish and Christian scholars. German 16th century woodcut. Such disputations were frequent throughout the Middle Ages. The Jews were forced to take part in them as defendants, while the accusers were often renegades, more or less conversant with the religious literature of their former faith.

immoral maxims. A delegation of rabbis, headed by Jehiel of Paris and Moses of Coucy, both recognized rabbinical authorities, in vain displayed their erudition and talent in refuting Donin's accusations. Following the disputation, the Talmud was declared an impious and obnoxious book. All the Talmud-manuscripts on which the monks could lay hands were confiscated and twenty-four cart-loads were publicly committed to the flames at Paris in 1242. The resulting shortage of Talmud-manuscripts led to the decline of the once famous Talmudic school of Paris. Its head, Rabbi Jehiel of Paris, left his inhospitable country and emigrated to Palestine.

Another apostate, Pablo Christiani, was the protagonist of the Disputation of Barcelona in 1263, which was held at the royal palace in the presence of King James I of Aragon. Pablo Christiani flaunted his ability in demonstrating, on the basis of Biblical and Talmudic texts, the truth of the Christian dogmas regarding the Messiah and the divine nature of Jesus, and of the Church-doctrine on the abrogation of the Jewish Law after the advent of the Redeemer. The Jewish spokesman in this disputation was Rabbi Moses ben Nahman of Gerona (generally known as the "Ramban"), the most renowned Talmudist and Bible exegete of his time. For four days, he courageously withstood the attacks of the apostate. Making full use of the freedom of speech granted to him by the king at the beginning of the disputation, Rabbi Moses ben Nahman skilfully and ironically refuted his adversary's arguments. Nevertheless, the friars later boasted that the Jews had given up, since

Interior of the "Ramban" — Synagogue in the Old City of Jerusalem, traditionally the synagogue restored by Rabbi Moses ben Nahman of Gerona, who went to Palestine after the Disputation of Barcelona in 1263 and re-established the community of Jerusalem, ruined by Tartar and Mongol raids.

they were unable to defend their cause. When Rabbi Moses ben Nahman published his report of the debate, in order to obviate misrepresentation, he was condemned to two years exile. He then decided, however, to leave his country for good. Although advanced in age, he undertook the long journey to Palestine, where he helped in the reconstruction of the community of Jerusalem, which had heavily suffered from the Tartar raid of 1244 and the Mongol attack of 1260.

The most spectacular disputation was that organized at Tortosa (Spain) in 1413–1414 by the antipope Benedict XIII, who personally presided at the browbeating of the representatives of the Jewish communities of the Kingdom of Aragon. It was again an apostate, the Talmudist Joshua of Lorca, called Geronimo de Santa Fé after his conversion, who confronted the Jews in the name of the Church. The Jewish delegation included such personalities as Vidal Benveniste, head of the community of Saragossa, a man of wide learning with a good knowledge of Latin, and the philosopher Joseph Albo, author of the famous work *Ikkarim* on the principles of the Jewish faith. The disputation began in February 1413 and lasted, with shorter and longer interruptions, until the autumn of 1414. Again attempts were made to prove the truth of the Christian dogmas by quoting passages from the Bible and the Talmud. The rabbis manfully maintained their position, but the physical pressure brought to bear on the Jews, meanwhile, had baleful results. Ultimately the enraged pontiff ordered the destruction of all the copies of the Talmud and of any other Jewish books allegedly hostile to Christian faith.

JEWISH INTELLECTUAL LIFE IN MEDIEVAL EUROPE

Jewish school in the Middle Ages. Miniature from a German 14th century manuscript of Pentateuch, Megilloth and Haphtaroth (British Museum Add. 19776). The lash has remained the attribute of the Jewish teacher in Eastern Europe, down to the end of the 19th century. But, on the whole, love of learning was for the Jewish children a more forceful incentive than the fear of punishment.

The main interest of medieval Jews was in their books. In all the townships of northern France, the Rhineland and England, the Jews, condemned by their Christian neighbors as usurers, dedicated all their spare-time to study. They immersed themselves chiefly in the Talmud, using as a guide the commentary of Rashi. This was an active and constructive discipline, which tended to enlarge and deepen the scope of Jewish learning and to keep it in permanent touch with the problems of Jewish life. The work of completing Rashi's commentary and elucidating unsolved difficulties in the text of the Talmud by additional explanatory glosses (the Tosaphoth), was assiduously continued by Talmudic authorities, mostly in France and Germany, throughout the twelfth and thirteenth centuries. The result of this collective effort invariably accompanies the text of the Talmud, along with Rashi's commentary, ever since Daniel Bomberg published the first complete edition of the Talmud at Venice in 1520/23. The Tosaphists (or Baale ha-Tosaphoth, as they are termed) made famous, for long after, the names of many small and otherwise unimportant places in which Jews lived and learned.

החבור הגדול מהלכות התלמוד לרבנו
יצחק אלפאסי עם חדושי הרב רבנו נסים
ברבי ראובן ופסקי הרב המרדכי זכר
צדיקים לברכה וחדושים לברכה

First page of R. Isaac Alfasi's Talmudic compendium "Halakhoth", printed in Constantinople, 1509, with decorative border first used in Hijar, Spain, before the expulsion of the Jews.

In southern Europe, particularly Spain, the humanistic influence of the environment led the Jews to interest themselves more in poetry, philosophy, grammar, and science.

In view of their broad and many-sided intellectual interests, the Jews of Spain could not devote their whole time to the Talmudic sources, to the exclusion of all else, as did their co-religionists in north-western Europe. The characteristic consequence was that the classical handy codes and compendia of Jewish religious practises were produced in Spain. In the eleventh century, Isaac Alfasi, a celebrated scholar from Northern Africa

153

who directed a famous school at Lucena, near Cordova, wrote his *Halakhoth* (Legal Decisions), which is in fact an abstract of the Talmud. Alfasi omitted all the haggadic material, which occupies such a large place in the Talmud, and all the lengthy controversies, and concentrated on the legal (halachic) portions, particularly those of practical importance. His work, which facilitates finding decisions applicable to specific cases, was readily accepted by his contemporaries, and the grateful posterity called the book "The Little Talmud."

It was this same Spanish trend towards codification which prompted Maimonides to compose his great code, the Mishneh Torah (Repetition of the Law). While Alfasi retained the Talmudic arrangement and followed the order of its tractates, Maimonides compiled a systematical compendium of Jewish law and ritual, dividing the whole material into fourteen books, each dealing with a certain range of subjects.

In the fourteenth century, the German Rabbi Asher ben Jehiel, who left his country to establish himself in Spain, first at Barcelona and then at Toledo, produced another code of *Halakhoth* (also known as *Piskei ha-Rosh*, "Decisions of the Rosh", Rosh being an abbreviation of the author's title *Rabbenu Asher*). In his compendium, Rabbi Asher ben Jehiel follows the order of Alfasi's "*Halakoth*." He also takes into account the opinions and decisions of German and French authorities, particularly the Tosaphists, and expresses views of his own as well.

The last Spanish code, and the most important, in view of later developments based on it, was composed by Rabbenu Asher's son, Rabbi Jacob ben Asher. This code, known as the *Arbaa Turim* ("The Four Rows," an allusion to the four rows of precious stones on the breast-plate of the High Priest, Exodus 28:17), owes its name to its division into four sections. Jacob ben Asher omitted Talmudic ordinances specifically applicable to Jewish life in Palestine in former centuries, and arranged systematically halakhic regulations of universal application regarding prayer, the Sabbath, holidays and related matters (*Orah Hayim*), dietary laws, family life, etc. (*Yoreh Deah*), marriage (*Even ha-Ezer*) and civil and criminal law (*Hoshen ha-Mishpat*). This division became generally accepted, when it was adopted by Joseph Caro's 16th century code, the *Shulhan Arukh*, which is considered as authoritative to this day.

Even more characteristic, perhaps, than the work of codification, was another function fulfilled by the Jews of southern Europe and the Mediterranean area. Straddling, as they did, the Christian and Moslem worlds and the Arabic speaking and Romance speaking lands, these Jewish communities, in Spain, Provence, and southern Italy, provided the translators of the great Arabic scientific classics (largely, indeed, of Greek origin) into Latin. In this language those fundamental works became known to the world of the Occident and helped to bring about

Page from R. Jacob ben Asher's religious code "Arbaa Turim", printed by Solomon ben Moses Soncino at Soncino in 1490.

להודך

בן תימא אומר הוי עז כנמר וקל כנשר ורץ
כצבי וגבור כארי לעשו' רצון אביך שבשמים
פרט ארבע' דברים בעבודת הבורא יתברך
והתחיל בעז כנמב כי שהוא כלל גדול ב
בעבודת הבורא ית' לפי שפעמים אדם חפץ
לעשות מצוה ונמנע לעשותה מפני בני אדם
שמלעינין עליו ועל כן הזהיר שתעיז פניך כ
כנגד המלעינים ואל תמנע מלעשות המצוה
וכן אמר רבן יוחנן בן זכא לתלמידיו הוי ר
רצון שתהא מורא שמים עליכם כמורא בשר
ודם וכן הוא אומר לענין הבושה שפעמים
אדם מתבייש מפני האדם ית' ממה שיתבייש
מפני הבורא ית' על כן הזהיר שתעיז פניך מצחך
כנגד המלעינים ולא תבוש וכן אמר דוד ע"ה
ואדברה בעדותיך נגד מלכים ולא אבוש אף
כי יהיה נרדף ובורח בין האומות היה מחזיק
בתורתו ולומד אף כי היו מלעיני עליו ואומר
קל כנשר כנגד ראו' העין דימה אותו לנשר
כי כאשר הנשר טט באויר כך הוא ראו' העין
לומר שתעצים עיניך מראות כרע כי הוא
תחילת העביר' שהעין רואה והלב חומד וכלי
המעשה גומרין ואמר גבר כארי כנגד הלב
כי הגבורה בעבודת הבורא יתברך וזו בלב
שתתחזק לבך בעבודתו ואמר רץ כצבי כנגד
הרגלים שרגליך לטוב ירוצו וכן דוד המלך
ע"ה היה מתפלל על שלשתם אלא ששנה
הסדר אמר אור הדריכני בנתיב מצותיך על ה
הרגלים ואמר אחר כך ודט לבי ואמר אחר כך
העבר עיני מראו' רע והזכי' כלב הנה ובען

העבירה כי הלב הוא כרשותו להטותו בדרך
הטובה או לרעה אף אחר שראה בעש' השוא
על כן התפלל שיעזרינג להטותו לדרך
הטובה אבל ראות השוא אינו ברשותו כי א
איפשר שיפגע בן פתאו' לכן ויראבו הת פל'
שיעזיד עינו מראו' שוא ולא יכמינד לפניו
כלל לכן צדיך האדם להתגבר כארי לעמוד
בבקר לעבודת בוראו ואף אם ישיאנו יצרו
בחורף לאבר איך תעמוד בבקר כי וקורן
גדו' או תשיאנו בקיץ לאב' איך תעמו' מטמתך
ועדיין לא שבעת משנתך התגבר עליו לקום
שתהא אתה מעירר השח' ולא יהא הוא מעיר'
כמו שאמר דוד ע"ה עורה כבודי עורה הנבל
וכנור אעירה שחר אבי מעיר השחר ואין ה
השחר מעיר אותי וכל שכן אם ישכים קדם
אור הבקר לקו' להתחנן לפני בוראו מה יופין
ומה טובו וטוב ט שטקרים שיכין לשעות ש
שמשתנגות ובמשמרת שהן בשליש הלילה נ
ולסוף שני שלישי הלילה ולסוף הלילה ש
שבאלו הםבי' הקדוש ברוך הוא נזכר הלילה
לחורבן הבית וגלות ישראל בין האומ' וט
והתפלה שיתפלל אדם באותה שעה על ה
החורבן הגל ר' רציה וקרובה להתקבל ומפיל
תחנתו לפני המקום אוד ומרבה ואחד ה
הממעיט וכלבך שיכון לבו בתחגוניו כי ט
מעט בכמונה מדרבות בזם שלא בכמונה וט
לוטר פרשת העקדה ופרשת המן ועשר ה
הדברו' ופרשת הקרבנות בכן פרשת העולה
ומנחה ושלמים וחטאת ואשם פרשת

Incipit phemium libri elhauy ad honorem dei cuius nomen sit bene dictum in secula seculorum amē.

Faraj ben Salem of Girgenti (Sicily) presents his translations of Arab medical works into Latin to his employer, Charles of Anjou, King of Naples (1265–1285). Miniature from a manuscript (Latin 6192) in the Bibliothèque Nationale, Paris.

the decisive earlier stages of the Renaissance. Usually, in the first instance, the Arabic works were rendered into Hebrew for the benefit of the translators' co-religionists. The Latin translations from Hebrew or directly from the Arabic original were frequently organized and patronized by Christian sovereigns interested in science. The Hohenstaufen Emperor Frederick II invited to his court in Sicily Jewish scholars from Spain and the Provence and took personal interest in the translations carried out by them. King Charles I of Naples employed as a translator the learned Jewish physician Faraj ben Salem of Girgenti (Sicily). The works translated were, to a large extent, philosophical, such as the writings of the 12th century Arab philosopher Ibn Rushd (Averroes), or medical, e.g., the compositions of the great 11th-century Arab physician and thinker Ibn Sina (Avicenna).

The Jewish scholars engaged in translation did not overlook the rich and important literature in Arabic created by Jewish authors in Moslem

First page of an illuminated 13th century Pentateuch manuscript of Franco-German origin, in the Schocken Library, Jerusalem. The lovely miniatures represent various Biblical scenes.

חג פסח מצה ומרור

Page from the 15th century "Second Nuremberg Haggadah", in the Schocken Library, Jerusalem. The miniature, showing Pharaoh and his host pursuing the Children of Israel, is a fine example of German-Jewish manuscript illumination.

Spain and other Arab countries, which was inaccessible to most of European Jewry. Various members of the Tibbon family at Lunel, in southern France, acquired everlasting renown by translating into Hebrew such books as Saadya ben Joseph's *Beliefs and Opinions*, Bahya ibn Pakuda's *Duties of the Heart*, Judah Halevi's *Kuzari* and Maimonides' *Guide of the Perplexed*.

Another remarkable family of Jewish scholars in southern France was that of Kimhi in Narbonne. Besides translating, they compiled dictionaries of the Hebrew language and wrote grammatical treatises, which were afterwards translated into Latin and proved most useful to the Christian Hebraists of the Renaissance period. The most famous member of this family was David Kimhi (1160–1235), whose Biblical commentaries enjoy to this day great popularity.

Besides the translations, original contributions of outstanding importance were made by Jews to medieval science. In the tenth century, Isaac Israeli of Kairouan was one of the foremost medical writers of his day. His works, which were translated into Hebrew, Latin, and Spanish, were current throughout the Middle Ages. The esteem in which they

Astrolabe of the 15th century, of Spanish origin, with Hebrew inscriptions, produced by a Jewish craftsman for the use of a Jewish astronomer. (M. Kugel Collection, Paris).

were held was so great that they were published at Lyons (France) as late as 1515.

It has already been mentioned that Maimonides was not only a Jewish religious philosopher, but also a prominent physician. His medical works were known and studied in Europe in Latin translation.

Jews were also greatly interested in astronomy and, of course, astrology, which was considered a science in the Middle Ages, although Maimonides denounced it as a superstition. It was a Jew who translated the great astronomical treatise of the Greek scholar Ptolemy (2nd century)—the *Almagest*, as the Arabs called it—into Arabic, and another Jew translated it into Hebrew. Jews drew up the astronomical tables used by Dante, and they were experts in the use of the astrolabe, the manufacture of which they perfected. Abraham bar Hiyya of Barcelona (12th century) and his contemporary the globe-trotting Abraham ibn Ezra, whom we already mentioned as a poet and Bible commentator, were key-figures in medieval science. The 14th century Provençal Jewish exegete and philosopher Levi ben Gershom invented the simple device for measuring the declivity of the sun, known as Jacob's staff. Instruments invented or perfected by Jews were largely used in navigation. In Majorca (Balearic Islands) there was an entire school of Jewish map-makers of rare ability, the most celebrated of whom were Abraham and Judah Cresques, who produced the already mentioned 14th century *Catalan Atlas*, now in the Bibliothèque Nationale in Paris.

To some extent Jews even contributed to the vernacular literature of the countries in which they lived. There were modest Jewish troubadors

az donde fue tomado: τ desterro a
adam τ asentolo fuera del parayso deleytoso
el angel cherubin cõ la flamante espada pꝰ
q̃ guardase el camino del arbol dela vida:

como el señor acato la ofren
da de abel τ non de chayn :

Adam orgulloso a eua su muger
conuiene saber durmio con ella
τ concibio τ pario a cayn τ di
xo ella cobre varõ de dios

τ torno a concebir τ parió
a su hermano abel el qual
abel pastor de ouejas fue τ chayn agricola cõ
uiene saber faziente enlas labores dela tri
a τ acabo de dias troxo chayn del fructo dela
tra presente a dios τ abel esso mesmo troxo
delos primos gemtos de sus ouejas τ delas
mejores dellos τ acato el señor a abel τ a su
presente τ chayn τ al su presente non acato

lo qual achayn mucho peso τ cuerõ se le la
fazes τ dixo el señor a chayn por rrazon qual
esto an peso τ por que tu fazes se cayeron :
por cierto sy tu bien usares perdon auras
como la tu faz alces τ sy bien usar non quisi
eres ala puerta tienes el tu pecado τ contra ti
sera el su apetito τ tu señoras en el τ dixo chay
a abel su hermano del ysla los mencion non fa
ze τ aunno asy q̃ ellos cul campo estando leua
to chayn contra el su hermano abel τ matolo
dixo el señor a chaym do es abel tu hermano
el qual respondio yo non se como señor so yo
guardador del mi hermano : τ el señor respon
diole τ dixo que as fecho q̃ la bos delas sangres
del tu hermano llaman mi dela tra τ bien
agora tu por aqueste mesmo fecho tu maldito se
ras sobre la tra q̃ abrio su boca para rescebir
las sangres del tu hermano de tu mano τ quan
do la tra labrares non tornara adar la su fuerça

comer. leuer. calçar. uestir. visitar. consolar. enterrar

Detail from a miniature in the Alba Bible. Below: Moses Arragel presents his Bible translation to Don Luiz de Guzman. — Above: Knights of the Order of Calatrava feed, clothe, tend and bury the needy.

Page from the Alba Bible, a Spanish Bible translation prepared by Moses Arragel in 1422–30 for Don Luiz de Guzman, Grand Master of the Order of Calatrava. The manuscript is adorned with fine miniatures. The miniatures on the page reproduced illustrate the story of Cain and Abel.

in the Provence. On the fringe, at least, of Dante's circle in Florence, there was a Jew, Manuel da Gubbio, known in Hebrew literature as Immanuel of Rome, author of the *Mahberoth* (Collections) containing Hebrew poetry in Italian verse-forms and short stories, sometimes reminiscent of Bacaccio's Decameron. Regrettably, not much has survived of his Italian poetry. The German Jewish Minnesinger Süsskind of Trimberg (13th century) has already been mentioned. A famous German manuscript, the Manessian collection of songs in the Heidelberg University Library, preserved not only his poems in medieval German, but also his portrait. In Spain, Judah Bonsenyor and especially Santob de Carrion (in his Hebrew liturgical poems, Shemtov ibn Ardutiel) wrote in the vernacular of the country. The latter is the author of the much-read *Proverbios Morales*, written for King Pedro of Castile. In Spain, too, Moses Arragel rendered the Bible into Spanish in 1422–30 for the Grand Master of the Order of Calatrava. The translation is accompanied by a short commentary and illuminated with over three hundred miniatures. The manuscript is known as the "Alba Bible".

The miniatures of the Alba Bible which reflect Jewish influence, illustrate incidentally, the fact that European Jews of the Middle Ages, whether in northern or southern lands, were by no means lacking in aesthetic appreciation. Persecution and destruction have wiped out part of the evidence for this, but illuminated manuscripts from the thirteenth century onwards which have survived in relatively considerable numbers were most probably, and in some cases provably, executed by Jewish hands. These manuscripts show a high technical competence as well as a keen artistic feeling.

THE EXPULSIONS FROM
ENGLAND AND FRANCE

Meanwhile, however, the vicious circle was turning more and more rapidly and with more and more distressing results. The operations of the Jewish money-lenders generated mounting prejudice resulting in attacks against the Jews as a whole. Physical violence and the destruction which came in its wake, as well as the royal rapacity in taking advantage of their financial operations and extorting from the Jews most of their profits, compelled the latter to be more stern in exacting their dues. This, in turn increased their unpopularity all the more.

In England, the Jews barely had time to recover somewhat from the excesses of the Third Crusade, when King John "Lackland" (1199–1216) inaugurated a policy of extortion on an unprecedented scale, which was carried out with refined cruelty. When a Jewish financier, Abraham of Bristol, was unwilling, or perhaps unable, to pay the extravagant contribution imposed upon him, the insatiable king ordered that every day one of his teeth should be extracted. After the seventh extraction, Abraham submitted to the royal will. During the war of the Barons against King John, Jewish property was considered by the Barons as belonging to the King and was, consequently, confiscated or destroyed.

The king's policy of extortion, coupled with the ill-treatment to which Jews were subjected by the Barons and the mob, continued unchanged throughout the reign of John's successor, King Henry III (1216–1272). Besides the progressively increasing "tallage" collected from the Jews, other heavy contributions were exacted periodically and property was frequently confiscated. The decisions of the Fourth Lateran Council, including the obligation to wear the distinctive Jewish badge, were now rigorously applied in England and from time to time mass-trials were staged. In 1230, the Jews of Norwich were accused of having circumcised a Christian child. In 1244, there was a murder trial in London. The Lincoln Trial of 1255 in connection with the alleged ritual murder of Little Hugh has already been mentioned. Under these circumstances, many English Jews thought of leaving the inhospitable island. But the king was not yet prepared to give up these profitable subjects, and their emigration was strictly forbidden.

As the thirteenth century advanced, the expanding power of the Italian bankers, operating in England as well as in Continental Europe on a most extensive scale and under the highest possible patronage (of the pope and the king), gradually reduced the importance of Jewish financial activity and its significance to the Exchequer. In the long run, therefore, it was proved possible to dispense with their services. When this happened, they were ruthlessly expelled. After tightening the repressive measures against his Jewish subjects, King Edward I (1272–1307) ordered the general expulsion of the Jews from England in 1290. Much of their property was confiscated for the benefit of the Crown. This was the first expulsion embracing an entire country.

Edward I, King of England (1272–1307), who expelled the Jews from his country, after having utterly ruined their economic position. The decree of expulsion was issued on July 18th, 1290, which happened to coincide with the Fast of the Ninth Ab, commemorating the destruction of Jerusalem.

Most of the expelled English Jews were admitted to France. But this country proved a temporary refuge only, and for a very short time indeed. In France the position of the Jews had gradually deteriorated since the reign of the fanatically pious King Louis IX (1226–1270). The decisions of the Fourth Lateran Council were relentlessly enforced. The Jews were exposed to all kinds of vexations, particularly on the part of the Inquisition, which accused them of encouraging former co-religionists who had embraced Christianity, to return to their ancient faith. From 1283 onwards, they were forbidden to live in the countryside, to prevent their coming in contact with the ignorant peasants, which could give rise to heresy. Philip the Fair (1285–1314) was a zealous Jew-hater, but also a cunning profiteer, who found many ways of extorting considerable amounts of money from his Jewish subjects.

Despite its precarious situation, French Jewry found leisure for grim ideological party-strife. The strictly conservative Talmudists, grouped around Solomon ben Abraham of Montpellier, pronounced (in 1231)

the excommunication against those who indulged in the study of profane sciences and in philosophic research. The attack was mainly directed against the spread of Maimonides' rationalistic philosophy. When the adherents of Maimonides retorted by the same weapon, the conservatives committed the fatal error of denouncing them to the Dominican friars as heretics and atheists. The effect was that Maimonides' writings were confiscated by the authorities and publicly burnt at Montpellier and Paris, Shame covered the faces even of his most fanatic opponents and for a time there was quiet. But about seventy years later the conflict flared up again. Abba Mari ben Moses of Lunel, the leader of the conservatives, succeeded in mobilizing Spanish authorities too, for instance Rabbi Solomon ben Adret of Barcelona, as allies in his fight against rationalism, The parties started anew excommunicating each other during several years, until a catastrophe which hit friend and foe indiscriminately, put an end to the strife.

In 1306 when King Philip the Fair was in desperate need of funds, he decided to replenish his empty coffers by means of a radical stroke. He ordered the expulsion of the Jews from his territories and the confiscation of their property. They were obliged to leave the country within one month and were allowed to take with them only their workday-clothes and a ridiculously small amount of cash for their immediate necessities.

The expulsion of the Jews, however, had a detrimental effect on the economic life of France, so that Philip's successor, Louis X (1314–1316) asked them to return. The edict which fixed the rights and duties of the returning Jews, limited their readmission to a period of 12 years. Some of the expelled Jews did indeed return, but before the term agreed upon was over, they were obliged to leave France again. The fanatical mob made their life unbearable and the appearance of the *Pastoureaux* (the shepherd's crusade), was followed by a series of horrible massacres of Jews at Toulon, Bordeaux, Albi, and elsewhere. The accusation levelled against the Jews in 1321, that they had poisoned wells and rivers, brought their martyrdom to a peak and most of them decided to leave France. After 1322, there were no more Jews in the country for many years.

In 1361, once again at a time of severe financial crisis for the royal treasury, the Jews were readmitted to France; but this time only a handful of financiers heeded the call. The Crown, however, again failed to keep the promises made to the returning Jews and was unable, or unwilling, to protect them from ill-treatment by the populace and the Church. They were expelled again, and for good, in 1394. Only in southern France, ruled by the Counts of Provence, were they allowed to remain for the time being. But in 1481 Provence was annexed to France and before long the Jews were expelled from this region, too.

Jewish types from Medieval France. Detail from a 15th century alabaster group in the Museum of Carcassonne.

Thereafter, the only Jewish settlements within the historic borders of France were those which persisted, under the relatively benevolent papal rule, in Avignon and the Comtat Venaissin.

Part of the Jews expelled from France established themselves in northern Italy. The three communities of Asti, Fossano and Moncalvo, constituted by those exiles, have preserved the French liturgical tradition almost to our own day.

The synagogue of Cavaillon (Southern France). Romanticized drawing by Georges Loukomsky, showing the building in 1773, before the reconstruction. Like Avignon and Carpentras, Cavaillon was under the jurisdiction of the popes and the expulsion of the Jews from France in 1306 did not apply to these communities. These towns even served as refuge to part of the Jews obliged to leave France.

LOCAL EXPULSIONS
IN GERMANY

The tombstones of R. Meir of Rothenburg (to the left) and Alexander ben Salomon Wimpfen in the old Jewish cemetery at Worms. R. Meir of Rothenburg, one of the most respected rabbinical authorities of the 13th century, died in captivity, having declined to be ransomed. Fourteen years after his death, Alexander Wimpfen succeeded in redeeming his body and acquired thereby the privilege of being buried by his side.

The record of the Jews in Germany differed from that elsewhere in northern Europe, largely because of the decline, there, of the central authority of the Holy Roman Emperors, which resulted in the fragmentation of the country. Hence, although exterminatory massacres took place periodically all over, and although there were expulsions from almost every region from time to time, there was never any general expulsion from the entire country at once, such as took place in England and in France. The paradox resulted that, although there was no country of Europe where the Jews were treated worse, there was also no country with which they were more tenaciously associated.

The first case of local expulsion in Germany seems to have been their temporary banishment from the city of Mainz in 1012, in the days of Rabbi Gershom ben Judah, the " Light of the Exile." A year later the expelled Jews were permitted to return to their homes. For the time being, this was an isolated event, but it was an earnest warning of things to come.

The massacres perpetrated in Germany during the Crusades, particularly the first one at the end of the eleventh century, destroyed numerous Jewish communities without the need for the authorities to resort to expulsions. Recurrent acts of violence against the Jews in various parts of Germany never subsided throughout the twelfth century. The protection extended to the Jews by the emperors, who considered them as "royal serfs" and a useful source of revenue, was not always of much avail. Besides, the emperors themselves did not refrain, at times, from shocking abuses. Emperor Rudolf von Habsburg, to cite a flagrant example, arrested in 1286 Rabbi Meir of Rothenburg, a highly respected

יזכור אל הרוגי וטרופי קהלות היידלבורג
יזכור אל הרוגי וטרופי קהלת כפרטום
יזכור אל הרוגי וטרופי קהלות שפיא
יזכור אל הרוגי וטרופי קהלות וירמש
יזכור אל הרוגי וטרופי קהלות אנגלן
יזכור אל הרוגי וטרופי קהלות טוהר
יזכור אל הרוגי וטרופי קהלת ודינקמרט
יזכור אל הרוגי וטרופי קהלת פולד
יזכור אל הרוגי וטרופי קהלת קאסיל
יזכור אל הרוגי וטרופי קהלת זוטע
יזכור אל הרוגי וטרופי קהלת דרטוויערא
יזכור אל הרוגי וטרופי קהלת זעין
יזכור אל הרוגי וטרופי קהלת עיטען נוימיעגן
יזכור אל הרוגי וטרופי קהלת אויזנבורק
יזכור אל הרוגי וטרופי קהלת לויבן
יזכור אל הרוגי וטרופי קהלת בריסל
יזכור אל הרוגי וטרופי קהלת העכיל
יזכור אל הרוגי וטרופי קהלות אוימטטר
יזכור אל הרוגי וטרופי קהלת פריון
יזכור אל הרוגי וטרופי קהלות לוונ
יזכור אל הרוגי וטרופי קהלות נייטטאט
יזכור אל הרוגי וטרופי קהלות וין
יזכור אל הרוגי וטרופי קהלות אלקבעת
יזכור אל הרוגי וטרופי קהלות זלצבורג
יזכור אל הרוגי וטרופי קהלת פסא וטובה עבור ועבין
ונטרפו על קדושת השם אסא אה ואפ על יהוד וואלבטוכר
זה יזכרם האל לטובה עש כד שובניאל ונואר אמן :

Page from the "Memorbuch" of the Community of Coblenz (Rhineland), with memorial prayers (Yiskor) for the communities destroyed in the persecution of 1348/49. (General Archives for Jewish History, Jerusalem).

Talmudic authority in Germany, hoping to extort from the Jews a high ransom for him. Rabbi Meir declined, however, to be ransomed and died in prison in 1293, Even his dead body was refused a Jewish burial for fourteen years, until a corresponding price was paid.

The situation became increasingly aggravated in the thirteenth century with the implementation of the decisions of the Fourth Lateran Council and the appearance of a wave of false accusations. Besides local acts of violence, which always involved bloodshed, there were also movements on a country-wide scale. Particularly devastating was the one initiated by a Bavarian noble, Rindfleisch, in Roettingen (southern Germany) in 1298, to avenge an alleged host desecration. In the course of six months Rindfleisch's gangs laid waste more than one hundred and forty communities in Bavaria and Austria, at a cost, it was said, of over one hundred thousand Jewish lives.

A similar movement came into being in 1336, again in southern Germany. Gangs of "Jew-slayers," as they shamelessly called themselves, found a leader in the person of an Alsatian inn-keeper. They were known as *Armleder,* on account of a leather-strap they used to wear around their arms, and their leader was styled "king of the Armleder." For over two years they marched to and fro between Alsace and Austria, murdering Jews and destroying property, before the Emperor could put a stop to the disorders and arrest the ringleader.

The suffering reached its peak in the years 1348–1349, when the Jews, accused of having provoked and spread the Black Death epidemic, were pitilessly murdered in masses throughout central Europe. The local authorities seldom made an effort to protect the Jews against the bloodthirsty mob. On the contrary, every accusation, however far-fetched, was considered a sufficient reason for expelling the Jews from towns or from whole provinces. They were driven out of Bavaria in 1314, Austria in 1420, Saxony in 1430, and Brandenburg in 1446. There were expulsions from Trier, Mainz, Cologne, Vienna, Augsburg, etc. Often the expulsion decrees were revoked after a certain time, and there are places from which the Jews were banished more than once during the Middle Ages.

The dismemberment of the German empire provided the Jews with islands of respite in their adversity. Whenever they were expelled from one place, they could generally find temporary asylum in the quasi-independent enclaves ruled by some knight or petty noble elsewhere, who would greedily permit them to settle under his protection for a price. They were thus able to continue residing in the same region or nearby, sometimes even on the outskirts of places from which they had been officially excluded.

The last of the great local expulsions in Germany in the Middle Ages occurred in Ratisbon (Regensburg) in 1519. Here they were permitted to take their movable property with them, but were obliged to yield up their claims against Christian debtors to the town council at a ridiculous price.

Of the major historic German Jewish communities which had attained distinction in the Middle Ages, only Worms and Frankfort-on-Main were left by now, both of which had been subject to numerous misfortunes. The community of Worms had been twice all but annihilated, once during the Crusades and again in the time of the Black Death. In Frankfort,

too, the old community had been massacred almost to the last man in 1349. When the Jews began to settle there again, they were granted only temporary residence and the renewal of the permits always involved financial sacrifices. They were ruthlessly fleeced, by the municipal council on the one hand, and by the Emperor on the other. At times, the financial burden was unbearable and once, at the beginning of the fifteenth century, the community dwindled to a few families. But despite all their difficulties the Jews persisted, and Frankfort-on-Main was to become, in a sense, the mother-city of German Jewry.

Notwithstanding local and regional expulsions, the Jews continued to be familiar everywhere in the country. This becomes obvious from scurrilous publications, broadsides, and engravings, remarkable for their grossness and virulence, which poured from the press after the invention of printing. In fact, the use of caricature as a weapon against the Jews seems to have originated in Germany. The plastic representation of the Synagogue under the image of the "Jews' Sow" on the walls of many a German cathedral has already been mentioned. This same sow figures on one of the earliest broadsheets published in Germany. Since the sixteenth century, anti-Jewish caricature has become a standing feature of German graphic art, spreading from there to other countries, later on.

In the eastern corner of the German Empire, the Jews of Vienna could look back on a long history. There have probably been Jews in Austria since Roman times (the first documentary evidence is from the tenth century) and they formed a prosperous community. The Crusades affected them less than their co-religionists elsewhere. In the thirteenth century their spiritual leader was the celebrated Rabbi Isaac ben Moses (known as the *Or Zarua* after the name of the comprehensive halakhic treatise to which he owes his fame). They had their share of suffering in the years of the Black Death. In 1370, they were banished temporarily. But the heavy blow came early in the fifteenth century. The heretic Hussite movement in Bohemia, which adopted a nationalist, anti-German character, aroused considerable ferment in Austria. This agitation vented itself upon the Jews, who were suspected of conniving with the heretics. In 1420, a rich Jew of Enns (Upper Austria) was

Interior of the "Altneuschul" Synagogue at Prague, built in the 14th century. According to a legend, it was founded in the 1st century by refugees from Jerusalem, who employed stones brought with them from the destroyed Temple, "on the condition" ("al-tenai" in Hebrew) that those stones would be brought back to Jerusalem on the advent of the Messiah. This is one of the explanations of the synagogue's name.

The "Altneuschul" Synagogue at Prague. Behind the synagogue the Jewish town hall with the famous clock with Hebrew letters instead of Arabic numerals, and inverse movement of the hands.

accused of having bought a host, for the purpose of desecration, from the wife of a sexton. All the Jews of Austria were arrested and their property confiscated. The proceedings were completed in March, 1421, when two hundred Jews, among them women, were solemnly burnt in Vienna and all the Jews who had survived were banished from the country "for ever". These events are known as the "Wiener Geserah." Jews were re-admitted to Vienna less than a hundred years later, but the town remained a center of virulent anti-Jewish feeling. The Jews were strictly obliged to wear the distinctive badge and the threat of expulsion always hung over them.

Prague with its important community, which has survived from the early Middle Ages down to modern times, was also in the German orbit. After the harrowing visitation of the First Crusade, the community knew relatively quiet times. Although outbursts of violence occurred now and then, the Jews enjoyed certain privileges, including a measure of autonomy in their famed "Judenstadt" centered around the legendary old synagogue, the "Altneuschul." Built in the fourteenth century, it was said to have been founded centuries earlier (in the eleventh century). According to one legend, it was even founded in the first century by refugees from Palestine, who built into the foundation stones which they had brought from the destroyed Temple of Jerusalem. Although the fourteenth and the beginning of the fifteenth centuries were marked by recurrent popular violence and administrative measures against the Jews, it was a Jew of Prague, Gerson ben Solomon Cohen, who in 1512 founded the first Hebrew printing house in Germany.

THE MIDDLE AGES
IN CHRISTIAN SPAIN

The history of the Jews in Spain differed fundamentally in many respects from that of their northern co-religionists. The rulers of the Christian states, slowly expanding their confines and progressively reducing Moslem areas, protected, and sometimes even favored, their Jewish subjects. In the twelfth century, Jewish refugees from the south, fleeing Almohade fanaticism, found a friendly welcome in Castile and Aragon. In Barcelona a Jewish cultural center was being established, which later achieved first rank in Spain. There were, of course, from time to time, eruptions of anti-Jewish feeling, stirred up by the clergy in various places, and tension sometimes ran high during the religious controversies, which became a fashion in the Middle Ages. But for the time being, this did not affect the economic position of the Jews.

The economic degradation, to which the Jews in northern Europe were subjected and which forced most of them to become money-lenders, never made any noticeable headway among the Spanish Jews, if only because of their number. Hence, though some of them were dependent on financial operations for a livelihood, there were many merchants among them and the great majority were artisans. There were Jewish masons and smiths, but most craftsmen, like the various classes of merchants, were chiefly engaged in all branches of the textile trade, the classical occupation of the Jews everywhere, down to our own day. In many places, there were Jewish craft-guilds similar to the gentile ones, sometimes maintaining their own synagogues and even, here and there, building their own guild-halls for storing their products. There

To the left: Jewish shop in Spain. To the right: The home of a Jewish money-lender in Spain. Miniatures from the manuscript of the "Cantigas" by Alfonso X "the Wise", King of Castile (1252–1284), in the Escorial Library.

were also Jewish farmers and dealers in agricultural produce, as well as Jewish ship-owners, engaged in the transport business between Mediterranean ports.

In the intellectual life, too, Jews occupied a prominent position as physicians, mathematicians, astronomers, and translators.

On the whole, the Jews formed a rather well-to-do community. But taxation was heavy and a considerable part of their earnings found its way into the royal treasury under different names.

As regards the Spanish Jewish financiers, their characteristic business did not consist of vulgar money-lending transactions, but of large-scale operations, such as farming the taxes, which became a common Jewish occupation. The principal tax-farmers naturally enjoyed considerable influence, since they were usually at the same time royal treasurers, finance ministers, and purveyors to the army. They would be consulted in other matters, too, and they were sometimes quite influential in determining policy. These Jewish financiers lived lavishly, building themselves palatial residences, which were sometimes strongly fortified. At the same time, they would be prominent among their co-religionists as munificent patrons of the sciences and arts. In the long run, however, it was not unusual for the success of the Jewish magnificos to invite the intrigues of their rivals, the hate of the Christian population, and

The entrance to the Palace of Samuel ha-Levy Abulafia of Toledo.

Inner court of the Residence of Samuel ha-Levi Abulafia of Toledo, finance-minister to King Pedro the Cruel of Castile (1350–1369). The famous painter El Greco, who settled in 1577 in Toledo, acquired the house and lived there. Formerly known as "The Palace of the Jew", it is now called "The House of Greco".

חישלביובשרינואלה

Detail of decoration of the El Transito Synagogue, Toledo, built by Samuel ha-Levi Abulafia. Although the synagogue was converted into a church after the expulsion of the Jews from Spain, the Hebrew inscriptions were not deleted.

the greed of their masters. Their fall was often as catastrophic as their rise was dazzling.

Typical was the case of Samuel ha-Levi Abulafia of Toledo. He was the finance-minister of king Pedro "the Cruel" of Castile (1350–1369) and reorganized the tax system, thus improving, within a short time, the ruinous financial situation of the kingdom. Besides his palace at Toledo, known to this day as the "Palace of the Jew," he built houses of worship, particularly the exquisite "El Transito" Synagogue near his residence, which was converted into a Catholic church after the expulsion of the Jews from Spain and is still standing. The beautifully carved Hebrew inscriptions at the side of the Ark in this synagogue embody the name of Abulafia's sovereign. Inevitably, Abulafia became involved in the court intrigues caused by the rivalry between King Pedro and his half-brother Henry of Trastamare. His faithful attachment to his king brought calamity on the Castilian Jews, who suffered heavily from the attacks of Henry's partisans. The attack on the Jewish quarter of Toledo alone (1355) is said to have cost one thousand two hundred lives. In the end, however, his unswerving loyalty was requited with ingratitude. King Pedro lent his ear to calumniators who accused Abulafia

A picturesque street in the old Jewish quarter (the Juderia) of Cordova.

Hebrew inscription from the Synagogue of Cordova, dated 1315.

Interior of the El Transito Synagogue at Toledo, a lovely building in "Mudejar" (Moresque) style, decorated with tasteful arabesques and bands inscribed with Biblical verses.

of embezzlement. The King confiscated the Jew's property and arrested him and his whole family. Abulafia was cruelly tortured to disclose the place where the rest of his fortune had allegedly been hidden in the ground, and died in the hands of his tormentors.

On the whole, however, the life of Spanish Jewry was far more ample than was the case in northern Europe. The Jewish groupings were larger, their relations with the general population easier, and their treatment by the sovereigns more equable. When Seville was conquered by King Ferdinand of Castile in 1248, he accepted a silver key from the Jews as a present. This key bore the inscription "God opens, the king enters",

in Spanish on one side and in Hebrew on the other. The inscription in Hebrew on his tomb in the Cathedral implies that he considered himself King in equal measure of all the peoples under his rule. Similarly, a Hebrew inscription is to be seen over the city gates at Medina del Campo.

The Jewish communities enjoyed a considerable amount of autonomy in matters of internal administration and jurisdiction. The anti-Jewish injunctions of the Church concerning the wearing of the Jewish badge, social segregation, etc. were often overlooked or imposed leniently. It took longer in Spain than elsewhere for anti-Jewish feeling to strike root, and it was not until the fourteenth century that hate poisoned the whole atmosphere and made Jewish life a nightmare.

Meanwhile, the Jewish quarters in the Spanish cities were spacious, sometimes surrounded by walls and partly fortified. Nowhere in the world did the Jewish artistic achievements in synagogue architecture or in the illumination of manuscripts reflect more faithfully and exquisitely the spirit of the environment.

In Jewish learning, too, Spanish Jewry occupied a place of honor. Authorities such as Rabbi Moses ben Nahman (Nahmanides), Rabbi Asher ben Jehiel, his son Rabbi Jacob ben Asher, and the philosopher Joseph Albo, known and esteemed far beyond the borders of Spain, have already been mentioned. In the thirteenth century the *Zohar*, a book

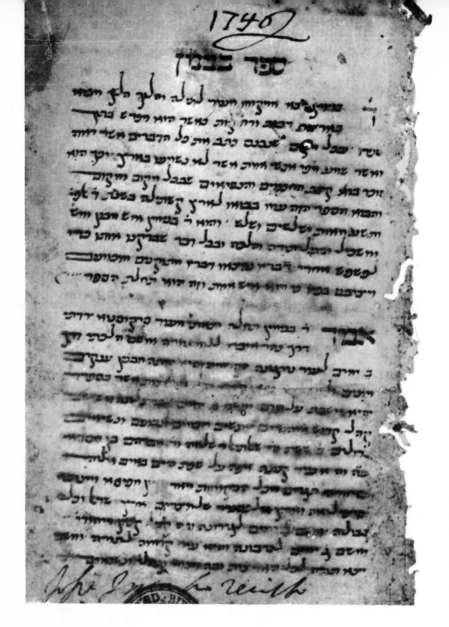

Page from a 15th century Manuscript of the Travels of Benjamin of Tudela (Vatican Library, Rome). In the second half of the 12th century, Benjamin toured Europe, Asia and Africa and left a noteworthy account of his travels, enlarging particularly on the Jewish communities visited.

to become the corner-stone of Jewish mystical philosophy, the Cabbala, came to light in Spain. Traditionally attributed to Rabbi Simon ben Jochai (second century), the Zohar, composed partly of much older material, was published by the Spanish cabbalist Moses de Leon. Its appearance greatly stimulated the cabbalistic studies, already cultivated in Spain by a large circle of scholars, including Rabbi Moses ben Nahman. While on the subject of the Jews in Christian Spain in the Middle Ages, mention should be made of the Jewish globe-trotter Benjamin of Tudela, who travelled extensively in the years 1165–1173 and left a noteworthy account of his voyage. Setting out from Tudela in northern Spain, he toured southern France, Italy, Greece, Constantinople, Palestine, Syria, Mesopotamia, Persia, India, Arabia, and Egypt. Everywhere he inquired about the number of Jews, their occupations, and their social and political status. He recorded in his notebook every detail which seemed to him of interest. His book provides a full, accurate, picturesque account of the Jewish Diaspora in the second half of the twelfth century.

THE MIDDLE AGES IN ITALY

The Jews of Rome used to offer to each new pope, on the occasion of his installation, a copy of the Scroll of the Law. The ceremony was sometimes accompanied by humiliating remarks on the part of the pope. Engraving by B. Picart.

The Jewish connection with Italy has remained unbroken since classical times. Rome was the oldest community in Europe which continued its existence uninterruptedly throughout the ages, from remote antiquity down to our own day. The Jewish population in Rome in the first centuries of the Christian era was estimated at about thirty thousand. They had many synagogues and their own cemeteries (mostly catacombs, some of them well known for their inscriptions and decoration).

From the sixth century on, the city of Rome was under the jurisdiction of the popes who, on the whole, showed tolerance and justice to their Jewish subjects. It was usual for a Jewish delegation to take part officially in the installation ceremony of a new pope and to pay homage on behalf of the Jewish community. The Jewish representatives would offer a scroll of the Law and ask for the renewal of their privileges.

From the tenth century, this practice was also observed on the occasion of the visits of the emperors of the Holy Roman Empire to Rome. When Henry VII came to Rome in 1312, the Jews went out to greet

181

The 13th century synagogue of Trapani, Sicily. Drawing by G. Loukomsky (C. Roth Collection).

him in procession and received from him the confirmation of their privileges. The scene is vividly depicted in a miniature in a contemporary manuscript.

Such ceremonies, however, did not always take place in an idyllic atmosphere. In 1138, when Pope Innocent II entered Rome after the death of his rival, Pope Anacletus II (the great-grandson of a Jewish convert), he replied to the homage of the Jewish delegation: "We honor the Holy Scripture which was given by God to your ancestors through Moses, but we loathe your religious customs and your exegetic artifices." The same indignity was inflicted on the Jewish delegation which attended the coronation of Pope Boniface VIII in 1295.

There were also sporadic acts of violence. The first persecution of Jews in papal Rome is recorded to have occurred in 1021. The mob attacked the Jews in the Trastevere quarter in 1268 and desecrated the cemetery. In 1298, Elias de Pomis, a prominent member of the Roman community, was executed by order of Pope Boniface VIII and his property was confiscated. There were serious riots in 1322, accompanied by the public burning of Talmud manuscripts. But on the whole, until the middle of the fifteenth century, the community of Rome was much better off than the Jewish communities in many other Christian countries. The decisions of the Lateran Councils were nowhere so leniently applied as in papal Rome. Jewish physicians and scholars were frequent visitors at the papal court. Jewish learning thrived among the Roman Jews who were, at the same time, receptive to general secular culture, science, philosophy, and poetry.

The entrance to the old Jewish quarter of Taormina, Sicily.

In the Middle Ages, the bulk of Italian Jewry outside Rome was located in the area south of this point. This southern part of the Italian peninsula, then called Apulia, was subsequently termed the Kingdom of the Two Sicilies; it included also the island-kingdom of Sicily itself. Here there are still to be seen in various places impressive architectural relics of medieval Jewish life, in particular at Trani, then one of the great Mediterranean ports. At various places in southern Italy, moreover, there have come to light medieval Jewish tombstones, on which are to be found some of the oldest evidences of Hebrew poetical creativity in Europe. South Italian Jewry, at this time, subsisted on the silk-weaving and dyeing crafts (in which they were considered experts) to such an extent that, when these industries were converted into state monopolies in the thirteenth century, Jews were left in control as managers. Jewish metal-workers, joiners, shoemakers, etc. were common. In Sicily, the bulk of the community followed even the humblest callings, earning a livelihood, as fishermen, porters, stevedores, and harbor-workers. There were, of course, also large-scale merchants. These, however, were squeezed out of business, in the course of time, by growing Venetian and Genoese competition.

Besides this keen participation in the economic life, there was also much intellectual activity. South Italian Jewry, straddling the Arab and Latin cultures, took a considerable share in translating the Arabo-Hellenic scientific classics.

Under Byzantine and Arab rule, the Jewish communities in southern Italy and Sicily enjoyed a period of relative security, in which they could develop, more or less undisturbed. When the Normans conquered these regions in the second half of the eleventh century, the change of rulers did not, for the moment, affect the Jewish population. They were

"Megillah" (Scroll) written to celebrate the deliverance of the Jews of Syracuse (Sicily) from a persecution which probably menaced them at the end of the 14th century The event used to be commemorated by a local annual feast called "Saragossa Purim" (Saragossa being a variant form of Syracuse), and the custom has been continued by some communities founded by Syracusan Jews after their expulsion from Sicily.

ויהי בימי המלך שאראגושאנוש מלך אדיר היה וחזק היה והיה רודה
ממשלתו כחמשת אלפי איש מבני ישראל כלם חכמים ונבונים
ראשי אלפי ישראל המה לבד מבחוריהם ונעריהם ונשיהם ובניהם
וטפם שתים עשרה קהלות קדושות בנים באבני גזית ועמוד
שיש כלילות יופי ממולאים כתרשיש וכה מנהג ומשפט היהודים
האלה בעבר המלך דרך שוק היהודים היו מוציאים שלשה ספרי
תורה מכל קהלה שלשים ושש ספרים מעוטפים בבגדי רקמה
ובתיקי כסף וזהב ורמונים ותפוחי כסף וזהב במשכיות כסף
בראשי ספרים ומברכים למלך בקול גדול ורם וכל העם ענים
אחריהם אמן ויהי היום נקהלו שנים עשר חכמי ישראל וארבעה
ועשרים דייניהם לאמר לא טוב אנחנו עושים לצאת עם תורת
אלהינו אלהים חיים ומלך עולם לפני עובד אלילים ופסילים מועדי
נסדרו יחדו להכין שלשה תיקין ריקים מכל קהלה וקהלה מעוטפים

במעילה וריממונה ולצאת עמהם לפני המלך יען כך רד יה
מנהגם להיות תופסי התורה חכם הקהל ושני דייני עמו ואיש
לא ידע את הדבר הזה רק חכמיו ודייניו וכך היו עושים ע
שנת י"ב למלך שאראגושאנוש בימים ההם נשתמד
איש ריב ומדון רשע וכל יעל חיים שאמי שמו ימח שמו
ויהי האיש ההוא נחמד בבית המלך כי משרת היה בשער המלך
לפנים בישראל בעת ההיא גדל המלך שאראגושאנוש את
חיים שאמי ימח שמו אשר שם שמו מארקוש וישם את כסאו
בין השרים אשר אתו בהיכל המלך ויהי היום ויצא המלך
שאראגושאנוש עם העם אשר אתו והשרים והפחתים כמו
ללכת בכל אות נפשו ויעבור בתוך העיר ויקר מקרהו לעבור בשוק
היהודים וימהרו היהודים ויגידו לראשי הכנסת ולחכמיו לאמר
הנה המלך עובר בשוק ויקומו חכמי הקהלות ודייניהם וכל העם

tuo delos iudios que enel habitan. Por ende nos hauiendo hauido sobre ello nuestro acuerdo y madura deliberacion hauemos acordado de mandar salir todos los dichos iudios y iudias del dicho Reyno paraque iamas tornen en el ⸿ Con tenor desta nuestra real pragmatica sanction statuto e ordinacion de nfa cierta scientia consultamente y deliberada queremos sancimos statuimos y ordinamos que todos los Judios y iudias de qualquier edad que sean que biuen y estan enel dicho nuestro Reyno assi enla ciudad de Napoles como en todas y qualesquier otras ciudades villas lugares casales y habitaciones del dicho reyno assi los naturales como los no naturales que en qualquier manera o por qualquier causa hasi venido y estan en el dicho reyno y en qualquiere parte del desdel dia dela publicacion delas presentes hasta por todo el mes de Marzo primero que verna de mil quinientos y onze años salgan del dicho nfo Reyno con sus fiIos y fiIas criados y criadas e familiares Judios y iudias assi grandes como pequeños de qualquier edad que sean E que no sean osados de tornar ael ni estar en el ni en parte alguna del dicho nfo Reyno de biuienda ni de passo ni en otra manera alguna. E si por auentura los dichos Judios y iudias no guardando la presente nuestra real pragmatica statuto y ordinacion passado el dicho tiempo fueren hallados estar en qualquier parte del dicho nfo Reyno o viuieren ael en qualquier manera incurran en pena de muerte y de confiscacion de todos sus bienes para la nfa Camara y fisco. En las quales penas incurran por esse mismo fecho sin otro processo sentencia ni declaracion E assi mismo mandamos a todos y qualesquiere personas de qualquiere estado preheminencia y condicion que no sean osados de recebir ni aceptar ni acoger defender ni hospedar passado el dicho termino de hasta por todo el dicho mes de Marzo adelante para siempre iamas iudio ni iudia en sus tierras ni en sus casas ni en otra parte alguna del dicho nfo reyno so pena de perdimiento de todos sus bienes muebles y rayzes vassallos fortalezas y otros heredamientos otrosi de perder qualesquiere diuisos responsiones y consignaciones que tengan de nos y de nfa corte para la dicha nfa camara y fisco. E porque los dichos iudios y iudias puedan durante el dicho tiempo que les assignamos para que salgan del dicho Reyno meior disponer deli y desus bienes y haziendas por las presentes los tomamos y recebimos so nfo seguro amparo defendimiento salua guarda y proteccio real e los aseguramos a ellos y a sus bienes para que durante el dicho tiempo de hasta per todo el dicho mes de Marzo puedan andar y estar seguros y

The decree of Ferdinand the Catholic, King of Spain and Naples (1452–1516), dated November 21st, 1510, ordering the expulsion of the Jews from Naples. The expulsion having been implemented only partially, it was decreed again and enforced by Ferdinand's successor, the Emperor Charles V, in 1540.

left entirely free to exercise their trades, and their religious and national autonomy was respected. The Spanish traveller Benjamin of Tudela, who visited the Normån Kingdom in the second half of the twelfth century, has sketched an impressive picture of its numerous prosperous communities.

At the end of the twelfth century, southern Italy came under the rule of the German emperors of the house of Hohenstaufen. This meant a deterioration in the position of the Jews. Even an enlightened emperor like Frederick II, who was a patron of science and was surrounded by Jewish and Arab scholars, found it necessary to enforce in his South Italian territories the anti-Jewish measures dictated by the Church, including the wearing of the Jewish badge.

Still more serious anti-Jewish reactions occurred at the end of the thirteenth century, at first under French influence, when Charles of Anjou conquered South Italy and Sicily after the downfall of the Hohenstaufen dynasty, and then under Spanish influence, when the French were driven out of Sicily in 1282 and the island was taken over by the kingdom of Aragon.

The fate of the Jews in Sicily from now on coincided with that of their Spanish co-religionists. The end came at the time of the expulsion of the Jews from Spain in 1492. The expulsion decree automatically had force in Sicily, as well as the island of Sardinia, likewise an Aragonese possession. The Jews had to leave both islands, never to return.

Later on, in 1505, Spanish rule was also extended to the Kingdom of Naples, and the Jews, already decimated, were expelled from there in 1540. From this time down to the present day, Jewish inhabitants have been a rarity in southern Italy. Their communities were henceforth restricted to the area from Rome northward.

By the middle of the 14th century, the northern Italian communities were solidly established. This was due mostly to the expansion of the activities of Jewish financiers. Generally starting business in Rome, they were taking advantage of the shortage of credit and setting up their establishments successively in other cities. The Italian burghers, the famous Lombards, by now notorious for their usurious activities throughout Europe, concentrated on large-scale operations and preferred

184

The 14th century synagogue of Siena. This town had a flourishing Jewish community at the close of the Middle Ages.

Seal of the Jewish Community of Verona, a town in which Jews were established since the 10th century, perhaps even earlier.

The ceiling of the Spanish Synagogue in the Ghetto of Venice.

to leave to the infidel the petty transactions at home and the obloquy attached to them. In many places the Jewish financiers were expressly invited
to establish themselves, in order to reduce the rate of interest on loans,
which the Italian bankers had driven up to incredible heights.
The Jewish loan-banker (in effect, the officially recognized pawn-broker
on a somewhat magnificent scale) now became a familiar figure in Italy.

Service in an Italian Sy-
nagogue, according to a minia-
ture in a 15th century manus-
cript of R. Jacob ben Asher's
code "Arbaa Turim" (Rossi
Collection No. 555 in the
Vatican Library, Rome).

Around him were built the various Jewish communities which henceforth were to be closely connected with Italian Jewish life, in Venice, Padua, Mantua, Florence, and so on; in effect, in all the classical cities of the Italian Quattrocento.

In some places, in Venice for instance, the municipal authorities strictly limited Jewish activity to financial operations and did not allow Jews to engage in commerce, in order to protect their own merchants from Jewish competition. Elsewhere, in Mantua or Ferrara for example, there was a more liberal spirit. Jews were allowed to work at various trades, and their influence made itself felt in the intellectual domain, too.

Although conditions of Jewish life in northern Italy were generally more favorable than elsewhere in Europe, there were occasionally some darker interludes. In the fifteenth century, the inflammatory sermons of the Dominican and Franciscan friars stirred up a wave of anti-Jewish feeling throughout northern Italy, which culminated in 1475 in the ritual murder accusation at Trent (already described in the chapter on False Accusations).

A characteristic episode took place at the close of the fifteenth century, when Francisco of Gonzaga, marquess of Mantua, to show thanks to the Virgin Mary for his somewhat equivocal "victory" at Fornovo in 1495, built a church dedicated to her on the site of a house confiscated from the Jewish loan-banker Daniel Norsa. The pretext for the confiscation was that Norsa had removed an image from the walls, although he had license for this from the Archbishop. It was for this church that Mantegna painted his great Madonna della Vittoria, now in the Louvre. One of his pupils adorned the church with an altar-piece showing the marquess presenting the church to the Madonna. Below are depicted Daniel Norsa and his family, downcast and wearing the Jewish badge of shame prescribed by law. The legend says: "The Jewish perfidy subdued."

The family of the Jewish banker Daniel Norsa of Mantua. Detail from an altar-piece in the church built on the site of his house, demolished in punishment for the removal of an image of the Virgin Mary (end of 15th century).

DETERIORATION IN SPAIN

In the course of time, the spirit of fanaticism triumphed in Spain, partly as a result of the unremitting war against the Moors in which, the Christian states were engaged. The clergy and the nobility persuaded themselves that the war against the infidels abroad had to be supplemented by the destruction of the internal foe, the infidels at home, the Jews. Towards the end of the fourteenth century, a zealous agitator, Ferrand Martinez, was preaching at Seville, inciting the people to merciless warfare against the enemies of Christ. Although the king and the archbishop of Seville opposed the agitation, in due time it bore fruit. In 1391 the Jewish quarter of Seville was set on fire and looted. Four thousand Jews lost their lives and others had to submit to baptism or were sold as slaves to the Arabs.

This attack sparked off a wave of massacres throughout the country, from south to north. Two thousand Jews were slaughtered at Cordova. Then came the turn of Toledo, Burgos, Valencia, Barcelona, etc., where thousands of Jews were pitilessly murdered. But besides the massacres, these attacks produced a peculiar, epoch-making result.

A street in Old Toledo.

Opening of Columbus' Letter to Gabriel Sanchez, Basle 1493. Columbus, himself apparently of Jewish descent, succeeded in performing his epochal voyage only owing to the active support of high-placed Marranos.

Very large numbers of Jews, instead of resisting to the end, as happened in most cases elsewhere, consented to accept baptism, and their synagogues were in many cases forthwith converted into churches.

Henceforth, attacks on Jews came at relatively frequent intervals, particularly at the beginning of the following century. At that time, the fiery, eloquent Dominican friar Vincent Ferrer appeared on the scene, preaching the "holy hate" against the infidels. He found a congenial ally in the Jewish apostate Paul of Burgos. Their conjoint influence induced the queen mother, Catherine, who held the regency during the minority of her son John II of Castile, to issue an ordinance, in 1412, depriving the Castilian Jews of all their rights, excluding them from public service and many trades, and imposing a strict separation between Jews and Christians. The emigration of Jews was also prohibited. Vincent Ferrer now initiated a campaign of conversion by intimidation. He swept through the country preaching conversionist sermons, often with an unruly mob at his heels. Sometimes he burst into synagogues at prayer-time, drove out the Jews and transformed the synagogues into churches on the spot. His successes in Castile induced Ferrer to extend his activity to the neighboring kingdom of Aragon as well. These assaults occurred in particular during the sessions of the disputation of Tortosa (1413—14) when the antipope Benedict XIII attempted to browbeat the Jews into conversion, so as to demonstrate the divine approval of his claims to the papacy.

The harsh provisions of the Ordinance of 1412 were partly mitigated in 1414, but meanwhile irreparable damage had been done. The number of Jews who had accepted baptism during this short period of terror has been estimated at over twenty thousand. They had done so to save their lives or to escape the unbearable restrictions imposed by the barbarous ordinance. The result was that, from now on, there existed in Spain, besides those Jews who remained true to their faith, a very large body of so-called "New Christians" of Jewish birth or origin. They were outwardly Christians, and as such achieved in many cases outstanding success in the world of politics, finance, letters, and even in the Church. But they were always suspected, and often with very good reason, of being secret adherents of Judaism and practisers of Jewish rites and of transmitting this taint to their children and grandchildren after them. This class now permeated all sections of society, from high prelates or ministers of state downwards.

Examination of prisoners under torture by the Inquisition tribunal.

The place of TORMENTS and manner of giving the TORTURE

Proclamation of the Inquisitor of Valencia, dated 1512, inviting all true sons of the Church to denounce persons suspect of observing in secret Jewish (or Mohammedan) rites

It is enough to take as an instance the little group of persons who supported Christopher Columbus, when everybody else considered him merely an obstreperous eccentric. Luis de Santangel and Gabriel Sanchez, both high dignitaries at the court of Aragon and both of Jewish descent, financed the enterprise, and Luis de Torres, the interpreter of the expedition and the first European to set foot on American soil, was a baptised Jew. It has been maintained by some authorities that Columbus himself belonged to a New Christian family which had emigrated to Italy.

The secret Judaizers were generally known by the names of *Conversos*, (Converts) "New Christians," or *Marranos*, originally a term of contempt meaning "swine."

During the reign of King John II of Castile (1418–1454) a breathing-pause was granted to the Spanish Jews. They were reinstated in their former rights, some of them again attained high positions, and the communities were reorganized. But the Church did not approve of his liberal policy, however beneficial it was to the economy of the country. The clergy uninterruptedly continued to nourish the hate which the people bore Jews and New Christians, suspected of insincerity, alike.

From the middle of the fifteenth century, the Church inaugurated a constantly intensifying propaganda campaign directed particularly against the New Christians, demanding the institution of an Inquisition, a tribunal of inquiry, to punish backsliders and prevent further defections. Among the leaders of the agitation was Alonso de Spina, head of the Franciscan order and rector of the University of Salamanca (himself reportedly of Jewish origin). His work *Fortalitium Fidei*, composed about 1460, had a great influence on his contemporaries. Alonso de Spina renewed in his book all the old charges against the Jews, including ritual murder, and advocated their expulsion from Spain and the institution of the Inquisition against the New Christians.

The following years witnessed a long series of trials and death sentences against New Christians, and of violent attacks against them and Jews, in many places and under various pretexts.

191

Thomas de Torquemada, confessor to Queen Isabella the Catholic, a fanatic hater of Jews and Marranos, was appointed Inquisitor General in 1483. By the time of his death, in 1498, vast numbers of "heretics", most of them Marranos, had been burnt alive and many more had been sentenced to various penalties by the Inquisition tribunals. Torquemada is responsible, to a great extent, for the expulsion of the Jews from Spain.

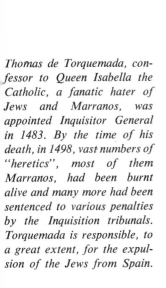

Auto da Fé presided over by St. Dominic de Guzman. Painting by P. Berruguete (1450–1503), Prado Museum, Madrid.

At last, in 1478, at the request of the Spanish sovereigns Isabella of Castile and her husband Ferdinand of Aragon, Pope Sixtus IV authorized, not without hesitation, the establishment of an Inquisitional tribunal in Spain, to deal with the problem of the New Christians. The first inquisitors were appointed in 1480 and the first auto-da-fé was celebrated at Seville on February 6, 1481. This was the earliest in a long series of autos-da-fé which continued down to the nineteenth century. Before the year was over, more than three hundred Marranos had been burnt at Seville alone and many more were rotting in the prisons of the Inquisition. The property of the condemned was, of course, confiscated in favor of the Crown. Even the Pope was shocked at the abuses of the Inquisition, which were prompted, as he expressed himself, "by cupidity more than by zeal for the faith." But he protested in vain. In 1483 the infamous Thomas de Torquemada (reputedly of Jewish extraction on one side) became Inquisitor General and the terror against the New Christians continued with incredible cruelty.

Professing Jews were not bothered by the Inquisition, the jurisdiction of which extended only to members of the Church. But the legal restrictions to which they were subject, were enforced with increasing severity during this period.

THE EXPULSION FROM SPAIN

It was obviously impossible, however, to cope adequately with the problem presented by the Marranos to the Church, as long as they were in constant touch with professing Jews, who could observe these same practices in public with impunity. Torquemada and his associates were hence constantly pressing the Spanish rulers to take drastic action against the latter as well.

For a long time they demurred. Ferdinand and Isabella saw their main task in the conquest of the kingdom of Granada, the last Moslem stronghold on Spanish soil. For the accomplishment of this purpose they still needed the Jews as a source of revenue and as experienced financial administrators. Ferdinand himself was said to have Jewish blood in his own veins. *Conversos* were prominent at court and the finances of the kingdom were administered by a Jew, Don Isaac Abrabanel, the last in the great tradition of Spanish Jewish scholar-statesmen.

Isaac Abrabanel was born at Lisbon of a noble and wealthy family, which traced back its origin to the Davidic dynasty. He received a choice education and excelled in Jewish learning as well as in worldly science and philosophy. Following his father's career, he distinguished himself in the financial administration of the kingdom of Portugal. In 1483, however, he was accused of having taken part in a conspiracy.

General view of Toledo. Since 1087 the residence of the Castilian kings, Toledo was the Capital of unified Spain till 1560. According to the Franciscan friar Aegidius de Zamora, there were 70.000 Jews in Toledo in the middle of the 13th century. This is a gross exaggeration and even the figure of 12.000, mentioned by Abraham ben Nathan ha-Yarhi at the beginning of the same century, is considered too high. But even so, this was an old established, wealthy and proud community.

Ferdinand the Catholic (1452–1516). Effigy in the Cathedral of Malaga (from a drawing by Otto Bacher).

Isabella the Catholic (1451–1504). Effigy in the Cathedral of Granada (from a drawing by Otto Bacher).

His property was confiscated, but Abrabanel himself succeeded in escaping trial by fleeing to neighboring Spain. Here he established himself at Toledo and, in a short time, succeeded in attaining a high position in the service of the Spanish crown. He was in great favor with Queen Isabella and King Ferdinand and exercised considerable influence. His enduring celebrity, however, is due, not to his political and financial activities in the service of Portugal and Spain, but to his Bible commentary and his philosophical writings (which include a commentary on Maimonides' *Guide of the Perplexed*.)

Abrabanel's influence was not sufficient to counteract the continual pressure of the Church, particularly of Torquemada. In the long run the adverse party carried the day. On January 2nd, 1492, Ferdinand and Isabella entered the conquered city of Granada in triumph, thus realizing the ideal for which generations had fought: the unity of Spain under Christian rule. Three months later, on March 31st, in the Court of the Lions of the captured Alhambra at Granada, the Spanish rulers signed a decree requiring all professing Jews to leave their dominions

*Reputed coat of arms of the
Abrabanel family.*

within four months. The decree "generously" allowed the Jews to
dispose of their property within this period and to take with them,
by land or by sea, whatever they possessed "except gold, silver, minted
gold and any other objects the export of which is prohibited." Any Jew
found on Spanish soil after the fatal date would have to choose between
death and baptism.

It was in vain that Abrabanel begged the sovereigns to reconsider
their decision. His offer to pay thirty thousand gold ducats for the
revocation made some impression and Ferdinand almost wavered.
But at that moment Torquemada is said to have flung his crucifix
at the king's feet exclaiming: "Judas sold his master for thirty pieces of
silver and you want to sell him for thirty thousand pieces of gold.
Take him and sell him."

The liquidation of Jewish property was, of course, a dismal parody.
The Jews left the country practically empty-handed. The friars took
advantage of the depressed state of mind among the Jews during these
last few months, and intensified their missionary propaganda, not
without a certain amount of success. The conversion of the rich and
influential Jewish tax-farmer Abraham Senior, who bore the title
"Crown Rabbi of Castile," was considered an outstanding achievement.
The royal couple consented to act as godfather and godmother at his
christening. But the bulk of the nation resisted the allurement of buying
themselves off at the price of baptism. About two hundred thousand Jews
left the country. By the end of July or the beginning of August the last
professing Jew had left Spain, the country with which Jews had been
connected since Roman times.

Part of the exiles found a temporary refuge in Portugal. Others journeyed
to North Africa, Italy, or even as far as Turkey. For most of them,
much suffering was still in store until they found a new home.

Don Isaac Abrabanel first went to Naples and then to Venice. In this
region he spent his last years, dividing his time, as he had always done
during his whole life, between political activity and his scholarly occupations. He died in 1508.

*The Church of Santa Maria
la Blanca at Toledo, formerly
a synagogue, founded by
Joseph ibn Shushan in the
13th century. In 1411 the
fanatic Dominican friar
Vicente Ferrer entered the
synagogue with a cross in his
hands, drove out the Jews
engaged in prayer and dedicated the house on the spot
to the service of the Im-
maculate Virgin.*

THE EXPULSION FROM PORTUGAL

The only countries adjoining Spain to which the exiles could go by land, were Portugal and the little Pyrenean kingdom of Navarre.

A handful of Jews from northern Spain went to Navarre. Here there was an ancient and relatively numerous Jewish community, which had experienced many ups and downs in its long history. Almost annihilated in a country-wide massacre in 1328, it had recovered and enjoyed quiet, and even a certain prosperity in the second half of the fourteenth century. But the fifteenth century was a period of economic and political decline for the kingdom, and the position of the Jews gradually deteriorated. The exiles from Spain who had been admitted to Navarre, could remain there only for a very short time. After having resisted the pressure of King Ferdinand of Castile (who was soon to annex this kingdom to united Spain) for several years, the king of Navarre had to yield in 1498 and the Jews, here too, were given the choice between expulsion and conversion.

Larger by far was the group which went to Portugal, whose vicissitudes partook of the nature of a Greek tragedy.

In Portugal, too, there was an old-established, numerous and well-organized Jewish community. From the thirteenth century on, it was directed by a Chief Rabbi the Arrabi-Mor, officially recognized as the head of the Jewish community and invested with considerable authority. But as in Spain, the clergy and part of the nobility advocated the restriction of the rights which the Jews were still enjoying, and their agitation achieved its aim in the course of time. In the fourteenth century, discriminatory laws against the Jews were decreed, and there were outbursts of violence in several places. Curiously enough, the fifteenth century, which brought about the rapid decline of Spanish Jewry, witnessed a considerable improvement in the position of the Portuguese community. King João I (1385–1433) protected his Jewish subjects, allowed the immigration of Jews fleeing from persecution in Spain, and even tolerated the return of baptized Jews to their former faith. The same policy, which proved most beneficial to the economy of the kingdom, was pursued by his successors. Jewish families attained not only wealth by means of large-scale commercial operations, but also high positions and considerable influence at court (e.g., members of the Abrabanel family). Even the alleged treason of Don Isaac Abrabanel and his flight to Spain in 1483, did not, for the moment, affect the friendly relations obtaining between the Crown and the Jews.

In 1492, about half of the Spanish exiles set out for Portugal. At first, they were admitted by King João II (1481–1495), subject to a heavy tax and for a time limited to eight months only. But their condition soon deteriorated. Early in 1493, popular animosity against the Jewish immigrants rose high and the authorities insisted on their leaving the country at the expiration of their term. But there were not enough ships

Street in the former Jewish quarter of Lisbon.

The Arrabi Mor (Chief Rabbi) of Portugal. Detail from a painting by Nuño Gonçalves (National Museum of Ancient Art, Lisbon).

and many of the exiles had no money left for the fare. Those who succeeded in embarking were exposed to the most disgraceful treatment on the part of unscrupulous captains and their rough crews. All the exiles who were still in Portugal when their time was expired, were declared to be the king's slaves. About two thousand children below the age of seven were deported to the island of São Thomé, to be brought up there in the Christian faith.

There was a short reprieve in 1495, when King Manoel "the Fortunate" ascended the throne, perhaps owing to his Jewish court-astrologer, the chronicler and mathematician Abraham Zacuto. He restored to the remaining exiles the liberty and took them under his protection. But when he married the daughter of Ferdinand and Isabella, the following year, he imbibed her religious fanaticism. However, he did not lose sight of the potential value of his Jewish subjects to his realm and, therefore, determined to force them into Christianity, thus retaining their services, while, at the same time, ridding his country of their disbelief. This new policy was directed, of course, against the entire Jewish population of Portugal, Portuguese Jews and Spanish exiles alike.

In December 1496, King Manoel signed an edict of expulsion ordering all the Jews to leave Portugal by the end of October 1497 at the latest. In fact this edict of expulsion was a farcical misnomer. What really took place in the course of the year 1497, was a forced conversion campaign on an enormous scale, embracing the quasi-entirety of Portuguese Jewry. Jewish children were baptized, by order of the king, against the will of their parents. About twenty thousand Jews who had refused to desert their faith and had gathered in Lisbon for emigration, but had been unable to leave Portugal before the fateful date, were baptized by force. The remnant of professing Jews who survived conversion and terror, were finally allowed to leave the country in the course of the year 1498.

The result of Manoel's zeal for the Catholic faith was that the phenomenon of crypto-Judaism or Marranism, already familiar in Spain, became implanted in the smaller country on a far vaster scale. Even the Inquisition, instituted here at the beginning of the sixteenth century, was able to cope with it only to a slight degree. This nucleus, which constituted the core of the Marrano groupings, was destined to play a great role in Jewish history in succeeding generations.

THE JEWS AND
THE RENAISSANCE

Jewish wedding in fifteenth century Italy. Miniature from Codex Rossi 555, Vatican Library, Rome.

In Italy, the country principally associated with the Renaissance, the Jews were solidly installed. Inevitably they were, on the one hand, deeply influenced by this movement and, on the other, they themselves participated in it to some extent. The luxury of the daily life of the wealthier elements among them reflected Renaissance standards. Their dress and costumes showed them to be true sons of their environment. Jews of aristocratic families would commission portrait-medallions from the most eminent artists of the time. The wealthy Jewish house-

Elia de Lattes and his mother Rica. Bronze medal executed in 1552. Such portrait-medallions were fashionable in high Jewish circles in Italy, during the Renaissance period.

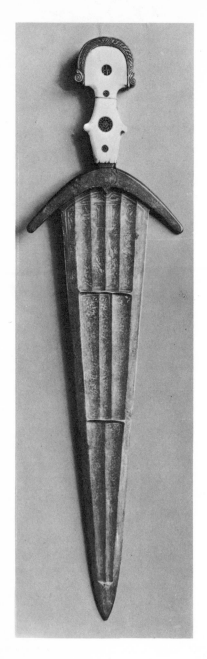

The Dagger of the Gonzagas (*Louvre, Paris*), *executed by the Jewish metal-worker Salamone da Sesso.*

Ivory Mezuzah-case, about 1500 (*Jewish Museum, London*).

Housewife's casket, 15th century, executed by Yeshurun Tovar (Israel Museum, Jerusalem).

Title-page of the French edition of the "Dialogues on Love" (Lyons, 1595) with portrait of the author, Leone Ebreo or Judah Abrabanel, son of Don Isaac Abrabanel. This was one of the most popular philosophical works of the Renaissance period.

holders would have their Hebrew manuscripts illuminated, regardless of expense, by the most skilled book-artists available. Even their house-hold-utensils reflected their keen aesthetic perception. A few Jewish artists of the period are known, though none of any great reputation, except for the eminent metal-worker Salamone da Sesso.

On the other hand, there were some aspects of the Renaissance in which Jewish participation was considerable.

The Jewish scholar Elijah Delmedigo, originally from Crete, taught philosophy at Padua in the second half of the fifteenth century and wrote in Latin philosophical treatises highly appreciated by his contemporaries. Judah Abrabanel, the son of Don Isaac Abrabanel, who, like his father, reached Italy after the expulsion from Spain, became famous there under the name of Leone Ebreo. While practising medicine, he was chiefly interested in philosophy, particularly in Neoplatonism. His treatise "Dialoghi di Amore" (Dialogues on Love), written in the Italian vernacular, was one of the most influential philosophical works of the sixteenth century.

Amatus Lusitanus (from a 17th century engraving), a famous Jewish physician and medical author of the 16th century. Of Marrano extraction, he left Portugal to flee the Inquisition, openly professed Judaism in Italy and died in Salonica.

Medal commemorating the Jewish physician Benjamin ben Elijah Beer (end of the 15th century), son of Elijah ben Sabbatai Beer, who had been court-physician to King Henry IV of England.

Jewish physicians, always notable, were particularly valued in this period. Many of them were in attendance on the numerous petty courts in Italy, and even on the popes, despite the ecclesiastic canon forbidding Jewish physicians to treat Christian patients. Some of them distinguished themselves as versatile scholars. Jacob Mantino, court-physician to Pope Paul III in the first half of the sixteenth century, translated into Latin the works of Arab and Jewish philosophers. The Marrano Amatus Lusitanus, a younger contemporary of Mantino who returned to Judaism in Italy and died at Salonica, where he had adopted the Hebrew name Habib (the beloved), not only made important contributions to medical research in his published works, but also to medical history. Some significant medical volumes were produced in Hebrew. Even the encyclopaedia of natural science *Maassei Tovia* by Tobias Cohen, the second part of which is dedicated to medicine, may be considered a fruit of this epoch, although not published until 1707. The author who was born in Metz and died in Jerusalem, studied medicine at Padua and imbibed the spirit of the late Italian Renaissance.

In the seventeenth century, the University of Padua had become the great center of Jewish students of medicine. It was not easy for Jews to obtain a doctorate, because graduation was an ecclesiastical ceremony which took place in the episcopal palace or sometimes in church. But in the course of time matters were made easier by the secularization of the graduating ceremony for non-Catholics. Even so Jewish, graduates were obliged to offer thirty-five substantial parcels of sweatmeats for distribution to the various corporations of Christian students, although the relations between Christian and Jewish fellow-students were at times far from friendly. In spite of all the difficulties, hundreds of Jews studied and graduated at Padua during the sixteenth and seventeenth centuries,

The fifteenth century Jewish dancing-master Guglielmo da Pesaro and his pupils (miniature in MS Ital. 973 of the Bibliothèque Nationale, Paris). He taught dancing at many princely courts in Italy, including Florence, and wrote a "Treatise on the Art of Dancing".

Setting for fête at Siena in honor of the Grand Duke, arranged by the Jews (Contemporary engraving).

and the diplomas which they received on graduation were indited and illuminated in the lavish fashion usual at that time. Some of the Jewish physicians hailing from Italy continued their activity in northern Europe, sometimes with memorable results.

But the Jews also contributed to the more frivolous aspects of the Renaissance. From the fifteenth century onwards, they had a high reputation throughout Italy as teachers of dancing. A treatise on the Art of Dancing by the Jew Guglielmo of Pesaro is among the most important Renaissance works in this field.

Jews played a role in the great pageants which were characteristic of Renaissance life. At the court of Mantua, especially, Jews took part in theatrical activities, and the community often had to undertake the

performance of plays in honor of visiting potentates or guests of the ducal house of Gonzaga.

As singers and musicians, too, the Jews were famous. Salamone de' Rossi, who was for forty-one years (1587–1628) in the service of the dukes of Mantua as conductor of the ducal orchestra, produced many volumes of original music. He was one of the most brilliant composers of his time and is regarded as one of the fathers of the symphony. He, moreover, attempted to introduce the new standards of Renaissance musical taste into the synagogue. His synagogal compositions were published under the title *Hashirim asher li-Shelomo* ("The Songs which are Solomon's", an allusion to the name of the biblical book "The Song of Songs, which is Solomon's").

Musical life among the Mantuan Jews seems to have been particularly intensive at the beginning of the seventeenth century and Salamone de' Rossi was by no means the only Jewish composer. Allegro Porto Ebreo, for instance, composed madrigals for several voices and dedicated them to members of the ducal family.

The Renaissance spirit permeated Jewish learning, too. An older member of the Rossi family, Azariah de' Rossi, the author of the famous book *Me'or Einayim*, brought Renaissance standards of historical criticism to Jewish scholarship. The majority of his contemporaries disapproved, it is true, of Azariah de' Rossi's rationalistic views, and many communities

Above to the left: "The Jewish Queen"; to the right: "The Mountain of the Jews". Details from the Sforza wedding pageant at Urbino in 1475 (from Cod. Urb. 899, Vatican Library, Rome).

Title-page of Salamone de' Rossi's synagogal compositions "Hashirim asher li-Shelomo", published at Venice in 1623, which first introduced Renaissance musical standards to the Synagogue.

The beginning of one of Salamone de' Rossi's synagogal compositions. The Hebrew text under the notes is to be read from left to right.

זה השער לﬣ

זה ספר
מאור עינים
לר' עזריה מן האדומי' יצ'ו
והוא נחלק לשלשה חלקיס
האחד מתואר
קול אלדים אשר כו ידבר על
הרעשי' שהתחילו בשורה יח
נוכימ'ס'ל'א' והשני מתואר
הדרת זקנים שהוא ספור
מעשה הזוקני' כותרי' התור' לתלמי
המלך נעתק מן היוני לרומיי'
וﬤﬦﬤ﬩ ללשון הקדם ·
והשלישי מתואר
אמרי בינה אשר יפרד וסיב
לארבע' מאמרי' כוללי' שמיס פרקי'
על דרושי' שונים ככל הנראה
מן הלוח בקצה הספר
נדפס פה מנטובה י'ס מנימר ש'לד

Title-page of Azariah de' Rossi's "Meor Einayim", published at Mantua in 1573. This controversial book marked the beginning of scientific critical study of Jewish antiquities.

put the book under ban. Later generations, however, recognized the high value of the book as a pioneering feat in overcoming the limitations of the Middle Ages and paving the way for modern scientific Jewish studies.

A characteristically picturesque episode of the Renaissance period in Italy was the appearance, in Venice in 1524, of a swarthy adventurer named David, claiming to be the brother of the king of the tribe of Reuben. He asserted that this tribe was living as an independent nation in the Wilderness of Habor (he may have meant the Khaibar Oasis in the northern part of the Arabian Peninsula, where a Jewish population had been living since ancient times) and called himself, in consequence, David Reubeni. The object of his mission was, he said, to obtain military support from the Pope and the princes of Europe, to stem the advance of the Turks, who were menacing his people's independent existence, and to deliver the Holy Land recently conquered by them. Mounted on a white horse, surrounded by servants, and speaking only Hebrew, David Reubeni made a deep impression on both Jews and Christians. It is remarkable that his preposterous story was credulously received as true by many people.

Reubeni proceeded from Venice to Rome and was granted an audience by Pope Clement VII, who gave him a letter of recommendation to the King of Portugal. In Portugal, he was sympathetically received by King João III, who even adjourned the impending institution of the Inquisition against the Marranos, so as not to disturb the negotiations being conducted with the Jewish ambassador. Reubeni's arrival could not fail to cause a sensation and to arouse hopes and illusions among the Marranos, although he carefully refrained from doing anything to encourage them.

One of the Marranos, the youthful royal notary Diogo Pires, had himself circumcised, openly professed Judaism and took the name of Solomon Molcho. Escaping to Turkey, he carried on a sort of Messianic propaganda centered on his own remarkable personality. After having visited Palestine, Molcho went to Italy, where he met David Reubeni in Venice. The latter had left Portugal without having achieved his aim, when he became suspect in the eyes of the court.

The episode now neared its tragic end. Reubeni lost the confidence of the Signoria and had to leave Venice. Molcho, who had irritated the less credulous Jews in Rome by his Messianic prophecies and had drawn on himself the suspicious eyes of the Inquisition, was obliged to leave Italy in haste. In 1532, at the Diet of Regensburg, Reubeni and Molcho unsuccessfully made a common dramatic attempt to win Emperor Charles V to their fantastic plans. But the emperor had them arrested and sent to Italy, where they were handed over to the Inquisition. Molcho died at the stake in Mantua. Reubeni was sent back to the Iberian Peninsula, where he perished in an auto-da-fé.

A popular legend claimed that Molcho had not died in the flames and would soon manifest himself again as the Messiah. Some of his personal effects, including his banner, were long preserved as pious relics in the ancient Altneuschul-synagogue of Prague.

CHRISTIAN HEBRAISTS OF THE RENAISSANCE AND REFORMATION PERIODS

One of the direct results of the revival of learning, which was an essential part of the Renaissance, was the growth of interest, in Christian circles, in the Hebrew language and literature. The movement is especially associated with the name of the Italian nobleman Giovanni Pico della Mirandola, the knight-errant of humanism in the second half of the fifteenth century. He brought to Florence, as his tutor, the Cretan scholar Elijah Delmedigo, who became a familiar figure in the circle of Florentine humanists. Delmedigo translated some of the writings of the Arab philosopher Ibn Rushd (Averroes) into Latin for his pupil, and also wrote some explanatory treatises on them in Hebrew and Latin.

Della Mirandola also had another Jewish tutor, Johanan Alemano of Constantinople, the author of a commentary on the Song of Songs. Alemano particularly introduced his pupil to the secrets of the Jewish mystical lore, the Cabbala. The Italian enthusiastically threw himself into this study, believing that it contained the key to the profoundest verities of theology and religion.

Elijah Delmedigo (detail from the fresco by Benozzo Gozzoli in the Palazzo Riccardi, Florence). A famous Jewish scholar, in the second half of the 15th century, he taught philosophy in Florence, translated the works of the Arab philosopher Averroes (Ibn Rushd, 12th century) and was the friend and tutor of the Christian Hebraist Pico della Mirandola.

Johann Reuchlin (1455—1522), German Christian Hebraist who gallantly took up the defence of the Talmud and other Jewish writings against the malevolent and slanderous attacks of the Jewish renegade Johann Joseph Pfefferkorn.

In due course, Pico infected the German scholar Johann Reuchlin, who was on a visit to Italy, with his enthusiasm. Reuchlin began his Hebrew studies under the direction of Jacob ben Jehiel Loans, court-physician to the German emperor Frederick III, and deepened his knowledge of Hebrew literature in Rome under the tuition of the Bible-exegete and talmudist Obadiah Sforno. As a result of his studies, Reuchlin published a number of works of Hebrew scholarship. Like Pico della Mirandola, Reuchlin was profoundly interested in the Cabbala and, like him, was far from being a friend of Judaism. But his noble spirit found violence against the Jews repulsive and his love of truth and sense of justice impelled him to be the defender of the Jews in a memorable battle.

In 1505, Johann Joseph Pfefferkorn, a Moravian Jew with dark antecedents in his homeland, turned Christian at Cologne, and consented to serve as the instrument of the Dominican friars there, in their agitation against the Jews. A series of libellous pamphlets now began to appear, allegedly written by this ignoramus, in which the "Jewish peril" was denounced and the Talmud was accused of being a most noxious and dangerous book. Pfefferkorn asked for the Talmud to be burnt, for the

Fu laudē et hono

rē dei omnipotētis domini nostri Jesu christi·bñdicere vgi
ni s matris eius marie:cremētū vtilitat۶ publice:ad mei
quoᵹᵹ ipᵒ honoris tuitionē in aim induxi ego Joannes
pfeffercorn professionis olim iudaice. nūc p misericordiam
dei christianus:libellū quendā edere post alios nōnullos
aduersum iudeos quē partitus sum in ptes tres. In pri
ma dicā conuitia ꝛtēptus probra:que iudaicū pecus qtti
die ingerit in deū ꝛ dñm nostrū Jesum christū matrē eᵘ
Mariā:sanctos celestis exercitᵒ:clez ꝛ populū sacramēta
et ritus christianos ex ipsoꝛmet hebraica litteratura ꝛ ser
mone quē inficias ire nequeūt. In parte scᵈa ostendā ap
tissime quanto damno iudei afficiāt terras ꝛ loca pl vsu
ras suas in qbus sultinenꝼ ꝛ quoquo mō defendunꝼ.ratō
nibus supputationibᵗ ꝛ numeris vt plane quisᵹ intelli
gere etiā rudis id possit. ¶ Tercio loco mōstrabo quo pa
cto ipsi christianos apud quos vsanꝼ corruptela dolorꝛ
et pecuniarum ad nefarios ꝛ minime christianos actus
hortēntur ꝛ inducāt(neᵹ emᵗvt id efficiant pecunijs par
cunt)atᵹ ibi ostendam quomodo mihi in famā in vitaᵶ
insidiati sint:ꝛ insidianꝼ adhuc vt a veridicis·ꝛ fide dig
nis accepi:vt tandeᵶ nō odio eoꝛ q̃uis meriti sint. sed ve
ritatis amore ꝛ iusticie hecme reuela n̄te ꝛ vulgo proden
te accipiant christiani. quales apud se serpētes in suo gre
mio alant ecclesiastici bisint aut laici(omnibus christia
nis cōmunes q̃pesuntiudei iudaisantes inimici) vt ab
hijs caueant sibi ꝛ eorum fraudibus obsistant.

Page from the Latin version of Pfefferkorn's book "Juden-feind" ("The Enemy of the Jews"), published in 1509, one of the pamphlets in which the author denounces the Talmud as a noxious book, which must be confiscated and destroyed.

Johann Joseph Pfeffer-korn (1469 — 1521), Jewish renegade and anti-Jewish agitator (from a contemporary engraving).

Jews to be converted, and for the stubborn ones, resisting conversion, to be expelled from Germany. He was assisted in his action by another Jewish renegade, Victor von Karben, a former rabbi, who likewise launched a violent attack on the Talmud in his book *Opus Aureum*. In 1509 Pfefferkorn was successful in obtaining an edict for the burning of Hebrew books from the German Emperor Maximilian I, on the ground that they contained matter offensive to Christianity. However, in view of the numerous protests which this edict aroused, the Emperor, on second thought, preferred to have the matter first investigated by experts. At this stage, Reuchlin came to the rescue and published a number of books in defense of Hebrew literature, in which he attacked the obscurantists who wanted to suppress it. This was the first rumbling of the intellectual conflict which was to result in the Reformation.

Another eminent Christian Hebraist in the sixteenth century was the Italian Cardinal Egidio da Viterbo. His tutor was the Jewish scholar Elijah Levita, also known as Elijah Bahur, a remarkable philologist and grammarian, originally from Germany, who was also an early contributor to Yiddish literature (he translated into this vernacular an Italian version of the English chivalry romance *Bevis of Hampton*). For ten years Elijah Levita was entertained in the palace of the Cardinal at Rome and had the leisure to dedicate himself to his scholarly occupations, while introducing his host to Cabḅala. Like most Christian Hebraists, Egidio da Viterbo was chiefly interested in this branch of Hebrew litera-

The Triumph of Reuchlin over anti-Jewish obscurantism (from a contemporary German woodcut). Among the humanists Reuchlin was known by the name of Capnion (the Greek translation of his German name).

Title-page of Martin Luther's book "Von den Juden und ihren Lügen" ("The Jews and their Lies"), published in 1543. Luther used to vent his enmity against the Jews in a coarse language and did not shrink from launching against them, in his sermons and in his books, the most vulgar invectives.

Martin Luther (1483–1546). His Reformation of the Church, epochal in the history of Christian Europe, marked no change in Christian attitude towards · the Jews and, if possible, even embittered the hatred against them in German lands.

ture, where he believed he had found allusions to Christian dogmas.

In Germany the Reformation greatly promoted the study of Hebrew. Martin Luther, who initiated the Reformation, translated the Bible into German, in order to enable his countrymen to read the Holy Scripture in their own language. In so doing, he rejected the official Latin translation employed by the Catholic Church (the Vulgate). His own translation was based on the original Hebrew text.

It is, however, noteworthy that, in the case of Luther too, the interest in the Hebrew language and literature did not imply friendly feelings towards Judaism and the Jewish people. At first, Luther hoped that his Reformation would make it easier for the Jews to enter the fold of Christianity. When he convinced himself that this was not the case and that the Jews persisted in their stubbornness, he became a ferocious Jew-hater. In his book *Von den Juden und ihren Lügen* ("The Jews and

their Lies"), Luther heaped monstrous accusations on the Jews with
incredible virulence and exhorted the Christian princes to destroy the
synagogues, confiscate Jewish books and property, and expel from
German lands "like mad dogs" all those who refused to submit to
baptism. Following the lead of the great reformer, Protestant Germany
proved no less intolerant than Catholic Germany and, in the long run,
Luther's recommendations were fully implemented.

Nevertheless, the interest in Hebrew literature persisted and a knowledge
of Hebrew became a point of pride among the Protestant theologians
during the Reformation and later.

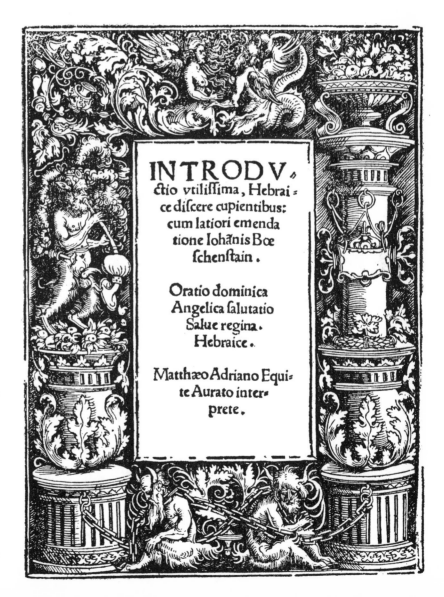

The "Introduction to the Study
of Hebrew" by the Christian
Hebraist Johann Boeschen-
stain, published in 1520; a
typical Hebrew grammar of
the Renaissance period.

HEBREW PRINTING

נסלם פ' תורת   סרטי פיתריה   וט זיית חורה   לכלתי חעריהס
חטיר עזיר לג   טר שדה עטל   חטיר מתן טל   עלו חבריהב
חן כמג חטיתי   כלטאות חמימת   דרטתי וחקרתי   כיג חבריהס
אך הטאי הזמן   בקטתי מעטה חמן   עטיר חטר מתן   טהים לחערסה
צמקוס למילתי   סמרים כתכתי   והנם הטלמתי   ילדט חבדיהס
כחמטשתם חול   חטותה מגהר חול   הלגחי והל   יהי מן לזהריס
רחה קדח ול   תעסם קטיעי לחל   כימה סבם נגל   לג מגל חברהב
הלג מגד חברה   אטה החטוך חורה   זעב גם עריה   הטיח על חדריהס
עטיר יטלח יח   מחזה ול תרחו   טחותם יחלי ,   מגד חבריהס
להר סתגרהטין   יקן לב ועטיטן   חב כן גרעון   כן יחק חבריהס
ברינו המטיה   דעל ימח מוחטא   כטוף קלגריזה   טס טר חבריהס
לטדרס ל שתם   ומחטים וה' וטלטס   כ כעוד מוף חטטים לחטטן חבריהס

Colophon of the first edition of Rashi's Commentary on the Pentateuch, printed by Abraham ben Isaac ben Garton at Reggio di Calabria in 1475. This is the earliest printed book in Hebrew.

On the preceding page: Decorated page from Pentateuch, printed about 1486 by Eliezer Alantansi at Hijar, Spain. This border was later taken by exiles to Constantinople and used for books printed there.

The beginning of the art of typography is generally associated with the famous Latin Bible produced by Johannes Gutenberg in 1456. There is, however, a record of an experiment in printing carried out by a Jew named Davin de Caderousse twelve years before this, in 1444, at Avignon, under the guidance of a Bohemian craftsman Procop Wildfoghel.

The earliest specimen of Hebrew typography that has survived is an edition of Rashi's commentary to the Pentateuch completed by Abraham Garton at Reggio di Calabria in southern Italy in 1475. In the same year Meshullam Cusi printed in Pieve di Sacco, near Padua, Jacob ben Asher's code *Arbaa Turim*.

Several Jewish printers were active, before long, not only in Italy, but also in Spain and Portugal, in the later of which the earliest books produced by the new art were in Hebrew.

In Italy the most zealous printers belonged to successive generations of the family of Soncino, who were active throughout the peninsula for over half a century. The printing-house was founded by Joshua Solomon

Printer's mark of Gerson ben Moses Soncino. The Soncino family started printing Hebrew books in 1483 in Soncino (North Italy). Members of the family continued the trade throughout the 16th century in Soncino, Brescia, Naples and other places. Some of them went to Constantinople and Cairo and founded, there too, Hebrew printing presses.

217

אֶל אֲשֶׁר יִהְיֶה שָּׁמָּה הָרוּחַ לָלֶכֶת יֵלֵכוּ לֹא יִסּ
יִסַּבּוּ בְּלֶכְתָּן: וּדְמוּת הַחַיּוֹת כְּמַרְאֵיהֶם כְּגַחֲלֵי
אֵשׁ בֹּעֲרֹת כְּמַרְאֵה הַלַּפִּדִים הִיא מִתְהַלֶּכֶת
בֵּין הַחַיּוֹת וְנֹגַהּ לָאֵשׁ וּמִן הָאֵשׁ יוֹצֵא בָרָק: וּ
וְהַחַיּוֹת רָצוֹא וָשׁוֹב כְּמַרְאֵה הַבָּזָק: וָאֵרֶא הַ
הַחַיּוֹת וְהִנֵּה אוֹפָן אֶחָד בָּאָרֶץ אֵצֶל הַחַיּוֹת ל
לְאַרְבַּעַת פָּנָיו: מַרְאֵה הָאוֹפַנִּים וּמַעֲשֵׂיהֶם
כְּעֵין תַּרְשִׁישׁ וּדְמוּת אֶחָד לְאַרְבַּעְתָּן וּמַרְאֵיהֶם
וּמַעֲשֵׂיהֶם כַּאֲשֶׁר יִהְיֶה הָאוֹפָן בְּתוֹךְ הָאוֹפָן:
עַל אַרְבַּעַת רִבְעֵיהֶן בְּלֶכְתָּם יֵלֵכוּ לֹא יִסַּבּוּ
בְּלֶכְתָּן וְגַבֵּיהֶן וְגֹבַהּ לָהֶם וְיִרְאָה לָהֶם וְגַבֹּתָם
מְלֵאֹת עֵינַיִם סָבִיב לְאַרְבַּעְתָּן: וּבְלֶכֶת הַחַיּוֹת
יֵלְכוּ הָאוֹפַנִּים אֶצְלָם וּבְהִנָּשֵׂא הַחַיּוֹת מֵעַל
הָאָרֶץ יִנָּשְׂאוּ הָאוֹפַנִּים: עַל אֲשֶׁר יִהְיֶה שָּׁם
הָרוּחַ לָלֶכֶת יֵלֵכוּ שָׁמָּה הָרוּחַ לָלֶכֶת וְהָאוֹ
וְהָאוֹפַנִּים יִנָּשְׂאוּ לְעֻמָּתָם כִּי רוּחַ הַחַיָּה בָּא
בָּאוֹפַנִּים: בְּלֶכְתָּם יֵלֵכוּ וּבְעָמְדָם יַעֲמֹדוּ וּבְה
וּבְהִנָּשְׂאָם מֵעַל הָאָרֶץ יִנָּשְׂאוּ הָאוֹפַנִּים לְעֻ
לְעֻמָּתָם כִּי רוּחַ הַחַיָּה בָּאוֹפַנִּים: וּדְמוּת עַל
רָאשֵׁי הַחַיָּה רָקִיעַ כְּעֵין הַקֶּרַח הַנּוֹרָא נָטוּי א
עַל רָאשֵׁיהֶם מִלְמָעְלָה: וְתַחַת הָרָקִיעַ פְּנֵי
פַנְפֵיהֶם יְשָׁרוֹת אִשָּׁה אֶל אֲחוֹתָהּ לְאִישׁ שְׁתַּיִם

בִּשְׁלֹשִׁים שָׁנָה בָּרְבִיעִי בַּחֲמִשָּׁה לַחֹדֶשׁ וַאֲנִי
בְּתוֹךְ הַגּוֹלָה עַל נְהַר כְּבָר נִפְתְּחוּ הַשָּׁמַיִם ו
וָאֶרְאֶה מַרְאוֹת אֱלֹהִים: בַּחֲמִשָּׁה לַחֹדֶשׁ הִיא
הַשָּׁנָה הַחֲמִישִׁית לְגָלוּת הַמֶּלֶךְ יוֹיָכִין: הָיֹה הָי
הָיָה דְבַר יְהוָד אֶל יְחֶזְקֵאל בֶּן בּוּזִי הַכֹּהֵן בְּ
אֶרֶץ כַּשְׂדִּים עַל נְהַר כְּבָר וַתְּהִי עָלָיו שָׁם יַד
יְהוָד: וָאֵרֶא וְהִנֵּה רוּחַ סְעָרָה בָּאָה מִן הַצָּפ
הַצָּפוֹן עָנָן גָּדוֹל וְאֵשׁ מִתְלַקַּחַת וְנֹגַהּ לוֹ סָבִיב
וּמִתּוֹכָהּ כְּעֵין הַחַשְׁמַל מִתּוֹךְ הָאֵשׁ: וּמִתּוֹכָהּ
דְּמוּת אַרְבַּע חַיּוֹת וְזֶה מַרְאֵיהֶן דְּמוּת אָדָם ל
לָהֵנָּה: וְאַרְבָּעָה פָנִים לְאֶחָת וְאַרְבַּע כְּנָפַיִם ל
לְאַחַת לָהֶם: וְרַגְלֵיהֶם רֶגֶל יְשָׁרָה וְכַף רַגְלֵ
רַגְלֵיהֶם כְּכַף רֶגֶל עֵגֶל וְנֹצְצִים כְּעֵין נְחֹשֶׁת ק
קָלָל: וִידֵי אָדָם מִתַּחַת כַּנְפֵיהֶם עַל אַרְבַּעַת

Soncino, with the aid of his father and brothers, and inaugurated its activity with the publication of the first tractate of the Babylonian Talmud with commentaries. In 1488 Joshua Solomon Soncino published the first Hebrew Bible. His nephew Gershom ben Moses Soncino continued to practise the art independently and printed many Hebrew books, including Maimonides' great code *Mishneh Torah* (1490). Early in the sixteenth century Gershom Soncino himself and other members of the family left Italy for Turkey and continued to print Hebrew books in Salonica and Constantinople. The decorative elements in some of the books printed by the Soncino family were sometimes magnificent artistic achievements, in particular the engraved borders to significant pages. The engravers were often Christian craftsmen of high reputation, but there is reason to believe that, in some cases, they were Jews.

First page of the Book of the Prophet Ezekiel, from the Bible printed by Josua Salomon Soncino in 1488. This is the first complete edition of the Hebrew Bible.

First page of Jacob ben Asher's rabbinical code "Arbaa Turim", printed in 1495 by Samuel Dortas and his sons in Leiria, Portugal. This is one of the earliest books printed in Portugal and the decorative border is probably by a Jewish artist.

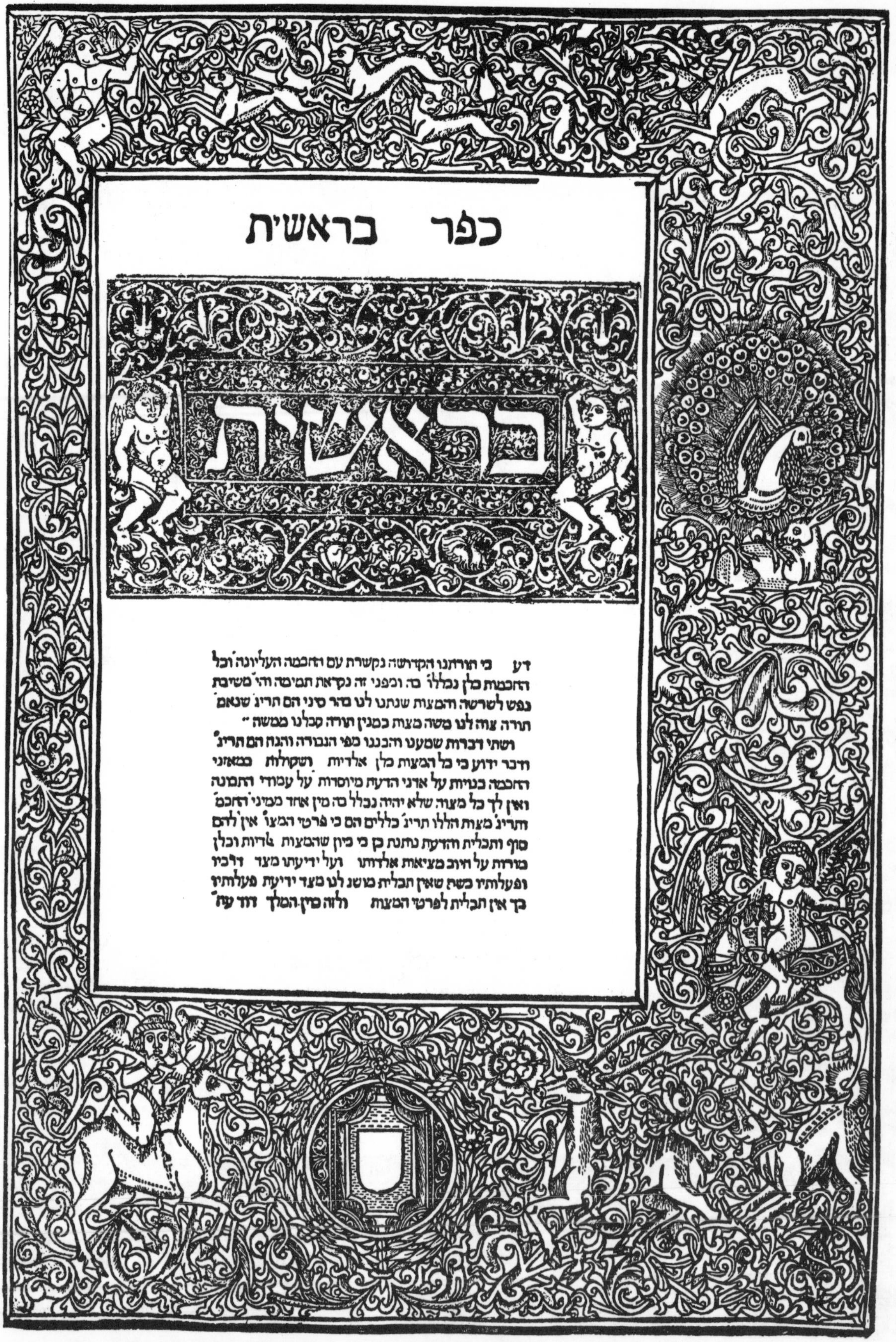

ספר בראשית

בראשית

דע כי תורתנו הקדושה נקשרת עם החכמה העליונה וכל
החכמות כלן נכללו בה. ומפני זה נקראת תמימה והי׳ משיבת
נפש לשרשה. והמצות שנתנו לנו בהר סיני הם תריג׳ שנאמ׳
תורה צוה לנו משה מצות כמנין תורה קבלנו ממשה ״
ושתי דברות שמענו והבננו מפי הגבורה והנה הם תריג׳
ודבר ידוע כי כל המצות כלן אלדיות ושקולות במאזני
החכמה בנויות על אדני הדעת מיוסדות על עמודי התמונה
ואין לך כל מצוה שלא יהיה נכלל בה מין אחד ממיני החכמ׳
ותריג׳ מצות הללו תריג׳ כללים הם כי פרטי המצו׳ אין להם
סוף ותכלית והדעת נותנת כן כי כיון שהמצות אלדיות וכלן
מורות על חיוב מציאות אלדותו ועל ידיעתו מצד דרכיו
ופעולותיו כשם שאין תכלית מושג לנו מצד ידיעת פעלותיו
כך אין תכלית לפרטי המצות ולזה כיון המלך דוד ע״ה

Page from the Häggadah printed by Gershon Cohen in Prague, in 1527.

First page of Bahya ben Asher's Commentary on the Pentateuch, printed by Azriel Gunzenhauser in Naples in 1492. The beautiful border was also used by Christian printers of the period.

The first Passover Haggadah printed with wood-cuts was produced by the Schwarz brothers at Gershon Cohen's printing-press at Prague in 1527. It is considered to be one of the most memorable specimens of sixteenth century German typography.

Towards the end of the sixteenth century, Hebrew printing also spread to eastern Europe.

In the sixteenth century some memorable Hebrew books were produced by devoted and skilful Christian printers, in particular the generous-minded Daniel Bomberg, founder of the great tradition of Hebrew printing at Venice.

ויקרא

Born in Antwerp, rich, and a great bibliophile, Daniel Bomberg established himself as a printer in Venice in the first years of the sixteenth century. Upon the advice of a learned Jewish convert, Felix Pratensis, he started printing the Bible. In 1517/8 he produced the first so-called Rabbinical Bible edited by Felix Pratensis himself, which comprised for

Page from the socalled "Rabbinical Bible" printed in Venice, in 1517–18, by the Christian printer Daniel Bomberg whose prints mark an epoch in the history of Hebrew scholarship.

222

יִהְיוּ לְרָצוֹן אִמְרֵי	Sint ad placēdū sermones	Et erunt vt complaceāt eloqa	Καὶ ἔσονται εἰς ἐυδοκίαν τὰ λόγια,
פִּי וְהֶגְיוֹן לִבִּי	oris mi̅, & meditatō cōdis mi̅	oris mei, & meditatio cordis mi̅	τοῦ σόματός μου. ἡ μελέτη τῆς καρδίας μου
לְפָנֶיךָ יְהֹוָה צוּרִי	i cōspectu tuo, Deo fortitu (	i cōspectu tuo sep. Dñe adiutor	ἐνώπιος διαπαντός. Κύρα βοηθός μου
וְגֹאֲלִי	& redēptor meus. (do mea,	meus, & redemptor meus.	καὶ λυτρωτά μου.

celerius quam lusitani fecissent nouas terras, nouosq̃ adire populos, regiones postremo ante hac incognitas penetrare. Fit celeriter de re hac uerbum regi, qui tum regum lusitanorum emulatione, tum studio huiusmodi nouarum rerum & glorie, que sibi ac posteris posset de ea re accedere pellectus diu re cum Columbo tractata, nauigia tandem exornari duo iubet quibus soluens Columbus ad insulaiq̃ fortunatas nauigans cursum instituit paululum ab occidentali linea sinister inter hibicum.s. ac zephirum remotior tamen longe a li̅ bico & ferme zephiro iunctus. Vbi copulrium dierum cursus exactus est & computata ratione cognitum quadragies se se iam cente na passuum millia esse permensum recto cursu ceteri quidem spe omni lapsi: referendum iam esse pedem & cursum in contra iam partem flectendum contendebant, ipse uero in incepto persistere & quantum coniectura assequi posset promittere haud longius diei unius nauigatione abesse uel continentes aliquas terras, uel insulas. Haud abfuit dictis fides. Quippe sequēti luce terras nescio quas conspicati naute eum laudibus efferre, & maximam in hominis opinione fiduciam reponere. Insule erant ut postea cognitum est ferme innumere, non longe a continentibus quibusdam terris ut prese ferebat aspectus. Ex huiusmodi insulis nonnullas animaduersum fer re homines incultos cognomento caniballos, humanis ad esum carnes minime abhorrentes, ac uicinos populos latrociniis infestantes, cauaris quibusdam magnarum arborum truncis quibus ad proximas trahicientes insulas homines quali lupi in cibum uenentur. Nec defuit fortuna ex his unam nauiculis cum suis huiusmodi ductoribus comprehendendi .idq̃ haud incruenta pugna qui postmodum usq̃ in hispaniam sospites uecti sunt. Que prima est inuenta ex insulis hispana est nuncupata. In eaq̃ inuenti mortales innumeri pau pertate & nuditate conspicui, quos primo nutribus ad congressum comiter inuitatos donisq̃ allectos, ubi propius accesserūt, facile ap parebat & dissimilem suo candorem, & habitum & inauditum antea ad eos accessum, ceteraq̃ omnia quali e celo aduenientium obstu pescere & mirari, quippe color illis lōge dissimilis nostro, minime tamen niger sed auro persimilis, lacerna illis collo pēdebat heretatq̃ pectori contegens pudenda quali uelamen, cui modicum annexū esset aurum, eaq̃ cōmunis manū & feminarū, no amplius uirginū.

Lower part of a page of the Polyglot Psalter published at Genoa in 1516. This page presents on four columns the original Hebrew text, a verbal translation into Latin, the Latin version of the Vulgate and the Greek version of the Septuagint. On the opposite page there are likewise four columns, presenting the Arab version, the Aramaic Targum with a literal Latin version and Latin glosses on the Psalms. The gloss at the bottom of the page reproduced above contains the first mention in Jewish literature of Columbus' discovery of America.

the first time the Aramaic version (Targum) to the entire Bible and several commentaries which had not been printed before. A second edition of the Rabbinical Bible appeared in 1524/5 edited by Jacob ben Hayyim of Tunis. Bomberg was also the first to print complete editions of the Babylonian and Palestinian Talmuds. His edition of the Babylonian Talmud became the archetype of all subsequent Talmud editions to this day, in respect of the pagination and the arrangement of the commentaries. As type-setters and correctors Bomberg employed only Jews.

Owing to the lively demand for Hebrew books in many countries, printing was good business and it is no wonder that there was soon a keen competition among several Christian printers of Hebrew books, for instance Marco Antonio Giustiniani and Aloisio Bragadini, leading even to law-suits before ecclesiastical tribunals. Those rivalries were among the causes which led to the burning of the Talmud and other Hebrew books in Rome and elsewhere in Italy in 1553, and to the temporary interdiction of the printing of Hebrew books.

For the sake of curiosity it may be mentioned that a polyglot Psalter produced by Agostino Giustiniani, Bishop of Nebbio, at Genoa in 1516 is the first document of Jewish literature to mention, in the marginal comment to Psalm XIX, the discovery of America by Columbus.

In northern Europe, too, there were Hebrew printing-presses managed by Christian scholars, particularly in Germany.

On the other hand, Jews began to participate in non-Jewish printing to some extent, as early as the fifteenth century. Thus, the fourth edition of Dante's *Divina Commedia*, produced in Naples in 1477, was the work of an anonymous Jewish printer. Later on, Gershom Soncino printed some memorable books in Italian, Latin, and even in Greek. The Portuguese Marrano Abraham Usque, who escaped to Italy and established, a printing press at Ferrara towards the middle of the sixteenth century, published books in Spanish and Portuguese. It was he who printed in 1553, a famous Spanish Bible translation, known as the Ferrara Bible.

THE JEWS IN EASTERN EUROPE

Many fugitives from persecution in Germany inevitably made their way to the lands of greater security farther east. Like the German merchants of the period (who brought with them to eastern Europe their native brand of anti-Jewish sentiment) — the Jews were also attracted eastward by the great commercial opportunities which opened up on this almost virgin soil.

One of the countries where fugitives from Germany found new homes was Hungary. Here there had been a Jewish population since Roman times. There is documentary evidence that there was, in the ninth century, a Jewish cemetery at Sopron (Odenburg), where recently remains of a medieval synagogue, too, have come to light. We have knowledge of other Jewish communities in Hungary in the tenth and eleventh centuries. The Jews in Hungary were not affected by the bloodshed which marked the Crusades in other European countries, and immigrants from the west increased their numbers in the course of the twelfth century. While the kings were friendly towards their Jewish subjects, who were contributing to the economic development of the country, and even employed Jews as financial agents, the clergy fomented hate against the unbelievers, and the nobles resented privileges being granted to anybody who did not belong to their class. The pressure from both quarters progressively increased during the thirteenth century and culminated, in 1279, in the introduction of the Jewish badge. This decree was ordered by the Council of Buda, convoked by Pope Nicholas III and presided over by his legate. Nevertheless, the kings of the Arpad dynasty continued to protect the Jews and to avail themselves of their industriousness and their financial talent. After the extinction of this dynasty in 1301, the kings who succeeded one another on the Hungarian throne followed, as a general rule, the same benevolent policy, down to the early sixteenth century, when the Turks defeated the Hungarian army at the battle of Mohacs (1526) and conquered the greater part of the country. Of course, the general rule was not without sad exceptions. The Jews suffered heavily in 1349, when the Black Death reached Hungary. In 1360 there was a temporary expulsion of the Jews. There were, in the fifteenth century, accusations of ritual murder with the usual issue of Jews being burnt at the stake. This notwithstanding, it can be fairly stated that, on the whole, the Jews suffered less in Hungary than in the western countries of Europe.

Another country which attracted Jews from the west was Bohemia. This country did not prove a safe shelter during the Crusades. But in the thirteenth century the Jews recovered under the protection of the Bohemian crown, although, as everywhere else, the clergy, did its best to incite the people against them. False accusations were not a rarity in the fourteenth and fifteenth centuries and the Armleder gangs devastated a number of communities in southern Bohemia. However, despite

Detail of the 13th century portal from the Altneuschul Synagoge at Prague (from the Guide to the Jewish Museum in Prague, 1957).

The tombstone of Rabbi Judah Löw ben Bezalel in the Jewish Cemetery at Prague. Rabbi Judah Löw (1520–1609), known also as the "Maharal of Prague", a famous rabbinical author and cabbalist, was for over thirty years the recognized spiritual leader of the Prague community. He was considered as a miracle-worker and numerous legends are associated with his personality.

all their difficulties, periodic attacks and spoliations, the Jewish communities held their ground in many places throughout the country, particularly in the capital. Prague with its lovely synagogues – the already mentioned *Altneuschul* was the most famous – its far-famed *Judenstadt*, and its spacious cemetery, where so many great scholars lay buried, was for centuries one of the greatest Jewish communities of Europe.

225

But it was the Kingdom of Poland, then extending from the Baltic to the Black Sea, which attracted the largest number of Jewish settlers. Jews had certainly been living in this area from remote antiquity, as is shown by the ancient inscriptions in Crimea, which go back to the first century C.E. In the tenth and eleventh centuries, the country was still economically undeveloped and badly in need of traders and craftsmen. The immigration of Jews in increasing numbers began in the twelfth century. The regional princes encouraged them to come and afforded them all possible protection and help. Jews were probably the first mint-masters in Poland, and some of the oldest Polish coinage of the thirteenth century bears inscriptions in Hebrew.

Later on, the immigration from Germany overwhelmed and absorbed the autochtonous Jewish element, with the result that Polish Jewry became to a great extent Germanized, at least in language and intellectual life. The language they spoke (Yiddish) was based upon medieval High German, although its vocabulary had been considerably enriched by innumerable words and locutions taken over from Hebrew. The Jewish immigrants from Germany also transplanted to their new country their zeal for the Talmud, which was studied here with an intensity hardly known in any other land or age.

The settlement of German Jews was sedulously encouraged, not only by regional Polish princes, but also, after the renewed unification of Poland in the fourteenth century, by the Polish sovereigns, who conferred on them comprehensive charters of privileges and protection. A model charter of protection was granted by Boleslaw V (1227–1279) in the year 1264. This charter laid down the judicial procedure in law-suits among Jews and between Jews and Christians, assured Jewish creditors full legal protection, and guaranteed Jewish life and property and the inviolability of synagogues and Jewish cemeteries. Accusations of ritual murder had to be proved by at least six witnesses, three of them Jews. King Casimir the Great (1333–1370) confirmed this charter in 1334 and, by the Statute of Kalisz, extended it validity, originally confined to the Principality of Great Poland, to the entire territory of the Polish kingdom. Jews were to be found in almost every village, where they kept the inns for the peasants and administered the estates of the nobles. Inevitably the Polish Jews adopted many of the habits, customs, and folkways of the

Polish coins minted by Jewish mintmasters at the beginning of the 13th century, bearing Hebrew inscriptions. These are silver coins struck on one side only (the type known in numismatics as "bracteates")

The "Rema" Synagogue at Cracow. Rema is the abbreviated name of Rabbi Moses Isserles (1520–1572) famous for his glosses called "Mappah" ("The Tablecloth") on Joseph Caro's religious code "Shulhan Arukh", adapting this code, based on Sephardic tradition, to the Ashkenazi practice.

Types of Polish Jews in their characteristic garb (from L. Hollaenderski, Les Israélites de Pologne).

Polish people. The normal dress of the local aristocracy, with long robes and fur-trimmed round hats, became their characteristic garb. Their religious and intellectual life, however, remained unaffected by the external assimilation. The Jews of Poland were famous for their devotion to study. There was no town without a rabbi and almost none without a Talmudic school *(yeshivah)*. Nearly every householder was in a way a scholar and every house that could afford it had a teacher for the children. No wonder that Poland became, from the sixteenth century on, the greatest center of Jewish scholarship in the world, producing famous rabbis, such as Shalom Shakhna, principal of the great Lubin Yeshivah, Moses Isserles, whose annotations to Joseph Caro's ritual code *Shulhan Arukh* to this day regulate the religious practice of all the Jews of

The Synagogue of Staro-Konstantin, Podolia, in the style of the fortress-synagogues of the 17th century

The fortress-synagogue of Luck, Poland, built 1626 (from a 19th century engraving).

Detail from the decoration of the wooden synagogue of Kapust, near Mohilev, 18th century.

228

Central and East European extraction (Ashkenazim) throughout the world, and Solomon Luria, whose chief merit is his painstaking philological study of the Talmud with a view to determining the most accurate texts.

The beautiful wooden synagogues of Poland, with high stepped roofs reminiscent of Far-Eastern pagodas, were unlike those anywhere else in the world. While, on the one hand, they reflected the style of the local churches, on the other, they possibly perpetuated the architectural tradition of the pagan temples of the area.

Another type of Polish synagogue was built of stone and presented many of the features of a military fortress with battlements and loop-holes. Their construction was authorized by the sovereigns on the express condition that they could be used not only for worship, but also for defence in case of enemy attack.

The frescos inside these buildings, sometimes admirably executed, curiously link up with the mural art of the classical period, which we have already seen in connection with the third century synagogue at Dura-Europos.

The Polish synagogues also served as centers of communal life and administration, in some cases even being provided with cells and stocks for the punishment of recalcitrants.

Wooden synagogue of Tebaki, near Sokol (now U.S.S.R.). Drawing by G. Loukomski (Roth Collection). A fine example of the pagoda-type with stepped roofs.

In due course, Polish Jewry developed one of the most remarkable instruments in the entire record of Jewish autonomous life in Diaspora history, the Council of the Four Lands. The Kingdom of Poland originated from the union of initially independent principalities. After the establishment of the Kingdom, the various regional organizations of the Jewish communities endeavored to set up a co-ordinating institution for the protection of their interests and the equitable distribution of the fiscal burden. The Council of the Four Lands (Great Poland, Little Poland, Podolia and Volhynia) was constituted in 1580 and served, between the sixteenth and eighteenth centuries, as a quasi-parliament of the Jews. At first, it met once every year; later it assembled semi-annually, at Jaroslav in Galicia in summer and at Lublin during the yearly local fair in the winter. The delegates apportioned the taxes among the communities, dealt with problems concerning the exercise of commerce, and settled communal and educational matters. Lithuania had, from 1623 on, a separate Jewish organization. But the two Councils often collaborated in matters of general Jewish interest. The economic degradation of Polish Jewry during the eighteenth century undermined the authority of the Council of the Four Lands, and in 1764 it was officially abolished by a vote of the Polish Parliament.

The house of Emmanuel (Simha Menahem), court-physician to John III Sobieski (1624–1696) King of Poland, at Lvov (Lemberg, now in U.S.S.R.).

Page from the Minute Book of the Council of the Four Lands.

THE SPANISH EXILES
IN NORTH-AFRICA

Many of the exiles from Spain and some of the few who managed to flee from Portugal found refuge in Morocco and the adjacent parts of North Africa, attracted by the brief and therefore inexpensive crossing. They were despoiled first by callous ship-captains and then by greedy sheikhs. However a considerable number ultimately managed to find new homes.

Here they found themeselves in an environment, in many ways similar to that in which their ancestors had lived in Spain in the so-called Golden Age under Moslem rule, four or five centuries before. Everywhere they encountered settled Jewish communities which had known better times. Jewish learning had flourished in North Africa during the tenth, eleventh, and first half of the twelfth centuries. The victory of the fanatically intolerant Almohade dynasty had put an end to the thriving Jewish life in North Africa, and the Jews had never recovered from this blow. To these stagnating communities the Spanish exiles brought Jewish learning and European culture. They settled chiefly in towns and once they had overcome the initial — often harrowing — difficulties, they formed a sort of aristocracy among the local Jews. Although they now lived in an Arabic-speaking environment, they continued to speak Spanish among themselves and have retained that vernacular to the present time.

The Jewish quarter of Tetuan, Morocco. The Jewish community of Tetuan, reinforced at the end of the 15th century by exiles from Spain, was for a long time, particularly in the 18th century, the largest in Morocco.

The interior of a Jewish house at Marrakesh, Morocco, (from a painting by G. Beauclerk.)

Jewish girl from Algiers. Drawing by B. Roubaud.

Some of the exiles did well as merchants and factors, especially in the coastal cities, in which they acted as intermediaries for the trade with Europe, chiefly exporting sugar in exchange for textiles. But even so, their situation was, on the whole, far from enviable. They were herded into fetid, overcrowded ghettos, known down to the present day as *mellahs*, and were not allowed to acquire houses or landed property outside these quarters. They were constantly exposed to the ill-treatment of the populace and the authorities and subjected to senseless degradations. They were forced to act as executioners and forbidden to wear white or colored clothing, so that long black robes and close-fitting skull-caps became the characteristic Jewish garb in many areas, particularly in Morocco. Farther east, however, in Tunisia, picturesque medieval Spanish costumes, especially among women, remained in common use almost to our own time.

Now and then, a Jew would achieve great wealth and even rise to a high position as the treasurer and confidential adviser to the ruler, sometimes serving as his ambassador to foreign powers. But, in general, the decline of such a personage would be rapid and catastrophic, as had commonly been the case in medieval Spain.

Jewish merchant from Algiers.
Drawing by Calix.

In the early sixteenth century, Spain conquered a number of regions on the North African coast, with a devastating effect for the Jewish communities there. Many of the exiles were obliged to resume their wanderings and most of them travelled to Palestine or other Turkish provinces. Among them was Abraham Zacuto, previously encountered as court-astrologer to King Manoel the Fortunate of Portugal. He had temporarily settled in Tunis and had completed there his chronicle *Sefer Yuhasin* (The Book of Genealogies), a memorable history of rabbinic scholarship in Europe.

A measure of security was restored to the Jews of North Africa in the second half of the sixteenth century, when the Turkish Empire extended its rule over the entire territory. However, in general, they led a wretched existence down to the middle of the nineteenth century, when European intervention caused some improvement.

Young Jewish girl from Marrakesh (from a drawing by G. Beauclerk).

233

THE SPANISH EXILES
IN TURKEY

Most important in every way was the body of Spanish exiles which found its way further east, to Turkey. Having conquered Constantinople half a century previously, in 1453, the Turkish Empire was now at the height of its power. The warlike Turks, deficient in the handicrafts, trade, and other arts of peace, ruled over a mosaic of recalcitrant subject peoples. To this ruling Turkish minority the Jewish immigrants, on whose loyalty they could rely and who excelled in precisely these callings which they themselves so regrettably lacked, were extremely welcome. Sultan Bayazid II is said to have exclaimed once, " What ! You call this Ferdinand wise, who depopulated his own dominions in order to enrich mine ?"

In Turkey, the Jews were, of course, subjected to the restrictions imposed by Moslem law on non-believers, but generally these were not enforced too strictly. Consequently, large Jewish settlements sprang up or were renewed all over the vast territories of the Ottoman Empire. The number of Spanish exiles (Jews and Marranos) who settled in Turkey at the end of the fifteenth and the beginning of the sixteenth century is estimated at about one hundred thousand. About forty thousand of them made their homes in Constantinople, where forty-four synagogues are reported to have existed in the sixteenth century. About twenty thousand settled in Salonica where they were relatively even more prominent than in the capital; it became a predominantly Jewish town, as it was to continue to be for centuries, almost until it was obliterated by the Nazis. Other important communities developed in Adrianople, Smyrna, Brusa and in many other places in the Balkans and Asia Minor.

In all these communities, the language, dress, balladry, folk-lore, lullabies, habits, and even dishes of medieval Spain were perpetuated with pathetic nostalgia down to our own day. In modern times, Spanish scholars went there to study Spanish life and speech of the fifteenth century.

Everywhere the Jews filled all walks of life. They almost monopolized the textile industry in all its branches. They were not only great merchants, but also the petty traders and craftsmen. In Salonica they were the fishermen and the harbor-workers. Down to the twentieth century, no ship that put into this port could be discharged on the Sabbath or on Jewish holidays.

The Jews were, of course, physicians and some of them gained political influence through their position as court-doctors, as, for instance, Joseph Hamon at the court of Sultan Bayazid II, and his son, Moses Hamon, as physician to Selim I and Suleiman the Magnificent.

The western immigrants were, moreover, extremely useful to the Sultans, owing to their knowledge of the languages and the circumstances of Christian Europe. A succession of them, consequently, played a significant part in the affairs of the Sublime Porte.

Turkish Jewish physician of the 16th century (from a 16th century woodcut).

The influx of Spanish immigrants brought in its wake a revival of Jewish scholarship in Turkey. Of the many illustrious names, a few must be cited. In Constantinople Elijah Mizrahi served as Chief Rabbi of the Turkish Empire. He was a a man of vast erudition and showed his tolerance by advocating less stringent treatment of the Karaites. He was the author of a famous super-commentary to the Bible commentary of Rashi.

In Salonica, Rabbi Joseph Taytazak represented the mystic and ascetic current of Jewish learning. One of his pupils, the cabbalist and poet Solomon Alkabetz, went to Palestine and joined there the prominent circle of Jewish mystics in Safed.

Fille Iuifue d'Andrinople.

Jewish girl from Adrianople
(from a 16th century woodcut)

The rapidly spreading preoccupation with mysticism made the aggadic
element of the Talmud, with its numerous reassuring legends and traditions on the Messianic redemption particularly popular. To meet the
demand of the simple man, who was impatient to immerse himself in the
Aggada without having to work through the intricacies of the legal texts
of the Halakha, another scholar from Salonica, Jacob ben Habib,
systematically excerpted and collected the aggadic material of the
Talmud in his *Eyn Yaakov*, a work still enjoying general currency.
The reign of the Sultan Suleiman the Magnificent (1520–1566) marked
the heyday of the Jewish community in the Turkish Empire. Their
flourishing economic situation could not fail to irritate their commercial
competitors, the Greek and Armenian merchants. In 1545 an attempt

was made by these circles in Amasia (Asia Minor) to arouse popular animosity against the Jews by staging a ritual murder affair. Several Jews lost their lives, owing to the zeal of the Turkish judge, but the Sultan's physician Moses Hamon obtained from his master a decree calculated to forestall further attempts of this nature in the future. The decree provided that local tribunals were henceforth forbidden to deal with such cases and that the Sultan himself was the only competent judiciary authority to hear accusations of ritual murder.

During Suleiman's reign, another Jew embarked on an outstanding career. Born a Marrano in Portugal, Micas João, later Joseph Nasi, was the nephew of the international banker Francisco Mendes, who had his head-office at Lisbon and branches in Flanders and France. After the death of Francisco, his widow Beatrice de Luna, who was to achieve fame as Gracia Mendes, thought it advisable to leave Portugal. In 1536 she went to Antwerp, which was then a great Marrano center, together with her daughter Reyna and her nephew João Micas. The whole family was animated by the desire to return publicly to Judaism, and their ultimate goal was Turkey, the only country where this was safely

Doña Gracia Nasi. Medal executed (about 1553) by Pastorino de' Pastorini in Ferrara (Musée de Cluny, Paris).

possible. However, settling the firm's affairs took many years. In 1544 Gracia moved to Venice, where she became involved in difficulties with the *Signoria*, when her intention to proceed to Turkey and profess Judaism became known. She was imprisoned for a while, and upon her release went to Ferrara, where the spirit was more liberal and she could abjure the Christian faith. In 1552 she finally proceeded to Constantinople. Here, her nephew João Micas joined her two years later, embracing Judaism publicly and adopting the name Nasi, which had been the original name of the Mendes family before its conversion. He then married his beauful cousin Reyna.

Joseph Nasi soon occupied a leading position in Turkey's Jewish community. At the same time he stood high in the Sultan's favor. Together with his redoubtable aunt, he organized an amazing underground system to assist Marranos to escape from Portugal. Their influence at court became manifest in 1556, when Pope Paul IV ordered the arrest of

Dedication of the "Ferrara Bible", a Spanish translation of the Bible printed by Abraham Usque at Ferrara in 1553, to Doña Gracia Nasi the Elder.

Prologo a la muy magnifica Señora
Doña Gracia Naci.

O parescia razon (muy magnifica Señora) que auiendose de ymprimir la Biblia en nuestra lengua Española (traduzida del Hebreo palabra por palabra obra tan rara y hasta nuestros tiempos nunca vista) fuesse a parar en personas de cuyo fauor no se pudiesse valer sino a alguna tan noble y magnanima que a su nobleza acrecentasse ornamiento. Por la qual causa la quesimos dirigir a vuestra merced como a persona que sus meritos entre todos los nuestros siempre tuuieron el mas sublime lugar: assi por sus grandezas lo merescer como por que la propria naturaleza y amor dela patria nos pone esta obligacion tan deuida; vuestra merced la acepte con la voluntad que nos se la offrecemos y la fauoresca y defienda conel animo que siempre fauorescio todos los que su ayuda hasta oy ympetraron. Y por que su nobleza naturalmente es acostumbrada a estos officios quedamos seguros de algun recelo que por la diuersidad de juizios podriamos tener: pidiendo que su memoria no se oluide de nuestro desseo que tan ynclinado es a su seruicio. Nuestro Señor por muy largos años guarde su persona y prospere su magnifico estado.

Seruidores de vuestra merced.

Yom Tob Atias y Abraham Usque.

Turkish Jewish merchant at Venice in the 17th century (from a drawing in the Museo Correr, Venice).

all the Marranos living at Ancona. At Gracia Mendes' request, the Sultan summoned the Pope to release all Marranos who were Turkish subjects, threatening reprisals against Christians living in Turkey, if he did not comply. The Pope yielded, but took his revenge on the remaining Marranos and had twenty-four of them burnt publicly. In retaliation for this outrage, the Jews proclaimed, at the instigation of Doña Gracia, a boycott against the port of Ancona. It was not her fault that this manifestation of Jewish solidarity and economic power finally collapsed.

The liberality of Don Joseph and his aunt was proverbial. They built synagogues and patronized Hebrew literature. His attempt to restore Jewish autonomy in Palestine will be described in the next chapter. As the boon companion and confidential adviser of Suleiman's successor, Selim II (1556–1574), his influence on Turkish policies was considerable. The Sultan made him Duke of Naxos and bestowed on him the Cyclades in the Aegean as a life-long fief. Since the Turkish conquest of Cyprus in 1571 was partly due to Nasi's prompting, the Sultan had wished to make him king of the island. This appointment, however, was foiled by the Grand Vizier Mohammed Sokolli.

Don Joseph's brilliant political career ended with the death of his friend and patron Selim II. During his last years, spent in retirement, he continued generously to support Jewish scholars and Talmudic schools. When he died in 1579, his widow continued his philanthropic work.

Don Joseph's career was the most spectacular, but he was not the only Jew to achieve distinction in Turkish politics. The physician Solomon Ashkenazi (1520–1602), an Italian Jew who had spent many years in Poland, at the courts of Sigismund I and II, became the adviser of the Grand Vizier Sokolli. He opposed the anti-Venetian policy of Don Joseph Nasi and was sent as Turkish ambassador, to conclude peace with reluctant Venice, where he was received with great honor. While representing Turkish interests, he also had the welfare of his fellow-Jews at heart. Owing to his intercession, the Signoria desisted from a projected expulsion of the Jews from Venetian territory. Ashkenazi was also busily engaged in international intrigues and twice tried to sway the elections to the throne of Poland.

Another remarkable Jewish statesman in Turkey was Solomon Abenaes (Ibn Yaish : 1520—1603). A Portuguese Marrano, he abandoned the name Alvaro Mendes and publicly professed Judaism upon his arrival in Turkey. Following in the path of Joseph Nasi, he advised successive sultans on foreign affairs, of which he had an intimate knowledge, and was made Duke of Mytilene. He was one of the architects of the Anglo-Turkish alliance against Spain at the time of the Great Armada, in 1588, and negotiated with Queen Elizabeth of England, almost as if he were an independent potentate.

NEW SETTLEMENT
IN PALESTINE

Many of the Spanish exiles, convinced that their sufferings betokened the dawn of Messianic days, turned their steps to Palestine. So did, later on, Marranos who felt that their sin in dissembling their faith could be expiated only on the all-atoning soil of the Holy Land. The attraction exercised by Palestine grew all the more after the Turkish conquest in 1517.

The Jewish settlement here had been almost obliterated during the period of the Crusades and the Mongol invasion in 1259–1260. Peace was not restored until the defeat of the Mongols by the Egyptian Mamelukes who overran the country. The Jews could now put their minds to reconstruction. In 1267, Rabbi Moses ben Nahman (known as "Ramban" or Nahmanides), the protagonist of the famous religious disputation at Barcelona, came to Palestine, and devoted himself to the task of renewing the Jewish settlement in Jerusalem. He induced the

Jerusalem in the 16th century, from a contemporary engraving.

Ezechielis. v.
Hæc est Ierusalem, Ego eam in medio Gentium posui, et in eius circuitu terras.

240

Jaffa in the year 1483 (from B. von Breidenbach, Peregrinationes ad Terram Sanctam, 1486).

dispersed Jerusalem Jews to return to the city, restored and inaugurated anew a destroyed synagogue, henceforth called after his name, and founded a Talmudic School which attracted students from distant places. Since this revival, the Jerusalem community has continued to our days without interruption. For the time being, however, the nervous Moslem rulers did their best to restrict the number of Jews authorized to live in the Holy City, and the Jewish settlement therefore concentrated mainly in the north of the country.

A community of some importance existed in the thirteenth century in Acre (Acco), one of the last strongholds of the Crusaders on Palestinian soil. Jewish immigrants from Europe had settled here. In the middle of the century the opponent of the renegade Nicholas Donin in the disputation of Paris, Rabbi Jehiel of Paris, came to Acre and transformed the community into a center of Jewish learning. The Talmudic school founded by him was known among the Jews of Europe as the "Paris Yeshivah." As the thirteenth century neared its end, the Mamelukes dealt the Crusaders a final blow. In 1291 Acre was conquered and destroyed by Al-Ashraf. The Jews left the ruined city and many fled to Safed in Upper Galilee.

During the fourteenth century the Palestinian Jews enjoyed a relatively quiet period and there was a constant influx of Jewish immigrants from Europe, where the Jews were cruelly harassed at that time. Among the illustrious immigrants was the physician Estori ha-Parhi, originally from Provence. After the expulsion of the Jews from France in 1306, he spent a few years in Spain and then proceeded to Palestine, where he settled at Beth Shean, in the Jordan valley south of Lake Tiberias. He toured the country extensively for years and, then wrote his famous book *Kaftor va-Ferah*, in which he laid the foundations of the geography and archaeology of Palestine.

In the fifteenth century the situation in Palestine deteriorated. The century opened with the raid of Timur Lang's Mongols, which sowed destruction everywhere. Moreover, Mameluke rule grew more and more burdensome and tyrannical. Heavy special contributions which were levied on the Jewish population, composed mostly of petty merchants, pedlars, and artisans, caused progressive impoverishment. Nevertheless, the Jewish population in Palestine was steadily increasing, owing to persecutions in Europe. One of the immigrants, Obadiah di Bertinoro, an Italian scholar who achieved great fame by his commentary on the Mishnah, exercised a decisive influence on the development of the Jewish settlement in Palestine, particularly in the Holy City. When he reached Jerusalem in 1488, this community, which had dwindled to about seventy

Safed and Meron (painted by an anonymous painter, about 1900). To the right, the town of Safed; to the left the mausoleum of Rabbi Simon bar Jochai at Meron.

families, was heavily in debt and the internal situation was chaotic. Bertinoro, whose fame was already well-established, assumed leadership, reconciled quarreling factions, inspired new courage and hope, and, moreover, succeeded in making favorable arrangements with the Egyptian authorities. In his day, some of the special taxes imposed on the Jews were abolished and restrictions on immigration lifted. Bertinoro's activity prepared the ground for the impending immigration of Spanish exiles, and he may, therefore, be considered the father of modern Jewish settlement in Palestine.

Had the Turkish conquest of Palestine taken place a quarter of a century earlier, the greater part of the Spanish exiles would probably have chosen to take advantage of Turkish hospitality in the Holy Land, preferring it to any other place in the Ottoman Empire. But even so, the expulsion of the Jews from Spain meant a substantial increase in the size of the Jewish population in Palestine. In 1495 there were already two hundred families in Jerusalem.

The immigration of Spanish Jews increased considerably after the conquest of Palestine by Sultan Selim I in 1517. However, despite the fascinating attraction of Jerusalem, only relatively few immigrants settled in the Holy City, which was always liable to be a hotbed of Moslem and Christian fanaticism. Most new-comers preferred the quieter atmosphere of Galilee. Consequently, in the sixteenth century, the greatest Jewish settlement was in the north, in the lovely and then important city of Safed.

Besides merchants and artisans, Jewish scholars gathered in this town, which soon became a spiritual center of moment. A Talmudic school was founded and directed by a remarkable Spanish exile, Rabbi Jacob Berab, who made an attempt to revive the Sanhedrin, to serve, as in ancient times, as the central religious authority of the whole Jewish people. His proposal, however, aroused vehement opposition, mainly among his colleagues in Jerusalem, and failed to materialize.

Safed had an additional attraction for devotees of the Cabbala because it is situated in the area associated with the great mystical classic, the Zohar, and near the grave – at Meron – of its reputed second century author, Rabbi Simon ben Johai. Hence it soon became the city of the mystics — "a revivalist camp in perpetual being." It is associated above all, with the names of Moses Cordovero (1522-1570) and Isaac Luria (1534–1572).

The Torah Shrine of the "Ari" Synagogue at Safed. The synagogue was built at the end of the 16th century on the place where the "Ari" (the Cabbalist Rabbi Isaac Luria), used to sit and discuss with his disciples, outside the town.

242

Moses Cordovero was the son of Spanish exiles and the brother-in-law, disciple and friend of the cabbalist and poet Solomon Alkabetz, the author of the beautiful liturgical hymn "Lekha Dodi", still recited on the eve of Sabbath in all synagogues. As a systematic thinker, Cordovero expounded his mystic philosophy in his book *Pardes Rimmonim* ("The Garden of Pomegranates"). But he was also a visionary who tried to reach the ultimate truth by ecstatic experiences.

Rabbi Isaac (Ashkenazi) Luria, known as the "Ari" from the initials of his name, was the founder of the so-called new or Lurianic Cabbala. Born in Jerusalem to a family of German Jews, he received his education in Cairo and, following his mystic impulse, he spent years in solitude on the banks of the Nile. In 1569 he returned to Palestine and joined the circle of mystics in Safed in the following year. The central point of his doctrine was a fervent Messianism. He taught that repentance, ascetic practices and the concentration of all the spiritual energy in prayer can hasten the advent of the Messianic redemption. Luria died at the age of thirty-eight, without having committed his doctrines to writing. His teachings were disseminated by his disciples, particularly by Hayyim Vital ("Calabrese") and exercised a profound influence on Jewish thinking, life, and ritual.

But Safed, the stronghold of mysticism, was at the same time the center of sober rabbinic learning. Rabbi Joseph Caro (1488–1575), himself a mystic, became immortal as the last in the series of great rabbinical codifiers. His non-mystical code, the *Shulhan Arukh*, has not been

The tomb of Rabbi Joseph Caro (1488–1575), the author of the "Shulhan Arukh", in the cemetery of Safed.

Tiberias in the seventeenth century. Since the 3rd century, when it was the seat of the Patriarchate, Tiberias has been one of the centers of spiritual life in Palestine. Here are the traditional burial-places of many illustrious Jewish scholars, among them Rabbi Akibah and Rabbi Moses ben Maimon, and it has, therefore, always been considered as one of the four Holy Cities of Palestine.

superseded and has remained to this day the ultimate authority in matters of religious practice for the Jews everywhere.

In the third quarter of the sixteenth century, Joseph Nasi, Duke of Naxos, obtained from the Sultan a grant of Tiberias and the surrounding area, to serve as the nucleus of an autonomous Jewish colony. He rebuilt and fortified the town, planted mulberry trees to develop silk-culture and invited European Jews to come and settle there. For various reasons, including the opposition of the local Arab population, the experiment had only a qualified success. But Tiberias was soon to take its place among the four recognized Jewish Holy Cities, by the side of Jerusalem, Safed and Hebron.

In Hebron, a sizeable community maintained the association with the City of the Tombs of the Patriarchs, until a shocking massacre at Arab hands in 1929.

Letter of recommendation for a "Shadar", an emissary sent abroad to collect funds for the Communities of the Holy Cities (Jerusalem, Safed, Hebron and Tiberias). This letter, dated 1811, is signed by the Rabbis of Hebron, who recommend the emissary Rabbi Israel ha-Levi to the Community of Carpi, Italy (General Archive for Jewish History, Jerusalem).

Haim Isaac Carigal (1733–1777), Palestinian Rabbi who traveled widely as an emissary of the Holy Cities, visited several times the British Colonies in North-America and died in the island of Barbados (Painting preserved in the Library of Yale University).

The Holy Cities sent out their emissaries to almost the entire world for the purpose of collecting funds for their maintenance. These emissaries, the so-called *Shadarim*, found a warm welcome in all the communities they visited, bringing to Jews everywhere something of the atmosphere and knowledge of the Holy Land. They were generally saintly men and some of them were outstanding scholars. One of them, Hayyim Joseph David Azulai, although belonging to a later period (the second half of the eighteenth century) deserves special mention. A mystic and, at the same time, a learned bibliographer, he left an invaluable account of his travels through Sephardi communities all over the world, including London. His contemporary, Isaac Carigal, even went to the British Colonies in North America twice and preached a memorable Pentecostal sermon in the synagogue at Newport, Rhode Island.

THE COMMUNITIES
OF THE ORIENT

The Great Synagogue of Bagdad.

East of Turkey, where Jewish life had so greatly flourished in former generations, there was, in this period, a good deal that was of interest, but hardly anything of importance for the general course of Jewish history.

In Iraq, Jewish life had recovered only slowly from the ravages caused by the disastrous Mongol rule. After the Turkish conquest of Bagdad in 1638, the condition of the Jews in Iraq was, as a general rule, similar to that of their co-religionists in other parts of the Ottoman Empire. Still, Iraq was a remote province in which the local governors wielded arbitrary power. Avaricious pashas were always on the look-out for any signs of prosperity in the Jewish community, and often found ways to remove those of its members who had been financially successful, appropriating their fortunes for themselves. Nevertheless, the community, with its ancient synagogues and shrines, was at least able to maintain its existence and even to expand slowly. Only the virulent anti-Jewish campaign which followed the establishment of the State of Israel in 1948 brought about its almost complete liquidation by emigration to the new country.

The very ancient Persian Jewry suffered heavily towards the middle of the twelfth century, as a consequence of the Messianic agitation of David Alroy. In the thirteenth century the Mongol conquest cruelly affected the Jews, although some of the Mongol khans manifested a certain amount of sympathy towards them. Their situation hardly improved in the sixteenth century, when Persia achieved independence under the rule of the intolerant Safawid dynasty, which raised the Shiite denomination of Islam to the rank of the Persian state religion. Considered impure by the Shiite clergy, the Jews could only continue a lethargic existence. In the first half of the seventeenth century, under the Shahs Abbas I and II,

Glass synagogue lamp with Hebrew inscription, Damascus 1694 (Jewish Museum, London).

Oriental glass bottle with Hebrew inscription, 18th century (Victoria and Albert Museum, London).

Page from a Persian-Jewish illuminated manuscript with miniatures on Persian style (Library of the Jewish Theological Seminary, New-York).

there were violent persecutions. Books were confiscated, scholars executed, and Jews forced to profess Islam. The hostile policy towards the Jews continued unmitigated under the successors of the Safawid rulers, and even the first half of the nineteenth century witnessed new massacres and forcible conversions. A great part of the Jews of Meshed were then driven into a Marrano-like existence as Jedid-al-Islam (Neo-Mohammedans).

Persian Jewry was, however, throughout this time, unique in the Moslem world, producing, in the spirit of the land, illuminated manuscripts of a high degree of competence, wholly Persian in style and execution.

In South Arabia there existed a large, isolated community of Yemenite Jews, largely in the capital city of Sana, but also in scores of smaller places. They were God-fearing, hard-working people, steeped in an environment not unlike that of their ancestors of Bible times. According to their own traditions, they had been living in the area since the time of the destruction of the First Temple.

In the fifth century, one of the kings of the Himyarite dynasty had become a convert to Judaism. His son, Joseph Dhu-Nuwas, was eager to disseminate the Jewish faith among his subjects and went even so far as to persecute the Christians in his kingdom. This kindled the wrath of the Byzantine Emperor and upon his instigation, the Negus of Ethiopia set out for Yemen to avenge the offense. He defeated Dhu-Nuwas, who lost his kingdom and his life, and thus put an end to Jewish rule in Yemen.

After the Moslem conquest in the seventh century, the Yemenite Jews experienced many periods of violent intolerance. In the twelfth century, the persecutions and forced conversions gave rise to Messianic agitations and the Yemenite Jews turned to Maimonides for advice. He replied by a famous epistle, *Iggeret Teman*, in which he exhorted them not to hasten or try to force the redemption, to bear their tribulations patiently and to remain true to their faith.

Throughout the centuries, the history of the Jews in Yemen has been a long series of persecutions and humiliations, which ended only in our day, when they left their inhospitable country, to start a new, free and productive life in the State of Israel.

Remarkably enough, during the long centuries of suffering, the Yemenite Jews succeeded in keeping abreast with all the spiritual developments of Judaism and in maintaining a relatively high standard of Jewish learning. The Yemenite Community was also in intermittent contact with those of India.

In southern India there was a remarkable Jewish community, which had been living since time immemorial at Cranganore (on the Malabar Coast). The Cochin Jews still have in their possession the famous Copper Tablets going back to the sixth, perhaps even to the third century. Engraved on these tablets, in the Tamil script and language, are the privileges granted by the Brahman king Bhaskara Ravi Varma of Malabar to the Jew Joseph Rabban, who seems to have been of Babylonian or Persian origin. Joseph Rabban is appointed hereditary Prince of Anjuvannam. All the picturesque feudal rights of an Indian princeling

251

are granted to him and his descendants, "as long as the sun shines upon the earth."

The Jews who had come to Cranganore with Joseph Rabban, already found there other Jews, who had settled in the country two or three centuries earlier.

When the Portuguese conquered Cranganore in 1523, the Jews had to remove themselves southward to Cochin, where they built their own quarter. These Jewish settlers were, by now, assimilated among their Indian neighbors to such an extent as to be physically indistinguishable from them. They are known as the "Black Jews." Besides them there was another group, known as the *Meshuhrarim* (the freedmen), descended from native slaves who had been converted to Judaism and then given freedom. In the seventeenth century, when trade flourished and Cochin was a place of economic importance, there was an immigration of Jews from Turkey, Syria, and Europe. The descendants of these immigrants came to be known as the "White Jews". The three groups into which the Jews of Cochin are divided, have retained their individuality and their separate rites down to our day. They have interesting ceremonies and customs, especially for the celebration of their weddings and the Simhat Torah holiday. Their prayer-books for these occasions include many liturgical poems by local poets and scholars.

In Cochin, the White Jews built a beautiful synagogue in Indian style near the palace of the Rajah. The street leading to the synagogue is known as the Jews' Street. The "Black Jews" had their own synagogues both in the capital and in smaller places in the vicinity.

The greatest part of the Cochin Jews have already emigrated to the State of Israel, where they continue to observe their customs and keep together as a distinct group.

Further north on the western coast of India, in Bombay and the neighboring villages, there is another Jewish group, the Bene Israel. According to their tradition, their ancestors. who came from the north, were ship-wrecked off the coast and settled there after their rescue. They engaged mainly in agriculture and oil- pressing. Since they strictly observed the sabbatical rest, they became known to their neighbors as the "seventh day oil-men." They had no contact with the rest of the Jewish world and in due course they not only adopted the Indian garb and way of life, but also lost their Jewish religious traditions almost entirely. The only vestiges of traditional practice were the observation of the Sabbath, the practice of circumcision and the prohibition of certain animals for food. They had no knowledge of Hebrew. At the close of the eighteenth century, Jews from Cochin and Baghdad taught them Hebrew and the tenets and practices of traditional Judaism. Since then the Bene Israel are eager observant Jews. Physically, however, they are indistinguishable from their Indian neighbors. Many of them have settled in Israel.

Interior of the Synagogue of the "white" Jews at Cochin.

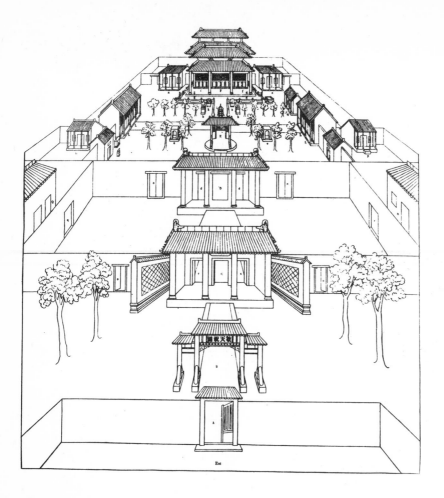

The Synagogue of the Chinese Jews at Kai-Feng-Fu, Province of Honan, after a drawing by Domenge, a Jesuit missionary who visited the place early in the 18th century and copied there several Hebrew inscriptions. The synagogue was already a heap of ruins in 1857, when the first European Jew, a certain Liebermann of Vienna, visited Kai-Feng-Fu, but there were still about 500 Jews in this remote town.

Christian missionaries who reached the Far East in the seventeenth century, were astonished to find in China Jews who outwardly resembled to the least detail the Chinese among whom they lived. The most remarkable group was the community of Kai-Feng-Fu in central China, which existed down to the nineteenth century. But it is probable that there were formerly many other Jewish communities in China. Their forefathers had presumably come from Persia in connection with the silk-trade. Their own tradition, that they had settled in China in the days of the Han dynasty (220 C.E.), may be legendary, but it is a fact that the Jewish ninth-century globe-trotter Soliman from Andalusia already encountered Jews in China.

In due course the Chinese Jews almost entirely isolated, became completely assimilated in every respect, They spoke the Chinese language, inditing their inscriptions in the tongue and script of the country, They wore Chinese costumes and fashion, down even to the pig-tail, and presented their religion in an acceptable Confucian light. When their synagogue at Kai-Feng-Fu was destroyed by a devastating flood in 1642, they rebuilt it in the style of architecture of the Confucian temples. Even their Hebrew manuscripts, all copied after this disaster, betray Chinese calligraphic influence and a solitary specimen of Chinese Hebrew illumination that has come down to us is wholly in the Chinese style.

Chinese Jews at prayer, from an 18th century engraving.

254

Chinese Megillah with illuminations in Chinese style, early 19th century. (Roth Collection).

The Chinese Jews were well treated by the government, and some of them rose to wealth and high rank. The destruction of the synagogue of Kai-Feng-Fu, however, seems to have dealt Chinese Jewry a serious blow. Many of their sacred books had been lost in this disaster. The community began to dwindle and they forgot the Hebrew language and most Jewish observances. In the first half of the nineteenth century the final decay set in. By now Chinese Jewry belongs to the past.

Mention must be made of another group, which preserved the Jewish faith to our day, although isolated for centuries from the main body of the Jewish people. These are the Falashas, the black Jews of Ethiopia. They are probably Jewish proselytes of Hamitic stock. According to their own tradition, they came to Ethiopia from Palestine in the days of King Solomon, together with the son whom the Queen of Sheba had borne him. The fact is that the Jewish faith appears to be older than Christianity in Ethiopia. The Falashas were organized for many centuries as an independent state under their own kings in the inaccessible mountains of Semien and the Ethiopian emperors had to fight many a destructive war, until they put an end to their independence in the seventeenth century. From time to time nebulous reports about the Falashas reached Palestine or Europe and contributed to perpetuate and enrich the legends concerning the Lost Ten Tribes of Israel. In modern times, worsening economic conditions and the zeal of Protestant missionaries have reduced their numbers. There are still about thirty or forty thousand of them left, clinging to their ancestral Biblical faith and customs. However, they readily accept the practices of traditional Judaism, when offered an opportunity to learn them, and dream of redemption in the form of a "return" to Zion.

255

THE JEWS IN GERMANY IN THE CENTURY OF REFORMATION

The end of the fifteenth and the beginning of the sixteenth century brought a certain improvement in the condition of the Jews in Germany. This was not due to a change of temperament or to a relaxation of the traditional anti-Jewish feelings of the German people, but there was a reassertion of respect for the rule of law which, to some extent, stemmed the unbridled displays of violence, The change in the atmosphere was felt by the Jews and they did their best to benefit from it.

The outstanding personality in this fight was Joseph ben Gershom Loans, better known as Joselman of Rosheim (1480–1554), an Alsatian Jew. Posterity has come to regard him as the prototype of the *Shtadlan*, the official representative of a community or a group of communities, who speaks to the authorities in their behalf, travelling about ceaselessly and indefatigably and making use of his talents, influence, and relations, to intercede whenever persecution or deprivation threaten. Joselman had seen the suffering of the Alsatian Jews in his youth. His own father had been involved in a charge of ritual murder. Owing to his dynamic temperament, he became a remarkable communal leader and, from

Charter granted by Emperor Charles V (1520–1558) to the Jews of Worms in 1551 (General Archive for Jewish History, Jerusalem).

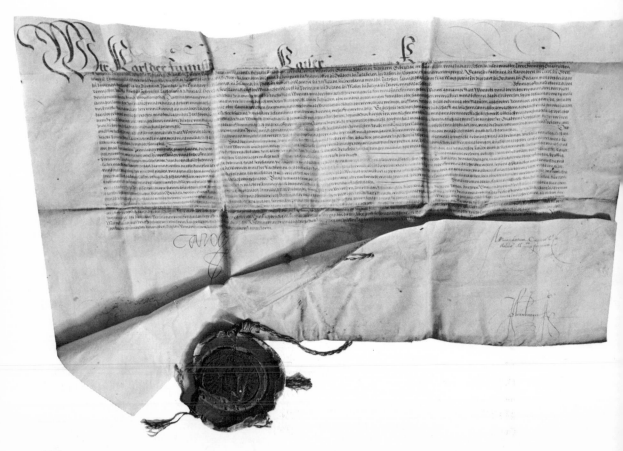

256

1510, began appearing before the emperor and princes as the authorized representative of the Alsatian communities, to intervene on behalf of his people wherever Jews were endangered in any way. His official Hebrew title was *Parnas u-Manhig* ("warden and leader"). He did not confine his intercession to the communities which had appointed him, but devoted himself to the defense of the interests of German Jewry at large.

After having averted, in 1515, the danger of an expulsion of the Jews of Alsace, he influenced Emperor Maximilian I, a year later, to abandon the project of a general expulsion from Germany. No wonder that he soon became known as the "Commander and Governor of all the Jews of the Empire." In this capacity Joselman attended the coronation ceremonies of Emperor Charles V and obtained his confirmation of the "rights and privileges" of the German Jews. The high regard in which he was held by the new emperor enhanced his prestige in the eyes of the regional and municipal authorities.

He had the courage to stand up even to the redoubtable Martin Luther in his later, virulently anti-Semitic days, and wrote a reasoned book

Derekh ha-Kodesh, to oppose the attacks of the Reformation leader. He even induced the Municipal Council of Strasbourg to forbid the publication of one of Luther's anti-Semitic books, which, of course, did not prevent Luther from having it printed in another place.

Joselman was present at the diet of Regensburg in 1532 and there met David Reubeni and Solomon Molcho. Foreseeing a tragic outcome, he tried to dissuade Molcho from submitting to the emperor his fantastic ideas, but the dreamer would not heed the voice of reason.

A contemporary caricature, not wholly unkind, shows how large Yoselman's figure loomed in the eyes of his contemporaries.

In the ensuing period there was a certain tendency to express anti-Jewish prejudices in more legal terms. The prejudices themselves, of course, persisted in Germany, and far from removing them, the Reformation only contributed to their strengthening.

In the Catholic provinces of Germany the Jews continued to be exposed to endless chicaneries and humiliations and from time to time, to local or regional expulsions as well. The emperors generally protected the rights of Jews, but their policy was often a vacillating one and their protection not always effective. Often enough violent outbreaks could not be avoided.

In Frankfort, for instance, an anti-Semitic agitator. Vincent Fettmilch, who was styled "the new Haman," tried for years to obtain the expulsion of the Jews from the city by legal means. He succeeded in intimidating the Municipal Council, but Emperor Matthias opposed this arbitrary measure. The imperial protection of the Jews incensed their enemies and Fettmilch resorted to violence. In 1614 the Jewish quarter of Frankfort was assaulted and sacked by the mob and the Jews were

The execution of Vincent Fettmilch and his accomplices at Frankfort, on February 28th, 1616 (Contemporary engraving).

258

obliged to leave the town abandoning all their property. It took the emperor almost two years to enforce his authority and arrange for the return of the Frankfort Jews to their homes.

Similar events occurred about the same time at Worms.

In Protestant Brandenburg the Jews were expelled in 1510, after a trial in which thirty-eight members of the community were burnt alive, having been convicted of host-desecration and ritual murder. Luther's friend, the learned Melanchthon, so different from Luther by the generosity of his spirit and by his sense of justice, convinced the Prince-Elector Joachim II of Brandenburg in 1539 that the Berlin trial had been a judicial murder, and thus prepared the ground for an appeal by Joselman of Rosheim for the readmission of Jewish residents. Towards the middle of the sixteenth century, there was again a modest Jewish community at Berlin and the Prince-Elector even employed a Jew, Lippold of Prague, as his treasurer and mint-master. Lippold's zeal in the collection of his master's taxes stirred up animosity against the Jews among the populace, who were anyhow aroused against them by the anti-Semitic pamphlets of Martin Luther, disseminated by the clergy. When the Elector died in 1571, Lippold was accused of having poisoned him. He was put on trial, confessed under torture anything demanded of him, and was executed with barbaric cruelty. The Jews were then again expelled from Brandenburg.

During the Thirty Years' War (1618–1648), which devastated Central Europe, the Jews suffered alike from Catholic and Protestant soldiery.

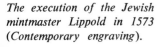

The execution of the Jewish mintmaster Lippold in 1573 (Contemporary engraving).

THE AGE OF THE GHETTO

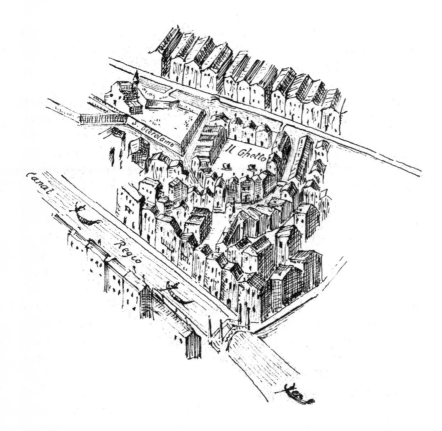

The Ghetto of Venice, the oldest of all Ghettos (from an 18th century plan).

Since the establishment of Jewish settlements outside their national territory, Jews had preferred to live among their own people. For religious, social and economic considerations, and later on for reasons of security as well, it became advisable not to disperse in an alien, and often unfriendly environment. There were Jewish quarters in Hellenistic Alexandria and ancient Rome. The same phenomenon occurred in Germany and France, as well as in Spain and Italy throughout the Middle Ages.

But there is a fundamental difference between this voluntary congregation around the synagogue and other communal institutions and the enforced segregation of the Jews in specially reserved quarters, which was mainly an innovation of the sixteenth century.

In 1555, Cardinal Pietro Caraffa became Pope as Paul IV. Before his coronation, the Cardinal had been known for his fanatic hatred of the Jews. Under his predecessor, Pope Julius III, he was already considered the chief representative of the nervous rather than obscurantist spirit of the Catholic reaction. It was he who had been responsible for the burning of the Talmud in Rome and many other places in Italy in 1553. One of his first acts after his accession to the papacy was to issue the famous bull "*Cum nimis absurdum*", in which he declared that it would

A quarter of Venice still bears the name "Ghetto Vecchio" (Old Ghetto).

Venice, The square of the Ghetto Nuovo.

be absurd and inadmissible to extend Christian love and tolerance to the people condemned by God for their sins. He relegated the Jews to the status of pariahs and demanded their complete segregation from the Christian population in separate, fenced quarters, within which no Christian would be allowed to dwell and outside which no Jew would be permitted to spend the night. The gates of the Jewish quarter were to be closed after dark and on the major solemnities of the Christian year. The Jews would be forbidden to have more than one synagogue in each town ; they were to be obliged to wear a distinctive yellow headgear to mark them off from other men, and would not be allowed to employ Christian servants or to have any social relations with Christians. They were to be prohibited from engaging in honorable occupations and would, in fact, be confined to peddling and old clothes

261

The "Judengasse" (Jews' Street) in Frankfort-on-Main.

dealing. Jewish physicians would no longer be permitted to treat Christian patients.

The institution created by this bull became known as the Ghetto.

The idea was not entirely new. The Church had protested for many centuries against free intercourse between Jews and Christians. In the fifteenth century segregation had already been enforced in several parts of the Iberian Peninsula, and the system was extended to the entire territory of Spain in 1480, almost on the eve of the expulsion. When the Municipal Council of Frankfort decided in 1462, to herd the Jews into a segregated area, its decision elicited the praise of Pope Pius II. But the classical age of the Ghetto really began in the sixteenth century, about forty years before the publication of Paul IV's bull.

The Signoria of Venice had shown the lead as early as 1516, when the Jews residing in this town were confined to the quarter of the former canon-foundry ("getto") and obliged to make themselves recognizable by wearing saffron-yellow hats. This was the prototype of the institution which was subsequently set up throughout Italy and elsewhere, and which also gave it its name. Rome followed suit a fortnight after the papal edict. Within a relatively short time, ghettos were instituted in all Italian towns with Jewish population. The system also spread throughout the rest of Europe, wheresoever segregation had not yet become a fact. Everywhere the Jews were concentrated in insalubrious, overcrowded areas. The authorities usually refused to allow the enlargement of the area and the growth of the population obliged the Jews to build many-storied houses separated by narrow, gloomy streets into which the sunlight seldom penetrated.

Portico d'Ottavia, the entrance to the Ghetto of Rome (18th century engraving).

Jew taking the oath before the Doge of Venice. Watercolor by Jan Grevembroeck (18th century), Museo Correr, Venice.

In most towns, confinement of the Jews to the ghetto involved all manners of additional degradation. In some places, brothels were obliged to be situated in the ghetto or its immediate neighborhood, as the fitting locality for houses of ill repute. Special payments would be exacted from the Jews by the civic authorities. Humiliating ceremonies were required when a Jew had to give testimony in court or, for instance at Venice, when he had to swear fealty. The Roman community was obliged to present a Scroll of the Law in front of the Arch of Titus to every newly elected pope, who would return it to them with the traditional insulting formula ; "We confirm the Law, but condemn the Jewish people and their interpretations."

The Jews were forced to attend conversionist sermons in church, aimed at breaking down their resistance to the dogmas of Christianity. This practice was continued at Rome almost down to 1870, when the city was incorporated into the kingdom of Italy. The Jews were driven to church by the papal *sbirri*, whose function it was also to keep them from falling asleep during the sermon.

Within the ghetto, raids were periodically made, to discover and destroy forbidden Hebrew literature. Not infrequently, Jewish children were seized and baptized against the will of their parents and, afterwards brought up as Christians. This abuse continued sometimes well into the second half of the nineteenth century. On one occasion, in the case of Edgardo Mortara, the kidnapping of a Jewish child in Bologna by the papal police in 1858 shook public opinion throughout the world. But Jewish protests, including a visit of Sir Moses Montefiore to Rome, and the intervention of Emperors Napoleon III of France and Franz Joseph I of Austria-Hungary, were of no avail. Pope Pius IX did not release the seven years old child, who was educated to become a Catholic priest.

Compulsory conversionist sermon to the Jews of Rome. Watercolor by Hieronymus Hess, in the Art-Museum of Basle.

Jewish wedding-procession in a German Ghetto, from a 17th century engraving.

Jewish festive procession at Prague, on the occasion of the birth of the archduke Leopold in 1716 (from a contemporary engraving).

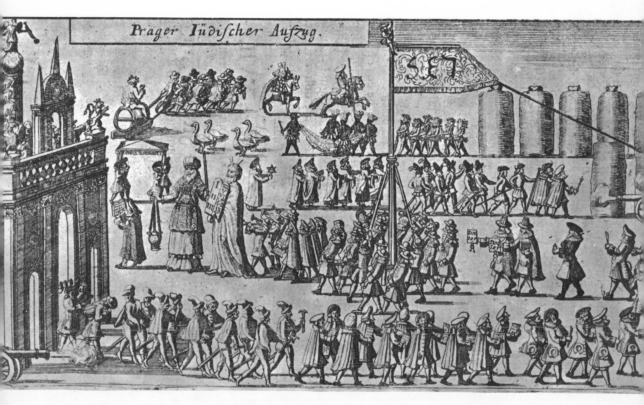

Prager Iüdischer Aufzug.

Yet everything was not darkness and misery in the ghetto. The Jews were able not only to maintain their individuality, but also to develop their institutions. The ghetto strengthened the inner solidarity of the community. The synagogues were the center of an intense religious and communal life. Traditional Jewish religious ceremonies continued to be zealously observed, though always in the spirit of the land and of the age. Italy and Germany, for instance, inevitably reflected contrasting attitudes in this respect. The community maintained philanthropic institutions and schools. The Jews still prided themselves on their standard of education. Adult study among the more mature continued the tradition of learning implanted among the young, and the ghetto still produced eminent scholars.

Although the vast majority of the Jews were on the border-line of poverty, some families attained a high degree of prosperity. Holidays and familiar celebrations afforded ample occasions for a merry social life. Music was cultivated in and outside the synagogue, and there were also theatrical performances and other kinds of entertainment.

Moreover, the ghetto was not really a hermetically sealed area. Jews left it to travel, and often visitors from other towns or from foreign countries, sometimes far-away, arrived. Despite all the restrictions, which were

The search for leaven on the eve of Passover (from a 17th century Minhagim-Book).

frequently relaxed, there were many contacts with the outside Christian environment. The inhabitants of the ghetto were thus always kept up to date on political and spiritual events in the world.

For Christians, the ghetto, a strange and, to a large extent, unknown world, was an object of curiosity. This explains the fact that artists of the period not infrequently tried to represent its diverse aspects.

Of course, there were also dark spots in the social life of the ghetto. One of them was the inclination to excessive gambling in certain circles, a vice which provoked many protests on the part of the rabbis, but which sometimes infected even some of them. One example is the wayward

Jacob Toorenvliet, (1641–1719), Jews studying the Law (Art Gallery, Oslo).

Rabbi Leon da Modena (1571–1648), a famous preacher, poet and rabbinical author, but an irremediable addict to gambling.

Rabbi Leone da Modena (1571–1648), the pride and the disgrace of the Venetian ghetto. This versatile scholar, who was for thirty-six years a member of the Venetian Rabbinate, excelled as a preacher, a liturgical poet, and a writer. He opposed the cabbalistic trend and wrote a vigorous polemic book against it, *Ari Nohem*. But it is not always easy to know his real beliefs and opinions. His talent for polemics carried him away, for instance, to write under a pseudonym a destructive criticism of the Talmudic tradition and under his own name, a refutation of this same criticism. Yet, he was prudent enough not to publish these two books in his lifetime, so that his contemporaries had no reason to doubt his orthodoxy. At the request of his Christian friends, Leone da Modena also wrote a book in Italian on the rites of the Jews, which was in fact destined for the information of King James I of England. The tragedy of Leone da Modena's life was, however, his passion for gambling, which often involved him in heavy debts. Although at the age of fourteen he had already written a dialogue against this vice, he never succeeded in resisting it for any length of time.

JEWISH RITUAL ART

Ghetto life could not stifle the aesthetic tastes and tendencies of the Jews, but it did restrict them, in the main, to the religious sphere. Jewish art, as it developed in the age of the ghetto, was necessarily a ritual art.

In architecture the aesthetic taste of the Jews found expression in the building of synagogues. Sometimes the synagogues were designed by Christian architects of outstanding reputation in the architectural fashion of the time. The Sephardic synagogue of Amsterdam, for instance, was constructed by the Dutch architect Elias Bowman the Elder, with a broad middle nave and two aisles, a plan which the Jews hitherto avoided, on account of its resemblance to churches. But Jewish architects, too, used to conform to the contemporary style of the environment, although at times an archaistic taste manifested itself. In Germany, for example, synagogues in the gothic style were erected in Frankfort, Altona, and elsewhere in the late seventeenth, and even in the early eighteenth, century. The interiors of the synagogues always corresponded to the requirements of Jewish worship and the arrangement breathes a Jewish traditional spirit, although outside influences could not always be avoided. The necessity to build women's galleries afforded an opportunity for the expression of various conceptions of interior architecture and decoration. The focus of the synagogue was, of course, the Ark, the shrine containing the Torah-scrolls, placed against the

Finials of Torah-scrolls, Venice 18th century (in the Tuck Collection, University College, London).

eastern wall (ideally facing Jerusalem). The ark was usually a welcome opportunity for the display of high skill and taste in wood-carving. In front of the doors of the Torah-shrine in Askenazic synagogues, or behind the doors in Italian and Sephardic synagogues, there were curtains made of richly and artistically embroidered brocades or velvets. The Torah-scrolls themselves, of which the Ark contained sometimes a great number, were enclosed in magnificent cases of wrought silver or covered with tastefully decorated wrappers of silk and velvet. They were, moreover, adorned with crowns, finials and breast-plates, all made of hammered or engraved silver.

Silver Kiddush goblets, 18th century. The one to the right especially for New Year, the other one for Sabbath and Holidays.

Synagogue Lamp, by Abraham d'Oliveyra, early 18th century (Jewish Museum, London).

Another object in the synagogue which invited Jewish artists to exert their fantasy and talent in the art of decoration, was the *bimah* or *almemor*, the platform facing the Torah-shrine, on which the reading of the Torah took place. It was usually provided with a balustrade of carved wood or wrought iron, and sometimes covered by a canopy supported by columns.

But Jewish ritual was not confined to the synagogue. The appurtenances for the domestic rituals characteristic of Judaism were similarly manufactured by expert craftsmen.

The Kiddush-goblets for the sanctification ceremony on the Sabbath eve, and the goblets for the celebration of the Seder ceremony were usually made of silver, with engraved arabesques and inscriptions.

Another object connected with the Sabbath ritual, which was to be found in every Jewish house, was the spice-container employed in the *Havdalah* benediction, which marks the end of the hallowed day. These boxes, as a rule of silver, were made in various sizes and shapes and there are, among those preserved in museums and private collections, real masterpieces. The most familiar form was that of a tower with a vane on its top and a door for the insertion of the spices. Other usual shapes were flowers and various fruits. There are also spice-boxes in the shape of fishes or birds. No other ritual object has challenged the imagination of Jewish artists to such an extent.

The most important requisite for the celebration of the Sabbath was, of course, the Sabbath-lamp or candlestick, which was kindled on Friday evening, when the day of rest began, Here, wrought brass successfully competed with silver to produce richly decorated many-branched hanging lamps or gracious candlesticks adorned with stylized animal and floral ornaments.

Spice-boxes for Havdalah. To the left: Ukrainian work (Israel Museum, Jerusalem). In the middle: tower-type box with symbols of Jewish feast (formerly Howitt collection, London). To the right: tower-type box in the form of the Eschenheimer Turm of Frankfort, 18th century (Roth Collection).

ויהי בימי אחשורוש הוא אחשורוש המלך מהדו ועד כוש
שבע ועשרים ומאה מדינה בימים ההם כשבת המלך
אחשורוש על כסא מלכותו אשר בשושן הבירה בשנת
שלוש למלכו עשה משתה לכל שריו ועבדיו חיל פרס ומדי
הפרתמים ושרי המדינות לפניו בהראתו את עשר כבוד
מלכותו ואת יקר תפארת גדולתו ימים רבים שמונים ומאת
יום ובמלאות הימים האלה עשה המלך לכל העם הנמצאו
בשושן הבירה למגדול ועד קטן משתה שבעת ימים בחצר
גנת ביתן המלך חור כרפס ותכלת אחוז בחבלי בוץ וארגמ
על גלילי כסף ועמודי שש מטות זהב וכסף על רצפת בהט
ושש ודר וסחרת והשקות בכלי זהב וכלים מכלים שונים וי
מלכות רב כיד המלך והשתיה כדת אין אנס כי כן יסד המ
על כל רב ביתו לעשות כרצון איש ואיש
ושתי המלכה עשתה משתה נשים בית המלכות אשר למ
אחשורוש ביום השביעי כטוב לב המלך ביין אמר למהום
מהומא חרבונא בגתא ואבגתא זתר וכרכס שבעת הסריס
המשרתים את פני המלך אחשורוש להביא את ושתי המ
לפני המלך בכתר מלכות להראות העמים והשרים את יפ
כי טובת מראה היא ותמאן המלכה ושתי לבוא בדבר המ
אשר ביד הסריסים ויקצף המלך מאד וחמתו בערה בו
ויאמר המלך לחכמים יודעי העתים כי כן דבר
המלך לפני כל יודעי דת ודין והקרב אליו כרשנא שתר
אדמתא תרשיש מרס מרסנא ממוכן שבעת שרי פרס ומ
ראי פני המלך הישבים ראשנה במלכות כדת מה לעשות

Italian Majolica Seder plate, by Isaac Cohn, Ancona 1673 (Roth Collection, Beth Zedaka Museum, Toronto, Canada).

Another candelabrum which was an obligatory appurtenance of the Jewish home, was the eight-branched Hanukkah-lamp kindled during the eight days of the feast of the Maccabees, in mid-winter. Here too, brass- and silver-smiths vied with one another to produce small masterpieces. Some of them are in the candelabrum- or menorah-type, imitating the golden candlestick in the Tent of Meeting and in the Temple of Jerusalem, as described in Exodus 25:31–40 (the Hanukkah-lamp, however, has eight branches besides the middle shaft, instead of the seven branches of the Temple menorah).

The Seder plates used on Passover eve were manufactured of majolica in Italy, or of pewter in Germany, in both cases decorated with appropriate designs and inscriptions.

The art of manuscript illumination was kept alive for inditing the hand-written scrolls of Esther for the recital on the hilarious feast of Purim, for rabbinical diplomas, and for the *ketubbah* or marriage contracts, which are sometimes splendid artistic achievements. Passover Haggadahs were often richly illuminated, as long as manuscript Haggadahs were used. When they began to be printed, they were adorned

Megillah with silver gilt case, Germany about 1650 (Jewish Museum, London).

275

Betrothal rings, gold filigree, engraved and enameled, probably Italian, Renaissance period, (British Museum London).

Silver book-binding with Biblical scenes (sacrifice of Isaac, temptation of Joseph and the dream of Pharaoh). Feinberg Collection, Detroit Mich.

Front-view of the ivory Mezuzah-case on page 202.

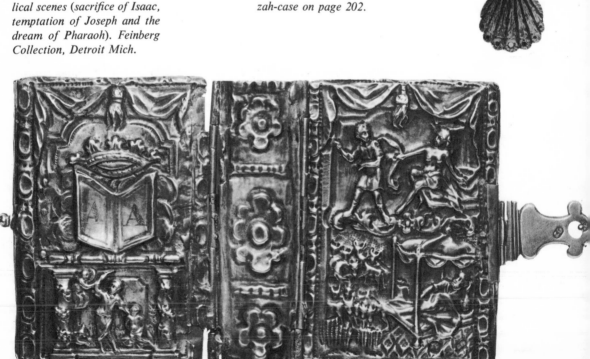

Enamel handle of circumcision knife, Poland or Germany, dated 1734 (Jewish Museum, New-York).

Polish-Jewish paper cut-out. Seven-branched candelabrum and a pair of doves (Ginza Museum, Tel-Aviv).

with tasteful woodcuts or engravings, and later there was a revival of manuscript art for this purpose as well.

For weddings, magnificent rings of gold and enamel were made in Germany and Italy, some of them elaborately chiselled and provided with inscriptions, like *mazal tov* (good luck).

At the circumcision ceremony, finely decorated implements would be used and the chair called by the name of the ever-present Prophet Elijah was also sometimes a remarkable piece of work.

Even the *mezuzah* affixed to the door of the Jewish house, in accordance with the biblical precept in Deuteronomy 6:8, often combined aesthetic taste with the expression of religious devotion.

In this way, the Jew endeavored in many ways to overcome the depressing influence, of the crowded and restricted ghetto-life He sought to achieve beauty in a sphere free from external coercion, if not always from outside influence.

THE MARRANOS AND THE COMMUNITIES THEY FOUNDED

Meanwhile, there had remained in Spain, and especially in Portugal, a large body of Marranos or New Christians. They proved unassimilable, being Christians in name, but Jewish at heart, transmitting from generation to generation their secret attachment to the ancient faith abandoned under compulsion, and continuing their clandestine observance of certain Jewish ceremonies. They were now, for a long time, the principal object of the Inquisitorial procedures in both countries. The Edicts of Faith, issued periodically by the Inquistion, called attention to the characteristic practices of the Judaizers: Sabbath-observance, abstention from certain foods, fasting on the Day of Atonement, etc., and invited every true son of the Catholic Church to denounce any one whom he knew to be guilty of such offenses.

Those denounced were arrested by the familiars of the Holy Office and incarcerated in the dungeons of magnificent Inquisitorial palaces. The trial was strictly secret. The procedure required that the accused confess his "waywardness." Extreme importance was attached to this confession, since the Inquistion was interested in learning the names of accomplices in heresy. If the accused did not confess of his free will, tortures were inflicted. An elaborate system of progressive torture was worked out in the course of time. No wonder that any kind of confession could be extorted, although the accused sometimes died under the torment to which he was submitted. Once convicted, the accused could profess repentance and ask for his reconciliation to the Church. In this case, he was obliged to suffer the humiliation of appearing as a "penitent" in one of the sumptuous autos-da-fé staged by the Inquitition. Clothed in the yellow garment called "sambenito," he had to express his "contrition" in public. Moreover, he was usually obliged to serve a term of imprisonment and was fortunate, if he was not sentenced to prison for life or sent to the galleys. His property was, as a rule, confiscated, at first for the State treasury, later on in favor of the Holy Office itself. Those who were convicted but did not repent, were liable to suffer the death penalty. Since, however, the Church was averse to bloodshed, they were handed over to the "secular arm" with the recommendation to put them to death without spilling blood. Their burning alive at the *quemadero* was the main attraction of the autos-da-fé. Those who repented after conviction were favored by being strangled before their public burning.

Marranos faithful to their ancestral creed escaped in a constant stream to lands where they could worship the God of their fathers in peace.

At first, they journeyed mainly to Italy, where they settled in areas not under Spanish rule. Many of them had the courage to profess Judaism openly even in territories belonging to the Pontifical State, for instance at Ancona. It is noteworthy that they did not suffer real persecution there until 1555, when Cardinal Caraffa became Pope as Paul IV. But even under his pontificate, they could continue to live in peace in other parts of Italy. At that time, tolerant Ferrara became their main center. In the chapter on Hebrew Printing reference has been made to the printing press established there by the Usque family. It was there that the earliest literature in Spanish and Portuguese for the use of Marranos made its appearance.

Other goals of Marrano emigration were the coastal regions of North Africa and Turkey, where they openly joined the communities founded by the Spanish and Portuguese exiles at the end of the fifteenth century. It has already been pointed out that many outstanding Jews in these countries in the sixteenth century were of Marrano origin.

An Auto-da-Fé at Lisbon in the 18th century (Contemporary engraving).

B. Picart delineavit et sculp direx 1721

The dedication of the Synagogue of the Spanish-Portuguese Community at Amsterdam in 1675 (Engraving by Picart).

The seal of the Portuguese Synagogue of Amsterdam.

Besides the stream of emigration eastward to Mediterranean countries, other groups traveled northward along the Atlantic coast, mainly to the Low Countries.

In Antwerp, New Christians settled as early as 1512, and established a there a flourishing and distinguished colony. However, under Spanish rule they could not think of dropping their mask and continued living outwardly as Christians.

After the winning of Dutch independence, the center of gravity of Marrano settlement moved from Antwerp to Amsterdam. A party of Portuguese Marranos arrived here about 1593, after an adventurous voyage, in the course of which they had been captured by an English ship. They were later joined by other Marranos and in 1597 they were granted permission to profess their Jewish faith openly. The community they founded was soon to become the most prosperous and most famous in Europe. Amsterdam bore deservingly and with pride the title "the Dutch Jerusalem."

The Amsterdam community attained a high degree of magnificence and evolved a cultural life of its own, in which the literary traditions of Spain and Portugal were perpetuated. At its head were armigerous merchant princes who lived in a sumptuous style and prided themselves on their family associations with the hidalgo aristocracy of the Iberian Peninsula. There were even cases in which some of them were raised to nobility by the rulers of the countries from which they had fled for their lives. Yet the shadow of the Inquisition continued to loom over them. At frequent intervals they would mourn those of their relatives and associates who had died the death of martyrs at some auto-da-fé in the Peninsula. Even in the present century, they still prayed, with curious conservatism, for their brethren in the prisons of the Inquistion.

Ephraim Bueno (died 1665), physician and scholar, friend of Rembrandt, founder of the society "Torah Or", one of the Marrano worthies of Amsterdam.

Abraham Zacuto, called Zacutus Lusitanus (1575–1642), famous physician and medical author. Born of a Marrano family, he left Portugal at the age of fifty, to escape the Inquisition, and joined the Jewish Community in Amsterdam.

The stream of Marrano migration also comprised — besides merchants — soldiers, and statesmen, poets, physicians, scholars, and renowned scientists. No wonder that the community maintained a high intellectual standard. A Talmudic academy, Etz Hayim, was founded and achieved wide fame. Countless books in Hebrew, Spanish and Portuguese were printed at Amsterdam.

The spirit of the Amsterdam community was strictly conservative and manifestations of free thinking on religious matters were severely repressed. A famous case was that of Uriel Acosta, a Portuguese Marrano who had joined the Jewish community of Amsterdam in 1618. He objected to certain Talmudic traditions which, in his opinion, did not conform to the spirit of Judaism, as he understood it. Excommunicated,

Benedict (Baruch) Spinoza (1632–1677). Excommunicated by the Amsterdam Community in 1656 for his heretical views, he spent the rest of his life in retirement at Hague, cutting optical lenses for his living and writing his immortal philosophical works.

he retracted after fifteen years, but soon relapsed into worse heresy, expressing doubts even in respect of the Mosaic law. Excommunicated a second time, he again declared his willingness to recant, after having resisted another seven years. Now, however, the penance imposed upon him was so humiliating that he broke down. After having gone through the ceremony, he committed suicide, leaving behind a moving autobiography.

Another case, no less famous but with a less tragic result, was that of the philosopher Benedict (Baruch) Spinoza. Born in Amsterdam, he received a thorough-going Jewish education and devoted himself to the study of the medieval Jewish philosophers. Having studied Latin, he extended his readings to the natural sciences and contemporary philosophic literature. He soon came under the influence of the Cartesian school and began to take a critical view of Judaism. After many vain endeavors to bring him back to orthodoxy, or at least to outward conformism, the community saw no other way than to pronounce, in 1656, the major excommunication. Spinoza took the sentence stoically and never retracted. Outside the synagogue and the community, he steadfastly continued the researches which secured him a place of honor in the history of philosophy.

The Synagogues of the Ashkenazi Community in Amsterdam (18th century engraving)

Portrait of a Rabbi by Rembrandt (painted 1657). Rembrandt spent part of his life in the Jewish quarter of Amsterdam, had many Jewish friends, painted, designed and etched with sympathy portraits of Jews and Biblical scenes.

Towards the middle of the seventeenth century, a steady immigration of Ashkenazic Jews from Germany and Poland to the Netherlands began. They soon outnumbered the Sephardim, who continued to consider themselves, however, the aristocracy of the Amsterdam community, which for almost three centuries, remained an important Jewish center.

Closely associated with the Amsterdam community was that of Hamburg, with its affiliates at Altona and Glückstadt. Here Portuguese Marranos had established themselves since the sixteenth century. Prosperous merchants, they contributed considerably to the city's economic development. By the beginning of the seventeenth century, they already had their own synagogues and burial ground; and in 1612 they finally obtained the formal recognition of the Senate of Hamburg.

Other Marrano communities, under somewhat different circumstances and long maintaining a transparent disguise of Catholicism, were to be found in Bordeaux and Bayonne, in south-western France. Although it was common knowledge that they were Catholics only outwardly, they had to wait until 1730 before being allowed to declare themselves officially as Jews.

In Spain the Marranos lost their identity in due course, except for the island of Majorca, where the so-called "Chuetas" still continue to preserve some degree of separatism and atavistic loyalty to a remote past. But in Portugal the phenomenon continued intensely long after. In the north of the country there are still thousands or tens of thousands of persons who recall their Jewish origins and practise at least some nostalgic Jewish rites. In the nineteen-twenties a distinguished Portuguese officer, Captain Arturo Carlos de Barros Basto, returned publicly to Judaism and initiated an organized movement to restore others like him to the Jewish faith.

THE RETURN OF THE JEWS
TO ENGLAND

One of the most remarkable members of the Amsterdam community in the first half of the seventeenth century was Rabbi Manasseh ben Israel. Brought to Holland as a child by his Marrano parents, he made rapid progress in the Jewish studies. At the age of eighteen (in 1622) he was awarded his rabbinical diploma and appointed preacher in the "Neveh Shalom" synagogue.

Like other scholars of the Amsterdam community, he knew many languages; Hebrew, Spanish, Portuguese, Dutch, Latin, and some Greek. This wide knowledge enabled him to become familiar with the classical and contemporary non-Jewish writers and to carry on a learned correspondence with many Christian scholars. The erudite and spirited Queen Christina of Sweden was among his correspondents. In 1627 he set up the first Hebrew printing press in Holland, where many important

Manasseh ben Israel (1604–1657), the promoter of the readmission of the Jews to England. Engraving by the Jewish artist Shalom Italia, 1643.

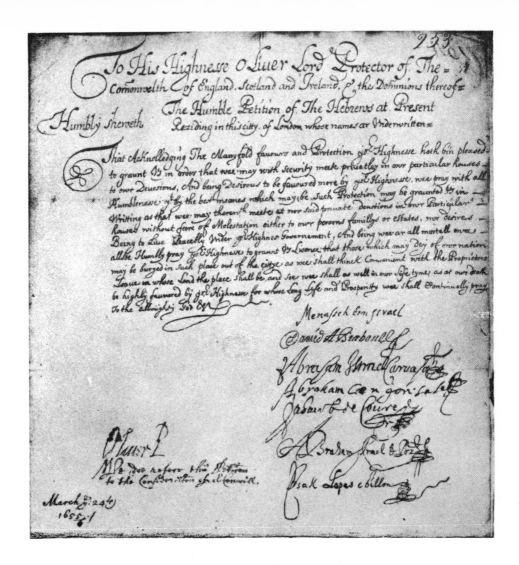

Petition to Oliver Cromwell, signed among others by Manasseh ben Israel and endorsed by Cromwell. The founders of the Spanish and Portuguese Jewish Congregation in London ask leave to open a synagogue and purchase a burial-ground. The petition is dated March 24th, 1656.

works were printed. His own books, in Spanish, Latin, and Hebrew, explained to the world at large the principles of Judaism and made him famous not only among his co-religionists, but also in Christian circles. Many visitors to the city of Amsterdam came to hear him preach; on one occasion the Queen of England listened to his sermon. Among his Dutch friends was the painter Rembrandt, who illustrated one of his books and painted and engraved his portrait.

In 1650 Manasseh ben Israel published his book "*Hope of Israel*" and dedicated its Latin edition to the English Parliament.

In this work he explained the reasons which justified the Messianic expectations of his time, He also pointed out that the advent of the Messiah must be preceded by the dispersion of the Jews in all the countries of the world and that their readmission to England — a country without Jews since their expulsion in 1290 — was one of the conditions for the fulfilment of the Messianic prophecies. The book also appeared in English and made a profound impression on Puritan readers.

In England the monarchy had been abolished in 1649 and replaced by a Puritan Republic headed by Oliver Cromwell, who became in due

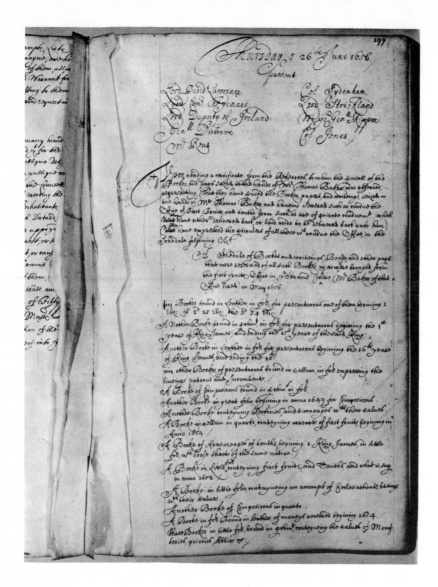

Minute-book of the Council of State, from which three pages have been torn out, for unknown reasons. These were the minutes of the sessions in which the Marranos established in England were allowed to maintain a synagogue and acquire a burial-ground.

course (1653) Lord Protector. The Puritans, who assiduously read and revered the Bible, were, for religious reasons, in favor of the readmission of the Jews to England. But there were also political reasons recommending this step; one of them was the desire to weaken Holland by attracting to London rich Jewish merchants and bankers, as well as Marranos from Spain and Portugal, who otherwise went to Amsterdam.

In 1655 Manasseh ben Israel went to England and opened personal negotiations with the Lord Protector, as a result of which a conference was summoned in Whitehall to consider the matter. The conference learned that there was no law preventing the recall of the Jews to England, but at the same time it became clear that there was no general inclination to bring them back. The main opponents were the London merchants, who found the idea of Jewish competition not to their liking. Despite Cromwell's generous advocacy in favor of the Jews, no decision was reached. Manasseh's hopes had not been realized. He left London in 1657, a disappointed man, and died at Middleburg (Holland) on his way home to Amsterdam.

But Manasseh ben Israel's endeavors had not been in vain. Cromwell conceded to Marranos who were already established in England, the permission to profess Judaism openly, to maintain a synagogue, and to acquire a cemetery in London. Although, for some mysterious reason, the pages of the Council minutes recording this decision were subsequently torn out of the volume, a Jewish community thus inconspicuously came into being. It grew slowly throughout the Restoration period and even under James II. In the days of William III, an already consolidated and wealthy Sephardic community could afford to construct its stately synagogue, still in use, in Bevis Marks (inaugurated in 1701).

Although he did not live to see his dream come true, Manasseh ben Israel is still reverently commemorated by the Jewish community of England as its true founder.

From 1690, there was also an Ashkenazic synagogue in London. The Ashkenazic community developed on separate lines and, in due course, outnumbered the Sephardim who, however, to this day retain something of their ancient luster and prestige.

The Synagogue in Bevis Marks, London (18th century engraving).

THE COSSACK MASSACRES

The relatively peaceful and prosperous life of Polish Jewry was shattered by the Cossack rising against the Poles in the Ukraine under the Hetman Bogdan Khmielnicki in 1648/9.

The Ukrainian peasants, who belonged to the Orthodox Church, had been cruelly oppressed and ruthlessly exploited by the Catholic Polish landlords and feudal nobility. The Jews, aliens in religion and race both to the oppressors and to the oppressed, had always served as the agents and factors of the Polish nobles and it is no wonder that they were among the first objectives of the hatred of the insurgents, who now rose to vent their resentment.

The embittered Ukrainians found a leader in the Hetman of the Cossacks, the warlike and bloodthirsty Bogdan Khmielnicki, who even concluded an alliance with the Khan of the Crimean Tartars, in order to secure his support in the "Holy War" which he declared against the Poles. In April, 1648, the onslaught of the Cossacks started with a fierce, apparently irresistible, vigor. The Polish armies were defeated. One town after the other was conquered and place after place witnessed massacres of the Jewish population on a scale that had no parallel in Europe, at least since the Black Death massacres in Germany, precisely 300 years before.

The contemporary chronicler Nathan Hannover recounts gruesome details of the atrocities committed by the Cossacks in the cities, villages, and country estates visited and pillaged by them. Having been informed that thousands of Jews had found refuge in the town of Nemirov, Khmielnicki sent a detachment in Polish disguise against the town. The Jews opened the gates to those whom they believed to have come to their relief, and thousands of them paid with their lives for their credulity. In many places the Jews took an active part in the armed defense of the towns, but were eventually overwhelmed because of insufficient support by the Polish military forces. Sometimes the Jews were betrayed and sacrificed by their Polish neighbors, who hoped thus to buy their own lives. The refusal of the citizens of Lemberg (Lwow) to deliver up their Jewish fellow-citizens, deserves to be mentioned as a praiseworthy exception. Khmielnicki, in this instance, contented himself with a high ransom. Towards the end of the ominous year 1648, hostilities subsided and peace negotiations between Poland and the Cossacks were initiated. For the time being, Khmielnicki retired to the Ukraine, but no stable peace was reached and year after year, henceforth, there were Cossack incursions, always involving a heavy loss of Jewish lives.

In 1654 war broke out again. This time, Khmielnicki was allied with the Russian Czar Alexei Mikhailovitch, who claimed large portions of Polish territory. Again there were frightful massacres of Jews in all places which fell into the hands of the allies.

To add to the misery of the Jews, the Swedes invaded Poland. They

Bogdan Khmielnicki (1595–1657), Hetman of the Cossacks and leader of the Ukrainian revolt against Polish rule. His war against the Poles was marked by frightful massacres of Jews in many places, particularly in the year 1648, which are remembered as the "Gezeroth Takh" (the disasters of 5408.

treated the Jews less brutally and were usually satisfied with imposing heavy war contributions. But the fact that the Jews submitted to the Swedish exactions without attempting to resist — a useless gesture in any case — made them appear as traitors and collaborators in the eyes of the Polish patriots. The fighters for the liberty of Poland now launched a series of massacres matching in cruelty those of the Cossacks and the Russians.

The result was the ruin of Polish Jewry, which was heavily reduced in numbers and completely impoverished. Poland, which had been a land of immigration for Jews, henceforth became a country from which Jews fled. Its Jewish population, long recruited from the West, began to return westwards. Polish refugees formed new communities in Germany, reached Palestine, were not unknown in Italy, and ultimately came as far as England, and even farther afield.

Moreover, the unprecedented suffering of Polish Jewry had important internal results. The Jews sought and found a compensation for the miseries of daily life in mystical speculations and artificially induced religious ecstasies. This mystical trend found its expression in the following century in the rise and rapid spread of the pietistic Hassidic movement.

On the other hand, the dreadful events known as *Gezerot Takh* ("The disasters of 5408" — the Jewish year corresponding to 1648) made a profound impression on the Jewish Diaspora at large and intensified the craving for deliverance. The massacres in Poland were considered part of the sufferings which, according to tradition, were bound to precede the advent of the Messiah. They were, therefore, largely responsible for the wave of Messianic excitement which swept over Europe and the Near East in the middle of the seventeenth century.

SABBATAI ZEVI

From certain points of view, the pseudo-Messianic movement associated with the name of Sabbatai Zevi was one of the great dividing lines in Jewish history. It marked the end of medieval romanticism, and, by shearing away the romantic, inaugurated an era of practical politics and local patriotisms.

The climate for the Sabbatean movement had been prepared by the spread among the Jews, in the period after the expulsion fron Spain, of the neo-cabbalistic teachings of Rabbi Isaac Ashkenazi Luria, the "Ari", of Safed, who also taught the mystical exercises by which the redemption could be hastened. Relying on an interpretation of Leviticus 25:13 in the Zohar, the classical text-book of the Cabbala, many cabbalists expected the year 1648 to be the year of salvation. Instead of fulfilling these hopes, the year brought the catastrophe in Poland. This invalidated the cabbalistic calculations, but enhanced and exalted Messianic expectations.

In those days, there lived in the Turkish town of Smyrna (Izmir) a young Sephardi Jew named Sabbatai Zevi (born 1626), who had immersed

Portrait of Sabbatai Zevi, from Th. Coenen, Ydele Verwachtinge der Joden Getoont in den Persoon van Sabbetai Zevi, Amsterdam 1669).

Den Nieuwen Iooden Koningh.   *Den Propheet der Iooden.*

Afbeelding, van den gewaenden, nieuwen Joodſchen Koning

SABETHA SEBI,

Met zijn byhebbende Profeet, opgeſtaen in den jare 1665, etc. zoo
vele daer van tot noch toe bekent is, of van de Joden geſeit wort,
uit de nauwkeurigſte brieven, en ſchriften opgeteekent.

Sabbatai Zevi and his prophet, Nathan of Gaza, from a contemporary Dutch broadsheet.

himself in the study of the Cabbala and indulged in ascetic exercises. A maniac-depressive, as is believed, of obviously remarkable personal attraction and physical beauty, he became convinced that he was the designated Savior. He proclaimed himself Messiah and, to assert his authority, dared to pronounce in public the ineffable name of God (the Tetragrammaton, in Hebrew the *Shem Ha-mephorash*). Excommunicated for this offense by the Smyrna rabbinate, Sabbatai Zevi left his native town and embarked upon years of wandering.

In Constantinople he was encouraged by the mystic Abraham Yakhini in his conviction that he was the Messiah. In Salonica he celebrated a mystical marriage with the Torah, the daughter of God, to the indignation of the local rabbis. In Palestine he prayed at the tombs of the Patriarchs and saints and lamented over the ruins of the Holy City. In Egypt he married Sara, a Polish girl who had escaped the massacres and had then wandered through Europe, declaring that she was destined to become the spouse of the King Messiah. On his way back to Palestine, he met at Gaza a young man of great genius, Nathan Ashkenazi, who became his "prophet," encouraged him to assert his claims, and supported him vigorously to the end. It was Nathan of Gaza who undertook the practical organization of the Messianic movement by despatching to many communities abroad his impassioned epistles announcing the advent of the Messiah.

Sabbatai Zevi in Smyrna in 1666 (Engraving from "Two Journeys to Jerusalem", London 1685).

In 1665 Sabbatai Zevi returned to his native Smyrna, where he was enthusiastically greeted as the Messianic King. His recognition by vast segments of the Jewish people all over the world, eminent scholars as well as simple folk, was instantaneous. Only a few realized the hollowness of his claims from the outset. The people crowded around him wherever he went and did whatever he told them to do. On the one side, he abolished traditional fasts and even turned them to days of rejoicing. On the other hand, Sabbatai set an example of self-flagellation, penitence, and prayer. There was a universal wave of penitential exercises meant to hasten the coming of the great day of deliverance. Amazing

Publication printed in England in the Messianic year 1666, reproducing a letter of the French Ambassador at Constantinople on "the Proceedings of the Israelites and the wonderful Miracles wrought by their Prophet".

reports swept the world, of the mustering of Jewish hosts and of the imminent return of the lost tribes of Israel to the Holy Land.

As far afield as England, there was a spate of publications to inform the excited readers of the newest developments, and wagers were made on the Exchange on the probabilities of Sabbatai's success. The Jewish community of London was only a small group at that time, but Christians, too, were highly interested in the events. Believing in computations based on the Apocalypse, many Puritans cherished the hope that the year 1666 would usher in the millennium of Christ's reign on earth. They did not doubt that there was a connection between their hopes and the Sabbatean movement.

In Holland, the great magnates of the Sephardi community declared their allegiance to Sabbatai Zevi. Books of penitential prayers were published there, containing ecstatic references to the newly arisen Deliverer, and with title-pages showing him sitting in glory.

In Germany people packed their property in barrels, ready for transference to Palestine, and young men dressed in green, the livery of Sabbatai Zevi, danced in the Sephardi synagogue at Hamburg. The sceptics aroused the indignation of the believers and sometimes nearly lost their lives.

Title-page of the prayer-book "Tikun ha-Keriah", Amsterdam 1666, showing Sabbatai Zevi enthroned as Messianic king.

Sabbatai Zevi in the prison of Abydos, receiving delegations of followers who come to render him homage (Contemporary engraving).

Rabbi Jacob Sasportas (1610–1698), the advocate of reason in a time of general exaltation, who constantly and forcefully opposed the Sabbatean agitation. (Painting by Isaack Luttichuijs, 1616–1673, Israel Museum, Jerusalem)

One of the relatively few outstanding European Jewish scholars who had maintained sobriety and a sense of proportion, was Rabbi Jacob Sasportas, formerly Haham of the newly established Spanish and Portuguese community in London, and later of Hamburg and Amsterdam. He carried on a constant and vigorous polemic against Sabbatai and his dupes.

In 1666 Sabbatai Zevi set out for Constantinople to take over his realm, having previously appointed princes of the twelve tribes of Israel, to assist him in the administration of the kingdom.

Immediately upon his arrival at Constantinople, he was, however, arrested by order the Grand Vizier and confined in the castle of Abydos, on the coast of the Dardanelles. The regime of the prison was a rather good-humored one. Sabbatai's adherents followed him to Abydos and converted his prison, which they called *Migdal Oz* ("Tower of Strength"), into a royal residence. His wife and his secretary were allowed

to join him in the tower and he received numberless individual visitors and official delegations from abroad, who came to render homage to the King Messiah.

When Sabbatai Zevi had sojourned at Abydos half a year, the patience of the Turkish authorities was exhausted. He was conducted to Adrianople, brought before Sultan Mehmed IV, and given the choice of either embracing Islam or dying as a rebel. In a moment of weakness he opted for life, put the turban on his head and left the royal presence as Mehmed Effendi, with the rank and emolument of a janitor of the court. Yet even now Sabbatai Zevi did not give up his pretensions, and his votaries, many of whom followed him in his new faith, refused to abandon their credence in him. They maintained that it was God's will that His Chosen One should experience even this lowly aspect of life, in order to expiate through humiliation the sins of his people. Thus Sabbatai Zevi continued to be the center of the loyalty of a wide circle of adherents. On account of his continued relations with his Jewish believers, the Turkish authorities sent him in 1673 into exile to Dulcigno in Albania (now Ulcinj, Jugoslavia), where he died in 1676.

The influence of his personality survived him. For almost one hundred years after Sabbatai's death, European Jewry, to whom the disappoint-

Zevi Ashkenazi, known as "Haham Zevi" (1658–1718), a famous talmudic scholar who was appointed in 1710 Rabbi of the Ashkenazi Community of Amsterdam. His uncompromising opposition to the Sabbatean propagandist Nehemia Hayun aroused against him the violent enmity of the heads of the Portuguese Community and obliged him to leave Amsterdam in 1714. His son, Jacob Emden (1697–1776), continued his father's war against the aftermath of the Sabbatean movement.

ment of their fervent hopes had been a heavy blow, continued to be convulsed by the propaganda of those who still believed in the apostate Messiah and diffused their faith publicly or secretly. Famous rabbis, among them particularly Haham Zevi Ashkenazi of Amsterdam, waged a tenacious war against these insidious propagandists. As late as the middle of the eighteenth century, the calm of the Jewish communities in Germany and Poland was disturbed by a virulent polemic between Rabbi Jacob Emden, the son of Haham Zevi, and Rabbi Jonathan Eybeschütz who was suspected, with good reason, of being a secret Sabbatean. This polemic commanded wide-spread attention even in non-Jewish circles and caused considerable damage to the prestige of Judaism. Meanwhile, in Turkey, chiefly at Salonica, but also at Adrianople, Constantinople, and Smyrna, those who had followed Sabbatai Zevi into Islam and their descendants formed a sect known by the name of Donmeh (converts, in Turkish). They continued to believe in Sabbatai Zevi as the Messiah and, while outwardly practising Islam, they preserved clandestine Jewish rites, as well as ceremonies instituted by their master. The members of the sect were prosperous and many of them played a considerable part in Turkish public life down to our days. When Salonica, which was their center and where they had their own quarter, became Greek in 1912, the Donmeh emigrated, mainly to Constantinople. They are now divided in three rival groups and their numbers (about 15,000 in 1920) are dwindling. Their existence is menaced by progressive assimilation to the Turkish environment.

Jonathan Eybeschütz (1690–1764), widely appreciated as a rabbinical scholar and a cabbalist, was accused by Jacob Emden of being a secret Sabbatean. The protracted polemic between the two rabbis caused considerable commotion in Jewish circles and aroused interest even among non-Jews.

MYSTIC MOVEMENTS
IN EASTERN EUROPE

In Poland the adherents of Sabbatai Zevi maintained their faith in him long after his death, although the persecution of the orthodox rabbis and the mockery to which they were subjected by their Jewish and Christian neighbors often obliged them to dissimulate their convictions. By a sort of chain reaction, a succession of mystics preached the impending advent of the Messiah or put forward, from time to time, more or less explicit Messianic claims.

Towards the end of the seventeenth century, the Polish Sabbateans centered mainly around the personality of the cabbalist Hayyim Malach, who was in close contact with the Donmeh circles in Turkey. Together with Judah Hassid, a fellow-cabbalist who had gathered around him a group of mystics styling themselves *Hassidim* ("The Devout Ones"), he organized in 1700 an exodus of their followers to Palestine. There they were to meet the Redeemer who was expected to return in 1706 (forty years after the apostasy of Sabbatai Zevi). After an exhausting journey,

Jacob Frank (1726–1791), claimed to be a reincarnation of Sabbatai Zevi, repudiated the Talmud, basing his teachings on the Zohar, and finally joined the Catholic Church together with his followers, without abandoning, however, his Messianic claims.

on which many perished and many others abandoned, the caravan reached the Holy City, where Judah Hassid died a few days later. The dire misery they endured there and the frustration of the year 1706, which came and went without bringing the awaited redemption, broke their spirit. Part of them followed the Donmeh into Islam, others including Hayyim Malach, who retained his faith in Sabbatai Zevi to the end, returned to Poland.

Evidently no disappointment was strong enough to extinguish the flame of the Sabbatean faith in certain circles. Towards the middle of the eighteenth century, another prophet, Leib Krysa of Nadworna, was preaching at Lemberg, announcing that the advent of the Messiah was at hand, and in 1755 he proclaimed Jacob Frank as the reincarnation of Sabbatai Zevi. Jacob Frank, a Podolian Jew who had spent several years in Turkey and had closely associated with Donmeh leaders there, based his confused teachings on the Zohar, which he established as the primary authority in Jewish life in place of the Talmud. He and his followers were soon accused, not only of disavowing Jewish religious tradition, but also of discarding all moral discipline, and the whole sect was solemnly excommunicated in 1756. But Frank's repudiation of the Talmud had aroused the interest of Christian circles. In 1757 Archbishop Dembowski arranged a public disputation at Kamienec-Podolsk between "Talmudists and Contra-Talmudists," which resulted in a verdict in favor of the Frankists. Many copies of the Talmud were confiscated and burned. A second disputation, held at Lemberg in 1759, in which the Frankists even dared to assert that the Talmud prescribed the ritual use of Christian blood, ended less triumphantly for them, for by now they had gone too far. There was no longer place for them in the fold of Judaism and Frank and his followers asked for admittance to the Catholic Church. Frank, who did not give up his Messianic claims and soon became suspect to the Church, was arrested and confined in the fortress Czenstochowa, where he spent thirteen years, continuing his agitation even from there. After his liberation, he organized, first at Brűnn (Brno in Czechoslovakia), and then at Offenbach, near Frankfort-on-Main, his "court" or "military camp." Living there in great style as the "Baron of Offenbach," he received the homage and oblations of numerous

followers until his death (1791). His daughter Eve inherited his status and only her death in 1816 marked the end of the movement.

The baptized Frankists became true sons of the Catholic Church. Some were raised to nobility and others intermarried with members of the Polish aristocracy.

While Frank was leading his adherents into apostasy, another mystical movement was being brought into the world, likewise by a Podolian Jew. This movement, Hassidism, was destined to effect a revival of intense religious life in Judaism.

Several years before Frank revealed himself as the reincarnation of Sabbatai Zevi, Israel Baal Shem Tov or "the Master of the Good Name" (usually known by his abbreviated name "Besht"), a loam-digger in the Carpathian mountains, settled at Miedzyboz. In this Podolian village, he collected around him disciples, whom he initiated in the way of reaching communion with God by ecstatic prayer and by concentration on the idea of divine omnipresence. He did not reject Jewish religious law, but asked that every observance be animated by a spiritual intention, instead of degenerating into a mere routine. The Besht's teachings changed the stern aspect of rabbinic Judaism and offered the distressed Polish Jews a glimpse of joy. His followers used to express their religious feelings by singing and dancing. Of course, not every Hassid was able to reach the summit of ecstatic union with God. This privilege was

The synagogue of Israel Baal Shem Tov (1700–1760), the initiator of Hassidism, in Miedziboz, Ukraine.

Rabbi Elijah, "the Gaon of Vilna" (1720–1797), the foremost rabbinical scholar of his time. An opponent to Hassidism, he was regarded by the "Mitnaggedim" as their spiritual leader.

reserved for a few *Zaddikim* ("Righteous Ones"). After the death of the founder, the *Zaddikim* soon assumed the role of mediators between God and the Hassidim, who considered them miracle-workers.

At first, the Hassidic movement aroused opposition in rabbinic circles and its adversaries even scornfully designated themselves as Mitnaggedim (Opponents). Among them were such outstanding personalities as Rabbi Elijah ben Solomon, known as the Gaon of Vilna (1720–1797). But neither persecution and derision nor excommunications succeeded in driving out the Hassidim from the Jewish fold. They clung to Judaism and, in the course of time, their way of worship was not only accepted as orthodox, but it also profoundly influenced the circles who had previously opposed it.

In the course of the eighteenth century, the Hassidic movement had a series of prominent leaders, among whom Elimelech of Lizensk, Levi Isaac of Berdichev and Shneur Zalman of Ladi, the initiator of the so-called "Habad" (ethical) current of Hassidism, deserve mention.

To-day Hassidism is still very much alive, but divided into many groups, each adhering to its own Zaddik. This dignity, which was originally charismatic, has become hereditary in certain families and regular dynasties have come into being.

Hassidism developed a fervent love of the Holy Land. In 1778 a group of Hassidim, led by their Rabbi Menahem Mendel of Vitebsk, settled in Palestine and many more subsequently followed their example. Their lead was soon followed by a group of "Mitnaggedim", disciples of the Gaon of Vilna, the Ashkenazi element in the Palestinian Jewish population henceforth assuming great importance.

Reputed portrait of Rabbi Shneur Zalman of Ladi (1746–1812), initiator of the "Habad" current of Hassidism.

303

THE COURT JEWS IN GERMANY

The crumbling of the last vestiges of the authority of the Holy Roman Emperors in Germany, as a result of the Thirty Years' War (1618–1648), filled the land with petty courts vying with one another in magnificence and aping, on a smaller scale, that of Versailles. All of them had need of jewellers, actors, military purveyors and financial experts — precisely those callings in which the Jews excelled. Hence from the middle of the seventeenth century, there emerged in Germany more and more prominently the class of "Court Jews," men of personal acceptability and financial adroitness, who devotedly and conscientiously served the interests of their princely masters, although not without securing important benefits for themselves.

In order to perform their functions, the Court Jews had to be freed from the restrictions to which other Jews were subject. They were allowed to live upon the same footing as the higher circles of society and mixed with them on terms of social equality. It was around these magnates and their ample households that fresh communities began to spring up throughout Germany in places from which Jews had been hitherto wholly excluded.

Among the most influential Court Jews were the factors of the Imperial Court at Vienna, particularly Samuel Oppenheimer (1630–1703) and

Expulsion of the Jews from Vienna in 1670 (Contemporary engraving).

David Oppenheimer (1664–1736), at first Chief Rabbi of Moravia, then of Bohemia. A nephew of the Vienna Court Jew Samuel Oppenheimer, he used his fortune to build up a most valuable library (about 7000 printed books and nearly 1000 manuscripts), which forms now the nucleus of the Hebrew collection of the Bodleian Library at Oxford.

DAVID BEN ABRAHAM OPPENHEIMER.

Samson Wertheimer (1658–1724), who were largely responsible for the organization of supplies for the Austrian armies in the War of Spanish Succession and the Turkish campaigns at the close of the seventeenth and the beginning of the eighteenth centuries.

A few years after the Jews had been expelled from Vienna in 1670 on no reasonable pretext except Catholic zeal, the same Emperor Leopold I, whose bigotry had brought about the expulsion, found it necessary to appoint Samuel Oppenheimer imperial factor and to grant the right of residence at Vienna to him and his numerous retainers — thus tacitly admitting the renewal of the Jewish community in his capital. Oppenheimer was in high favor with the Emperor and even succeeded in inducing him to confiscate Johann Eisenmenger's anti-Semitic book *Entdecktes Judentum* ("Judaism Unmasked"). But the Emperor's favor could not protect him against the Vienna mob which, instigated by the clergy, stormed and ransacked his house in 1700.

After Oppenheimer's death, his collaborator Samson Wertheimer inherited his position and did much for the development and consolidation of the Jewish community at Vienna.

By means of the fortune which Samuel Oppenheimer had left him, his nephew David Oppenheimer, who was Chief Rabbi of Moravia, was able to build up the greatest collection of Hebrew manuscripts and printed books the world had even seen. This collection now belongs to the Bodleian Library at Oxford.

Wer groſser Herren Gunst misbraucht mit bösen Rath.
Wie dieser fréche Iud Süeß Oppenheimer that.
Wen Geitz und Übermuth auch Wollust eingenomen.
Der mus wie Haman dort zu letzt an Galgen komen.

Joseph Süss Oppenheimer (1698–1738), remembered as "Jew Süss", a tragic figure among the 18th century Court Jews. His rapid ascent at the court of the Duke of Wurttemberg aroused envy and hatred. At the death of his patron, he was arrested and sentenced to death.

More typical was the tragic career of the Oppenheimer's kinsman, Joseph Süss Oppenheimer (1698–1738), better remembered as "Jew Süss." After having occupied similar positions and proved his talents at the courts of the Palatinate and Hesse, Joseph Süss was, in 1732, appointed factor of the Duke of Württemberg, later becoming his all-powerful minister. He carried out financial reforms and set up a great number of industrial and commercial enterprises, which yielded him considerable profits, but at the same time consolidated the economical situation of the country. His high position and powerful influence aroused a great deal of hatred against him. When his patron and protector, the Duke Karl Alexander, suddenly died in 1737, Joseph Süss was arrested and accused of peculation and many other sins, to which he all confessed under torture. Condemned to death by hanging, he refused the proposal to change his faith, protested his innocence to the last and died with a proud "*Shema Yisrael*" on his lips. His death was followed by a howling storm of anti-Jewish feeling and the Jews were expelled from Wurttemberg, not to be readmitted until the end of the eighteenth century.

Although such expulsions could still happen, the dawning of a new age made itself felt when, in 1745, the ancient community of Prague was struck by a similar fate. The pretext was, in this case, that Rabbi Jonathan Eybeschütz, a famous although controversial scholar (because of putative Sabbatean inclinations), had left Prague to accept the appointment as Chief Rabbi of the community of Metz. This was interpreted by the authorities as a manifestation of anti-Austrian sentiments among the Jews and the Empress Maria Theresa issued a decree obliging the Jews to leave Prague within a month in deep winter. This time, the cruel decree elicited indignation throughout Europe and was followed by international diplomatic interventions. England and the Netherlands made representations at Vienna, efficiently supported by influential Jewish financiers at home and abroad, Finally the Empress was obliged to recall the Jews to Prague, although only after three years of Jewish suffering.

The death of Duke Karl Alexander of Wurttemberg (contemporary engraving). 'Jew Süss' holds in his right hand a paper inscribed "Es fällt mein Freund. Oweih! Oweih!" (My friend falls. Woe! Woe!) Two other Jews gesticulate excitedly, while the townfolk stream into the room and joyfully clasp the hands.

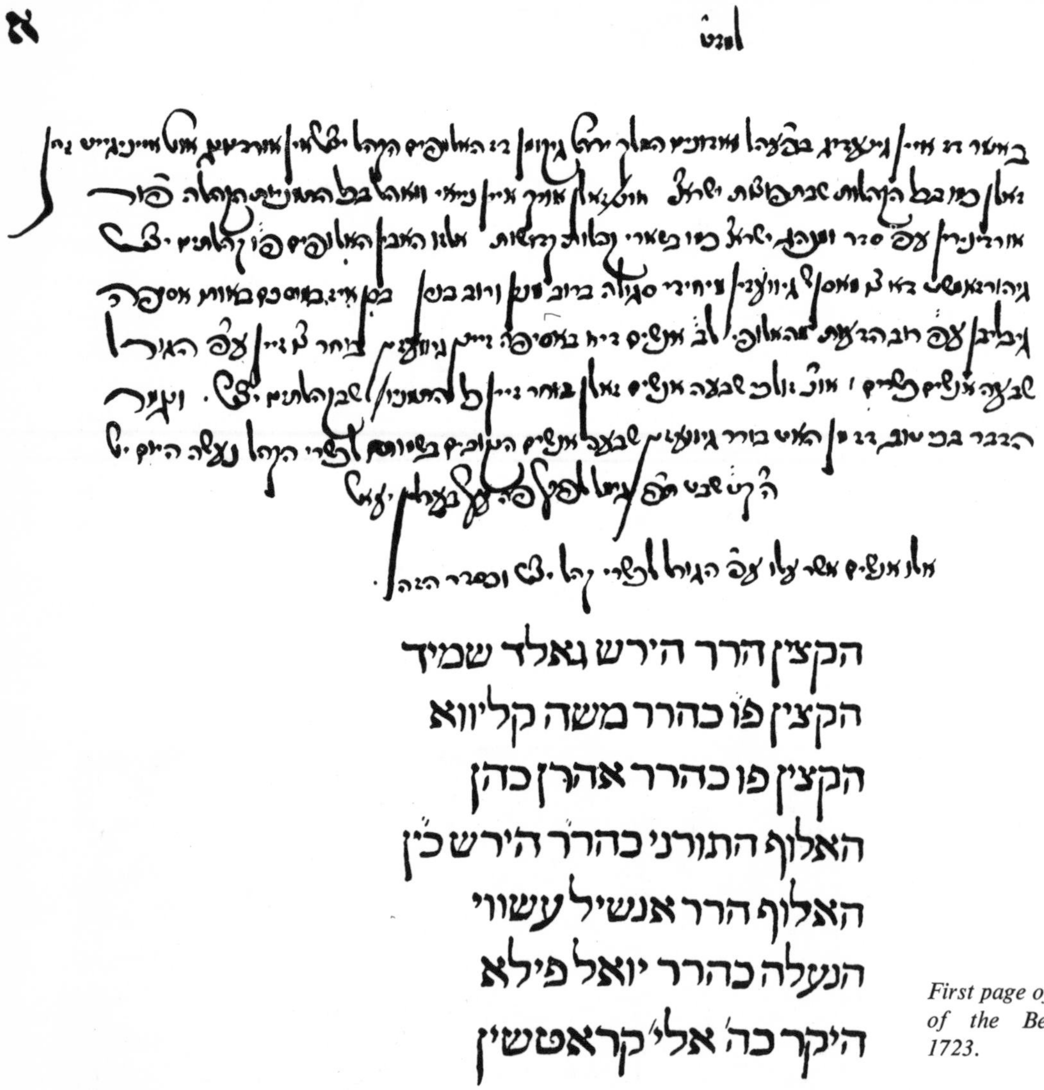

הקצין הרר הירש נאלד שמיד
הקצין פו כהרר משה קליווא
הקצין פו כהרר אהרן כהן
האלוף התורני כהרר הירש כ׳ץ
האלוף הרר אנשיל עשוי
הנעלה כהרר יואל פילא
היקר כה׳ אלי׳ קראטשין

First page of the Minute Book of the Berlin Community, 1723.

Sometimes such expulsion had far-reaching consequences in respect of future developments. This was the case of the already mentioned temporary expulsion of the Jews from Vienna in 1670. Besides reinforcing numerous other existing Jewish communities of Germany, part of the exiles were admitted to Brandenburg, where there had been no Jewish settlement since the expulsion of 1573, and founded the community of Berlin, soon to become one of Germany's most important Jewish centers.

The Berlin community became, in the eighteenth century, the point of departure of a spiritual ferment destined to revolutionize European Jewry at large, the Haskalah (Enlightenment) movement. Its initiator was the Jewish philosopher Moses Mendelssohn (1729–1786), who settled in Berlin in 1743. Setting aside the prejudices of his time and environment, Mendelssohn had also acquired, besides the usual Jewish learning, a thorough knowledge of the German and Latin languages and a comprehensive grounding in philosophy. Encouraged by his friend, the German poet Lessing, he soon became a philosophical author in the German language, highly appreciated in wide non-Jewish literary and intellectual circles. Mendelssohn considered it his task, to put an end to the intellectual isolation of his co-religionsists by opening the way to European culture for them. For this purpose he rendered the Bible into literary German and published this translation in Hebrew letters together with a Hebrew commentary ("Biur"), written with the help of several like-minded collaborators. In this way, Mendelssohn wanted to make the Jews familiar, on the one side, with the grammatical, non-allegorical interpretation of the biblical text and, on the other, with the German instead

Moses Mendelssohn (1729–1786), famous as a philosophical and theological author, as a translator and commentator of the Bible, he raised the prestige of Judaism in the eyes of the gentiles and ushered in the movement called "Enlightenment" (Haskalah), which aimed at integrating the Jews into European culture.

Salomon Maimon (1754–1800). Passionately devoted to philosophic research, he left his native Lithuania for Germany and joined Mendelssohn's circle in Berlin. He distinguished himself as a critic of Kantian philosophy and influenced the development of the idealistic philosophy in Germany. But his autobiography illustrates the danger of the abrupt passage from Jewish seclusion to European culture.

of the Yiddish tongue, exclusively used by them till then. Although fanatically opposed by orthodox circles, Mendelssohn's Bible translation was widely used and, together with his other writings, helped to model a new Jewish type. At the same time, Mendelssohn taught his German compatriots that the Jews possessed the elements of the finest citizenship in the modern sense. He, his family, and his disciples symbolized the end of the old Ghetto in Germany, even though it betokened the approach of a new one. The demolition of the barrier which had hitherto separated the Jews from the Christians was, however, not free of danger to Judaism. Many members of Mendelssohn's family and some of his disciples too wavered on the border line that divided Judaism from Christianity. Some of them even crossed the line, abandoning their people and faith in order to enter Christian society.

Among the intellectuals in Mendelssohn's circle, one at least, Salomon Maimon, deserves a special mention. His criticism of Kantian philosophy wrested from Kant himself the avowal that none of his adversaries had so well understood him. Maimon exercised considerable influence on German philosophy, but the sudden jump into European culture proved disastrous to his character and finally estranged him from Judaism. He left an autobiography, which is a moving confession.

The vast majority of the German Jews in the eighteenth century formed a proletariat of petty merchants and pedlars living on the verge of indigence. But high above them there was the numerically small, but financially powerful, class of Court Jews and their associates, a tightly-knit oligarchy which, in some cases, led a life of real magnificence, with numerous servants and superbly furnished houses. They sometimes maintained their private synagogues, which they furnished resplendently. For this purpose they patronized Jewish silversmiths and craftsmen, artists and engravers.

A German Jewish household in the 18th century (from the Second Cincinnati Haggadah).

311

Title-page of the Minute Book of the Ashkenazi Community of Hamburg-Altona, 1726 (General Archives for Jewish History, Jerusalem).

Jewish pedlar, Derby ware, about 1760 (Jewish Museum, London).

Germany's largest Jewish community was in Hamburg. With the communities in Amsterdam and London, it formed a sort of Jewish Hansa, which played a significant part in eighteenth century trade. The Hamburg community, with its hidalgo Sephardim, its Ashkenazi merchants and jewellers and its vast proletariat, illustrated, to a greater extent than almost any other place, the deep contrast in the way of life between the social classes into which German Jewry was divided. At that time, Hamburg also became the seat of a flourishing Jewish spiritual life, owing particularly to the personality of the great rabbinic authority Haham Zevi Ashkenazi, who settled there in 1690 and founded a Talmudic school which he headed for twenty years, before he was appointed Rabbi in Amsterdam. His son, Jacob Emden, who was born in Hamburg returned to his native town in 1733 and made it the center of his fierce campaign against the aftermath of the Sabbatean movement.

The history of Jewish life in Hamburg is particularly well known thanks to two extremely interesting autobiographies. The first is that of a Jewish woman, Glückel of Hameln, describing the second half of the seventeenth century, when the Messianic excitement was running high. The second is the autobiography of Rabbi Jacob Emden covering the greater part of the eighteenth century. The former, with its warmth and its mass of intimate domestic detail, is among the classics of Jewish literature.

THE JEWS IN EIGHTEENTH-CENTURY ENGLAND

The Jewish community in England was meanwhile developing along different lines. Owing to the informal circumstances of the Jewish resettlement in England, there were from the outset no legal restrictions on Jewish life in this country. They were mostly able to live where they pleased, to dress as other men did, to mix with others on normal terms, and to follow any calling according to their inclinations. From the moment the Jews returned to live in England, the upper crust of brokers and merchants, Ashkenazim as well as Sephardim, lived lives not very different from those of their gentile neighbors.

On the other hand, a stream of poor Jews, mostly refugees from the ghettos of Germany and Eastern Europe, followed at their heels, earning their living in the new country as best they could, as pedlars and old-clothes men performing what was then a most useful economic function. These modest immigrants made their way later to provincial towns and founded the earliest Anglo-Jewish communities in places like Birmingham, Bristol, Canterbury, Liverpool, Plymouth, Portsmouth and elsewhere. The beginnings of these communities date from the middle of the eighteenth century. From these towns, they ranged about the countryside as provincial pedlars.

Rag Fair in London (Drawing by Thomas Rawlinson). The trade in old clothes was a Jewish specialty.

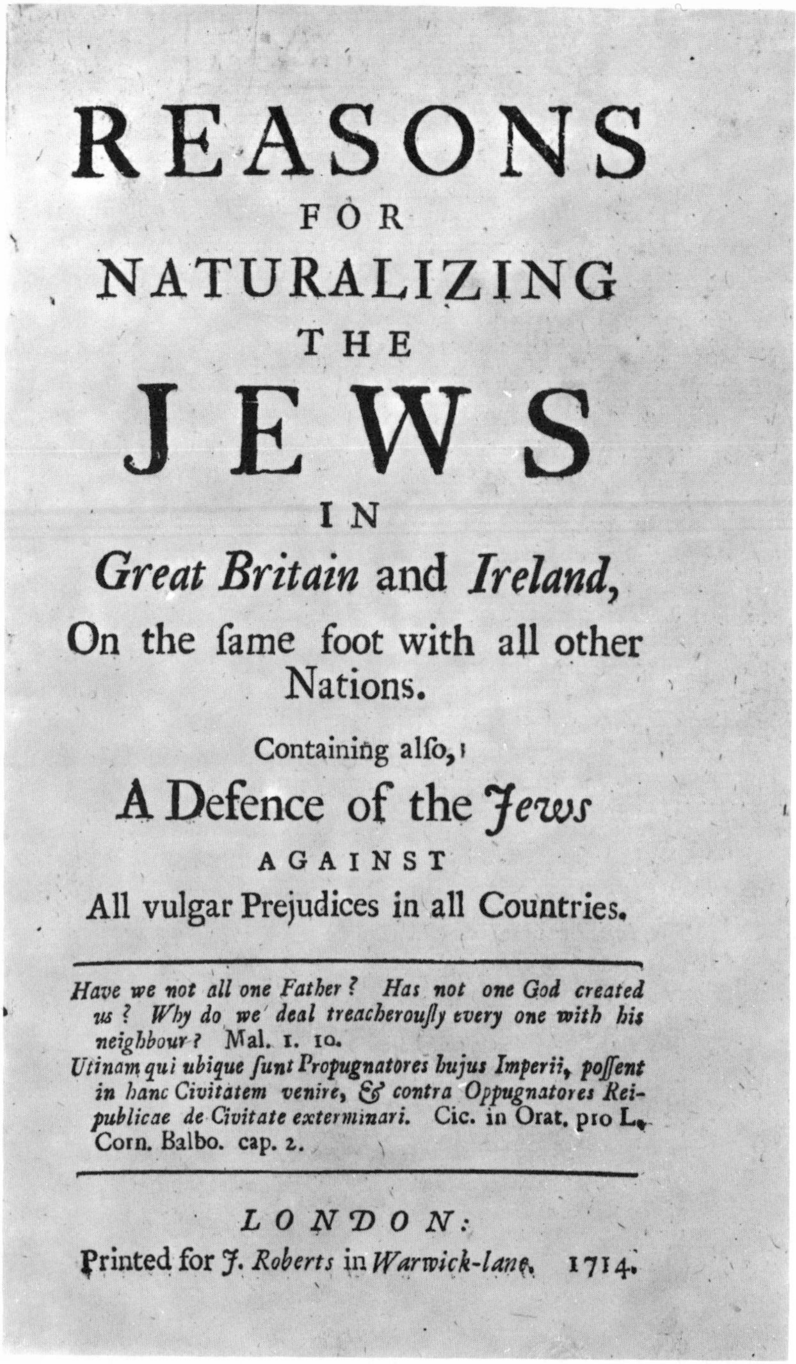

REASONS
FOR
NATURALIZING
THE
JEWS
IN
Great Britain and *Ireland,*

On the fame foot with all other
Nations.

Containing alfo,

A Defence of the *Jews*
AGAINST
All vulgar Prejudices in all Countries.

---

*Have we not all one Father? Has not one God created
us? Why do we deal treacheroufly every one with his
neighbour?* Mal. I. 10.
*Utinam qui ubique funt Propugnatores bujus Imperii, poffent
in hanc Civitatem venire, & contra Oppugnatores Rei-
publicae de Civitate exterminari.* Cic. in Orat. pro L.
Corn. Balbo. cap. 2.

LONDON:
Printed for *J. Roberts* in *Warwick-lane.* 1714.

*Title-page of John Toland's
"Reasons for Naturalizing the
Jews in Great Britain and
Ireland", published anony-
mously in 1714.*

This part of the Jewish population (whose total hardly exceeded ten
thousand souls in the middle of the eighteenth century) was, naturally,
far more in the public eye than their fashionable Sephardic co-religionists
in London. The social history of England's Jewry of the lower orders in
that period may be traced in the brutal productions of the English caricaturists of the time, who spared them no more than they did other
strata of society.

The great majority of the English Jews were, at that time, foreign born,
and it was suggested that a more liberal policy in regard to naturalization

Sampson Gideon (1699–1762), the London banker who helped maintain public credit in England and offered to equip five vessels for the defence of the British coasts, at the time of the Jacobite rebellion of 1745. (Portrait by Allan Ramsay, Collection of Lt. Col. D. E. Fremantle).

would not only accelerate the process of assimilation, but would also encourage a larger immigration of the wealthier elements, who were considered to be most valuable economically. The first to advocate the naturalization of the Jews in England was the deistic philosopher John Toland, who in 1714 published an anonymous pamphlet, "Reasons for naturalizing the Jews in Great Britain and Ireland, on the same foot with all other Nations, containing also a defence of the Jews against all vulgar prejudices in all countries." The motto of this remarkable pamphlet was: "Have we not all one father? Has not one God created us?" (*Malachi 2:10*). Although not, as is generally imagined, advocating full civil rights for the Jews, the pamphlet was, nevertheless, a remarkable plea for tolerance.

In 1753, the Government submitted to Parliament a rather innocuous bill on the naturalization of foreign Jews, which more or less implemented Toland's modest proposals. The supporters of this bill pointed out the part played by Jews in the development of British trade and the patriotic contribution of the Jewish financial magnates to the improvement of the country's finances. They also mentioned the special merit of the Jewish broker Sampson Gideon, who in 1745 offered to the Admiralty five vessels, fully equipped at his expense, for the defence of the British coasts.

The bill was passed and granted Jews who had been living in England for at least three years, the right to apply for naturalization. The ludicrous anti-Jewish storm raised by the opposition against this

The JERUSALEM INFIRMARY.
Alias, a JOURNEY to the Valley of JEHOSAPHAT.

bill, may have had the purpose of embarrassing the Government more than of vexing the Jews. However, it led to the bill's revocation in 1754. This set-back caused profound disappointment in higher Jewish circles. The fight was, nevertheless, continued with energy and patience and victory was achieved towards the middle of the nineteenth century.

The Board of Deputies of British Jews, established in 1760 for purely ceremonial and formal objects, later developed in scale and extended its scope, so that in the Victorian period it was able to take an active part in the struggle for Jewish emancipation and the protection of persecuted Jews abroad.

Anglo-Jewish communal life was evolving during all this time on characteristic English lines. Even internal criticism, for instance objections to the administration of the "Beth Holim" Hospital of the Spanish and Portuguese community, established in 1745, manifested themselves in typically British caricaturistic expression. The portraits of Anglo-Jewish rabbis and ministers of religion, too, showed them in a British guise, which was as much Anglo- as it was Jewish.

Later in the century, the emergence of a succession of Jewish prize-fighters, such as Daniel Mendoza, the first English scientific boxer, presented the Jew in somewhat of a new light to the man in the street.

The same may be said of one of the most amazing events in the late eighteenth century, the conversion to Judaism of the English aristocrat

Caricature by a Jewish artist criticizing the administration of the "Beth Holim" Hospital of the Spanish and Portuguese Community of London (18th century engraving).

Lord George Gordon (1751–1793), the English aristocrat who became a convert to Judaism in 1787 and spent the rest of his short life as a strictly observant Jew (Copper token, 1793).

Lord George Gordon. After having been known for many years as the militant representative of Protestant intolerance against Catholicism, Lord George became in 1787 a most orthodox Jew, grew a beard and sidelocks, and changed his name to Israel ben Abraham On account of his virulent attacks against the Government, he was sentenced to imprisonment for libel and died in prison, where he continued to his last day to observe scrupulously all the minute prescriptions of Jewish law. His conversion to Judaism, of course, afforded a golden opportunity to the ever-vigilant caricaturists, who did not scruple to present him as an old-clothes man. But it also demonstrated the attraction which Judaism was capable of exercising on a thoroughly religious nature.

Caricature on the prize-fight between Humphreys and the Jewish boxer Daniel Mendoza in 1787. Lord Gordon, the noble convert to Judaism, is shown on the extreme left.

The TRIUMPH

THE SETTLEMENT OF THE JEWS
IN AMERICA

The association of the Jews with America goes back to Christopher Columbus. It is believed that Columbus himself belonged to a Marrano family, and there seem to be fairly strong grounds for this assumption. His Jewish descent was possibly one reason for the deliberate mystery in which he concealed his origins. Many of his private letters bear at the top corner a mysterious sign, which some persons hold to be the traditional abbreviation of the Hebrew words "with the help of God," with which Jews were, and are, accustomed to begin their correspondence. What is certain, in any case, is that Columbus had what may be termed

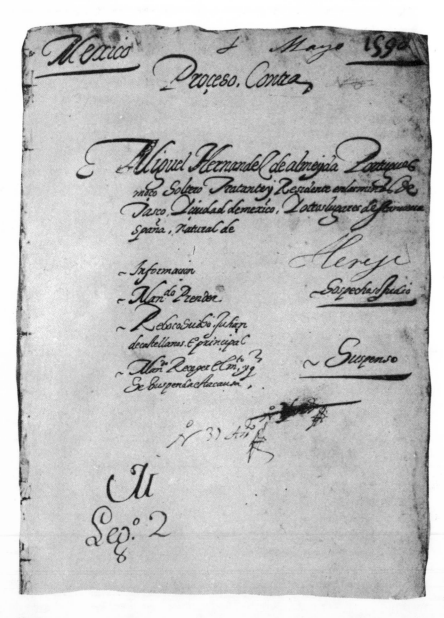

Trial of the Marrano Miguel Hernandez de Almeida by the Inquisition in Mexico, 1590 (Archives of the American Jewish Historical Society).

a penchant for Jewish society. He received his most solid and consistent support from a group of Jews and crypto-Jews, and his earliest reports, through which the discovery of the new continent became known in the world, were addressed to his Marrano or New-Christian patrons, Luis de Santangel, chancellor and comptroller of the royal household in Aragon, and Gabriel Sanchez, high treasurer of the kingdom.

A baptized Jew, Luis de Torres, who served as interpreter to Columbus' expedition, was the first European known to have set foot in the New World. There was at least one Marrano among the Conquistadores who fought under Cortes in Mexico, and Marranos were known, too, among the earliest settlers in central and southern America. Their numbers increased when the ban on their emigration from Spain and Portugal to the oversea colonies was lifted, at the beginning of the seventeenth century

But the Church was on guard and the Inquisition followed hard on the heels of the Marranos. As early as 1539 a group of Marranos was among those who appeared at an auto-da-fé in Mexico. In the last decade of the sixteenth century, Luis de Carvajal, a Marrano who had been appointed governor of the Mexican province of New Leon, was prosecuted by the Inquisition and died in prison. His nephew and namesake, who had been the leader of the Judaizing Marrano group, was burned at an auto-da-fé together with many members of the family.

In the second half of the sixteenth century, tribunals of the Holy Office were established throughout the Spanish colonies, amassing great wealth and building, out of the confiscated fortunes, impressive palaces as their headquarters. Some of them still stand as monuments to intolerance.

Inquisitional activities reached their climax towards the middle of the seventeenth century. In 1639 in Lima, about sixty Judaizers were involved in a great auto-da-fé. Seven of them were burnt alive and forty-four sentenced to various punishments. Hundreds of Marranos stood trial in Mexico between the years 1642 and 1649 and a number of spectacular autos-da-fé were held. These mass-trials effectively checked the spreading of the Judaizing movement in that country.

In Brazil there were numerous Marranos, a number of them deported from Portugal for the crime of Judaizing. When, early in the seventeenth century, the Dutch temporarily conquered Brazil from the Portuguese, many of the local Marranos openly professed Judaism. Jewish communities were established in different regions. Immigrants from the Netherlands came to join their Brazilian co-religionists and bolster their congregations. The first and most important among the communities in Brazil was "Zur Israel" at Recife (Pernambuco). At its head stood Rabbi Isaac Aboab da Fonseca, who had come from the Netherlands in 1642. With him came the learned head of the Amsterdam Talmud Tora, Moses Raphel d'Aguilar, to act as reader in the synagogue.

Isaac Aboab da Fonseca (1605–1693), "the first American Rabbi". He was the spiritual head of the Jewish Community at Recife (Pernambuco) in Brazil. When the Portuguese conquered Brazil, in 1654, and the Jewish Community there came to an end, he returned to Holland, where he became Rabbi of the Sephardi Community.

But this period of religious freedom was only a short interlude. In 1645 the Portuguese launched a counter-attack for the reconquest of Brazil and drove out the Dutch after a protracted war. Pernambuco was twice besieged and the Jews valiantly participated in the defence of the city. Relief from the first siege was the occasion for the first literary production in Hebrew on American soil, a lengthy poem of thanksgiving by Rabbi Aboab. In 1654, however, the city was recaptured by the Portuguese and the community broke up. Aboab, Aguilar, and other Jews who had come from the Netherlands, returned to their former country. The rest of the community scattered throughout the New World and established the earliest enduring communities in territories which were under the more tolerant rule of the Protestant powers, England and the Netherlands.

Some went to Curaçao to reinforce an already existing small community, to the island of Barbados, where congregations were set up at Bridgetown, Speightstown and elsewhere, and in due course to Jamaica, where communities sprang up at Kingston, Spanish Town and other places. Some of these communities still survive.

In Surinam there was, besides the still extant mercantile community at Paramaribo on the sea-coast, a flourishing agricultural colony up-river, at the Savanna of the Jews (Joden Savanne) enjoying quite a remarkable degree of autonomy. A splendid synagogue was built there in 1685. This settlement was, however, abandoned in the eighteenth century, mainly owing to successive Negro revolts.

320

Tombstones in the Sephardi cemetery of Curaçao, 1726.

The synagogue of Surinam, built about 1700.

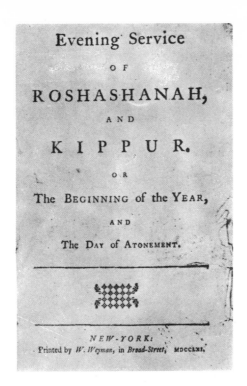

Evening Service

OF

ROSHASHANAH,

AND

KIPPUR.

OR

The BEGINNING of the YEAR,

AND

The DAY of ATONEMENT.

NEW-YORK:
Printed by *W. Weyman*, in *Broad-Street*, MDCCLXI.

Title-page of the Services for the New Year and the Day of Atonement, New York, 1761. This is the first translation of the Jewish prayer-book printed in the English language. No Hebrew appears in this volume.

Interior of the Touro Synagogue at Newport R. I., built in 1763, the earliest synagogue erected in the United States outside New York. In 1946 the synagogue was dedicated as a national historic shrine (Photograph by Kerschner, Newport R.I.).

The most memorable communities founded by Brazilian refugees, and Jews who joined them later on were those of the North American mainland. In September 1654, a small group of twenty-three Jews arrived at New Amsterdam (later New York) after a four months' sea voyage, in the course of which their vessel had been captured by Spanish pirates and subsequently released by a French privateer. This was the origin of the Spanish and Portuguese congregation of New York, later to become numerically the greatest Jewish community of all times.

Further communities were established elsewhere in the American colonies in the course of time, the earliest of which was in Newport (Rhode Island). The Newport community was augmented in the eighteenth century by Ashkenazi immigrants and a lovely synagogue, which still stands, was dedicated there in 1763. In Charleston, Savannah, Philadelphia and some smaller places too, communities were established. Everywhere Ashkenazi immigrants from Germany and Poland, in many cases coming via the Netherlands and England, arrived in due course to reinforce the original settlers who were, as a rule, Sephardim. Some of these Ashkenazic immigrants — the Levy, Franks, Philips and other families — became veritable merchant princes, as their dignified portraits amply demonstrate. The Town of Aaronsburg, Pa., is named after Aaron Levy, a merchant who arrived in America from the Netherlands about 1760.

By the time of the American Revolution, there were some two thousand Jews in the British North American colonies, scattered in about half a dozen communities along the Atlantic seaboard, with a few isolated families in the smaller commercial centers that were now coming into being. In addition, there was a Jewish community in Montreal, Canada, established almost immediately after the British occupation in 1761.

323

The Mill Street Synagogue of Shearith Israel Congregation, New York, built in 1729, consecrated in April 1730 (American Jewish Archives, Cincinnati).

During the American War of Independence (1775–1783), the majority of the Jewish population embraced the patriot cause. Many fought bravely under Washington in the ranks of the continental forces and some performed important services in other ways. David Salisbury Franks, a resident of Montreal, threw in his lot with the Americans, served with distinction in the U.S. Army and thereafter was sent on important diplomatic missions abroad. His cousin, Isaac Franks, was one of Washington's adjutants. Colonels Solomon Bush and Mordecai Sheftall likewise deserve mention.

To the left:
Colonel David Salisbury Franks (1750–1790), joined the American revolutionary army and was Benedict Arnold's aide-de-camp. When Arnold went over to the English, he remained faithful to the American cause. After the war, he accomplished diplomatic missions abroad (American Jewish Historic Society).

To the right:
Colonel Isaac Franks (1759–1822), aide-de-camp of General George Washington. Painting by Gilbert Stuart.

To the Hebrew Congregation in Newport
Rhode Island

Gentlemen.

While I receive, with much satisfaction, your Address replete with expressions of affection and esteem, I rejoice in the opportunity of assuring you, that I shall always retain a grateful remembrance of the cordial welcome I experienced in my visit to Newport, from all classes of Citizens

The reflection on the days of difficulty and danger which are past is rendered the more sweet, from a consciousness that they are succeeded by days of uncommon prosperity and security If we have wisdom to make the best use of the advantages with which we are now favored, we cannot fail, under the just administration of a good Government: to become a great and a happy people

The Citizens of the United States of America have a right to applaud themselves for having given to mankind examples of an enlarged and liberal policy a policy worthy of imitation All possess alike Liberty of conscience and immunities of citizenship It is now no more that toleration is spoken of, as if it was by the indulgence of one class of people that another enjoyed the exercise of their inherent natural rights For happily the Government of the United States, which gives to bigotry no sanction, to persecution no assistance requires only that they who live under its protection should demean themselves as good Citizens, in giving it on all occasions their effectual support.

It would be inconsistent with the frankness of my character not to avow that I am pleased with your favorable opinion of my administration, and fervent wishes for my felicity. May the Children of the Stock of Abraham, who dwell in this land, continue to merit and enjoy the good will of the other Inhabitants; while every one shall sit in safety under his own vine and figtree, and there shall be none to make him afraid May the father of all mercies scatter light and not darkness in our paths, and make us all in our several vocations useful here, and in his own due time and way everlastingly happy.

G Washington

But the outstanding Jewish figure of the period was Polish-born Haym Solomon, who heroically collaborated with Washington's finance minister Robert Morris in maintaining public credit during the period of emergency, as official broker to the Office of Finance. His devoted assistance in this sphere helped to consolidate the American Republic in its formative years. He advanced to the revolutionary government more than half a million dollars without interest or security, and generously assisted from his own pocket patriot leaders such as James Madison and Thomas Jefferson.

When the period of emergency was over, the Jewish community of Newport addressed to George Washington, as President of the newly-founded United States, a congratulatory address, to which he replied in a document that may be counted among the most memorable in American Jewish history.

The Declaration of Independence and the original Constitution of the United States assured, on principle, full civil rights to the Jewish citizens. But when independence was achieved, years of struggle were still necessary. in many states, to make these assurances a fact, Some of them removed all disabilities only in the course of the nineteenth century.

THE FRENCH REVOLUTION

By the second half of the eighteenth century, Jewish emancipation was in the air.

In Germany Moses Mendelssohn's noble friend, the poet and philosophic author Gotthold Ephraim Lessing, pleaded in his famous play "*Nathan the Wise*" for genuine religious toleration and a new human approach to the Jews. It is true that this lofty plea did not meet with an enthusiastic reception on the part of the German public and that Lessing was even accused of having been bribed by Amsterdam's Jewry. But once so vigorously expressed, the idea slowly permeated minds, if not hearts.

Another friend of Mendelssohn's, the political author Christian Wilhelm von Dohm, argued concretely for the cause of emancipation in his influential publication "Über die bürgerliche Verbesserung der Juden" ("On the civil improvement of the Jews") in which he analyzed the influence of the discriminative anti-Jewish legislation on the Jewish character and social structure and concluded that, if they were granted full civil rights, the Jews could be transformed into useful citizens.

In France, the idealistic Abbé Henri Grégoire published his "Essai sur la régénération physique, morale et politique des juifs" ("Essay on the physical, moral and political regeneration of the Jews") Like Dohm he

Abbé Grégoire (1750–1831), the champion of Jewish emancipation at the time of the French Revolution.

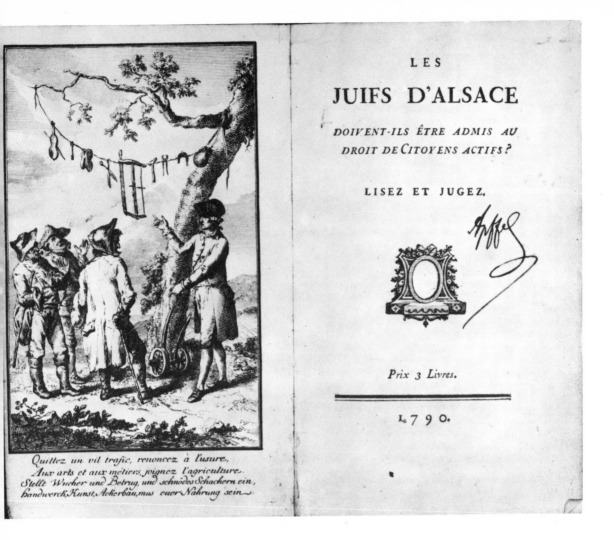

LES

JUIFS D'ALSACE

DOIVENT-ILS ÊTRE ADMIS AU
DROIT DE CITOYENS ACTIFS?

LISEZ ET JUGEZ.

Prix 3 Livres.

I790.

Quittez un vil trafic, renoncez à l'usure,
Aux arts et aux métiers, joignez l'agriculture.
Stellt Wucher und Betrug, und schnödes Schachern ein,
Handwerck, Kunst, Ackerbau, muss euer Nahrung sein.

Anonymous French pamphlet on the problem of the grant of civil rights to the Jews of Alsatia. The illustration invites the Jews to prefer agriculture and handicrafts to commerce and money-lending.

saw the cause of Jewish degeneration in the persecution and contempt to which they had been subjected for centuries, and he invited the Christians to put an end to the groundless hatred and embrace the Jews as fellow-citizens and friends.

In 1782 the German Emperor Joseph II, the enlightened son of that same Maria Theresa who had expelled the Jews from Prague in 1745, issued the famous "Toleranzpatent," by which the Jews of the Austrian dominions were relieved of the most galling disabilities. This act was greeted by his Jewish subjects with jubilation. Joseph's idea of toleration, however, was far from generous, and was in a way a danger to Jewish religious and cultural life. It pursued, in fact, the purpose of gradually absorbing the Jewish population by Germanization and Christianization. Nevertheless it may be considered as a step towards emancipation.

On the part of Jews, too, steps were taken to create the conditions deemed indispensable for the granting of full civil rights, particularly, the introduction of a revised system of Jewish education along western lines. The movement started in the circle which had gathered round Moses Mendelssohn and its chief promoter was one of his closest

LOI

RELATIVE AUX JUIFS.

Donnée à Paris, le 13 Novembre 1791.

LOUIS, par la grâce de Dieu & par la Loi constitutionnelle de l'État, ROI DES FRANÇOIS : A tous présens & à venir ; SALUT.

L'ASSEMBLÉE NATIONALE a décrété, & Nous voulons & ordonnons ce qui suit :

DÉCRET DE L'ASSEMBLÉE NATIONALE, du 27 Septembre 1791.

L'ASSEMBLÉE NATIONALE considérant que les conditions nécessaires pour être citoyen François & pour devenir

The decree of November 13th, 1791, granting the Jews of France full equality of political and civil rights.

collaborators, Naphtali Herz (Hartwig) Wessely. The latter was among the supporters of the principles of the "Toleranzpatent" and in his *Divre Shalom ve-Emet* ("Words of Peace and Truth"), published in 1782, he stressed the necessity for the Jews to acquire a thorough mastery of the German language and the elements, at least, of natural science, geography, and history, in addition to the traditional study of Bible and Talmud. Despite the vehement opposition of conservative rabbinical circles, his ideas soon began to make considerable progress in central Europe.

But the greatest breach in the old system was made by the French Revolution. True to the principles which he had represented before the outbreak of the Revolution, brave Abbé Grégoire pleaded in the National Assembly for the emancipation of the French Jews. There was no particular enthusiasm for the cause in the Assembly and considerable

Come Come Surrender!

*Vat Shurender Jean Boots property— never while I am a Shew.
— I'll let you know Mounsheer, dat I fight for King Sheorge, and
de Shynagogue!!*

London Publ. Sept. 1803. by W. Holland. No 11 Cockspur Street - Pall Mall.

THE LOYAL JEW - and FRENCH SOLDIER or BEARD against WHISKERS!!

English caricature of the time of the Napoleonic wars; in fact a bland joke on the manifestations of Jewish loyalty in England.

opposition in the press and public opinion. But the Declaration of the Rights of Man and the proclamation of the ideal of "Liberty, Equality and Fraternity" necessarily had to be followed out to their logical conclusion. Slowly and even, to some extent, reluctantly, equality of political and civil rights was extended, notwithstanding local opposition, first in 1790 to the Sephardim of Bordeaux, Bayonne and the old-established "Comtadin" Jews of Avignon and the former Papal territories, then in 1791 to the Ashkenazim of Alsace, a population which may have appeared somewhat uncouth in French eyes. This time there was no question of relieving the Jews of certain disabilities, hitherto the utmost that could have been expected. The Jews asked and were granted the same rights as enjoyed by every French citizen.

Moreover, the armies of the French Revolution took these principles in their knapsacks and propagated and applied them, at least for a time, wherever they penetrated in the course of their triumphant campaigns. In the Netherlands, the Batavian Republic was proclaimed and, in 1795. granted full equality of rights to all citizens irrespective of their religion. The emancipation of the Jews was maintained and fully implemented when the Republic was transformed into the Kingdom of Holland under Louis Bonaparte, the brother of Napoleon I.

In Italy the gates of the ghettos were everywhere broken down by the French armies and their denizens were summoned forth to enjoy the same rights as other men.

In Germany the Jews were emancipated in those territories which were under French dominion during the short-lived Napoleonic era: in the Kingdom of Westphalia under King Jerome, another brother of Napoleon, in the Rhineland, and in Hamburg. Here a reaction set in immediately after Napoleon's downfall and the emancipation of the Jews was revoked, so that the fight for equal rights had to be started over again.

Even where French influence did not become dominant, it still penetrated to a certain extent and brought more or less profound changes in the condition of the Jews. In Prussia, for instance, in the national resurgence which accompanied the war of liberation of 1812–15, the Jews received almost complete civil emancipation. They were allowed the honor to fight in the ranks of the patriot armies — in fact the necessity of rebuilding the Prussian military force after the defeat of Jena had been a principal

M. Oppenheim (1799-1882): The Return of the Volunteer (Jewish museum, New-York). Many Jewish volunteers served in the German armies in the war of liberation against Napoleon.

Berek Joselewicz (1765–1809), commanded a Jewish regiment in the Polish revolt of 1794, then joined the French army and took part with distinction in the Napoleonic campains. Returned to Poland in 1807 to serve the Grand Duchy of Warsaw, he fell in the battle of Kock against Austrian troops, in 1809.

reason for issuing the Edict of Emancipation of 1812 — and the Jews signalized their new-found equality by fighting bravely.

Theoretically the new spirit came to Poland as well. Equality of rights for the Jews was among the principles of the Polish revolution of 1794 headed by Kosciuszko, to which the Polish Jews contributed a regiment of volunteers under command of Berek Joselewicz. The Jewish regiment was almost annihilated in the battle for the defense of Warsaw. Berek Joselewicz himself subsequently achieved military distinction in the Napoleonic army. He returned in 1807 to Poland, to serve the Grand Duchy of Warsaw and to die for it in battle in 1809. The constitution of this Polish Grand Duchy, set up by Napoleon, provided on the paper equality of rights for all citizens, but to the end of its existence (1813), the Jews vainly struggled for their rights against the cynical bad will of the Government and Senate.

In France, the Republic had been replaced by now by the Empire of Napoleon I. Before attaining the imperial crown, Napoleon had already displayed some interest in the Jewish people. In 1798, fighting in Palestine against the Turks, he issued a proclamation to the Jews of Asia and Africa promising them to re-establish the Jewish State and inviting them to co-operate with the French Army. It is difficult to know, how seriously the promise was meant, but in any case the proclamation remained without any practical effect.

SANHÉDRIN DES JUIFS
de l'Empire.

A session of the Great Sanhedrin of 1807, convoked by Napoleon I (Engraving by David after a painting by Monnet).

In 1806 numerous complaints against the Jews in Alsace reached the Emperor. It was alleged that they were unscrupulously exploiting Alsatian peasants. But the irritating aspect of the problem for Napoleon was the fact that the Alsatian Jews formed a distinct ethnic and cultural body, "a nation within the nation," as he expressed himself. His tidy mind could not tolerate the apparent anomaly of the Jewish position. He summoned to Paris first an Assembly of Jewish Notables, which convened in July 1806 under the chairmanship of Abraham Furtado of Bordeaux. Other prominent personalities among the Notables were the army-purveyor Berr-Isaac Berr of Nancy and Rabbi David Joseph Sinzheim of Strasbourg. The Assembly was required to answer a series of questions determining and defining the position of the emancipated Jew in the modern state. When he had obtained satisfactory answers to his questions from the Notables, Napoleon decided to convoke a "Great Sanhedrin" in the following year, carefully modelled on the ancient institution of post-biblical times, to confer authoritative sanction upon the resolutions of the Assembly of Notables. The "Great Sanhedrin," consisting of the traditional number of seventy-one members and presided over by Rabbi David Sinzheim, who bore the time-honored title of Nasi, held its inaugural session on the February 9th, 1807 and completed its transactions a month later. Actually the Sanhedrin accomplished little. It did no more than approve — as was expected of it — the resolutions formulated by the Notables, thus submitting Jewish religious and cultural life entirely to the control of the state. But the gesture of convoking such a forum impressed contemporary opinion profoundly and the Emperor was celebrated as the restorer of Judaism to a place of dignity among the religions of the world.

The praise was, however, entirely undeserved, as Napoleon was soon to prove to his Jewish admirers. One year after the adjournment of the Sanhedrin's sessions, on March 17th, 1808, the Emperor signed a decree drastically limiting for a ten years period the rights of the Jews to exercise trade and handicrafts, and denied them freedom of movement This decree, which tried to nullify in practice the principle of equal rights is known in history as the *décret infâme* ("*infamous decree*").

But one by one certain French " départments ", particularly those inhabited by Sephardi Jews, were exempted, until in the end the restrictions applied effectively only to Alsace with its numerous Jewish proletariat population.

Medal commemorating the convocation of the Great Sanhedrin by Napoleon I.

NINETEENTH CENTURY EMANCIPATION

After Waterloo, reaction swept over Europe. Except for France and Holland, where the status quo remained unaltered, the Jews lost a good many of the rights they had been granted in the past quarter of a century. The situation was worst in Italy. In the Papal State, where the popes were fighting a vigorous rear-guard action to re-establish their position and stem the advance of liberalism, the reaction was most extreme. The old regime was restored, down to almost the last detail. The Jews were thrust back into the ghettos and again subjected to the traditional humiliations and restrictions. Even the periodical conversionist sermons, with the compulsory church-attendance of reluctant Jews, were renewed. There were, from time to time, deplorable cases of kidnapping of Jewish children for baptism. Though formally unofficial, they were subsequently endorsed by the Church. The most notorious instance was the Mortara case in 1858, already mentioned in the chapter on the Age of the Ghetto. It was late in the day for such a flagrant abuse and the case stirred a wave of protest throughout much of the civilized world. But Pope Pius IX, notwithstanding his earlier liberal leanings and his fundamental humanity, remained adamant.

The position of the Jews was hardly a better one in the Kingdom of Sardinia and other parts of Italy. The only concession the Jews managed to obtain, was a promise not to reimpose the wearing of the Jewish

The kidnapping of Edgardo Mortara (Drawing by M. Oppenheim).

"Hep; Hep;" Anti-Jewish riot at Frankfort-on-Main, 1819 (Contemporary engraving).

badge. The reaction was somewhat more lenient only in the Grand Duchy of Tuscany and the northern areas under Austrian rule.

In Germany, the ghetto regime was not reinstated, but the rights conceded to the Jews in the Napoleonic era were retracted. In some areas, for instance in the Hanseatic ports of Bremen and Lübeck, the Jews who had settled there under the French regime were expelled. In 1819, anti-Jewish riots, accompanied by destruction of property and even some loss of life, swept the country. They erupted in Würzburg and spread to many towns, including Frankfort-on-Main and Hamburg. The mob, led by rowdy students, broke into Jewish houses or attacked Jews in the streets, Their battle-cry was "Hep, Hep," alleged to be the abbreviation of an old Crusader slogan "Hierosolyma est perdita" ("Jerusalem is lost").

In Prussia, the Edict of Emancipation of 1812 was not revoked, as far as the ancient Prussian territory was concerned, but far-reaching restrictions were imposed upon the Jews of the territories annexed after Napoleon's downfall. All kinds of chicanery were used to scale down Jewish rights everywhere.

The illogicality of the situation was emphasized by the fact that in the past generation a new class of Jewish capitalists had emerged. Owing to the advance of the industrial revolution and its demands for capital, as well as in consequence of the requirements of the French revolutionary

335

wars, they had become an important factor in the economic life of Europe. Among the Jewish financiers of international significance, the most important were the Rothschilds. The father, Meyer Amschel Rothschild (1743–1812) had amassed a considerable fortune as the Court Jew of the Prince Elector of Hesse and had founded a banking-house at Frankfort-on-Main. After his death, his five sons continued and vastly enlarged the business. The eldest son stayed in Frankfort, while his four brothers established banks at Vienna, London, Paris and Naples, which maintained close co-operation with one another. The Rothschilds treated with the governments in every country, and also with the Papal Court as though they themselves constituted an independent political force. To continue to exclude the Jews from the elementary rights enjoyed by their fellow-citizens, when some of them played such a weighty part in the economic development of the European countries, was, to say the least, paradoxical. It was obvious that a change was bound to come.

To the left:
The Rothschild House at Frankfort-on-Main.

To the right:
Nathan Meyer Rothschild (1777–1836), founder of the English branch of the family. In 1814 he assisted financially England and her allies in their war against Napoleon.

Jews in the revolutionary Polish National Guard in 1830/31 (from L. Hollaenders-ki, Les Israélites de Pologne-Paris, 1846). There was a special Jewish detachment in the National Guard and the Warsaw Community granted the revolutionary Government generous financial support.

By the middle of the nineteenth century, the cause of the full emancipation of the Jews had become part of the creed of the liberals who were struggling for national freedom and constitutional government through-out Europe. Everywhere, therefore, the Jews threw in their lot with the liberals, striving, fighting and suffering with them. At times of revolutionary successes, in 1830, and then again in 1848, they temporarily achieved their aims. In subsequent periods of reaction, their hopes receded again.

Gabriel Riesser (1806–1863) the champion of Jewish emancipation in Germany. He pleaded the cause in numerous publications, and particularly in his speeches in the National Assembly at Frankfort-on-Main, 1848/49.

In Germany, the outstanding fighter for the Jewish cause was Gabriel Riesser. Originally from Hamburg, he had studied law, but prevented by the prevailing discriminatory regulations from becoming a lawyer or engaging in a university career, he dedicated his life to the struggle for emancipation. In numerous fiery publications he polemized against anti-Semitic agitators, refuted their arguments, stigmatized abuses against the Jews, and pleaded for their rights. After the revolution of March 1848, Riesser was one of the four Jews elected to the National Assembly which convened at Frankfort-on-Main, as a leader of German liberalism. One of his stirring speeches was supported by a large majority of the members, and the Constitution proclaimed by the Assembly in the spring of 1849 provided full equality of rights. However the tide had already turned. The National Assembly was dispersed, a few months later, and its decisions remained, for the time being, on paper only. Another twenty years of struggle were needed, until emancipation was achieved throughout Germany in1869, on the eve of the proclamation of the German Reich. Gabriel Riesser had meanwhile become the first Jewish judge appointed in that country and had died in 1863, without seeing the final victory.

In the Austro-Hungarian Monarchy, too, emancipation was formally granted after the revolution of 1848, but, as in Germany, it required a

The Synagogue of Rome. inaugurated 1904. It stands in the center of the area which was once the Ghetto of Rome.

further period of twenty years, until it became a reality under the Constitution promulgated in 1867.

In Italy, Jewish participation in the wars of the Risorgimento was out of all proportion to their numbers. The idealistic revival of the Venetian Republic, under the leadership of the half-Jew Daniel Manin, in 1848 numbered a noble group of Jews among its principal leaders. But in Italy as a whole, the emancipation of the Jews was largely the result of the active support of gentile liberal politicians, such as the Marquess Massimo d'Azeglio, the prime minister of the liberal-minded King Victor Emanuel II and the author of a pamphlet "On the civil emancipation of the Jews." D'Azeglio's policy was continued by his successor Cavour and emancipation came into force in all the territories successively liberated by the army of the King of Sardinia, who became King of Italy in 1861. The work was completed in 1870 when Victor Emmanuel occupied Rome and put an end to the temporal power of the pope and to the last vestige of a ghetto regime on Italian soil.

In England, the disabilities from which the Jews had suffered had never been enormous. Ever since the resettlement, they had been admitted to terms of general social equality with their neighbors, as we have seen. From the eighteen-thirties, minor disabilities began to be removed. This was largely accomplished through the direct methods employed by Sir David Salomons. His persistence resulted in his successive admission, after election, to the offices of Sheriff and Alderman, without having to pronounce the traditional Christian oath formula. In due course, he became, in 1855, the first Jewish Lord Mayor of London. He failed, however, in his attempt, to secure admission to the House of Commons, in 1851, without taking the oath. He tried to insist on his right, but finally had to leave the House and was even obliged to pay a heavy fine.

This was not the first time that the problem had cropped up in the House of Commons. From 1847 onward, Baron Lionel de Rothschild had been elected, year after year, to represent the City of London in the House of Commons, but could not take his seat, because he refused to pronounce the Christian oath-formula, Several times the Liberal Party submitted a bill for the modification of the formula. Each time, however, the bill, approved by the House of Commons, was turned down by the House of Lords. After long and tiresome debates, a compromise was

Baron Lionel de Rothschild introduced into the House of Commons (1858). Painting by H. Barraud. This was the victorious conclusion of a ten years' struggle, which began in 1847, when Lionel de Rothschild was first elected to the House, but was not admitted to take his seat, because of his refusal to pronounce the Christian oath-formula.

The Reward. Queen Victoria raises Disraeli to the peerage. Caricature from "Punch".

Benjamin Disraeli, Earl of Beaconsfield (1804–1881). Painting by J. E. Millais. The brilliant leader of the Conservative Party and the seer of the British Empire, whom Bismarck nicknamed "the old Jew", never concealed his attachment to the people from which he was descended.

reached in 1858 and Baron Lionel de Rothschild was at last permitted to take his seat in the House of Commons. In effect, this completed Jewish emancipation in England. In 1885 his son, Nathaniel, became the first Anglo-Jewish peer and took his seat in the House of Lords.

The emancipation of the Jews in England was, without doubt, facilitated by the kaleidoscopic career of Benjamin Disraeli. Son of a Jewish author who quarrelled with the Synagogue, he had been baptized as a boy. but he manifested throughout his life a strong sympathy for the Jewish people. At the beginning of his parliamentary career, he was unmercifully ridiculed and howled down. His Jewish antecedents were sneeringly referred to. But in due course he proved to be one of the most brilliant speakers in the House of Commons and he became the leader, if not the idol, of the aristocratic Conservative Party. In 1868, and again in 1874-80 he was Queen Victoria's well-liked premier and the champion of a new conception of the British Empire.

341

One of the most prominent personalities in England at the time was Sir Moses Montefiore, a relative of the Rothschilds and chairman of the Board of Deputies of the British Jews from 1835 till 1874. A strictly observant Jew, he was highly sensitive to Jewish suffering everywhere. Until nearly the end of his long life of over a century, he never ceased travelling to countries where Jews were oppressed — Russia, Morocco, the near East — in order to plead the cause of his brethren. Most remarkable was his intervention, in 1840, in the so-called Damascus-Affair, when the notables of the Jewish community of Damascus were arrested as guilty of the murder of a Franciscan friar, submitted to inhuman treatment and threatened with the death penalty. He travelled to Cairo and Constantinople and obtained not only the acquittal of the accused, but also a decree from the Sultan, protecting the Jews for the future from the accusation of ritual murder. Above all, Sir Moses Montefiore was attached to the Holy Land, which he visited several times, establishing there agricultural settlements and charitable foundations.

THE JEWRY OF EMANCIPATION

The emancipation of west European Jewry released a prodigious store of pent-up ability, which had previously no outlet. As a result, the Jews of Europe attained a many-sided distinction in almost every walk of life. There was no branch of human activity which they did not enter, and although progress was not equal in every sector, it was extraordinarily marked in some.

However, in a very large number of cases, the Jews achieved their new positions at the expense of their Jewish loyalties, which were implicitly or explicitly discarded.

The Synagogue of Florence, a fine example of 19th century synagogal architecture.

In politics many Jews soon attained the highest ranks. In England, Benjamin Disraeli was called to steer the destiny of the Empire, despite his Jewish descent and his undisguised Jewish sympathies.

In Italy Luigi Luzzatti served his country in many capacities, including that of prime minister. Although far from Jewish religious practices, he had a warm heart for his people, interceded on behalf of the Jews wherever they were persecuted, and even manifested, in his later years, considerable interest in the new Jewish settlement in Palestine. Giuseppe Ottolenghi achieved military distinction in the wars against Austria, was the first Jew on the Italian general staff, and rose to become Senator and Minister of War. Less than forty years after the abolition of the Roman ghetto, the Jew Ernesto Nathan was elected Mayor of Rome.

In France, Adolphe Crémieux was twice Minister of Justice and then Senator for life. Although first of all a French politician, he was a courageous defender of Jewish interests. In the Damascus Affair he actively colloborated with Sir Moses Montifiore and accompanied him in his voyages to Egypt and Turkey.

Together with Montefiore, again, Crémieux was among those who raised their voices in protest against papal abuse in the Mortara case. He was also one of the founders of the Alliance Israélite Universelle, an association founded for the purpose of raising the educational standard of the Jews in under-developed countries, alleviating Jewish distress, and protecting Jewish rights wherever they were menaced. It is, however, symptomatic of the danger of emancipation to the national and spiritual survival of the Jewish people in Europe, that Crémieux, this generous advocate of the Jewish cause, had his children brought up as Catholics.

Many other Jews entered French political life, making brilliant careers as party leaders, members of parliament, or ministers. The best known among them, in the generations after Crémieux, was Léon Blum, the man who directed the destinies of France in the fateful years of 1936–38.

In Germany, where social prejudices against the Jews did not easily give way, it was more difficult for them to attain leading positions. But from 1848 on, there were always Jews in the parliaments of the various German states, and after 1871, in the Reichstag. A number of them played a conspicuous part in the political life of the country, for instamce Ludwig Bamberger, the brilliant adversary of Bismarck's policy. Jewish participation in German political life increased after World War I. This was the period of personalities such as Walther Rathenau and Kurt Eisner, both of whom paid for their devotion to Germany with their lives.

Jewish contributions to European art before the emancipation were negligible. Now, Jewish artists emerged everywhere and were often

Luigi Luzzatti (1841–1927)

Benjamin Disraeli (1804–1881)

Ludwig Bamberger (1823–1899)

Adolphe Cremieux (1796–1880)

Kurt Eisner (1867–1919)

Léon Blum (1872–1950)

Walter Rathenau (1867–1922)

Camille Pissaro (1831–1903)

Joseph Israels (1824–1911)

Max Liebermann (1847–1935)

Marc Chagall (born 1887)

Lesser Ury (1861–1931)

responsible for profound changes in artistic concepts. Jewish painters like Camille Pissaro in France, Jozef Israels in Holland, and Max Liebermann and Lesser Ury in Germany were prominent among the Impressionists at the end of the nineteenth and the beginning of the twentieth centuries. In the following generation, too, Jews from Modigliani to Max Chagall were among the most brilliant representatives of the School of Paris. In sculpture, Jacob Epstein opened new paths. In music, Felix Mendelssohn-Bartholdy, the baptized grandson of Moses Mendelssohn, was celebrated as one of the greatest musicians of the first half of the nineteenth century, to be followed later by Gustav Mahler, Darius Milhaud, Ernest Bloch, and many others.

Gustav Mahler (1860–1911)

Darius Milhaud (born 1892)

Felix Mendelssohn-Bartholdy (1809–1847)

Ernest Bloch (born 1880)

Paul Ehrlich (1854–1915)

A. v. Wassermann (1866–1925)

Sigmund Freud (1856–1939)

Siegfried Marcus (1831–1898)   *Heinrich Hertz (1857–1894)*

Albert Einstein (1879–1955)

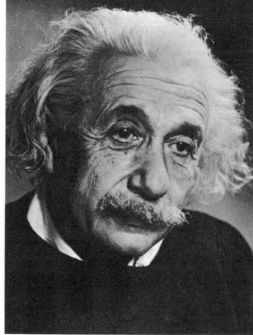

David Schwarz (1845–1897)   *Fritz Haber (1868–1934)*

The fame of German medicine throughout Europe, towards the end of the nineteenth and the first part of our century, was largely due to the contributions of many Jewish medical pioneers such, as Paul Ehrlich, the inventor of Salvarsan, or August von Wassermann, the discoverer of the blood-reaction bearing his name. It was Sigmund Freud who revealed the world of the unconscious, created the method of treating mental disorders by psychoanalysis, and exercised an unprecedented influence on many domains outside medicine, particularly on literature and art.

Numerous Jews distinguished themselves in the natural sciences and their practical application. Heinrich Hertz's experiments on the propagation of electro-magnetic waves laid the foundation of wireless telegraphy. Albert Einstein revolutionized physics by his theory of relativity. Fritz Haber produced artificial fertilizers and developed a method for extracting nitrogen from the air. The first dirigible airship (an invention afterwards exploited by Graf Zeppelin), was constructed by David Schwarz and the first car propelled by a gasoline motor was built by Siegfried Marcus in 1875.

In literary creation Jews took an ever increasing part since the days when Heinrich Heine, baptized but irremediably Jewish at heart, brought

Max Reinhardt (1873–1943)

to the German language and literature a charm and wit which it had never previously known. Many Jewish poets, playwrights, novelists, critics, and philosophic authors enriched the literatures of England, France, Italy, Germany, and other countries. Even a simple enumeration of the most important names would exceed by far the limits of this short survey. Great was also the Jewish contribution to the theater, where Max Reinhardt showed new ways in the art of the stage. Actresses like Rachel and Sarah Bernhardt and actors like Sonnenthal and Schildkraut interpreted the great classics of world literature.

While the Jews thus added to the cultural life of the peoples among whom they dwelt, changes took place in the inner life of the Jewish community too. The progressive assimilation loosened the personal allegiance of the individual to his community. The better he mastered the language of his neighbors, the more he forgot his Hebrew, and the Jew began to feel a stranger in his synagogue. To cater to these estranged Jews, a Reform Movement arose in Germany and later spread to other countries.

Rachel (*1820–1858*)

Ad. v. Sonnenthal (1832–1909)

Heinrich Heine (1797–1856)

Sarah Bernhardt (1844–1923)   *R. Schildkraut (1862–1930)*

Sermons in German were added to the service. Prayers in Hebrew were replaced by prayers in German. The burden of ritual prescriptions was eased. It is difficult to assess, whether or no the Reform movement saved Jews for Judaism, but it aroused the violent opposition of the conservative orthodoxy and was the cause of much internal strife and discord.

This same period saw the rise of a new discipline, the Science of Judaism (Wissenschaft des Judentums), an expression coined by Leopold Zunz (1794–1886), the explorer of homiletic and liturgic medieval literature. Together with his collaborators and pupils he endeavored to study and popularize Jewish spiritual values. Moritz Steinschneider plumbed the treasure of Jewish medieval literature. Heinrich Graetz wrote the "History of the Jews." Zacharias Frankel and Abraham Geiger investigated the Jewish tradition. These were the forerunners of generations of Jewish scholars and scientifically trained rabbis, who commanded the respect of their co-religionists and enhanced the prestige of Judaism in the eyes of their Christian neighbors.

Of great significance were such bodies as the already mentioned *Board of Deputies of British Jews* in London, the *Alliance Israélite Universelle* in Paris, and the *Hilfsverein der Deutschen Juden* in Berlin. Even Jews who had lost the religious contact with Judaism, found in these organizations a field of activity which fostered the tradition of Jewish solidarity on a humanitarian basis, offering it a wide scope and achieving useful results in many domains.

In some respects, England became the ideal pattern of Jewry under emancipation. It had its ecclesiastical hierarchy under the Chief Rabbi, who exercised almost the authority of a rabbinical bishop, being assisted by his rabbinical court or Beth Din. The Board of Deputies, besides taking care of Jewish interests abroad, served almost as an Anglo-Jewish parliament. The Board of Guardians for the Relief of the Jewish Poor in London (founded in 1859) administered poor-relief in a spirit which combined Victorian almsgiving with Jewish soft-heartedness. The United Synagogue (founded in 1870) provided a perfectly co-ordinated central organization for the old-established Ashkenazi synagogues of the capital and ultimately became the greatest organization of its sort in the world. In 1841 two Anglo-Jewish periodicals began to appear, the *Voice of Jacob* and the *Jewish Chronicle*. While the *Voice of Jacob* suspended publication after a few years, the *Jewish Chronicle* became an influential organ of English Jewry and is today the oldest Jewish periodical in existence.

The model network set up by English Jewry was uniquely able to withstand the strains placed upon it by the mass immigration at the end of the nineteenth century. In its main lines it still maintains itself unbroken, though not wholly unmodified, even at the present time.

The first issue of the "Jewish Chronicle", November 12th, 1841; the oldest Jewish periodical still appearing.

M. Steinschneider (1816–1907)   Z. Frankel (1801–1875)

Abraham Geiger (1819–1874)

Leopold Zunz (1794–1886)   Heinrich Graetz (1817–1891)

סֵפֶר זִכָּרוֹן
THE JEWISH CHRONICLE

דבר בעתו מה טוב משלי טו' כג'   " A word in its season how good it is." Proverbs, chap. 15, ver. 23,

No. 1.]   כח" מרחשון תרב" לפק'   NOVEMBER 12th, 5602.—1841.   [PRICE 2d.

TO OUR READERS.

WE have always anticipated the appearance of a truly Jewish paper, with the most lively satisfaction; for we knew, that the existence among us, of an organ of mutual communication, was a desideratum of such magnitude, that the person supplying it would be entitled to the thanks of his brethren, and be a man to be to our publication, the less matter of fact, but not less honorable productions of their well stored minds; indeed, we have already received a tale, which we purpose commencing at the earliest opportunity.

4thly.   Our Text Books will not, we dare venture to assert, form the least attractive part of our information :—nay, they will perhaps, be the most essentially

351

EASTERN EUROPE
IN THE NINETEENTH CENTURY

The movement for Jewish emancipation in western Europe hardly affected the eastern part of the Continent, where the vast Jewish community of Poland, as a result of the partitions of this country at the end of the eighteenth century, had now come preponderantly under the rule of Russia.

This reactionary power, barely issued from sheer barbarism, had done its utmost, during the past centuries, to exclude Jews entirely from its lands. Until the end of the sixteenth century, there was practically no Jewish settlement in the Grand Principality of Moscow, the kernel of the future Russian Empire. The only Jews in the area were stray court-physicians or visiting merchants from Poland, trading under the protection of their kings. Russian expansion in the seventeenth century inevitably brought a Jewish population within the borders of the country, but the Czars refused to accord the right of settlement even to old-established communities and instituted all kinds of harrassing measures against them. Peter the Great, at the beginning of the eighteenth century, personally displayed some benevolence to the Jews in certain cases, but did not even consider a change in the legal principle forbidding Jewish settlement in Russian territory. His successor, Catherine I, attempted to enforce this principle in practice by a general expulsion of the Jews (1727). When the impossibility of fully implementing this decree became evident, the Czars resorted to economic measures and endeavored to make life unbearable for Jews by drastically restricting their commercial activities. Despite these highly unfavorable conditions, the Jewish population not only survived, but even managed to increase numerically.

The situation changed profoundly, as the eighteenth century neared its end. The first partition of Poland (1772) brought about 100,000 Jews under Russian sway. The second (1793) and the third (1795) partitions meant an even greater increase in the Jewish population, whose solid religious orthodoxy, ethnic solidarity, linguistic separation and striking folk-ways marked it out as a perpetual minority. After much fumbling, which amply proved the incompetence and bad will of the Russian authorities and caused endless Jewish suffering, a general solution was tried at the beginning of the nineteenth century. The Jews were expelled from the villages, to eliminate their "harmful" influence on the peasant population, and they were allowed to live in towns only in a restricted number of western frontier provinces, the so-called "Pale of Settlement."

Under the impression of the loyal behavior of the Jews during the Napoleonic invasion in 1812, there was an ephemeral wave of good will. Czar Alexandér I (1801—1825) for a time lent his ear to proposals of liberalization and even toyed with the idea of emancipation, although in his mind this was closely linked with a mass conversion of the Jews to Christianity. But in his later years he returned to the inveterate methods

Czar Alexander I (1801–1825), whose liberal views, manifested at the beginning of his reign, aroused vain hopes among the Jews of Russia.

Jewish types from Galicia at the beginning of the 19th century.

of harshness. His brother and successor, Czar Nicholas I (1825–1855), the "drill-sergeant of Europe," who personified the traditional Russian policy of resistance to any external, particularly occidental and liberal, influence whatsoever, deliberately attempted to crush the spirit of the Russian Jews and to coerce them into giving up their separatism, religious as well as social. In the thirty years of his reign, no fewer than six hundred edicts concerning the Jews were published, almost all of them malevolent. Even the medieval Church regulations, heavily restricting Jewish rights and forbidding the employment of Christian servants, the construction of new synagogues, and the retention of uncensored books, were all enacted and enforced. The nadir was reached by a series of injunctions extending conscription for a twenty-five years period to Jewish children from the age of twelve, or sometimes even eight. These were the so-called "Cantonists." Although everything was done to drive the youthful recruits into despair and baptism, and many did not survive the treatment, most of them resisted the assimilatory coercion. Their heroic struggle with the forces brought against them became one of the subjects of the rich Russian-Jewish folk-lore. The Jewry of western Europe vainly protested against the worst abuses and even a visit of Sir Moses Montefiore to Russia, undertaken in 1846, remained without any practical result.

An amelioration took place only in the reign of Alexander II (1855-1881) when the westernization of the country was allowed to make considerable headway. As a logical element of this process, some of the restrictions were eased or lifted and the Jews were to a certain extent allowed, and even encouraged to normalize their lives, an opportunity which the richer classes avidly seized. At the beginning of the last quarter of the nineteenth

A group of Polish Hassidim.

Market-place in Cracow in the 19th century. Engraving by William Unger (Israel Museum, Jerusalem).

century, it seemed that east European Jewry was about to follow, somewhat tardily, in the footsteps of the West, and that the Jewish problem throughout the world was on the verge of a tranquil solution.

Meanwhile, the inner life of this vast Russian Jewry was undergoing deep changes. The pressure from without, which tended to crush and disintegrate this formidable ethnic and religious body, provoked by reaction a more obstinate attachment to traditional Judaism. The greatest part of this Jewry refused any cultural contact with the outside world and concentrated on the study of the Bible and the Talmud. The great Yeshivot of Eastern Europe were the stronghold of Talmudic erudition. Considerable portions of the Jewish population consisted of adherents of the Hassidic movement, grouped around their respective *Zaddikim,* who were often in conflict with one another and always at war with the *Mitnaggedim* (the opponents of Hassidism). But Hassidim and Mitnaggedim were united in their opposition to another movement, which they both considered the most dangerous internal foe, the Haskalah (Enlightenment). Taking its inspiration from the works of Moses Mendelssohn and his Berlin circle, the Haskalah slowly made its way in Russia, trying to open the minds to western culture and let fresh air into the suffocating atmosphere of the spiritual ghetto in which the Russian Jews were living. Notwithstanding the vigorous opposition from religious quarters, the Haskalah succeeded in giving birth to a secular literature in

355

Hebrew and in the Yiddish vernacular. On the one hand, there were learned contributions to what was styled in Germany *Science of Judaism*. On the other hand, poets, novelists and publicists began criticizing abuses and anomalies in Jewish life and stressing the necessity for reforms. One of the founders of this secular literature in eastern Europe was Isaac Baer Levinsohn (1788–1860), who undertook to prove in his books that Judaism was essentially not obscurantist and has never opposed the acquisition of secular culture. The first novelist was Abraham Mapu (1808-1867), who wrote the historical romance *Ahavat Zion* ("Love of Zion"), and the first genuine poet, Judah Loeb Gordon (1830–1892), who combined revolutionary pathos with biting satire. They prepared the way for the next generation, which included figures like the Hebrew novelist and publicist Peretz Smolenskin (1842–1885), as well as Mendele Mokher Seforim (1835–1917), the folk writer and satirist, and Shalom Aleikhem (1859–1916) the humorist. While Mendele wrote only his early works in Yiddish, and turned later on to Hebrew, Shalom Aleikhem consistently preferred Yiddish as a literary vehicle.

To the left:
Mendele Mokher Seforim (1836–1917), the creator of the satiric story in Yiddish and one of the fathers of modern Hebrew literature.

To the right:
Shalom Aleikhem (1859–1916), the creator of the humoristic short story in Yiddish.

ANTI-SEMITISM

The prodigious progress made by the emancipated Jews, their advance in economic well-being, and their prominence in so many fields of activity in which they had formerly been unknown, had the inevitable result of stimulating jealousy against them. This was the case especially in Germany, where their numbers were greater than elsewhere in western Europe (about half a million in 1871), and their progress, particularly in literature, journalism, and politics, the more striking.

The commercial crisis which followed on the post-war depression of 1873, resulted therefore in the rise of an organized anti-Jewish movement. Anti-Jewish feeling was no novelty in Germany, but now it was no longer directed, as in the Middle Ages, only against those professing the Jewish faith. It was extended to all persons belonging to or descended from the Jewish "Race," thus including Jews by birth who no longer professed Judaism, and even descendants of Jews who had given up Judaism a generation previously. This movement was termed "Anti-Semitism."

Secretly favored by Bismarck, who was furious at the criticism of his policy in the liberal newspapers, which were termed the "Jewish Press" by reactionary circles, the anti-Semitic movement attained, within a short time, a menacing degree of popular support. By 1879, it had organized itself as a powerful political faction, the Christian-Social Party, which soon took its place among the other reactionary elements on the Reichstag and bluntly demanded the abolition of Jewish emancipation. The founder of the party was Adolf Stöcker, chaplain to the imperial court, who endowed anti-Semitism with a certain cachet of religious respectability. A "scientific" foundation was supplied by the English-born German author Houston Stewart Chamberlain. In his brilliantly written *Die Grundlagen des XIX. Jahrhunderts* ("The foundations of the 19th century"), he contrasted the noble Aryan race — the purest representatives of which he considered the Germans — with the depraved Semitic race represented in its entire vileness by the Jews. He showed that the Jews were waging a permanent war for the destruction of Aryan civilization, and proclaimed the necessity of expelling this alien and noxious element from the body of European society. In order to avoid giving offence to believing Christians, Chamberlain undertook to prove that Jesus Christ was an Aryan.

So much venomous propaganda could not fail to call forth outbreaks of violence, especially in Prussia. There were even several abortive attempts to stage accusations of ritual murder: in Skurz (Pomerania) in 1884, at Xanten on the Rhine in 1891 and at Konitz (Prussia) in 1900. All these developments were still on a relatively mild scale, compared with what was to happen later, but they already echoed an audible rumble of the terrible storm to come.

Jews and well-intentioned Germans joined in warding off anti-Semitic

Dr. Lueger.

Dr. Joseph Bloch (1850–1923), the Jewish scholar who unmasked the lies of the anti-Semitic Professor A. Rohling.

The reception of Dr. K. Lueger, the leader of the Austrian anti-Semites, after his election as Vice-Burgermeister of Vienna, 1895 (Drawing from the Illustrated London News).

attacks and promoting a better understanding between the two peoples. But the subsequent course of events proved that these noble efforts had been to no avail.

The German example was imitated in the neighboring lands. In Austria anti-Semitism was propagated by August Rohling, professor of theology at Prague. His ignorance and impudent lies having been publicly denounced by the Jewish scholar Dr. Joseph Bloch, Rohling was obliged to sue him for libel, but the trial took such an unpleasant turn for the anti-Semitic theorist, that he thought it advisable, in the end, to withdraw his complaint. This fiasco, however, did not weaken the anti-Semitic movement in Austria. In Vienna, its protagonist was the lawyer Dr. Karl Lueger, who became the mayor of the Austrian capital in 1897. It is true that the anti-Semitic municipal government in Vienna did not push matters to an extreme and that Lueger himself, outwardly at least, displayed respectable moderation. But in the economic sphere discrimination against the Jews soon assumed tangible proportions.

In Austria, too, the anti-Semitic movement was organized as a Christian-Social Party, which soon entered the Austrian parliament and repeatedly proposed to deprive the Jews of their civic rights.

The Austro-Hungarian Monarchy shares with Germany the distinction of having unsheathed, at the end of the nineteenth century, the medieval weapon of the ritual murder accusation. In 1882 Jews were arrested at

Tisza-Eszlar (Hungary) and tried for having murdered a Christian girl for ritual purposes. The accused were even submitted to torture, to extract from them an admission of their guilt. But in this case, too, the anti-Semites failed. All the accused were acquitted and the court's decision emphasized that ritual murder did not exist.

In France, the defeat of 1870/1 had prepared a fertile ground for anti-Semitic propaganda. An anti-Semitic press came into being and Édouard Drumont, a gifted but unscrupulous journalist, published his *La France Juive* ("Jewish France"). This book is a tendentiously distorted representation of the history of the Jews in France, showing how they had finally succeeded in subjugating the French nation. The passions aroused by such publications found an outlet in the Dreyfus Affair.

The Dreyfus Case. The opening of the Court Martial.

HISTOIRE D'UN INNOCENT

Paris. — Imp. Pothy

Il y avait en 1894, à l'État-Major français, un jeune officier alsacien très savant, patriote et de bonne conduite appelé Dreyfus.

Par malheur, il y avait aussi, dans son bureau, deux autres officiers: Du Paty de Clam et Henry, jaloux, intrigants, fourbes. Ils complotèrent de le perdre à la première occasion.

Un jour, un agent dévoué à la France réussit à dérober un papier chez l'ambassadeur prussien. C'était justement une lettre d'un Français qui offrait de vendre sa patrie à l'Allemagne.

Du Paty et Henry en profitèrent aussitôt pour faire croire à leurs chefs et à la France que ce traître était Dreyfus.

Les chefs, confiants en leur parole d'honneur, se laissèrent tromper et, croyant venger la patrie, condamnèrent Dreyfus.

Il fut condamné à perpétuité, mais le jour où on lui arracha ses galons, il cria fièrement: « On dégrade un innocent, vive la France! » Et beaucoup de gens versèrent des larmes.

Voilà quatre ans qu'un brave et honnête officier alsacien, qui ignore pourquoi on l'a condamné, vit désespéré sur un rocher au milieu du grand Océan.

Pendant ce temps, sa pauvre jeune femme pleure toutes les larmes de son corps et ses deux orphelins crient: « Maman! où est mon papa? »

Un beau matin, un colonel d'État-Major, le brave et magnifique colonel Picquart, découvrit le vrai traître. Il s'écria alors: « Il faut sauver l'innocent et punir le coupable! »

Il y eut aussi des civils comme Zola, Bernard Lazare, Jaurès, Duclaux (celui qui guérit la rage), qui réclamèrent la justice pour l'innocent, car eux aussi avaient découvert le vrai traître.

C'était un autre officier, le pire des mauvais sujets, appelé Esterhazy, à la solde de la Prusse et qui voulait se faire uhlan pour massacrer des Français.

Mais Du Paty et Henry, qui ne voulaient pas voir revenir Dreyfus, se mirent à fabriquer de faux papiers qu'ils mirent sur son compte et protégèrent Esterhazy, le traître.

Pour mieux tromper la France, ils firent emprisonner le colonel Picquart et voulurent faire condamner Zola, sous prétexte d'insultes à l'armée, mais ils n'y réussirent pas.

Les mensonges ont les jambes courtes. Henry, pris la main dans le sac, avoue avoir fabriqué les faux papiers. On l'arrête, mais ses remords sont si terribles qu'il se coupe la gorge.

L'autre faussaire, Du Paty, fut chassé de l'armée. Quant au vrai traître, Esterhazy, il s'enfuit en Allemagne. Bon voyage! monsieur le uhlan!

Au jour prochain, on rendra ses galons à Dreyfus et la France glorieuse réparera noblement l'injustice faite à un de ses soldats les plus dévoués.

"Truth and Lie". Drawing by M. Lilien on the Dreyfus case, 1868. Truth turns its back, Justice stops the scale of the balance. The struggle between Truth and Lie goes on.

The story of the Dreyfus Case. Contemporary presentation of the facts from the "Dreyfusard" point of view.

In 1894, a Jewish staff-officer, Captain Alfred Dreyfus, was arrested on a charge of espionage. On trumped up evidence, he was sentenced to life imprisonment and deported to French Guiana. The forgeries which had led to Dreyfus' conviction were soon unmasked and Jewish and French personalities, among whom the French author Émile Zola played a prominent part, asked for a retrial and the rehabilitation of Dreyfus. But reactionary and military circles stubbornly opposed a new trial. France was divided into "Dreyfusards" and "Anti-Dreyfusards" who carried on a raging polemic. Instances of anti-Jewish violence occurred in several places, the most serious ones in Algeria. The affair shook the whole of the French Republic to its foundation, until, at last, after two retrials, the verdict was reversed in 1906. Thus, justice was finally done, but it had become apparent that even in the land in which Jewish emancipation had originated, the most virulent anti-Jewish agitation could be renewed and put into effect.

THE RUSSIAN POGROMS

The new German anti-Semitism, as yet more or less theoretical, found a fertile ground in reactionary Russia. Here it combined with a medieval religious obscurantism and became, in the hands of the Government, an instrument to oppose not only Jewish emancipation, but also any liberal tendency whatsoever in politics.

The alleviation of some of the most oppressing restrictions by Czar Alexander II in the first years of his reign, which had aroused such elated hopes in the hearts of the Russian Jewry, had stirred, on the other hand, a recrudescence of anti-Jewish feelings in many circles. The large commercial and industrial enterprises feared Jewish competition and their anxiety found a willing ear and ready support in the official bureaucracy, which shunned any deviation from the traditional line of conduct. The press, inspired and encouraged by high quarters, began denouncing the "Jewish peril" and inflaming the passions of the ignorant people, among whom the hatred of the Jews was anyway endemic and violent enough. Reaction gradually gained the upper hand again, in the second part of the reign of Alexander II, and the assassination of the Czar by terrorists in March 1881 put an end to whatever was left of Russian liberal aspirations. The unfortunate fact that the terrorist group responsible for the act included a Jewess was amply exploited by anti-Semitic propagandists. Under the new Czar, Alexander III (1881–1894), a general reactionary movement gained impetus and found vehement expression in a wave of pogroms, that year and the subsequent one.

Pogrom was a new term for a very old phenomenon — Jew baiting, usually ending in massacres. The Russian word means riot and was used with the intention of conveying the impression that these were spontaneous outbreaks of popular indignation against abuses perpetrated by the Jews. In fact, however, a pogrom was an organized performance with governmental connivance and active police support, whether open or disguised.

The wave of pogroms began in April 1881 in Elisavetgrad and swept over Kiev, Berdichev, Odessa, Warsaw, Balti, etc. By the autumn of 1882, no fewer than 160 localities in southern Russia had witnessed this violence. Protest meetings were held in London and New York. Influential Jewish and Christian personalities everywhere emphatically expressed their abhorrence of the Russian methods. But all these protest made little impression on those in charge of Russia's domestic policy. Henceforth the pogroms became an endemic feature of Russian Jewish life, constantly recurring throughout the country and actually sponsored by the authorities.

In May 1882, the "Provisional Regulations," a code of crushing and humiliating anti-Jewish rulings, were enacted. They purported to impose a temporary check on those aspects of Jewish life alleged to have been

Meeting at the London Guildhall, 1890, in protest against the persecution of the Jews in Russia. The Bishop of Ripon is addressing the meeting. (Illustrated London News).

Duchess of   Bishop of Ripon.   Sir J. Pease.   Rev. Dr. H. Adler.   Sir J. Simon.   Dean of Westminster.

utts. Westminster.   Duke of   Lord Mayor. Lady Mayoress.   Earl of Meath.   Sir R. Fowler.   Mr. H. J. Atkinson.   Rev. H. P. Hughes.
       Westminster.

MEETING AT GUILDHALL ON BEHALF OF THE JEWS IN RUSSIA.

1890

English caricature of Czar Alexander III and his oppressive policy against the Jews.

E. M. Lilien: In Memory of the Martyrs of Kishinev.

A street in Kishinev after the pogrom of 1903.

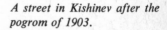

Oscar Gruzenberg (1866–1940), the advocate who pleaded successfully in the cases of the ritual murder charges brought against Blondes (1900–02) and Beilis (1913).

responsible for the outbreaks. This formed the nucleus of the so-called May Laws, which henceforth governed Jewish life in the empire of the Czars, as long as it continued to exist, and caused a terrible amount of Jewish suffering. The Jews found themselves excluded from the greater part of the Russian Empire, and from rural areas and centers even in those provinces in which they were allowed to reside. They were subject to ruthless sudden expulsions, almost at the whim of the local authorities, shut out almost entirely from higher education and most liberal professions and barred from any sort of social progress. In effect, they were confined to great urban and semi urban ghettos along the western frontier of the Empire. There were places, like Berdichev, for instance, where at least eighty percent of the Jewish population consisted of poverty-stricken, hopeless individuals. Nevertheless, they managed to maintain human dignity in the midst of their misery. The image of the East European *shtetl* (small town) with its folkways and values and the warm-hearted life among the deeply religious Jewish poor, has been immortalized in the novels and short stories of the Yiddish author Shalom Aleikhem.

There were about five million Jews in Russia in the eighties, and the absurdity of the regime to which such a body of population was submitted became evident even to some of the high Russian functionaries. A commission was appointed, under the chairmanship of Count Pahlen in 1883, to revise the laws concerning the Jews. After five years of examining and discussing the situation, the majority of the members recommended a gradual reform towards normalizing Jewish life in Russia. The Government, however, and the Czar himself, sided with the conservative minority and, under the inspiration of von Plehwe, the German born Chief of Police and afterwards Minister of the Interior, the coming years brought a series of even harsher anti-Jewish measures. In 1891, many thousands of Jews were deported in mid-winter from Moscow to the Pale of Settlement. Expulsions from areas outside the Pale followed throughout the years 1892-1898. From time to time, pogroms were organized, and even a ritual murder charge, the Blondes case, was raised in Vilna. However, owing to the talent and devotion of

MOSES FEITELES TRÖDLER
VERKAUFT ALLE GATTUNGEN WAARE

the Jewish lawyer Oscar Israel Gruzenberg, Blondes was acquitted. Gruzenberg had the opportunity, later on, of appearing a second time in court to defend successfully a Jew accused of ritual murder, in the famous Beilis case of Kiev in 1913.

Czar Nicholas II (1895-1918), who had meanwhile succeeded Alexander III, marched in his father's footsteps. His ministers combined blind hatred of the Jews with fear of an imminent revolution. The stratagem was to drown the revolution in Jewish blood. No wonder anti-Jewish violence soon reached an uprecedented peak in the 1903 pogrom at Kishinev (forty-five dead, about six hundred wounded, not to speak of the material damage) which shook the whole civilized world and even a number of Russian intellectuals, including Count Tolstoi. But nothing could induce the Russian authorities to change their policy. Further pogroms followed: Homel in 1903, Kishinev (again), Odessa and many other places in 1905, Bialystok in 1906, to mention only the major scenes of attack. In each case there was a heavy toll of Jewish lives.

Jewish refugees from Russia in the Jewish quarter of Vienna (Contemporary English engraving).

THE BREAKING OF THE DAM

The cumulative result of the events in Russia from 1881 onwards—the recurrent outbursts of violence, as well as the hopelessness of life under the May Laws, was that vast numbers of persons sought refuge in flight. At that time, the United States of America seemed to be the land of freedom and boundless opportunity to all the down-trodden and poverty-stricken masses throughout the world. In the circumstances, it had a particularly powerful attraction for the Russian and Polish Jews, and later on also for the Jews of Rumania, Galicia, Austria, and Hungary. Something of a mass emigration movement developed in eastern Europe. Jews began leaving the lands of their birth and crossing the Atlantic, animated by the hope that all their troubles would end in the New World and that they would be able to establish themselves there as self-respecting human beings.

This emigration reached considerable proportions. About 400,000 Jews entered the United States during the period 1881—90. In the following two years 1891—92, emigration to the United States achieved a record figure of 250,000 persons. However, the natural increase of eastern European Jewry was so great, that the mass emigration hardly seemed to diminish the bulk of the Jewish population remaining behind, which continued to live and suffer as before, down to the outbreak of World War I.

On the other hand, the emigrants to the United States soon learned that hard reality in the New World was far from the paradise they had anticipated. Adjustments to the new mode of life were fraught with much suffering. Most of the immigrants had to earn a meager living by laboring long hours in factories or in the so-called sweat-shops of the needle trade, in which the newcomers were largely concentrated. Many of them became pedlars. A number of experiments to establish agricultural settlements failed. Relatively few succeeded in completing their education and entering a profession, at great sacrifice. Nevertheless the Jewish immigrant to the U.S. had his physical security, civil rights, and the hope that his children would advance on the social and economic ladder.

A new Jewish life began to develop in the United States with amazing rapidity. The immigrants brought with them not only their native customs and folkways but also their religious and social institutions. They set up manifold little synagogues, communal charity foundations, religious schools for their children, Talmudic academies, and rabbinical seminaries. Since the immigrants were still unfamiliar with the English language and felt uneasy in the company of non-Jews, they crowded into the same neighborhoods and clung together economically and socially, forming great population centers in several large cities, first and foremost in New York. A Yiddish press and theater developed for this public in due course. In a short time the Jewish workers

began to organize themselves into labor unions, which gradually helped to establish more decent working conditions and which, later on, exercised a vast influence on the trade-union movement generally.

Other places of settlement for Jewish emigration from eastern Europe were, at that time, Canada, South America, particularly Argentina, and South Africa. Each of them drew large numbers of Jews in search of a new home, but none of these countries could possibly compare with the irresistible surge toward the United States.

An eddy of this migration naturally also reached the countries of western Europe, particularly England. Here their old-established co-religionists set up a network of charitable institutions to help the new arrivals, although their main purpose was to direct the stream to the countries overseas. Nevertheless, part of the immigrants overcame their difficulties and settled in western Europe, numerically and spiritually reinforcing the existing Jewish communities there. But in doing so, they also supplied new fuel to anti-Semitic reaction everywhere.

Jewish refugees from Russia passing the Statue of Liberty. Engraving, 1892 (Bittmann Archive, New-York).

BARON DE HIRSCH AND
THE ARGENTINE COLONIES

Life in the overcrowded Pale of Settlement painfully evidenced the unsound economic structure of the Jewish people. There were some who thought that it was necessary and possible to reverse the historical process which had caused this anomaly, and to regenerate and normalize Jewish life by re-establishing the lost contact with the soil. A return to agricultural settlements were established by Jews in southern provinces. putting a halt to the suffering of the Jew and solving the problems of his peculiar existence.

The first steps to translate this ideal into facts were made in Russia in the days of the Czars Alexander I and Nicholas I, when a series of agricultural settlements were established by Jews in southern provinces. At first, the Government encouraged this movement, but it soon withdrew its support and thus put a stop to further development. The colonies, however, continued to subsist down to the Russian Revolution, when most of the settlers perished in the pogroms which accompanied the civil war. Later on, courageous attempts were made, with serious American support, to renew the process, but they proved futile in their effects.

The two most remarkable experiments to realize the ideal of a return to the soil were made outside Russia, one in the ancient homeland, in Palestine, the other overseas, in Argentina.

Baron Maurice de Hirsch (1831–1896), the founder of the Jewish Colonization Association (Vanity Fair cartoon by 'Lib').

The experiment in Argentina was initiated on a vast scale, owing to the generosity of Baron Maurice de Hirsch, a noble-hearted Jewish philanthropist. Baron de Hirsch had accumulated an enormous fortune from railway construction in Turkey and elsewhere and from other successful business ventures, and he spent his time and money trying to help his persecuted co-religionists. He attempted at first to improve the condition of the Jews in Russia by negotiations with the Russian Government. His proposals to establish professional schools and agricultural farms in Russia met with little sympathy in governmental circles, and he finally reached the conclusion that the emigration of Russian Jewry, coupled with a return to agriculture in a new country, was the only solution. The reports of his experts made him decide that Argentina, with its vast expanses of undeveloped land, offered the best conditions and prospects for a Jewish settlement on agricultural basis.

In 1891 Baron de Hirsch set up the Jewish Colonization Association (I.C.A.) with a capital of £2,000,000 (then equivalent to some 10,000,000$; ten times as much in to-day's values) as the instrument for carrying out his plans. His ambition was to transfer and settle on the soil a million Jews from eastern Europe. The Russian Government permitted the activity of the I.C.A. in Russia and even displayed a readiness to authorize and encourage Jewish emigration. But when emigration to

Administration buildings of Mauricio, one of the colonies founded by I.C.A. in Argentina.

Co-operative grain elevator in a I.C.A. colony in Argentina.

Argentina really got under way, it soon became evident that the opportunities had been over-estimated. Matters proceeded much more slowly than had been anticipated and the difficulties were greater than had been foreseen. By the turn of the century, only some 30,000 east-European immigrants had been transferred there and only part of them were actually engaged in agriculture. A number of Jewish townships and colonies based on agriculture (Rosario, Mauricia, etc.) had been founded, some of which still survive, but the experiment had, as a whole, only a limited success and the result did not justify the enormous expenditure (about $100,000,000 in 1914 value) lavished upon it. The development of the agricultural colonies soon came to a standstill and the attraction of the large cities and the easier opportunites offered by them have since contributed to diminish the number of Jews tilling the soil in Argentina.

The I.C.A. made similar experiments in other areas, too. Under its auspices, agricultural settlements were set up in Brazil, the United States, Canada, Cyprus, and eastern Europe (Soviet Russia, the former Rumanian province of Bessarabia, and Poland), but everywhere success was either modest or temporary. It was only in Palestine that the movement for a return to the soil led to durable and far-reaching results, because it laid the foundation for the revival of the Jewish people as a free nation.

THE BILU

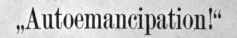

„Autoemancipation!"

Mahnruf an seine Stammesgenossen

von

einem russischen Juden.

Berlin SW.
Commissions-Verlag von W. Issleib (G. Schuhr).
1882.

One of the least conspicuous eddies of the tide of emigration from Russia, after the pogroms of 1881, was that which reached Palestine but, in the long run, was to prove the most significant.

In 1882, Leon Pinsker, an Odessa physician and journalist who had previously held assimilationist views and favored the diffusion of Russian culture among the Jews as an instrument to stem the growth of anti-Semitism published a pamphlet entitled "Auto-Emancipation." In contradiction to his former opinions, he now proclaimed his conviction that there was only one way to put an end to anti-Semitism: The Jews must again become a normal nation established in an independent territory of their own, preferably in Palestine.

In the same year, a group of Jewish students, who met at Kharkov, decided to become farmers in the ancient Jewish homeland and founded an organization which they called " Bilu " (the initials of the four Hebrew words *Beit Yaakov Lekhu ve-Nelkha*, " House of Jacob, come let us depart " — *Isaiah 2 : 5*).

Leon Pinsker (1821–1891) and the title-page of his pamphlet "Auto-Emancipation", a landmark in the history of the nation revival of the Jewish people.

The idea was not new. It had been propagated since the seventies by the Jewish publicists David Gordon (1831—1886) and Peretz Smolenskin (1842—1885). But the pogrom wave of 1881/2 gave it the deciding impulse. Everywhere groups of *Hovevei Zion* ("Lovers of Zion") came into existence and soon formed an organized movement known as *Hibbat Zion* ("the Love of Zion"). But what singled out the Bilu-group was the earnest intention of its members to make an immediate beginning to realize their idea.

In the summer of 1881, the first group, consisting of fifteen young men and one woman, reached Jaffa. It was subsequently followed by others. When the Biluim (Hebrew plural of "Bilu") came to Palestine, they found some fifty thousand Jews in the country, most of them in the so-called Holy Cities of Jerusalem, Hebron, Safed and Tiberias and in the coastal towns of Jaffa and Haifa, while the countryside belonged to the Arab peasants, the fellaheen, and the bedouin herdsmen. The Jews were mainly living off the charity of their co-religionists in other lands and justifying their existence by constant prayer and study of the Talmud.

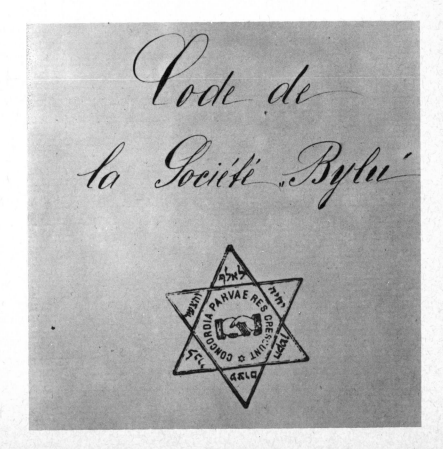

Title-page of the original Statutes of the "Bilu„ Organization. The Hebrew motto means: "The little one shall become a thousand and the small one a strong nation" (Isaiah 60:22), and the Latin one: "Little things grow big by union".

The noble-hearted British philanthropist Sir Moses Montefiore, who visited Palestine seven times between 1827 and 1874, assisted by persons such as the American Jew Judah Touro, had worked hard to rehabilitate them by improving their living conditions and creating a sounder economic basis for their existence. He had founded modern residential quarters, established a number of small industries and even tried to set up agricultural colonies in the purlieus of the cities. But the results had been entirely out of proportion to the efforts, because local orthodox circles fanatically opposed any change in the traditional way of life. In 1870, the Alliance Israélite Universelle had founded an agricultural school at Mikveh Israel, but the local Jews boycotted the school and the Alliance was obliged to recruit students mainly in Eastern Europe.

In such circumstances, it is no wonder that the new immigrants were accorded a cool reception by their co-religionists. Furthermore, the Turkish authorities were suspicious and heaped difficulties in their way. Some of the groups were even refused permission to land at Jaffa and were obliged to infiltrate into the country by way of Egypt. But the Biluim were a resolute lot. They had come to settle on the soil of their forefathers and so they did, despite official chicanery, the lack of security prevailing in the country, the unaccustomed climate, and the physical strain and malaria which took a toll of many victims. Further groups from Russia, Poland and Roumania followed in their

The beginnings of Rishon-le-Zion, founded as an agricultural colony in 1882, now a thriving township.

Baron Edmond de Rothschild (1845–1934), "the well-known philanthropist" who supported the first colonies financially and contributed to the consolidation and extension of the Jewish settlement in Palestine. (Painting by A. Moro).

wake and a number of colonies were established : Rishon le-Zion (First in Zion), Zikhron Yaakov (In memory of James Rothschild), Rosh Pinnah (the Corner-stone), Yessud ha Maalah (the Foundation of the Going up), Ness Zionah (a Standard toward Zion) and Gederah. The abandoned settlement of Petah Tikvah (the Door of Hope) was renewed. Most colonies reflected in their names the idealism of their founders and they were destined to form the basis for the revitalization of the Jewish people on the ancestral soil.

The financial situation of the young colonies was, however, precarious from the outset and soon became hopeless. The Russian Hovevei Zion who, at the Kattowitz Conference in 1894, had established a fund to assist the Jewish agricultural colonies in Palestine, did their best, but their financial means were modest. The success of the whole experiment would have been doubtful, but for the devoted material support of Baron Edmond de Rothschild, head of the Paris branch of this great family. This noble man, who is gratefully remembered in Israel to this day as *ha-Nadiv ha-yadua* ("the well-known philanthropist"), lent a willing ear to the appeal of the Hovevei Zion. He not only opened his purse to provide the most urgent needs, but also helped found new colonies and reorganize the economic basis of the old ones. He sent experts to Palestine to advice the colonists, and initiated new branches of agricultural activity, *e.g.*, vine-growing.

To the right:
Ahad ha-Am (1856–1927), the ideologist of cultural Zionism.

To the left:
Eliezer Ben-Yehudah (1858–1922). Thanks to his obstinacy, Hebrew became again a spoken language in Palestine.

The first house in Haderah, a colony founded in 1891 by members of the Hovevei Zion Organization. Despite malaria, the colonists held on and the colony developed, in course of time, into a town which has now about 30,000 inhabitants.

The generous intentions of the Baron de Rothschild were not always correctly understood and interpreted by his numerous officials who had daily contact with the colonists, and conflicts were frequent and complaints sometimes justified. His intervention, however, saved Jewish colonization in Palestine from a serious crisis. The expansion of colonization could now be continued by the Odessa Committee of the Hovevei Zion, in which the Hebrew author Ahad ha-Am (pseudonym of Asher Ginzburg), the ideologist of cultural Zionism, had a decisive say. Under the auspices of this committee, a series of additional colonies sprang up (Rehovot, Hadera, Metulla, etc.). By the end of the nineteenth century, there were in Palestine about thirty Jewish agricultural colonies with a population of nearly six thousand. The Jewish population in the towns had likewise increased by immigration, and industrial enterprises were springing up. All this was the work of the so-called First Aliyah (the first wave of immigration).

Besides the hard work on the ungrateful soil and the war against malaria, the new settlements often had to cope with the enmity of jealous or rapacious Arab neighbors. There were many casualties until, a system of armed Jewish watchmen was evolved, to culminate later on in the institution called *Ha-Shomer* ("The Watchman"), which was in effect a Jewish militia for the defense of the settlements.

Another problem was that of language. In 1879, Eliezer Ben-Yehudah had advocated the revival of the Hebrew language for the daily use of the Jewish people, in Peretz Smolenskin's Hebrew monthly *Ha-Shahar*. After he settled in Jerusalem in 1881, his home became the first in which Hebrew was the exclusive language. Through his unrelenting efforts, Hebrew was established as the language of the new community of Jews drawn from many parts of the world. The ancestral language was revived together with the return of the people to the land. Thus the new settlement, to be reinforced after the renewal of the pogroms in the early twentieth century by the Second Aliyah of 1904-14, began to acquire the characteristics of a nation.

A group of "Watchmen", members of the "Ha-Shomer" Organization in Galilee.

377

ZIONISM

Theodor Herzl (1860–1904), the founder of modern political Zionism and the prophet of the Jewish State.

The passions aroused by the Dreyfus case, showing to what extent anti-Jewish prejudice was still alive in the country which had been the first in Europe to grant the Jews civil rights, made a profound impression on a brilliant Austrian journalist and playwright, Theodor Herzl, the Paris correspondent of the Viennese newspaper *Neue Freie Presse*.

Born in 1860 in Budapest in a fairly assimilated family, Herzl had not received much of a Jewish education. He had witnessed the growth of anti-Semitism in Austria, while studying law at Vienna, and knew from his own experience how difficult it was for a Jew to become an official in that country, despite emancipation. But all this had not perturbed him too deeply. Having failed to enter upon a judiciary career, he devoted himself to writing and his feuilletons and plays were widely

DER

JUDENSTAAT.

VERSUCH

EINER

MODERNEN LÖSUNG DER JUDENFRAGE

VON

THEODOR HERZL

DOCTOR DER RECHTE.

LEIPZIG und WIEN 1896.

M. BREITENSTEIN'S VERLAGS-BUCHHANDLUNG

WIEN, IX., WÄHRINGERSTRASSE 5.

In a letter dated 1897, Herzl wrote about the establishment of a Jewish State in the near future: "Should I say this aloud to-day, the reply would be universal laughter. In five years perhaps, but at any rate in fifty years, everybody will understand." Fifty years later, the State of Israel was an accomplished fact.

Wenn ich das heute laut sagte, würde mir ein universelles Gelächter ant-worten. Vielleicht in fünf Jahren, jedenfalls in fünfzig wird es Jeder einsehen.

Title-page of the first edition of Herzl's book "The Jewish State", 1896.

appreciated. In 1891 he went to Paris, whence he sent his newspaper interesting reports on events in France and on the debates of the French parliament. In the middle of these peaceful pursuits, the Dreyfus case came as a shock. If such a virulent anti-Jewish agitation was possible in France, if pogroms were raging in Eastern Europe and anti-Semitism was spreading and growing stronger in Germany, there was, it suddenly dawned upon Herzl, no secure hope for the future of the Jewish people, except in the reconstruction of Jewish nationhood in a Jewish state, the independence of which was to be guaranteed by international agreements. At the beginning, Herzl wavered between Palestine and Argentina, but afterwards he determined on Palestine.

Baron de Hirsch refused to listen to his plans and he was discouraged by friends from approaching the Rothschilds. But the idea had taken possession of him and he embodied it in a work written at white-heat, under the impression of recent events, the *Judenstaat* ("The Jewish State"), published in 1896.

His was not a new conception. The Jewish political author Moses Hess (1812-1875), one of the founders of modern socialism, had preceded him in 1862 in his book *Rome and Jerusalem*, in which he advocated, as the solution of the Jewish problem, the renewal of an independent national life in the land of the Bible. In this work, Hess sketched a plan for the practical realization of mass-colonization in Palestine with the assistance of Jewish high finance and the consent of the Powers, particularly France. Leon Pinsker, in his *Auto-Emancipation* of 1882, had the same objectives in view. Herzl was, however, unaware of these predecessors when he wrote the *Judenstaat*. The idea had come to him as a revelation, and under its impact the feuilletonist became a man of action and an inspiring leader. Herzl presented the issue dramatically, backed it with his remarkable personal charm, worked out the details, and devoted his short life to putting his ideas into execution.

Immediately after the appearance of the *Judestaat*, numerous Hovevei Zion in Eastern Europe accepted Herzl's ideas and acknowledged his leadership. From now on, the movement became known as Zionism (a term coined by Nathan Birnbaum, a versatile author, who afterwards abandoned Zionism and turned to extreme orthodoxy). Among the assimilated Jews of central and western Europe, the movement generally met either with indifference or with active resistance. Nevertheless, some outstanding personalities joined the movement, adding to it the weight of their names. Among these was Max Nordau (1840-1923), already famous as an essayist and critic.

In order to mobilize Jewish opinion and obtain practical backing for his proposals, Herzl convoked the first Zionist Congress. This Congress met at Basle in 1897, founded the World Zionist Organization under the chairmanship of Herzl, and formulated the program of the Zionist movement (the so-called Basle Program): "The aim of Zionism is to create for the Jewish people a home in Palestine secured by public law."

During Herzl's lifetime, the Zionist Congress convened every year from then on, with one interruption in 1902.

The official text of the "Basle Program", formulated by the first Zionist Congress in 1897. It set as the purpose of Zionism the settlement of Jewish agriculturists, artisans and tradesmen in Palestine and the securing of Governmental approval necessary for the realization of Zionist aims.

Programm.

Der Zionismus erstrebt für das jüdische Volk die Schaffung einer rechtlich gesicherten Heimstätte in Palästina.

Zur Erreichung dieses Zieles nimmt der Congress folgende Mittel in Aussicht:

I. Die zweckdienliche Förderung der Besiedlung Palästinas mit jüdischen Ackerbauern, Handwerkern und Gewerbetreibenden.

II. Die Gliederung und Zusammenfassung der gesammten Judenschaft durch geeignete örtliche und allgemeine Veranstaltungen nach den Landesgesetzen.

III. Die Stärkung des jüdischen Volksgefühls und Volksbewusstseins.

IV. Vorbereitende Schritte zur Erlangung der Regierungszustimmung, die nötig sind, um das Ziel des Zionismus zu erreichen.

Herzl opens the Second Zionist Congress in Basle, 1898.

THE JEWISH COLONIAL TRUST

(JUEDISCHE COLONIALBANK)

LIMITED.

(Incorporated under the Companies Acts, 1862 to 1898, whereby the liability of Shareholders is limited to the amount of their Shares.)

CAPITAL - - - £2,000,000

DIVIDED INTO

£1,999,900 ORDINARY SHARES of £1 each, and
£100 FOUNDERS' SHARES of £1 each.

THE FOUNDERS' SHARES will be vested in the Council of the Company or their nominees and can only be transferred with the approval of the Council. They will not confer any right to participate in the profits of the Company.

PRESENT ISSUE—£1,999,900 IN £1 SHARES

Payable at the option of the Applicant in any one of the following modes, namely :—

(a) 20 per cent., or 4s. per Share, on Application, and the balance in four instalments of 20 per cent., or 4s. per Share, each at intervals of 3 months from the date of the first payment, with 6 per cent. interest in the meantime payable with the last instalment.

(b) 20 per cent., 4s. per Share on Application, and the balance on Allotment.

(c) The full amount of £1 per Share on Application.

Prospectus of the Jewish Colonial Trust, 1899.

Herzl on his way to Palestine in 1898.

Herzl greets Emperor William II at Mikveh Israel, 1898.

Herzl believed that it was not opportune to continue Jewish colonization in Palestine before obtaining an appropriate charter from the Turkish Government, and he persisted in his policy, despite the violent opposition of many Hovevei Zion.   The rest of his brief life Herzl entirely devoted to the cause in which he believed so passionately. He created the Jewish Colonial Trust, for the purpose of providing the Zionist Organization with a solid financial basis, independent of Jewish financiers, who could not easily be won over.   Displaying a lively interest in Herzl's plans, Grand Duke Frederick of Baden arranged a meeting between him and the German Emperor William II during the latter's visit to Palestine.   Herzl met the Emperor in 1898 at the entrance to the Agricultural School of Mikveh Israel and was then granted an audience in Jerusalem.   He went to Constantinople, where he was accorded a friendly reception by Sultan Abdul-Hamid II, and to Rome, where he interviewed the King of Italy and the Pope.   He also made contacts with the British Government, where he found a certain amount of sympathy for his ideas.

Thus far, Herzl's endeavors to obtain a charter from the Sultan had failed. He received his first concrete proposal from England. The British offer was remote from the aim of Zionism, but it, at least, demonstrated that the Zionist movement was being taken seriously by one of the Great Powers. In 1903, the British Government declared its readiness to consider the establishment of an autonomous Jewish colony in British East Africa (the area was commonly, though inaccurately, spoken of as Uganda). When this proposal was submitted by Herzl to the Sixth Zionist Congress, which met in Basle in 1903, it aroused a storm of indignation. Although Herzl stressed the fact that this was meant only as a temporary solution, until political conditions for settlement in Palestine could be secured, the overwhelming majority of the delegates opposed the so-called Uganda scheme as a betrayal of the Zionist ideal. However, it was agreed to send a delegation to investigate conditions in the area. The Congress then decided to initiate practical undertakings in Palestine and to authorize the Jewish National Fund, which had been set up at the Fifth Zionist Congress in 1901, to begin purchasing land. The Seventh Zionist Congress (1905) definitely rejected the Uganda scheme, This outcome was, in fact, providential. Had the scheme been carried into execution, there is no doubt that it would have met a disastrous end when Great Britain withdrew from the area in the anti-colonial reaction after World War II.

Unfortunately, overwork and the excessive strain of the last years aggravated Herzl's heart-disease and he died prematurely in July 1904, at the age of fourty-four. His death provoked an almost unprecedented display of grief in the whole Jewish world.

The funeral of Theodor Herzl at Vienna, July 7th (24th Thamuz) 1904. His body was transferred to Israel in 1949 and re-interred in Jerusalem, in accordance with his will.

The farm-yard at Kinnereth in 1910. This colony, on the southeastern shore of the Lake of Tiberias, was founded in 1909 by immigrants belonging to the so-called "Second Aliyah".

A. D. Gordon (1856–1922), the theoretician of the Zionist labor movement. He preached and exemplified the idea that the return to the soil is the foundation of national revival.

However, the movement which he had created continued to grow, with results of inestimable importance. David Wolffsohn, a rich merchant of Cologne, who succeeded Herzl as Chairman of the Zionist Organization, faithfully adhered to his predecessor's policy of striving to secure a charter as the political guarantee of the Jewish homeland. However, at the Congresses held after Herzl's death, the faction advocating immediate colonization work in Palestine prevailed more and more. Its leaders were Chaim Weizmann and Menahem Ussishkin, men who were from now on to play decisive roles in the further course of Zionist policy. Their victory obtained official sanction at the Tenth Zionist Congress (1911), when Wolffsohn resigned and Professor Otto Warburg, an eminent botanist and a partisan of " practical Zionism ", was elected in his place.

When rejecting the Uganda scheme, the Seventh Congress (1905), the first after Herzl's death, accepted, at the same time, the principle of excluding forever colonization outside Palestine. This had then caused the secession of a group led by the Anglo-Jewish author Israel Zangwill, who held the opinion that any proposal for a Jewish home, no matter where, should be considered upon its merits, because the Jews had no time to wait for the illusive charter. They founded the Jewish Territorial Organization, which dissolved, however, in 1918, after the Balfour Declaration was issued.

In the meantime, a new wave of immigrants, mainly from Russia and largely motivated by socialist idealism, came to Palestine in the years 1904-1914. This is the so-called " Second Aliyah." These were the people who founded such settlements as Kinneret and Deganiah, where

a new form of socialist communal living began to emerge. The ideologist of the movement was the patriarchal Aaron David Gordon (1856-1922), who preached the religion of labor as an ideal and an end in itself. By 1914, there was in Palestine, besides the old-established traditional communities in the Holy Cities, a body of about twelve thousand Jews of the new type, living in the agricultural settlements and speaking the renewed Hebrew language.

In 1909, Jewish residents of Jaffa founded a garden-suburb which they named Tel-Aviv ("The Hill of Spring"), a name inspired by Ezekiel 3:15 and the Hebrew title of Herzl's utopist novel "Altneuland" ("Old New Land").

Clay houses built in Arab fashion by the first colonists of Deganiah, established in 1909 on the left bank of the Jordan, near the point where the river emerges from the Lake of Tiberias.

The founders of Tel-Aviv meet on the city's site and cast lots for their building plots (11.4.1909).

AMERICAN JEWRY
AND ITS INSTITUTIONS

While the nucleus of the Jewish settlement in Palestine was being formed, greater significance was attached at that time, to the mass-migration to the United States, already mentioned before. This country of hope had assumed great consequence in Jewish life even before the arrival of the East European refugees.

The middle years of the nineteenth century had been characterized by a massive Jewish emigration to the United States, mainly from Germany, where conditions continued in many ways to be highly unfavorable for the Jews. By the period of the American Civil War (1861-1865), in which about ten thousand Jews valiantly served in both camps, communities, mainly deriving from Central Europe, had become established throughout the country. Many were the cities in which Jewish traders were among the earliest pioneers.

The old Temple Emanu-El, New York (built 1868).

The anti-traditional currents of their new land of residence inevitably exercised considerable influence on the Jewish immigrants. Many of them had also brought over from Germany ideas of religious reform which had been spreading there for several decades. Among the immigrants were several rabbis, like David Einhorn (1809-1879) and others, who had been the protagonists of the reform movement in their native land and naturally steered their synagogues towards Reform Judaism, sometimes of an extremist type.

The great organizing spirit of American Reform Jewry in this period was the single-minded, ambitious, enormously competent Isaac Mayer Wise. Born in Bohemia in 1819, he had come to the United States in 1846, was at first rabbi in Albany and then, from 1854 to his death in 1900, in Cincinnati. He endeavored for many years to unite in a single organization the various currents of the reform movement and finally succeeded in establishing, in 1873, the Union of American Hebrew Congregations. Two years later, he founded in Cincinnati a training seminary for reform rabbis, the Hebrew Union College, which he directed until his death. At Wise's suggestion the graduates of this seminary formed the Central Conference of American Rabbis in 1889.

In the opposite camp, Isaac Leeser (1806-1897) of Philadelphia. also originally from Germany, tried with the same ardor, although with less success than Wise, to organize those who adhered to traditional Judaism. This same Isaac Leeser was the first rabbi to preach in English, when German was still the language of the reform synagogues. In 1886 the Jewish Theological Seminary of America was founded in New York by Leeser's successor, Sabato Morais (1823-1897), as a traditionalist counterpart to the Hebrew Union College. The seminary was subsequently to

Hebrew Union College, Cincinnati, founded in 1875 by the Reform movement as a rabbinical seminary.

Hester Street, in the heart of the Jewish quarter of New York, 1898.

Solomon Schechter (1850–1915), the scholar who investigated the Cairo Genizah, was from 1902 to his death at the head of the (Conservative) Jewish Theological Seminary of America in New York.

attain a great reputation under Solomon Schechter, the investigator of the Cairo Genizah, who was brought over from England to act as its president in 1902.

The independent order of B'nai B'rith was founded in New York in 1843 by a German immigrant, Henry Jones, for the purpose of promoting harmony and brotherly love among the immigrants and extending assistance to the needy. After modest beginnings, the order soon attained impressive proportions, spreading to Europe and becoming an institution of international importance.

By the closing decades of the nineteenth century, the basic institutions of the older stratum of American Jewry which were to be of permanent importance had, more or less, reached their definitive form. At the beginning of the twentieth century, three additional institutions of primary importance came into being.

In the wake of the 1905 pogroms in Russia, the American Jewish Committee was founded in 1906. The purpose of the Committee was to prevent the infraction of the civil and religious rights of Jews in any part of the world. By its purpose it parallelled such bodies as the Alliance Israélite Universelle in France, the Board of Deputies of British Jews and the Anglo-Jewish Association in England. At the time of the peace negotiations at Versailles (1919), which followed the conclusion of World War I, its significance was to be very great in fighting for minority rights for the Jews in various countries.

The American Joint Distribution Committee, established in 1914 under the chairmanship of Felix M. Warburg for the purpose of granting relief to war sufferers in Europe, was to become the largest voluntary charitable body in existence. It has to its credit during the next half century not only the relief of a great deal of human suffering, but also the saving of Jewish morale from collapse in some areas of the world.

The American Jewish Congress was established in 1917, largely through the efforts of the dynamic New York Reform Rabbi Stephen Wise, to serve as spokesman for the aspirations and aims of pro-Zionist Eastern European groups. Originally intended to represent American Jewry on a larger basis than the American Jewish Committee at the Peace Conference after World War I, it was transformed in 1922 into a permanent organization, which subsequently developed an activity on a very large scale for the defense of Jewish interests everywhere, active participation in Zionist work, and adult Jewish education.

The Orthodox "Yeshiva University" of New York.

THE BALFOUR DECLARATION

The Zion Mule Corps, a Jewish military formation in the British Army during World War I, which took part in the Gallipoli Campaign, 1915.

When World War I broke out in 1914, all Zionist activity was temporarily paralyzed because the leaders of the movement were dispersed in the various belligerent countries. In order to demonstrate the neutrality of the Zionist movement in the European conflict and to create a possibility of communication and co-ordination among the leaders, a Central Office was set up early in 1915, at Copenhagen in neutral Denmark. Besides support for the colonies in Palestine, this Office also organized relief to Jewish war sufferers in Eastern Europe.

The entry of Turkey into the World War as an ally of the Central Powers, however, created a very difficult situation for the Jews of Palestine. The Turkish Commander in Chief, Jemal Pasha, closed the Zionist institutions, deported or expelled Jews who were not Ottoman subjects and oppressed the Jewish community in many ways, because he suspected the Jews of being in sympathy with the cause of the enemy.

Nor was Jemal Pasha entirely wrong. It had soon become clear to everybody that one of the consequences of the World War would be the breaking up of the Sultan's empire. In Zionist circles there was a growing tendency to abandon the neutral and passive attitude in favor of active participation in the war on the side of England and her Allies. A Jewish military formation, the Zion Mule Corps, under Joseph Trumpeldor, took part, under the British flag, in the Gallipoli campaign.

391

Owing to the agitation of Vladimir (Zeev) Jabotinsky, the 38th Battalion of the Royal Fusiliers (later to be joined by two other battalions), which afterwards, took part in the conquest of Palestine, was formed in England by Jewish volunteers. In Palestine, a group of Jewish settlers, headed by the agronomist Aaron Aaronson, set up an espionage organization (the so-called "Nili" group) which conveyed valuable information to the British Command in Egypt. It was, however, finally discovered and several of its members paid with their lives for their devotion to the cause of the liberation of Palestine.

Meanwhile, no less fruitful work was being done on the diplomatic front. Outstanding among these Zionist diplomats was the brilliant chemist Chaim Weizmann.

Born in 1874 in Motol near Pinsk (Poland), he had studied chemistry in Germany and Switzerland and had adhered to the Zionist movement from its inception. Since the second Congress in 1898, he had been active in Zionist work. He had been one of the opponents of the Uganda scheme and, after Herzl's death, one of the principal supporters of the idea that active colonization work was to be carried out in Palestine without waiting for a charter. Weizmann established himself in England in 1903 as lecturer in biochemistry at the University of Manchester. It was there there that, in 1906, he met Arthur James (later Lord) Balfour, the man destined to play a decisive part in the history

Chaim Weizmann (1874–1952). It is due chiefly to him that the Balfour Declaration was issued in 1917, laying the foundation-stone for the future State of Israel, of which he was to become the first President.

392

Major-General Allenby, Commander of the British Expeditionary Forces, conquered Palestine in World War I and entered Jerusalem on December 9th, 1917, being greeted by the Jews as a "liberator".

Lord Balfour (1840–1930), who issued in 1917, in his capacity as Foreign Secretary, the declaration approving the creation of a Jewish National Home in Palestine.

of Zionism and of the Jewish people, and had the opportunity to present to him his views on the Jewish problem and its solution. Balfour never forgot this interview. During the World War, Weizmann became more and more the recognized leader of the Zionist movement in England. At the same time, he made important contributions to the British war effort with his scientific work, thus securing the sympathy of influential members of the Government. There is a nice story, told by Lloyd George, that to his question, how he wished to be honored for his services, Weizmann replied, he wanted nothing for himself, but a country for his people.

On November 2nd, 1917, Arthur James Balfour, then British Foreign Secretary, issued on behalf of the Government the famous declaration known by his name, in which approval was expressed for the idea of the establishment in Palestine of " a National Home for the Jewish People." A month later, on December 9th, the victorious British Army entered Jerusalem and was enthusiastically received by the Jewish population.

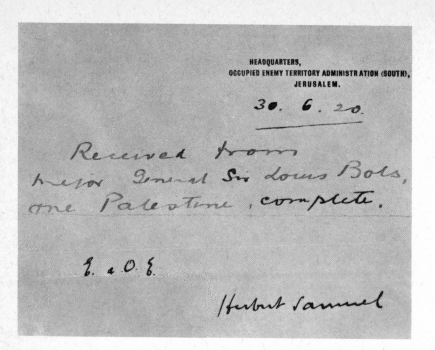

HEADQUARTERS,
OCCUPIED ENEMY TERRITORY ADMINISTRATION (SOUTH),
JERUSALEM.

30. 6. 20.

Received from
Major General Sir Louis Bols,
one Palestine, complete.

E. & O. E.

Herbert Samuel

The facetious receipt signed by Sir Herbert Samuel, the first High Commissioner, confirming that he had received "one Palestine complete" from the Military Commander, Major-General Sir Louis Bols. Sir Herbert humorously added the initials E. & O.E. (Errors and Omissions Excepted). When he left Palestine to his successor, Lord Plumer, in 1925, it was no longer complete, Transjordan having been detached, by the White Book of 1922, from the mandated territory in which Jewish settlement was to be fostered.

The installation of Sir Herbert Samuel as first High Commissioner of Palestine, in 1920.

Nahalal, in the Valley of Jezreel (the Emek), a co-operative village founded in 1921.

The Balfour Declaration was endorsed in due course by the other Allied Powers and subsequently by the Peace Conference in Paris. In 1920, the " Mandate " for administering Palestine, in order to implement the Declaration, was assigned by the League of Nations to Great Britain, and a prominent English Jew, Herbert (later Lord) Samuel, who had filled several high government offices and been the first Jewish Cabinet Minister in England, was appointed High Commissioner. For the first time in two thousand years, a Jew again headed the government of the Holy Land. In the following years, development was rapid enough, though less so than had been hoped. The British administration, at first hopefully hailed by the Jewish population, proved to be temporizing.

Arab leaders had from the outset opposed the creation of a Jewish National Home in Palestine, and from the beginning of 1920 there had been Arab attacks on Jewish settlements. In the defense of Tel Hai, in the north of the country, Joseph Trumpeldor and seven of his comrades met a hero's death on the 29th of February (11th Adar) of that year. There were additional attacks the following year. Despite the good will and Jewish loyalty of the High Commissioner, the British Administration did not display much understanding for the Jewish point of view, but was extremely sensitive to the objections of the Arab population, whose opposition to the realization of the promises embodied in the Balfour

Declaration was favored, if not actually fostered, by part of the mandatory authorities. In 1922, Transjordan was detached from Palestine, in order to end Arab criticism once for all, but this meant a drastic reduction of the territory destined to become the Jewish National Home. Jewish political rights were restricted and Jewish immigration and expansion arbitrarily limited. Order was, however, more or less maintained under Herbert Samuel and his successor, Lord Plumer (1925-1928). Afterwards the situation deteriorated rapidly and anti-Jewish agitation among the Arabs led to outbursts of violence and bloodshed. The most outrageous was that of 1929 with its wholesale massacres at Safed and particularly in the venerated Holy City of Hebron, whose ancient Jewish settlement henceforth ceased to exist.

Nevertheless, in spite of administrative sabotage on the part of the British and open enmity on the part of the Arabs, there was a considerable influx of Jewish labor, mainly from Eastern Europe. The Jewish National Fund purchased and developed additional tracts of land, hitherto swamp and malaria-stricken, and many new agricultural settlements were established. Tel Aviv developed enormously, with a Jewish press, a pulsating Jewish intellectual and artistic life, a symphonic orchestra and Hebrew theatres. In 1925, the Hebrew University was opened in Jerusalem.

"Palestine was not Jewish, but there was a Jewish Palestine again."

The Israel (former Palestine) Philharmonic Orchestra. The inaugural concert, in December 26th, 1936, directed by Maestro Arturo Toscanini, with violinist Bronislav Hubermann as soloist.

EASTERN EUROPE
BETWEEN THE WORLD WARS

Up to the outbreak of World War I in 1914, the Russian Empire still constituted the great center of Jewish life and a huge reservoir of Jewish population for the entire world. This historic phase was now to be irretrievably closed.

Concentrated in the western provinces of Russia, where fighting was actually centered, the Jews suffered terribly throughout the war, so much the more since the Russians considered them an unreliable element and frequently took revenge on them for their military failures.

The Russian defeat gave birth to the revolution of 1917, which was at first hopefully welcomed by the Jewish population, but soon revealed its destructive character, at least as far as Jews were concerned. It is true that the revolution put an end to the Czarist regime's discriminating legislation against the Jews. But this was only in theory. The Bolshevik system, which ultimately triumphed, after the overthrow of the democratic revolutionary elements, had no place for Jews who retained Jewish allegiances in the old sense. Both religious observance and Zionism were heavily punished as counter-revolutionary offenses. Moreover, the Jews belonged, to a large extent, to the bourgeois middle class which the Communist Party was pledged to destroy. Although a number of Jews occupied prominent positions in the party, Judaism as such was forthwith doomed in Russia.

Jewish suffering reached its peak during the years of the Civil War, which devastated the country in 1917-1921. The Communist " Red " troops and the " White " troops of the reactionary forces waged a grim, merciless war against each other, mainly in the Ukraine, but both of

Irregular Ukrainian soldiers photographed together with their Jewish victims after a pogrom, during the Civil War of 1918–1920.

them found time for easy victories over the Jewish population. Frightful pogroms were perpetrated, particularly by the White armies of Petlura and Denikin in Berdichev, Zhitomir, Proskurov and numerous other places. The number of Jews slain in these pogroms probably exceeded sixty thousand. When the murder subsided, there was widespread distress, to which even the generous succor of overseas Jewry could bring only slight relief.

After settled conditions were restored, one half of the Jews of the former Czarist dominions (together with those of formerly Austrian Galicia and the Prussian province of Posen) were in the territory of the newly resuscitated Republic of Poland. On the other hand, the Jews of Russia proper, formerly so significant, were now cut off almost completely from the mass of the Jewish people. They were to be henceforth a factor of rapidly diminishing importance. In 1924, there was a tendency to settle on the land part of the urban Jewish population, which was economically ruined. The tendency was encouraged by the Soviet Government and lavishly supported by the American Joint Distribution Committee. A number of agricultural settlements were established at that time, but they did not develop and were soon to disappear.

As a sort of face-saving substitute for Zionism, to which it was relentlessly opposed, the Soviet government set up in Birobidjan, in Siberia, a nominally autonomous Jewish region. The idea was, of course, to base the Jewish community there on a wholly secularized Yiddish culture, instead of Hebrew and the universal Jewish tradition. The

The Talmud Torah in Bratislava (formerly Pressburg), Capital of Slovakia.

Calea Vacaresti, main street of the Jewish quarter of Bucharest, Roumania.

experiment, not unnaturally, failed to arouse any enthusiasm among the Jewish masses and the project maintained only a symbolic existence. Otherwise, the outward signs of Jewish life in the vast domains subject to Soviet rule constantly diminished year after year. Only in some of the great cities, isolated synagogues still continued to cater nostalgically to the requirements of the dwindling minority who still recalled the tradition in which they had been reared.

In most of Central and Eastern Europe, Jewish rights were nominally guaranteed, after the Peace Settlement of 1920, by the Minority Treaties, which had been agreed upon at the insistence of the delegates from the Jewish communities of the western countries, who had been present at the negotiations in Paris. In fact, however, the Minority Treaties were to a great extent flouted, except in Czechoslovakia. In this country, which had a population of about three hundred fifty thousand Jews, a thoroughly democratic regime was set up, which endured down to the German occupation in 1939 and strictly respected Jewish minority rights.

In Poland, on the contrary, with a population of about three million Jews (ten per cent of the total population of the country), equal rights existed only on paper. Endemic Polish anti-Semitism manifested itself in many ways, particularly at the universities, where Christian students, with the benevolent assistance of their professors, attempted to exclude Jewish students from the lecture-halls, and in the economic sphere, where it took the form of an organized and government-supported anti-Jewish boycott. The consequence was a growing impoverishment of the Jewish population, which finally reached a terrible degree.

A workshop in the "ORT" trade-school in Vilna, Poland.

In Rumania, with about nine hundred thousand Jews, conditions were similar, although at the beginning perhaps not quite as harrowing as in Poland. Here, too, anti-Semitism held complete sway and the Jews were gradually expelled from their economic positions.

The effect of this growing pauperization of the Jews in Eastern Europe would have been more appalling still, but for the noble efforts of the American Joint Distribution Committee and other similar organizations. Among them ORT (the abbreviation of a Russian name meaning "Society for the Encouragement of Handicraft"), deserves a special mention. It had been founded in Russia in 1880 for the promotion of skilled trades and agriculture among the Jews. Until the war, it confined its activity to Russia alone, but afterwards it developed into an international organization and became increasingly active throughout the whole of Eastern Europe, assisting Jewish craftsmen and farmers and directing Jewish youth to productive occupations.

In the midst of the poverty caused by economic anti-Semitism, and notwithstanding the progress of secularization and modernization in large circles, the Jewish communities of Poland and the neighboring states were still able to carry on a vigorous religious and intellectual life in the traditional sense, with schools, synagogues and yeshivot. The old Jewish world was still able to maintain itself, hardly touched, in some places, by the eroding influences of the modern world. On the other hand, the Jews also developed a rich secular literature in Yiddish, which created works of lasting value, partly describing contemporary Jewish life and partly evoking memories of the Jewish past.

DEVELOPMENTS
OUTSIDE EUROPE

The period between the two World Wars witnessed significant developments in the lands beyond the seas.

In the United States, the economic depression which followed World War I was accompanied by a reactionary trend directed against foreigners generally and against Jews in particular. Social discrimination and tacit restrictions against the Jewish population made themselves felt in various economic and cultural spheres.

American Jewry did not accept this new situation. The American Jewish Congress and the Anti-Defamation League, created by the Order of B'nai Brith, fought back courageously. The economic recovery of the United States gradually quieted the agitation. Anti-Semitism began to subside and the return to a more liberal spirit was promoted by the reaction against the rise of Nazism in Germany.

In the inter-war years American Jewry reached its maturity, consolidated its forces, and developed a notable communal life on a scale far greater than had ever been known in the world before. This received its outward expression in the construction of monumental sygnagogues and in the creation or expansion of important cultural institutions. The activities of a network of great charitable and political organizations were constantly growing and began to loom more and more significantly in the life of Jews throughout the world.

Meanwhile Jewish immigration to the various countries of Latin America, given an enormous impetus by conditions in Europe and spurred on

The Great Synagogue in Sidney, Australia, opened in 1878.

401

by the restrictions on immigration to the United States, brought into being great communities in these regions as well. It seemed as if the great tradition of Hispano-Jewish culture of the Middle Ages were about to revive. The greatest Jewish community in Latin America (about 320,000 at the outbreak of World War II and about 400,000 to-day) developed in Argentina, particularly in the capital Buenos Aires, which has become an active cultural center.

The American pattern was duplicated in several parts of the British Commonwealth.

In Canada a liberal immigration policy allowed the Jewish community to expand from barely 16,000 in 1901 to a quarter of a million.

South Africa had become one of the goals of Jewish emigration from Eastern Europe since the eighties of the nineteenth century. By World War I about sixty thousand Jews had found a new home there.

This number doubled in the period between the World Wars and South Africa's Jews contributed in a considerable measure to the development of the economic resources of their country.

Australia was less conspicuous as a country of Jewish immigration. But even so, its Jewish population grew between the wars from about twenty thousand to about thirty thousand souls, a number since doubled. Owing to this process, English-speaking Jewry, which a century before had numbered probably no more than two per cent of the Jews of the world, increased in an astonishing proportion. It now comprises something approaching one half of the Jewish people.

THE NEW ANTI-SEMITISM

The wave of anti-Semitism which had begun to rise in many parts of Europe after World War I gained momentum from year to year. The new states established on the principle of national autonomy eyed their Jewish citizens askance, and the minority treaties proved ineffective in protecting them from the manifestations of a racial policy ranging from social discrimination and minor molestations to economic boycott and physical violence.

Although the triumph of Communism in Russia had proved disastrous for the Jews of that country, the fact that a number of Jews were among the leaders of the Communist movement was elsewhere a sufficient pretext to identify the Jewish people at large with the revolution and its outrages. The Jews were accused of having created Communism and of propagating its ideas in order to undermine and destroy Christian civilization, and broad masses believed these ridiculous allegations.

Unscrupulous anti-Semitic agitators stooped to all means to reach their goal and sow destructive hatred. It was in the post-war period that an enormous circulation in many languages was attained throughout Europe, and even in America, by a ludicrous fabrication entitled "The Protocols of the Elders of Zion." This pamphlet claimed to report the deliberations of a conference which had allegedly taken place in 1897, the year of the first Zionist Congress in Basle, and in which representatives of World Jewry had plotted to achieve universal domination, using among their instruments both Zionism and Communism. Although it was irrefutably proved, in 1921, that the Protocols were a brazen forgery, they were still given credence by a large public and continued to be used as an efficient weapon by anti-Semites, particularly in Germany.

Advertising poster for the German anti-Semitic motion picture "Der Ewige Jude" ("The Eternal Jew").

Adolf Hitler addressing a meeting of the National Socialist Party.

In that country conditions gradually deteriorated after a first hopeful start. The Weimar Republic, set up after the war, made a sincere attempt to discard all traces of administrative anti-Jewish prejudice inherited from the former German Reich. As a result of this liberal policy, scientists — foremost among them Albert Einstein — brought fame to German Universities. Jewish poets, authors, and critics endowed German liberature with a new brilliance. There were also Jewish statesmen. Walter Rathenau, Minister for Reconstruction, did more than anybody else to secure Germany's ecomonic recovery and its re-acceptance in the comity of nations. But proud imperial Germany had suffered a crushing defeat and the people, exasperated by inflation and un-employment, was looking for a scapegoat for the humiliating military disaster which had brought about this situation. There was nothing easier than to blame it all, absurdly, on the Jews, who had become so conspicuous of late. Rathenau was assassinated in 1922 by anti-Semitic thugs and from then on conditions in Germany constantly worsened, as far as the Jews were concerned. Anti-Semitism became one of the main planks of the National Socialist Party, which had been founded in 1919 and counted among its first members an obscure Austrian-born ex-corporal destined to rise very soon to notoriety : Adolf Hitler. After an abortive attempt to seize power in Munich in 1923 and about a year in prison, Hitler re-formed the dispersed party in 1925, ushering in two decades which were to be a nightmare for the greatest part of mankind, but most of all for the Jewish people. Hitler's avowed purpose was from the outset the realization of a program in which the crusade against Judaism figured prominently and was to be carried out most conscientiously.

Julius Streicher, the Editor of the anti-Semitic weekly "Der Stürmer", was one of the main educators of the German people. In May 1934, a special issue was devoted to the subject of "Ritual Murder".

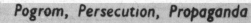

Preis 30 Pfennig

Der Stürmer

Ritualmord-Nummer

Deutsches Wochenblatt zum Kampfe um die Wahrheit

HERAUSGEBER: JULIUS STREICHER

Sonder-Nummer 1 — Nürnberg, im Mai 1934 — 12. Jahr 1934

Jüdischer Mordplan

gegen die nichtjüdische Menschheit aufgedeckt

Das Mördervolk

Die Juden stehen in der ganzen Welt in einem furchtbaren Verdacht. Wer ihn nicht kennt, der kennt die Judenfrage nicht. Wer die Juden nur ansieht, wie Heinrich Heine (Chaim Bückeburg) sie beschreibt: „Ein Volk, das zu seinem Unterhalt mit Wechseln und alten Hosen handelt und dessen Uniform die langen Nasen sind," der ist auf falscher Wäge. Wer aber weiß, welch eine ungeheuerliche Anklage schon seit Anbeginn gegen die Juden erhoben wird, dem erscheint dieses Volk in einem anderen Lichte. Er sieht in ihnen nicht nur ein eigenartiges, seltsam anmutendes Volk, er sieht in ihnen Verbrecher und Mörder und Teufel in Menschengestalt. Und es überkommt ihn gegen dieses Volk ein heiliger Zorn und Haß.

Der Verdacht, in dem die Juden stehen, ist der des Menschenmordes. Sie werden beschuldigt, nichtjüdische Kinder und nichtjüdische Erwachsene an sich zu locken, sie zu schlachten und ihnen das Blut abzuzapfen. Sie werden beschuldigt, dieses Blut in die Mazzen (ungesäuertes Brot) zu verbacken und auch sonstige abergläubische Zauberei damit zu treiben. Sie werden beschuldigt, ihre Opfer, besonders die Kinder, dabei furchtbar zu martern und zu foltern. Und während dieses Folterns Drohungen, Flüche und Verwünschungen gegen die Nichtjuden auszustoßen. Dieser planmäßig betriebene Menschenmord hat eine besondere Bezeichnung, er heißt

Ritualmord.

Das Wissen vom jüdischen Ritualmord ist schon Jahrtausende alt. Es ist so alt wie die Juden selbst. Die Nichtjuden haben es von Generation zu Generation übertragen. Es ist und durch Schriften überliefert. Es ist aber auch in der breiten Volksmasse vorhanden. In den verschiedenen Bauerndörfern ruht man auf dieses Wissen. Der Ahne sprach von ihm zu seinem Enkel. Und dieser wieder trug es weiter auf Kinder und Kindeskinder. So vererbte es sich bis zum heutigen Tag.

Es ist auch in den anderen Völkern vorhanden. Wo irgendwo in der Welt eine Leiche gefunden wird, die die Anzeichen des Ritualmordes trägt, erhebt sich sofort laut und groß die Anklage. Sie richtet sich überall nur gegen die Juden. Hunderte und aberhunderte von Völkern, Stämmen und Rassen bewohnen den Erdball. Niemand denkt daran, sie des planmäßigen Kindermordes zu beschuldigen und sie als Mördervolk zu bezeichnen. Den Juden allein wird diese Anklage aus allen Völkern entgegengeschleudert. Und viele große Männer haben

Judenopfer

Durch die Jahrtausende vergoß der Jud, geheimem Ritus folgend, Menschenblut
Der Teufel sitzt uns heute noch im Nacken, es liegt an Euch, die Teufelsbrut zu packen.

Die Juden sind unser Unglück!

"The Jews are our Misfortune!"

THE NAZIS IN POWER

After a few promising years of economic recovery, conditions suddenly deteriorated again in Germany in 1930. Large-scale bankruptcy became widespread and unemployment assumed fantastic proportions (rising to six million unemployed in 1933). This desperate situation and the fear of a Communist revolution drove Paul von Hindenburg, President of the German Republic since 1925, and the circle around him to accept drastic solutions. On January 30th, 1933, Adolf Hitler was appointed "Reichskanzler".

As soon as the National Socialist Party seized control, the parliamentary regime was practically abolished and replaced by a brutal Nazi dictatorship. By the end of 1933 the National Socialist Party had become the sole exponent of the political will of the German people and Adolf Hitler its omnipotent leader (Fuehrer). The swastika, which had been hitherto the emblem of the party, became from now on the German national emblem.

The boycott against Jewish shops in Germany, April 1st, 1933.

"Rassenschande" ("Race profanation") became a major crime in Germany. This woman, exposed to public abuse, wears a placard with the inscription: "I am the biggest sow in this place and have relations only with Jews."

With the accession of Hitler to power, a reign of terror against the Jews set in. They were thrust out of public and intellectual life. A boycott was enforced against Jewish shops and business enterprises. Elaborately organized "spontaneous" outbreaks of popular indignation against the Jews became frequent. One of the first institutions set up by Nazis was a network of concentration camps for political opponents and, of course, for Jews.

Outside Germany, the only reaction was a number of protest meetings convoked by Jewish organizations, in the United States and elsewhere. The civilized peoples and their leaders watched the events with indifference, and no voice was raised to recall Hitler to the bounds of humanity and reason.

In September 1935 a solemn gathering of the Nazi Party took place at Nuremberg and on this occasion the so-called " Nuremberg Laws " were issued. They defined as Jew any person of Jewish extraction (even if only one of the grand-parents was Jewish) irrespective of religious affiliation. The Jews were deprived of German citizenship. Inter-marriage was prohibited. A new crime called *Rassenschande* (race profanation) was created to stamp out sexual relations between Jews and Germans, and violators were liable to severe penalities.

Henceforth, each year further humiliations and restrictions came into being. The German Jews, who had been attached to their country for generations and deeply rooted in German culture, began to emigrate and very soon the world became filled with hopeless refugees in search of new homes.

The general lack of concern with the fate of the Jews, manifested by the so-called civilized world, encouraged the Nazi leaders to proceed from one stage of horror to the next. In March 1938 Hitler annexed Austria to the German " Third Reich." The event was marked by violence against the Jews throughout Austria, particularly in Vienna. Later in the year, the Sudetenland was ripped off Czechoslovakia and annexed to Germany, as a first step towards the total abolition of Czecho-slovak independence, which followed in March 1939. German anti-Semitic policy was now applied in this country, too, the only one in Central Europe where the minorities treaties had been honorably observed and the Jews had been able to develop their potentialities to the full. Meanwhile, an event took place which gave the Nazis a welcome pretext to deal the Jews a new spectacular blow. In Paris a seventeen years old Jewish boy, Herschell Grynspan, burning to avenge the sufferings of his parents who had been deported from Germany, shot and killed a diplomatic official of the German Embassy. On November 9th, 1938, when the news reached Germany, a country-wide pogrom was staged. About six hundred synagogues were burned or demolished. Jewish organizations, shops, and lodgings were pillaged. Numerous Jews were beaten up and sent to concentration camps.

Even those Jews who had continued to hope that conditions would quieten down, now understood that emigration, while there was still time, was the only solution. The German authorities did not oppose emigration, which they regarded as one way of getting rid of the Jews, but they made sure, as much as possible, that the Jews should leave Germany in utter destitution. Jews were rounded up throughout the country and released only on condition that they emigrate forthwith, leaving their property behind. Until the outbreak of World War II in 1939, more than three hundred thousand Jews left Germany. Another sixty or seventy thousand succeeded in emigrating during the first two war-years, despite the disturbed international situation. An appreciable

The burning of the Synagogue in the Oranienburger Strasse, Berlin, November 9th, 1938.

portion of these emigrants directed their steps towards Palestine, where they helped build a home, not only for themselves, but for the Jewish people at large.

The Nazis did not content themselves with applying the anti-Jewish policy in Germany and the annexed territories. Their agents abroad were at work in many countries, endeavoring to recruit adherents and introduce similar conceptions and methods elsehwere. They found a willing ear in many circles, which later, during the war, collaborated with Germany in the effort to annihilate European Jewry. Even in a country such as England a Fascist movement, led by Sir Oswald Mosley, could rise and temporarily generate a certain amount of unrest and anxiety.

Queue of German Jews preparing for emigration to Palestine, in front of the Berlin Agency of the Palestine & Orient Lloyd (1939).

THE FINAL SOLUTION

On September 1st, 1939, the Nazis irrupted into Poland, thus sparking off World War II, the most murderous struggle mankind has ever seen. Within less than a month Poland ceased to exist. All of western Poland was overrun by the Nazi military machine. Soviet Russia marched in and occupied the eastern part of the country. Out of Poland's three and a half million Jews, more than two millions were now in the zone under German occupation, and for them disaster ensued immediately. Wherever the German army arrived, there were wide-spread outbreaks of violence, and brutal killings, in which the local Polish population often zealously co-operated with the German invader. After the completion of the conquest, those territories which had belonged to Germany before World War I were incorporated into the Reich, and the rest of

The Jewish badge was first enforced by the Nazis in Wloclawek, Poland. It was, at the beginning, a triangular patch worn on the back and on the chest.

Humiliation and annihilation—
Above: A Jew wearing "tallith" and "tephillin" is obliged to stand near the bodies of his slaughtered co-religionists.
Below: A German soldier clips the beard of a pious Jew.

"Umsiedlung" ("transfer-ence") was the Nazi technical term for the deportation of Jews from their homes and their concentration into urban ghettos. The photograph shows a group of Jews deported to the Ghetto of Lodz.

Poland was organized under the so-called General Government. The Jews in the annexed territories—over half a million souls—were deported to the General Government's territory under the most inhuman conditions. Many of them perished on the way. In the General Government area Jews were excluded from normal human intercourse and systematically humiliated. They were wholly expelled from many towns and regions. In others they were segregated in heavily over-populated urban ghettos. The largest, in Warsaw, was established in the autum of 1940. From the outset its population numbered more than 350,000 persons and at a certain moment even reached the half million mark. There were also numerous labor camps for Jews. Their inmates had to perform the most exhausting labors under a regime of terror and starvation. Sanitary conditions and lack of food in ghettos and labor camps became more and more appalling and many were those who succumbed. Yet somehow the Jews mostly managed to keep their spirit unbroken and their Jewish life intact, at least at the initial stage.

On the opposite page: Jewish children in the Warsaw Ghetto.

The Warsaw Ghetto is isolated from the outer world by an unscalable wall. The Jews were, of course, compelled to pay for the materials and the labor.

The gate of the Ghetto of Lodz.

The denizens of the ghettos who were still able to work were led each morning under escort to hard labor.

In the course of 1940 and 1941 the greatest part of Europe fell under the Nazi heel, from the Arctic Ocean to the Mediterranean and from the Pyrenees to the Caucasus. Everywhere the Jewish problem was immediately tackled by the German occupation authorities along the same Nazi lines. It is gratifiying to know that they sometimes failed. The undaunted attitude of the Danish people, from the king down to the last fisherman, saved the lives of their Jewish fellow citizens. Much was done by the Dutch people and by many Belgians and Frenchmen to preserve Jewish lives and to alleviate Jewish suffering. But as a general rule the Nazis did as they wished, even in a country like France, where Jewish emancipation was first established. Almost everywhere the Jews were segregated from normal life, allotted grotesquely inadequate food rations, robbed of their property, cruelly maltreated and marked off from other persons by the wearing of a yellow Badge' of Shame, as in the Middle Ages, but now in the form of the traditional Shield of David.

As the German triumphs extended, the persecution of the Jews increased and became more systematic. In most countries concentration camps were established, in which Jews were herded together prior to their being despatched to a special reservation, which the Germans had decided to set up in the General Government area, in the region of Lublin.

If the fate of the Jews in the invaded countries to the west was bitter enough, it in no way approached the ghastly tragedy in the East. When Germany turned against Soviet Russia in June 1941 and in a short time conquered vast territories with a large Jewish population, a more summary procedure was applied. Here the Germans did not think it necessary to save face and make a pretence to civilized conduct. The Jews were relentlessly butchered on an enormous scale. Especially notorious was the great massacre at Babbiyar, outside Kiev, when in two days in that autum of 1941, upwards of thirty thousand Jews were ruthlessly shot. Many of them had been rounded up on the Day of Atonement in synagogues.

Among the many Jewish intellectuals who lost their lives in those days was the famous Jewish historian Simon Dubnow, over 80 years of age, who was casually murdered by a German trooper when Riga was occupied.

In these eastern territories the Germans found willing and efficient assistants in their Rumanian allies, who fought on the southern sector of the front, and particularly in the local Ukrainian population, ever-thirsty for Jewish blood and so experienced in pogroms.

While the deportation from many parts of Europe to the projected Jewish reservation in Poland was in full swing, a fateful change took place in the anti-Jewish policy of Nazi Germany. The idea of a Jewish

The mass execution of Jews at Lijepaia, Latvia.

A convoy of Jews arriving at the death-camp at Oswiecim (Auschwitz)

reservation was abandoned and the Nazi leaders who met in Wannsee, a suburb of Berlin, on January 20th, 1942, decided to put into effect what they termed " the final solution." What was meant by this ominous term was the total physical annihilation of that part of the Jewish people which was within reach of the German executioners. The officer in charge of this sinister operation was to be Adolf Eichmann, a man who had already proved his capacity in the organization of deportations.

Death camps were now arranged in Majdanek, Belzec, Treblinka, Oswiecim (Auschwitz) and elsewhere. After trying out other methods, the conclusion was reached that mass-asphyxiation in gas chambers was the quickest and probably the most economic way for killing Jews. The corpses were then burnt in huge furnaces. Convoys from everywhere in Europe supplied a steady flow of deportees for extermination. Those who were not sent immediately to the gas chambers died sometimes of starvation or maltreatment, or were shot or hanged for some minor offense against the camp-regulations. Some of them had to submit to sadistic medical experiments which they seldom survived.

Adolf Eichmann, responsible for organizing the "Final Solution", was tracked down by a Jewish commando, brought to Israel, tried and executed in 1961.

Above:
"Selection" in the Osiwecim death-camp. Jews still able to work were allowed to survive for a while for further exploitation, the others were sent forthwith to death.
In the middle:
The crematorium of the Oswiecim death-camp.
Below:
Huge quantities of shoes and other articles of dress piled up in the death-camps. Everything was carefully sorted and registered.

German soldiers clear the "bunkers" of the Warsaw Ghetto of Jewish fighters.

All the countries in German-occupied Europe furnished the material for the running of this satanic machinery in which a whole people was being systematically, scientifically annihilated. Famous European communities, which had played a glorious part in Jewish life in the past, were liquidated, one after the other, or reduced to insignificant remnants: Salonica and Cracow, Frankfort and Lublin, Sarajevo and Amsterdam, Lodz and Vienna.

There were isolated attempts at resistance. Jews succeeded in escaping from ghettos and joining Russian or Polish partisans, or forming separate Jewish partisan groups to take part in the guerilla warfare against the Nazis. Revolts flared up, from time to time, in ghettos and even in death camps. They were, of course, cruelly quelled, but sometimes not without loss of life to the Nazis. As the most glorious episode of Jewish resistance, the revolt of the Warsaw ghetto will always be remembered. It broke out on April 19th, 1943 and the fighters held out five weeks against an incomparably superior enemy, upon whom they inflicted serious losses. The Germans had to conquer the area house by house and bunker by bunker, while the defenders resisted to the last. What was left of the non-combatant ghetto population was rounded up and sent to the death camps.

Jewish women who fought in the revolt of the Warsaw Ghetto.

But, after all, even this revolt was not more than a heroic gesture. Nothing could stop Germany from carrying out its plan of destruction. Anti-Jewish terror raged on inexorably in all the territories occupied by the Nazis, including the Balkan and the Greek islands, and in nominally independent countries like Slovakia, Hungary, Bulgaria and Rumania, where Nazi supported puppet governments obediently followed the instructions of their overlords. In Italy, where the Jews had lived in peace under the Fascist regime, their situation suddenly deteriorated in 1938, when Mussolini concluded a military alliance with Germany and pleased Hitler by introducing anti-Jewish legislation, and a step further in 1940, when Italy joined Germany in war. Yet the catastrophe came here in 1943, when the German army took over, after the collapse of the Fascist regime.

From all these countries Jews were deported to the death-camps in Poland. The gruesome massacre ended only with the downfall of the German Reich. By that time six million Jews, two thirds of all European Jewry, had perished. In some countries, such as Poland, Greece, or Czechoslovakia, not more than one tenth of the Jewish population had survived. It was the most terrifying disaster in the annals of any people since the beginning of recorded history.

Fighters of the Warsaw Ghetto. taken away for execution

The Warsaw Ghetto in flames. German official photograph, with the subscription: "There is no more a Jewish district in Warsaw."

422

Es gibt keinen
jüdischen Wohnbezirk
— in Warschau mehr!

THE STRUGGLE FOR INDEPENDENCE IN PALESTINE

The appalling tragedy that had overtaken European Jewry from 1933 onwards, and the difficulties of the harried emigrants in finding a land of refuge in a world filled with suspicions, resentments, and distress, resulted in exactly that situation with which the conception of Zionism and the foundation of the Jewish National Home had been intended to cope. Many of the refugees turned to Palestine, but the nervous British authorities, anxious to avoid offending Arab susceptibilities, only half-opened the gates. Moreover, the German and Italian governments, wishing to embarrass British administration in the Middle East, fomented Arab opposition to Jewish immigration and to the consolidation of the Jewish National Home. This antagonism gradually assumed more violent forms, until in 1936 it developed into an armed revolt. Bands of Arab volunteers were organized and trained by officers from neighbouring Arab countries for the purpose of disrupting communications in Palestine and attacking Jewish settlements.

Jewish policemen in armored cars and tenders, accompany a convoy at the time of the Arab attacks in 1936–39.

At the beginning, the Jewish self-defense organization, the Haganah, persisted in its policy of not using violence as far as possible (in Hebrew *havlagah*, restraint), and confined itself to defensive action only. But this attitude merely encouraged the British to make increasing concessions to artificially fomented Arab opposition. Concessions proved, however, ineffective in restoring peace and order. A partition plan brought forward in 1937 by the British Government, on the basis of the findings of a commission of enquiry presided over by Lord Peel, was rejected by both Jews and Arabs. A second commission, under the presidency of Sir John Woodhead, came to Palestine in 1938 and the result was the publication of the " White Paper " of 1939. Jewish immigration and the right to acquire land for settlement in Palestine were ruthlessly restricted, just at a time when they were needed so desperately as a condition for survival for tens of thousands of homeless refugees.

One of the "Special Night Squads" of Jewish policemen and volunteers, organized by Orde Wingate, a British officer who had become an enthusiastic supporter of Zionist aspirations.

The attitude and actions of the British administration constituted a flagrant breach of the obligations towards the Jewish people which Great Britain had undertaken by accepting the mandate for Palestine. Without satisfying the high-flown pretensions of the Arabs, they deeply offended and actually endangered the Jewish community. No wonder that the actions the British authorities provoked armed resistance which, in the course of time, developed into a struggle for independence.

The Haganah soon abandoned the *havlagah* policy and began to react to Arab attacks by reprisals. Members of the Revisionist party, headed by Zeev Jabotinsky, who believed that even the new tactics of the Haganah were not firm enough, founded a separate " National Military Organization " in 1937 (*Irgun Tzevai Leumi*, known usually as " Etzel"). Both organizations gradually intensified the struggle against the Arab gangs on the one hand, and against British suppression on the other.

From 1938 on they also began to organize on a vast scale what was termed " illegal immigration." The ready absorption of all the "illegal" immigrants into the Palestinian Jewish Community (the "Yishuv") constituted conclusive evidence that the absorptive capacity of the country was far from being exceeded, notwithstanding the contrary conclusions reached by commissions of inquiry. In spite of all administrative obstacles and Arab terrorist attacks, the Palestinian Jewish community continued to grow, constantly developing its national institutions in the face of opposition and threats.

When World War II broke out in Europe, in 1939, the Yishuv declared itself ready to lay aside, for the time being, its grudge against Great Britain and co-operate with her whole-heartedly in the fight against the common foe, Nazi Germany. The Jews threw themselves solidly into the war effort, organizing in Palestine workshops and industrial enterprises for supplying many of the needs of the Allied Forces. Jewish volunteers served under British command in Greece and North Africa. In 1944 a Jewish Brigade was finally formed, which fought with distinction in Italy and took part in the liberation of Europe, bringing aid to Jewish survivors and helping many of them to reach Palestine.

Arab attacks did not prevent the establishment of new settlements. They only gave rise, in the years 1936–39, to a different type of settlements, the so-called "wall and tower colonies", in which the protective fence and the watch-tower were the essential features and the first construction to be set up. One of them was Tirat Zvi, in the Beth Shean Valley, set up in 1937.

Notwithstanding British official coolness and even opposition, a Jewish Brigade was finally set up and served with distinction on the Italian front.

When fighting was over, the soldiers of the Jewish Brigade concentrated their efforts on assistance to the survivors of the Nazi concentration- and extermination-camps.

Despite the sincere and valuable co-operation of the Jews, which contrasted sharply with the passive and wavering attitude of the Arab sector in Palestine, the Mandatory Government continued to pursue the same restrictive immigration policy during the war, although it was obvious that those excluded from Palestine were virtually condemned to a cruel fate. Illegal immigration was carried on, in the first war-years, with mounting intensity. But the British authorities, too, increased their vigilance and severity. Dreadful tragedies sometimes overtook prospective immigrants who were refused admission. Over 1,700 illegal immigrants seized by the British were embarked in 1940 at Haifa on the s.s. "Patria" to be deported to the island of Mauritius. Only when the ship was blown up and more than two hundred persons met their death in the explosion, were the survivors allowed to remain in the country as an "exceptional" case. But another group of about 1,600 illegal immigrants was actually deported to Mauritius, to spend years there living under adverse conditions. The most tragic case was that of the s.s. "Struma". Under British pressure, the Turkish authorities at Istanbul refused this ship, carrying 769 refugees from Rumania, permission to proceed or to land passengers. After two months of vain negotiations, the ship was obliged to return to the Black Sea and finally foundered there in February, 1942. Only one refugee survived to tell the story.

This obstinate adherence to a callous policy on the part of the British Government succeeded in suppressing illegal immigration during the

After the war, the survivors of the Nazi terror flocked to Palestine, crowded in inadequate, often unseaworthy craft. But the British authorities refused them admittance, diverted part of the transports to Cyprus and set up huge concentration-camps in that island.

The most famous "illegal" immigrant-ship was "Exodus 1947". The immigrants opposed resistance to the boarding-party of the British Navy and there were killed and wounded. In Haifa the immigrants were transferred to prison-ships and sent back to Germany.

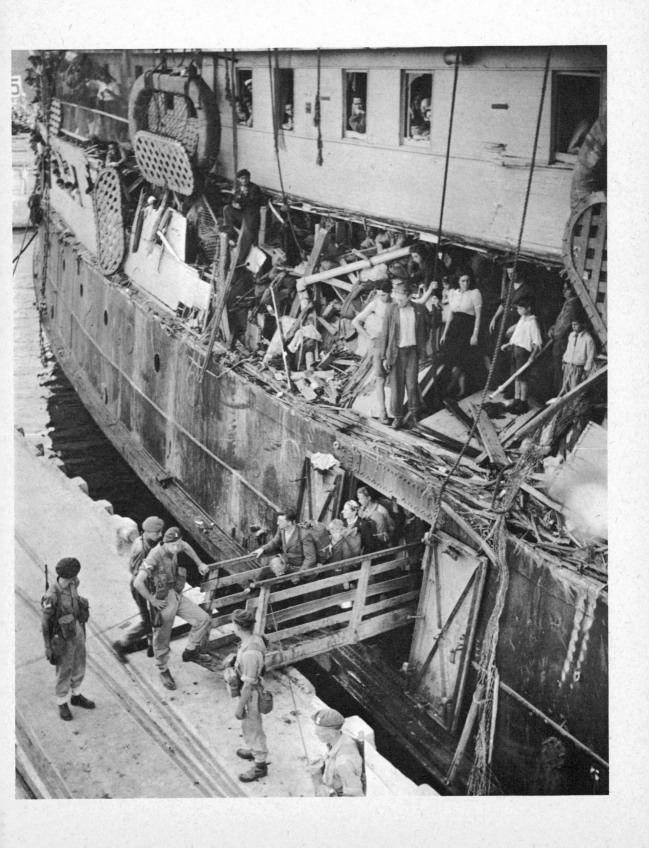

British Police and Army search the Jewish settlements for arms.

remaining war years. After the defeat of Germany, however, there was a universal and irresistible desire among the survivors of the death-camps to leave Europe for the only land where they hoped to find mental and physical safety in the future. Yet they were excluded from there by the Mandatory Government, which was animated, above all, by the desire to placate the Arab states, in the hope of thus strengthening Britain's position in the Middle East.

The accession of the Labor Party to power in Great Britain, after the close of the war, did not improve the situation, as far as Palestine was concerned. The policy of Ernest Bevin, foreign minister in the Labor Government, was decidedly hostile to Zionist aspirations and impervious to arguments of sheer humanity. A joint British-American commission, which examined the situation in 1945, recommended that 100.000, displaced persons be immediately admitted to Palestine. Britain, however, rejected this recommendation. Ships loaded with thousands of illegal immigrants were converging on Palestine. But the British Navy was allotted the inglorious task of intercepting them, forcing them to return, or diverting them to Cyprus, where the immigrants were interned in concentration camps.

Britain's obstinacy in enforcing the restrictions on immigration, without regard for her international obligations and humanitarian considerations, provoked extreme indignation throughout the Jewish world and exasperation among the Jews in Palestine. There were increasing tension and mounting bloodshed, and the Jewish defense-organizations clashed more and more often with the British forces employed to prevent immigration and with Arab guerrillas who had resumed their terrorist activities.

THE JEWISH STATE

The increased activity of the Haganah and the two dissident extremist organizations, the already mentioned Irgun Tzevai Leumi and the small, but resolute and efficient group called "Lehi" (abbreviation of Lohamei Herut Israel—the Fighters for the Freedom of Israel), provoked more severe and relentless repressive measures on the part of the British administration. Ultimately, it became clear to the Jewish leaders that there was no solution to the problem, except a return to the original objectives of Zionism : the constitution in Palestine of a sovereign Jewish State, which would be the master of its own destiny and in a position to alleviate the suffering of European Jewry without resorting to outside approval and control. The demand for a solution of this sort grew more and more insistent, and the clashes between the frustrated Jews and the forces of the mandatory power became increasingly more bitter.

Finally, the British Government, too, reached the conclusion that it was unable to master the situation, and referred the problem to the United Nations in April, 1947. A United Nations commission composed of the delegates of eleven states, excluding the Big Five (Great Britain, the United States, France, Soviet Russia and China), was designated to investigate the situation in Palestine and in the Displaced

Dr. Chaim Weizmann sums up the Zionist views before the United Nations Committee on the Palestinian Question (October 18th, 1947). Seven months later, Dr. Weizmann was elected the first President of the State of Israel (U.N. Photo, Dept. of Public Information).

The United Nations decision of November 29th, 1947, that an independent Jewish State should be set up in Palestine, was greeted with enthusiasm by the Jewish population.

Persons' camps in Europe. In its report, a majority of the commission's members recommended the partition of Palestine and the establishment of two separate, but economically co-ordinated, Jewish and Arab States. The Jewish State was to comprise the Valley of Jezreel (the Emek), eastern Galilee, the Plain of Sharon, the Coastal Plain and a great part of the Negev. Jerusalem was to belong to neither state, but to form a separate territory administered by a U.N. Commissioner.

In a historic session, held on November 29th, 1947, the United Nations approved these recommendations. The United States and Soviet Russia, in an unprecedented step, joined hands and voted in favor of it. The Arabs immediately announced their refusal to accept the plan and their determination to oppose its realization by force of arms. Great Britain declared that it was unable to implement the recommendation and would terminate the Mandate and withdraw all its forces from Palestine by May 15th, 1948.

The Arabs, on the other hand, fiercely opposed the United Nations decision. Armed Arab gangs concentrate in the neighborhood of Jerusalem.

The Old Commercial Center of Jerusalem set on fire and looted by Arab gangs (2.12. 1947).

The British administration now began to wind up its activities. But while restrictions and repressive measures against the Jewish sector were maintained to the very last, the organization of Arab forces in Palestine, with the active aid of the neighboring Arab States, was benevolently tolerated. Ferocious Arab attacks on Jewish settlements, on interurban traffic, and on the Jewish population in the towns started forthwith and caused numerous casualties. The Jews could not rely on British protection and had to depend entirely on their own forces.

Above to the left:
Haganah group patrols the occupied Arab quarter of Haifa (April 1948).

Above to the right:
Haifa Arabs carry away a dead comrade.

In the middle:
The Flour Mill at Abu Kebir, on the border between Tel-Aviv and Jaffa, seen through the loop-hole of a Jewish defence position.

To the right:
Forces of the Irgun Zvai Leumi attack Jaffa (April 1948). Jaffa capitulated on May 13th, 1948

Jerusalem was cut off from the rest of the country, besieged and constantly shelled by Arab forces, Food supplies ran short and even water was rationed

Palmach soldiers of the Negev Brigade

The emblem of the "Arab Liberation Army, under the command of Fawzi Kawukji, which operated in the North.

The Haganah and the two dissident organizations now co-ordinated their actions. The Palmach (i.e., Plugot Mahatz—Commando forces), under the command of its founder Yitzhak Sadeh, proved itself a superb fighting force, admirably trained to serve as the spearhead of a regular army. Even before the British troops left Palestine, the War of Independence had virtually begun.

The Jewish forces soon took the initiative and seized Tiberias, Haifa, Safed, and Jaffa, Tel Aviv's neighbor. Many Arab villages were conquered. Acre was isolated. In Jerusalem, however, the situation was critical. The New City had been occupied by Jewish forces following the evacuation of the British, but communications between Jerusalem and the Coastal Plain were interrupted and all efforts to re-establish them failed. In the Old City, the defenders of the Jewish Quarter still held out, but they were cut off from the New City.

The proclamation of the establishment of the State of Israel, in Tel-Aviv, on May 14th, 1948.
The proclamation is read by David Ben Gurion, Prime Minister of the New State.

In Jerusalem, Jewish forces occupy the fortified British sector
(popularly called "Bevingrad", , after the evacuation of the British forces (14.5.1948).

Above:
A unit of the Israeli Defence Army taking the oath of loyalty.

To the left:
General Jacob Dori, the first Commander-in-Chief of the Israeli Defence Army (till November 1949).

To the right:
General Yigal Yadin, Commander-in-Chief of the Israeli Defence Army from 1949 to 1952.

This was the situation in the country, as the fateful date of the termination of the British Mandate drew near. One day before, on the 14th of May 1948, at a gathering of Jewish representatives in Tel Aviv, the State of Israel was proclaimed. The veteran statesman Chaim Weizmann was elected its first President. The Palestinian Jewish leader David Ben-Gurion became Prime Minister and formed the first government of the new state. The United States and Soviet Russia immediately recognized the State of Israel and other countries, with few exceptions outside the Arab States, successively followed suit.

The first problem of the new state was defense. The Arab guerrilla forces were now joined by the regular armies of Egypt, Iraq, Lebanon, Syria, and Transjordan, which crossed the frontier as soon as the British Mandate ended, to crush the newly born Jewish state. The former Jewish underground formations were now rapidly organized into a regular army, the Tseva Hagana le-Israel (the Israel Defense Army). Compulsory conscription was introduced, and volunteers came from many countries to help Israel in its war of survival.

437

The young army soon proved its worth. In a series of brilliant operations, during the next half year, the Jewish forces not only defended themselves triumphantly on all fronts, but extended the area of the Jewish-held region beyond the limits originally specified by the United Nations recommendation. They even advanced into enemy territory, invading Egypt at one point, and, but for British intervention, would have reached the Suez Canal and perhaps penetrated far beyond. Communications with besieged Jerusalem, subjected to shelling by Transjordanian and Egyptian forces and for a long time practically cut off from the outside world, were re-established. But the Old City, in which Jews had been living for centuries, had to be given up.

To the left:
Preparing for action during the War of Liberation.

To the right:
The attack on Irak el-Manshie, a village east of the Egyptian bastion of Faluja.

The "Burmah Road", built in the summer of 1948, in order to break the isolation of Jerusalem. By this road provisions, arms and ammunitions finally reached the besieged city.

To the left:
Israeli armoured cars advance in the Negev (October 1948).

To the right:
In March 1949 the Israeli flag was hoisted at Elath, on the Red Sea.

"Operation Horeb" (22.12. 1948 — 7.1.1949), the last in the war against Egypt, drove the Egyptians out of all their positions, except the Gaza Strip, and brought the Israeli Army into Egyptian territory, where they captured the airport of El Arish.

UNITED NATIONS   NATIONS UNIES

Mission of the United Nations Mission du Médiateur des Nations
Mediator on Palestine   Unies pour la Palestine

EGYPTIAN-ISRAELI GENERAL CEASE-FIRE AGREEMENT

We, the undersigned, do hereby agree that:

1. The general cease-fire agreement between the two parties which became effective on 7 January 1949 at 1200 GMT is hereby formally confirmed as a complete and enduring cease-fire between all elements of our military or para-military forces - land, sea and air - wherever located.

2. No element of the ground or air forces of either party shall advance beyond or pass over the line now held by the foremost elements of its ground forces, and no element of naval or air forces of either party shall enter into or pass over the waters adjacent to the coastline now held by the other party for any purpose whatsoever.

3. In pursuance of the resolution of the Security Council of 29 December 1948, complete supervision of the truce by the United Nations Observers shall be allowed and facilitated.

4. Movements of civilians shall not occur from one side to the other.

Done and signed in quadruplicate at Rhodes, Island of Rhodes, Greece, on the 24 January 1949, in the presence of the United Nations Acting Mediator on Palestine and the Chief of Staff of the United Nations Truce Supervision Organisation.

Signed: _____ Signed: _____
For and on behalf of the   For and on behalf of the Pro-
Government of Egypt   visional Government of Israel

Signed: _____ Signed: _____
For and on behalf of the   For and on behalf of the Pro-
Government of Egypt   visional Government of Israel

Rhodes, 24 January 1949

The Cease Fire Agreement between Israel and Egypt, signed at Rhodes on January 24th, 1949.

In the end, the efforts of the United Nations resulted in a general cease-fire, followed in January 1949 by a conference at Rhodes, where a series of armistice agreements were signed with the defeated Arab States in the course of the following months. The last agreement to be signed was the one with Syria, in July, 1949, marking the end of the War of Independence.

The State of Israel had, meanwhile, been admitted to membership in the United Nations. A legislative assembly (*Knesset*) was elected. In 1950, despite numerous foreign protests, the seat of government was transferred to Jerusalem, which was declared the capital of the State of Israel.

On May 12th, 1949, Israel became the fifty-ninth member of the United Nations. The Israeli flag is hoisted in the presence of Moshe Sharet, first Foreign Minister of Israel, and Abba Eban, Israeli delegate to the United Nations (U.N. photo, Dept. of Public Information).

THE CONSOLIDATION
OF THE STATE OF ISRAEL

There now followed a period of consolidation and development.
The new state considered the " Ingathering of the Exiles " its prime
duty. It threw the doors wide open to immigration and the inflow
began immediately, while the War of Independence was still in progress.
In the interval between May 15th, 1948, and the end of the same year,
over one hundred thousand Jewish immigrants entered the country.
The Displaced Persons' camps in Europe were at last emptied and their
inmates brought to the land to which they aspired.

At the same time, immigrants came in large numbers from Arab countries,
particularly Iraq and the Yemen, from Persia and Turkey, as well
as from North Africa and India. Whole communities were systematically transferred to Israel and countries in which Jews had lived since
time immemorial, such as the Yemen, were now to lose nearly their entire
Jewish population.

Immigration from Eastern Europe occured on a lesser scale, because
the Communist regimes prevailing there opposed Zionism on principle.
Some countries in that area softened their attitude in the course
of time and allowed a trickle of their Jewish citizens to emigrate to
Israel. But Soviet Russia has hitherto remained adamant in this
respect.

The Jewish population of Israel, which numbered about six hundred
thousand souls on May 16, 1948, increased steadily. By 1955 it had
reached 1,600,000 and in 1964 it passed the $2\frac{1}{2}$ million mark.

Mass immigration raised numerous problems of an economic, cultural,
and social character. The economic problem of creating means of
subsistence for so many new immigrants, many of whom came from
backward countries, was solved partly by the united effort and spirit
of sacrifice of the population already rooted in the country, which
willingly accepted for years a regime of hard work and strict austerity,
and partly by the aid from Jewish communities abroad, particularly
the United States, Great Britain and South Africa. Substantial and
continuous aid from the Government of the Unites States also helped to
overcome financial difficulties created by the necessity of absorbing
large-scale immigration, on the one hand, and of maintaining at the
same time a strong and well equipped army, on the other.

The problem of cultural and social absorption of the immigrants requires
more time for its solution. Here school and military service play a
decisive part. By and large, the younger generation is assuming the
characteristics of a homogeneous Israeli people, in which uniting factors
prevail over differences in background.

With the help of foreign loans and investments, old industries were
modernized and new ones founded. The country began not only to
produce, but also to export on a large scale. In 1962 an agreement
was concluded with West Germany, providing for the indemnification

*Types of Jewish immigrants
from various countries.*
*Upper row (from the left to
the right): Rumania, Cochin,
Yemen;*
*Middle row: Hadhramaut,
Persia, Yemen;*
*Lower row: United States,
Morocco, Turkey.*

Modern port-installations in the Port of Haifa.

Elath, the Israeli port on the Red Sea, is a fast-developing town.

Israeli industry developes. Above: Tubes for supplying water to the Negev, manufactured by the Yuval Gad Factory. Below: Fertilizers and Chemicals Ltd., Haifa, the country's biggest chemical plant.

of the State of Israel for the confiscation by the Nazis, of Jewish property to which there are no heirs. The subsequent payment of more than 700 million dollars in goods over the next 12-14 years, contributed, of course, to the process of economic consolidation. The occupation of the port of Elath, in the extreme south of the country, at the end of the War of Independence, provided the new state with an outlet to the East through the Red Sea and the Indian Ocean. It also opened up the vast areas of the Negev, the parched southern part of the country, for colonization and industrial development.

Itzhak Ben-Zvi, second President of Israel, from 1952 to his death in 1963.

In 1952, Chaim Weizmann died and in his place, Itzhak Ben-Zvi, a distinguished scholar and one of the recognized leaders of Jewish Palestine during the Mandate period, was elected second President of the State of Israel.

Meanwhile, the Arab States, unable to swallow the defeat suffered in 1948 and the existence of the Jewish State, openly declared on every occasion that they were preparing a "second round." Armed raids undertaken by Arab infiltrators constantly endangered the security of settlements situated near the borders. Sometimes murderous attacks were perpetrated on road transport even in the interior of the country. In order to destroy the bases of marauders, and eliminate the constant threat of a war of extermination, which had become more imminent with the formation of a military alliance between Egypt, Syria, and Jordan, the Israeli Army undertook in October 1956 a brilliant offensive against Egypt in the Sinai peninsula. France and Great Britain joined the attack on Egypt, for the purpose of regaining control of the Suez Canal, which had been nationalized by the Egyptian Government.

The campaign had to be ended prematurely under the pressure of the United Nations, and Israel was obliged to withdraw its victorious forces, abandoning the territories conquered, the Gaza strip and the Sinai peninsula. Nevertheless the campaign brought about an enduring result. Order on the frontiers, particularly on the southern border, was restored and sea-communications with the Far East and East Africa through the port of Elath were secured.

After the death of President Ben-Zvi in 1963, another scholar and veteran representative of the Labor movement in Israel, Zalman Shazar, was elected in his place as Israel's third President.

The Sinai Campaign, in 1956, proved that Israel had the power to enforce respect for its sovereignty.   Above: Israeli tanks move across the Sinai desert. — Below: The captured Egyptian destroyer "Ibrahim al-Awal", is towed into the Port of Haifa.

The Haifa Technical Institute.

The Hebrew University, Jerusalem.

The Hadassah Hospital, the Hebrew University's Medical Center in Jerusalem.

Hechal Shlomo, the seat of the Israeli Chief Rabbinate, in Jerusalem.

The Atomic Reactor at Nabi Rubin, where atomic research is harnessed to the service of peace,

"The Shrine of the Book", in which the Dead Sea Scrolls are on exhibition. It forms part of the Israel Museum, Jerusalem.

Despite a number of financial and political crises, the unavoidable childhood diseases of a new state, Israel has followed, on the whole a continuously ascending line of development and has manifested remarkable political stability in an area where revolutions and counter-revolutions and violent changes of rulers and governments are endemic. It has set up a thoroughly democratic, progressive society and already serves as a model and guide to states of more recent formation. Although its Arab neighbors still manifest enmity, Israel has not lost hope in the realization of the prophecy, that finally the nations "shall beat their swords into ploughshares and their spears into pruninghooks; nation shall not lift up sword against nation, neither shall they learn war any more" (*Isaiah 2 : 4*).

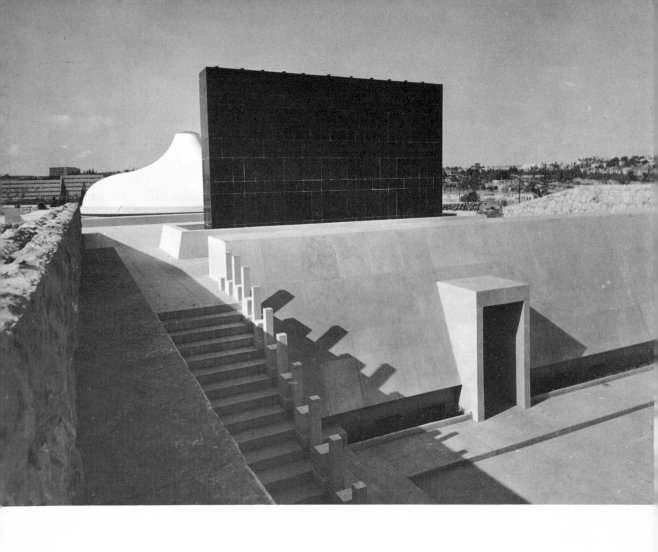

General view of the Israel Museum, Jerusalem.

CONTENTS:

CONTENTS

INDEX: